KU-660-073

Microsoft®
Office 97
Small Business
Edition
6-in-1

by Peter Aitken, Jennifer Fulton, Sherry Kinkoph,
Joe Lowery, Sue Plumley, Faithe Wempen

A Division of Macmillan Computer Publishing
201 West 103rd Street, Indianapolis, Indiana 46290 USA

Microsoft® Office 97 Small Business Edition 6-in-1

©1997 by Que® Corporation

All rights reserved. No part of this book shall be reproduced, stored in a retrieval system, or transmitted by any means, electronic, mechanical, photocopying, recording, or otherwise, without written permission from the publisher. No patent liability is assumed with respect to the use of the information contained herein. While every precaution has been taken in the preparation of this book, the publisher and author assume no responsibility for errors or omissions. Neither is any liability assumed for damages resulting from the use of the information contained herein. For information, address Que Corporation, 201 West 103rd Street, Indianapolis, IN 46290. You can reach Que's direct sales line by calling 1-800-428-5331.

Library of Congress Catalog Card Number: 97-68086

International Standard Book Number: 0-7897-1352-7

This book is sold as is, without warranty of any kind, either express or implied, respecting the contents of this book, including but not limited to implied warranties for the book's quality, performance, merchantability, or fitness for any particular purpose. Neither Que Corporation nor its dealers or distributors shall be liable to the purchaser or any other person or entity with respect to any liability, loss, or damage caused or alleged to have been caused directly or indirectly by this book.

99 98 97   8 7 6 5 4 3

Interpretation of the printing code: the rightmost double-digit number is the year of the book's first printing; the rightmost single-digit number is the number of the book's printing. For example, a printing code of 97-1 shows that this copy of the book was printed during the first printing of the book in 1997.

Printed in the United States of America

Screen reproductions in this book were created by means of the program Collage Complete from Inner Media, Inc., Hollis, NH.

President
Roland Elgey

Senior Vice President/Publishing
Don Fowley

Publisher
Joseph B. Wikert

Publishing Director
Karen Reinisch

Manager of Publishing Operations
Linda H. Buehler

General Manager
Joe Muldoon

Editorial Services Director
Carla Hall

Managing Editor
Thomas Hayes

Director of Acquisitions
Cheryl D. Willoughby

Acquisitions Editor
Lisa Swayne

Product Director
Melanie Palaisa

Production Editor
Kate Givens

Editors
Lisa Gebken
San Dee Phillips

Product Marketing Manager
Kourtnaye Sturgeon

Assistant Product Marketing Manager
Gretchen Schlesinger

Technical Editor
Kyle Bryant

Media Development Specialist
David Garratt

Acquisitions Coordinator
Michelle R. Newcomb

Software Relations Coordinator
Susan D. Gallagher

Editorial Assistant
Jennifer L. Chisolm

Book Designer
Glenn Larsen

Cover Designer
Dan Armstrong

Production Team
Marcia Deboy, Maribeth Echard,
Brian Grossman, Kay Hoskin

Indexer
Greg Pearson

Composed in *Palatino* and *Helvetica* by Que Corporation.

Acknowledgments

Que Corporation would like to acknowledge the contributing authors of this book: Peter Aitken, Jennifer Fulton, Sherry Kinkoph, Joe Lowery, Sue Plumley, and Faithe Wempen.

And finally, thanks to our hard-working Que production team: Marcia Deboy, Maribeth Echard, Brian Grossman, Kay Hoskin, and Greg Pearson.

Trademarks

All terms mentioned in this book that are known to be or are suspected of being trademarks or service marks have been appropriately capitalized. Que Corporation cannot attest to the accuracy of this information. Use of a term in this book should not be regarded as affecting the validity of any trademark or service mark.

We'd Like to Hear from You!

As part of our continuing effort to produce books of the highest possible quality, Que would like to hear your comments. To stay competitive, we *really* want you, as a computer book reader and user, to let us know what you like or dislike most about this book or other Que products.

You can mail comments, ideas, or suggestions for improving future editions to the address below, or send us a fax at (317) 581-4663. For the online inclined, Macmillan Computer Publishing has a forum on CompuServe (type **GO QUEBOOKS** at any prompt) through which our staff and authors are available for questions and comments. The address of our Internet site is **http:// www.quecorp.com** (World Wide Web).

In addition to exploring our forum, please feel free to contact me personally to discuss your opinions of this book: I'm **73353,2061** on CompuServe, and **mpalaisa@que.mcp.com** on the Internet.

Thanks in advance—your comments will help us to continue publishing the best books available on computer topics in today's market.

Melanie Palaisa
Product Development Specialist
Que Corporation
201 W. 103rd Street
Indianapolis, Indiana 46290
USA

Contents

Part II: Excel 97   135

Part III: Outlook   307

Part IV: Publisher 97   421

xix

Appendixes   673

Introduction

Small business users, rejoice! The Microsoft Corporation has packaged five of their most powerful and useful software products into one impressive package called Microsoft Office 97 Small Business Edition—a package designed exclusively with you in mind. With these software products and Windows 95, you can save time and money as you create impressive business documents and forms, financial statements, brochures and newsletters, plus manage your daily schedule, and hop on to the Internet. You can now do all of these things with one great package!

The Microsoft Office 97 Small Business Edition includes:

- **Word 97**   Arguably the best Windows-based word processing program on the market. Word has features that enable you to create everything from a one-page memo to a 500-page report. You can quickly generate business correspondence, mass mailings, and even customized business forms.

- **Excel 97**   A powerful yet easy-to-maneuver spreadsheet program you can use to create impressive financial statements, databases, charts, and graphs, and share the information with other software packages. Plus, you can tap into the power of the Small Business Financial Manager, a program that works alongside Excel to whip up financial reports and what-if scenarios based on your accounting data.

- **Publisher 97**   An easy-to-use desktop publishing program that lets you create newsletters, brochures, advertisements, and even Web pages. If it's eye-catching materials you want, Publisher is the tool to use.

- **Outlook**   A daily planner, calendar, and to-do list that helps you get the most out of your day through careful schedule management. Use this program to track tasks, compile contact lists, and juggle appointments.

- **Internet Explorer**   A new and improved Web browser that lets you plug in to the Internet and surf the Web with the greatest of ease. Download the latest files, read the latest online news, and communicate with other Internet users. You can even conduct your own business on the Web.

- **Automap Streets Plus**   A helpful tool that lets you locate addresses around the country, plan out the easiest routes, and mark places you've been.

This powerful suite of programs also comes with the Office 97 ValuPack, a collection of useful tools and information to help you get the most out of your Office programs.

As you can see, the Office 97 Small Business Edition is a dynamic software package that can help you and your company make the most out of the ever-evolving computer technologies.

Using This Book

Microsoft Office 97 Small Business Edition 6-in-1 is designed to help you learn these programs quickly and apply them to your business needs. You don't have to spend any time figuring out what to learn. All the most important tasks are covered in this book. Forget about long classes or thick manuals; acquire the skills you need in short, easy-to-follow lessons.

The book is organized into six parts—one for each of the five software packages, with 15–20 lessons in each part, and a final part that shows you how to integrate the various programs and offers you practical ways to put them to use for your company. Because each of these lessons takes 10 minutes or fewer to complete, you can quickly master the basic skills you need to create documents and business forms, financial statements, advertisements, and flyers; or send and reply to e-mail messages.

If this is the first time you've ever used Windows 95 (or NT 3.51) or a dependent product, begin with the Windows appendix at the back of this book. If you haven't yet installed the package onto your computer, you'll also find installation steps at the back of the book.

This book's usefulness doesn't end with the last page. You can also find updated information on the Web at Que's Office 97 Online Resource Center, **http://www.mcp.com/que/msoffice**. Here you'll find additional business solutions, practical advice and tips, the latest information about Microsoft Office 97 products and updates, plus links to other small business sites. Be sure to check out this Web site often.

Conventions Used in This Book

Each of the short lessons in this book includes step-by-step instructions for performing specific tasks. The following *icons* (small graphic symbols) are included to help you quickly identify particular types of information:

 TIP These icons indicate ways you can save time when you're using any of the Microsoft Office 97 products.

 These icons point out easy-to-follow definitions that you'll need to know in order to understand how to use a software package.

 Watch out for these icons that can help you avoid making mistakes.

CAUTION

 These icons point out associated programs or features found in the Office 97 ValuPack that you may find useful as a small business user.

In addition to the icons, the following conventions are also used:

`On-screen text`	On-screen text appears in monospace.
What you type	Information you type appears in bold type.
Items you select	Items you select, buttons you click, or keys you press appear in bold type.

Word 97

Getting Started with Word

In this lesson, you learn how to start and exit Word, and identify the parts of the Word screen.

Introducing Word

Microsoft Word is the most popular word processing program available today. As a small business user, you'll find plenty of ways to harness Word's powerful features and use them to generate all kinds of documents. You can use Word to create business forms, office documentation, professional and personal correspondence, marketing materials, memos, reports, and much more. The new and improved Word 97 offers you easy-to-use tools for building customized business documents that fit your needs; plus, there are new tools for creating e-mail and Internet documents.

In this section of the book, you'll find lessons to help you get Word 97 up and running fast, plus all the basic information you need to start creating your own business documents. In no time at all, you'll consider Word 97 an invaluable part of your business team.

 TIP   **More Word Power**   There are dozens of other ways you can use Word when you integrate it with the other Microsoft Office 97 programs. Turn to Part IV for some practical ideas and suggestions.

Starting Word 97

You start Word from the Windows Start menu. Follow these steps:

1. Open the Start menu by clicking the **Start** button.

2. On the Start menu, click **Programs**.

3. On the next menu, click **Microsoft Word**.

Another way to start Word is to open the **Start** menu and click **New Office Document**. The New dialog box appears. In this dialog box, click the **General** tab (if necessary), and then double-click the **Blank Document** icon.

CAUTION

Can't Find Microsoft Word on the Menu? You must install Word 97 on your system before you can use it. Refer to Appendix D for installation instructions.

Understanding the Word Screen

When you start Word, you see a blank document ready for you to enter text. Before you begin, however, you need to know about the various parts of the screen (see Figure 1.1). You'll use these screen elements, described in Table 1.1, as you work on your business documents.

Table 1.1 Parts of the Word Screen

Screen Element	Function
Work area	Your document displays here for text entry and editing. Figure 1.1 shows a blank document.
Title bar	The program name, user name, and the name of the current document appear here. At the right end of the title bar are buttons to minimize, restore, and close the program.
Menu bar	Menu headings on this bar let you access Word's menu commands.
Toolbars	The small pictures, or *buttons*, on the toolbars let you select commonly needed commands by clicking the mouse.
Status bar	Word displays information about the document and the state of the keyboard lock keys on the status bar.
Scroll bars	You click the scroll bars to move around in your document.

Screen Element	Function
Minimize button	Click this button to temporarily hide Word (to shrink it to an icon on the taskbar). You can then click the Microsoft Word button on the taskbar at the bottom of your screen to redisplay Word.
Close button	Click this button to close Word.
Restore/Maximize button	Click this button to enlarge Word to full-screen or to shrink Word to a partial-screen window.

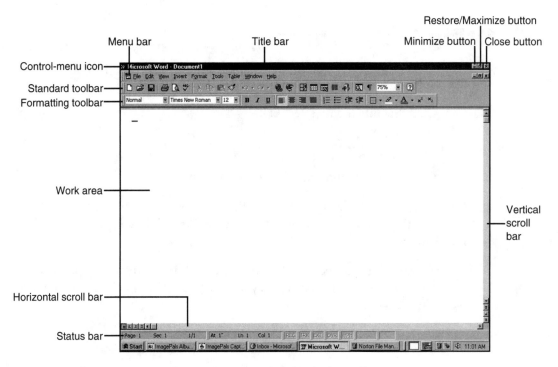

Figure 1.1   Word's opening screen is a blank document.

As you can see from Figure 1.1, Word 97 contains all the basic screen elements you're used to using with other Windows 95 programs. You issue commands through menus and dialog boxes, as well as by clicking toolbar buttons. All of the Office 97 programs use toolbars; some start out with one or two by default and other toolbars may appear when performing certain tasks. Word's Standard toolbar has buttons for common tasks, such as printing and saving, while the Formatting toolbar has buttons associated with formatting commands.

Office 97 has made it very easy to identify toolbar buttons. If you're ever in doubt about what a particular button does, simply move your mouse pointer over the button and pause. Word will display a ScreenTip next to the button identifying its function.

TIP **Are You a New User?** If you're brand new to Windows 95, check out Appendix C at the back of this book for a quick lesson in Windows basics.

Quitting the Program

When you are finished working with Word, you have several options for exiting the program. All of these methods have the same result:

- Open the **File** menu, select **Exit**.
- Press **Alt+F4**.
- Click the **Close** button at the right end of the title bar.
- Click the **Control-menu** icon and select **Close**.

If you are saving the document for the first time, Word prompts you to save it before exiting. For now, you can just select **No**. You'll learn about saving documents in Lesson 4.

In this lesson, you learned how to start and exit Word, and identify parts of the Word screen. The next lesson shows you how to create new Word documents using templates.

Creating a New Document

In this lesson, you learn how to create a new Word document and about the relationship between documents and templates. You also learn how to build new documents with wizards.

Understanding Document Templates

To work effectively with Word 97, you must understand that every Word document is based on a *template*. As the name suggests, a template is a model for a document.

 TERM   **Template**   A model for a new document that may contain text or formatting instructions.

Some templates contain no text, giving you a blank document with some basic formatting specifications; you are responsible for entering all of the text. Other templates contain text or detailed formatting specifications. For example, if you write a lot of business letters, you could use a template that contains the date, your return address, and a closing salutation. When you create a new document based on that template, all of those elements will automatically be in the document—all you need to do is add the other parts. If a template contains formatting, all documents based on that template will have a uniform appearance (for example, the same font and margins).

Word comes with a variety of predefined templates that are ready for you to use. These templates cover a range of common document needs, such as fax forms, memos, business letters, and Web pages. You can also create your own

templates. In this lesson, you will learn how to use Word's predefined templates. Lesson 12 shows you how to create your own templates.

 More Templates You'll find even more templates in the Small Business
Edition ValuPack. Turn to Appendix B to learn more about using the ValuPack.

Starting a New Document

 Many of the documents you create will be based on the Normal template, which
creates a blank document. When you start Word, it automatically opens a blank
document for you to work with. If Word is already running, you can create a
blank document by clicking the **New** button on the toolbar.

When you create a document based on a template, the template's text and
formatting will be displayed in the new document. There's nothing special
about document text that comes from a template—you can edit it just like any
other text. You can also edit the actual templates, as you'll learn in Lesson 12.

To start a document based on a template other than the Normal template, follow
these steps:

1. Open the **File** menu and select **New**. The New dialog box appears (see
   Figure 2.1).
2. The tabs along the top of the dialog box list the different template categories. Click the tab corresponding to the category of document you want to
   create.
3. Click the icon that corresponds to the template you want. If a preview of
   the template's appearance is available, it will appear in the Preview area.
   Figure 2.1 shows a preview of the Contemporary Fax template.
4. Click **OK**. Word creates the document and displays it on-screen, ready for
   adding your own text.

 TIP **Word on the Web: Web Templates** Select the **Web Pages** tab in the
New dialog box for templates that are useful for Web documents. If you don't
see such a tab, you will need to run the Setup program again and install the
templates. Refer to Appendix D for installation instructions.

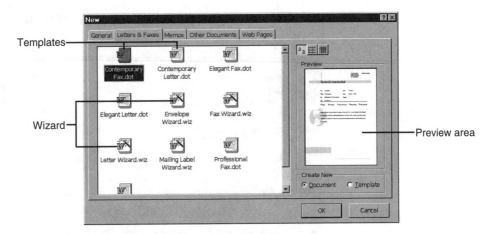

Templates

Wizard

Preview area

Figure 2.1   The New dialog box.

Some templates contain *placeholder* text that you must replace. For example, the résumé template contains a dummy name and biography that you must delete and replace with your own information. For example, the document might display [Click here and type your name]. Simply follow the instructions displayed in brackets.

No Templates or Wizards?   If you can't find any templates, they probably were not installed with Word. You can reinstall Word, choose the Custom installation option, and specify which templates and wizards you want installed.

CAUTION

Using Wizards

Some of Word's templates are a special kind of template called a *wizard*. Whereas a standard template is a static combination of text and formatting, a wizard is an active tool that asks you questions about the document you want to create, and then uses your answers to create the new document. When you're starting a new document, you can recognize a wizard in the New dialog box by its title. You can see several wizard templates in Figure 2.1.

Each wizard is unique, but they all follow the same basic procedures. There are a number of steps in a wizard; each step asks you for certain information about the document you want to create. Figure 2.2 shows an example; this is a step in the Fax Wizard.

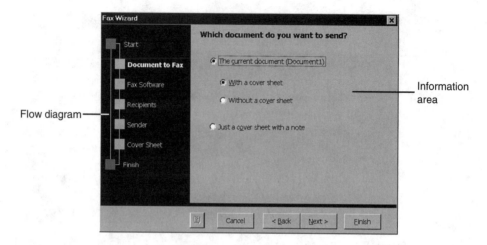

Figure 2.2   The Fax Wizard dialog box.

Table 2.1 describes the different components of the wizard dialog box.

Table 2.1   The Parts of a Wizard Dialog Box

Wizard Component	Function
Title bar	Shows the name of the wizard that is running.
Flow diagram	Graphically represents the wizard steps, with the current step highlighted. Click any step to go directly to it.
Information area	Requests document information from you.
Cancel button	Cancels the wizard without creating a new document.
Back button	Moves to the previous wizard step.
Next Button	Moves to the next wizard step.
Finish button	Ends the wizard and creates the new document based on the information you have entered so far.
Help button	Click to display Help information about using the wizard.

To create a new document using a wizard, follow these steps:

1. Open the **File** menu and select **New** to open the New dialog box (refer to Figure 2.1).

2. Click the tab corresponding to the category of document you are creating. (Not all tabs contain wizards, however.)

3. Click the wizard you want to use, and then click **OK**.

4. In the wizard dialog box, enter the information Word needs, based on how you want the document created. Then click **Next**.

5. Repeat step 4 for each of the wizard steps. If needed, click **Back** one or more times to return to an earlier step to make changes in the information.

6. At the last wizard step, click **Finish** to close the wizard and create the new document.

 TIP   **Know Your Templates**   Spend some time becoming familiar with Word's various predefined templates; they can save you a lot of time. You should also check out the extra templates available in the Office 97 ValuPack (see Appendix B for more information).

In this lesson, you learned about document templates and how to create a new document. You also learned how to use wizards. The next lesson teaches you how to perform basic editing tasks in Word.

Performing Basic Editing Tasks

In this lesson, you learn how to enter text, move around in a document, and perform other basic editing tasks.

Entering Text

When you start a new Word document based on the Normal template, you see a blank work area that contains only two items:

- **Blinking vertical line** This is the cursor, or insertion point, which marks the location where the text you type appears in the document and where certain editing actions occur.
- **Horizontal line** This marks the end of the document.

In a new empty document, these two markers start at the same location. To enter text, simply type it using the keyboard. As you type, the text appears on-screen, and the insertion point moves to the right. If the line of text reaches the right edge of the screen, Word automatically starts a new line for you; this is called *word wrapping*. There's no need to press **Enter** unless you want to start a new paragraph.

If you enter more lines than will fit on the screen, Word scrolls previously entered text upward to keep the cursor in view. Figure 3.1 shows word wrap as well as the end of document marker and cursor. If you make a mistake while typing, there are a couple of ways you can delete it:

- Press the **Backspace** key on your keyboard to erase characters to the left of the cursor.
- Press the **Delete** key to erase characters to the right of the cursor.

TIP **Leave It to Word Wrap** Press **Enter** only when you want to start a new paragraph.

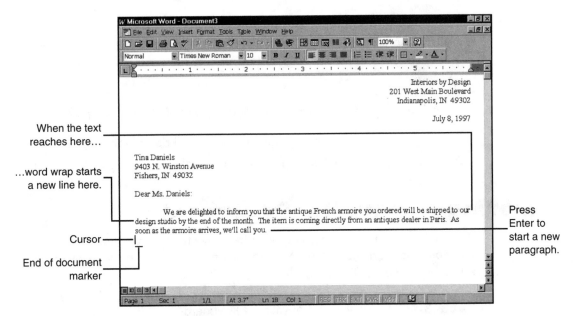

When the text reaches here...

...word wrap starts a new line here.

Cursor

End of document marker

Press Enter to start a new paragraph.

Figure 3.1 Using Enter and word wrap.

Try an Animated Cursor Office 97's ValuPack comes with an animated cursor you can install to help liven up your Office tasks or make your pointer easier to see while using the Office 97 programs. Check out Appendix B for more information.

Paragraphs in Word

The idea of paragraphs is important in Word because certain types of formatting apply to individual paragraphs. In Word, you end one paragraph and start a new one by pressing **Enter**. Word inserts a new, blank line and positions the cursor at the beginning of it.

 On your screen, the result may look the same as if word wrap had started the new line, but the difference is that Word has inserted a *paragraph mark*. These marks are normally invisible, but you can display them by clicking the

Show/Hide ¶ button on the Standard toolbar. Click the button again to hide the marks. This tool is very useful when you need to see exactly where the paragraphs begin and end in your document.

 TIP Other Marks? When you display paragraph marks, Word also displays spaces as dots and tabs as arrows.

To combine two paragraphs into a single paragraph, follow these steps:

1. Move the cursor to the beginning of the second paragraph.

2. Press **Backspace** to delete the paragraph mark.

Moving Around the Document

As you work on a document, you will often have to move the cursor to view or work on other parts of the text. Most of the time you'll use the keyboard to do this, as explained in Table 3.1.

Table 3.1 Moving the Cursor with the Keyboard

To Move...	Perform this Action
Left or right one character	Press ← or →
Left or right one word	Press **Ctrl+←** or **Ctrl+→**
Up or down one line	Press ↑ or ↓
Up or down one paragraph	Press **Ctrl+↑** or **Ctrl+↓**
To the start or end of a line	Press **Home** or **End**
Up or down one screen	Press **Page Up** or **Page Down**
To the top or bottom of the current screen	Press **Ctrl+Page Up** or **Ctrl+Page Down**
To the start or end of the document	Press **Ctrl+Home** or **Ctrl+End**

You can also navigate with the mouse. If the desired cursor location is in view on the screen, simply click the location. If the desired location is not in view, you must scroll to bring it into view and then click the location. Table 3.2 describes how to scroll with the mouse.

Table 3.2 Scrolling with the Mouse

To Scroll…	*Do This*
Up or down one line	Click the up or down arrow on the vertical scroll bar.
Up or down one screen	Click the vertical scroll bar between the box and the up or down arrow.
Up or down any amount	Drag the scroll box up or down.
Up or down one page	Click the **Previous Page** or **Next Page** button on the vertical scroll bar.

Note that scrolling with the scroll bar does not move the cursor, only the view of the document; the cursor remains in its original location while the screen displays another part of the document. You must click the new location to move the cursor there.

TIP **Quick Go To** Press **Shift+F5** one or more times to move the cursor to locations in the document that you edited most recently.

Selecting Text

Many tasks you'll perform in Word will require that you first select the text you want to modify. For example, to underline a sentence, you must select the sentence first and then click the **Underline** button on the toolbar. Selected text appears highlighted on the screen with white letters on a black background, as shown in Figure 3.2. Note the phrase **Dear Ms. Kennedy:** is selected in the figure.

You can select text with either the mouse or the keyboard. With the mouse, you can use the selection bar, an unmarked column in the left document margin. When the mouse pointer moves from the document to the selection bar, it changes from an I-beam to a northeast-pointing arrow. Table 3.3 lists the methods you can use to select text.

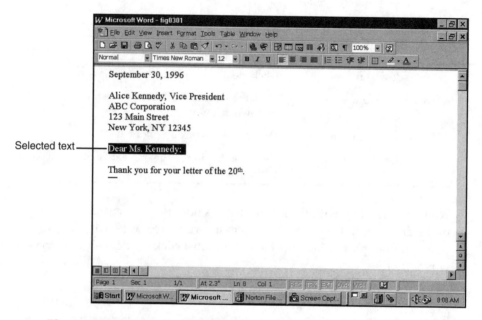

Selected text

Figure 3.2   Selected text appears highlighted.

Table 3.3   Methods of Selecting Text

To Select Text	*Perform this Action*
One word	Double-click anywhere on the word.
One sentence	Press and hold **Ctrl** and click anywhere in the sentence, or simply triple-click the sentence.
One line	Click the selection bar next to the line.
Multiple lines	Drag in the selection bar next to the lines.
One paragraph	Double-click the selection bar next to the paragraph.
Entire document	Press and hold **Ctrl** and click anywhere in the selection bar.
Any amount	Move the insertion point to the start of the text, press and hold Shift, and move the insertion point to the end of the desired text using the movement keys described in Table 3.1.
Entire document	Triple-click the selection bar, or press **Ctrl+A**.

To cancel a selection, click anywhere on the screen or use the keyboard to move the insertion point.

When you are selecting text by dragging with the mouse, Word's default is to automatically select entire words. If you need to select partial words, you can turn this option off (or back on) as described here:

1. Open the **Tools** menu and select **Options** to open the Options dialog box.
2. Click the **Edit** tab.
3. Click the **When Selecting, Automatically Select Entire Word** check box to turn it on or off.
4. Click **OK**.

Deleting, Copying, and Pasting Text

You have already learned how to use the Delete and Backspace keys to delete single characters. In addition, you can delete larger amounts of text, and you can move or copy text from one document location to another.

To delete a block of text, first select the text. Then do one of these things:

- To simply delete the text, press **Delete** or **Backspace**.
- To delete the text and replace it with new text, just start typing in the new text.

To move or copy text, start by selecting the text. Then follow these steps:

1. To *copy* the text, click **Edit**, **Copy**; or click the **Copy** button on the Standard toolbar; or press **Ctrl+C** on the keyboard.

   To *move* the text, click **Edit**, **Cut**; or click the **Cut** button on the Standard toolbar; or press **Ctrl+X**.

2. Move the cursor to the location where you want the text moved or copied.

3. Choose **Edit**, **Paste**; or click the **Paste** button on the Standard toolbar; or press **Ctrl+V**.

You can also use the mouse to move and copy text. This technique, called drag and drop, is most convenient for small amounts of text and when both the "from" and "to" locations are visible on-screen. Here's how you drag and drop:

1. Select the text.
2. Point at the text with the mouse. The mouse pointer changes from an I-beam to an arrow.

3. To copy the text, press and hold **Ctrl**. To move the text, do not press any key.

4. Drag to the new location. As you drag, a vertical dotted line indicates the text's new location.

5. Release the mouse button and, if you are copying, the **Ctrl** key.

Make a Mistake?   You can recover from most editing actions (such as deleting text) by clicking the **Undo** button on the toolbar, or opening the **Edit** menu and selecting **Undo**, or by pressing **Ctrl+Z** on the keyboard.

CAUTION

In this lesson, you learned how to enter text, move around in the document, and perform other basic editing tasks. In the next lesson, you'll learn how to save and retrieve documents.

Saving and Opening Documents

In this lesson, you learn how to name your document, save it to disk, and open a document you saved earlier.

Saving a New Document

When you create a new document in Word, it is stored temporarily in your computer's memory under the default name Document*n*, where *n* is a number that increases by 1 for each new unnamed document you open during a session. Word only "remembers" the document until you quit the program or turn off the computer. To save a document permanently so you can retrieve it later, you must assign a name and save it to hard or floppy disk. These steps show you how to do just that:

1. Open the **File** menu and select **Save** or click the **Save** button on the Standard toolbar. The Save As dialog box appears (see Figure 4.1).

2. In the **File Name** text box, enter the name you want to assign to the document file. The name can be up to 256 characters long and should be descriptive of the document's contents.

3. If you want to save the document in a different folder or drive, click the **Save In** drop-down arrow and select a different folder or drive.

4. Click **Save**. The document is saved to disk, and the name you assigned now appears in the title bar.

Save In list box

File Name text box

Figure 4.1 The Save As dialog box.

TIP **Word on the Web** Documents you make publicly available on your Web site must be saved in Hypertext Markup Language (HTML) format. Word provides a separate command for saving in this format: **File**, **Save as HTML**.

Saving a Document as You Work

After naming and saving a document, you still need to save it periodically as you work to minimize data loss in the event of a power failure or other system problem. After you name a document, you can easily save the current version:

- Open the **File** menu and select **Save**.
- Click the **Save** button on the Standard toolbar.
- Press **Ctrl+S** on the keyboard.

Word automatically saves the document with its current name, and no dialog boxes appear.

Don't Forget! Save your document regularly as you work on it. If you don't, you may lose your work if there is a power outage or other problem.

CAUTION

Changing a Document's Name

After you name a document, you may need to change its name. For example, you might want to keep an old version of a document under its original name and then save a revised version under a new name. To rename an existing document, follow these steps:

1. Open the **File** menu, and select **Save As**. The Save As dialog box appears, showing the current document name in the File Name text box.

2. In the **File Name** box, give the file a new name.

3. (Optional) Select a different folder in the **Save In** list box to save the document in a different folder.

4. Click **Save**, and Word saves the document under the new name.

Opening a Document

You can open any document created with Word 97 to work on it again. You can also open documents that were created with other programs, such as WordPerfect.

 To open an existing file, select **File**, **Open** or click the **Open** button on the Standard toolbar. The Open dialog box appears (see Figure 4.2).

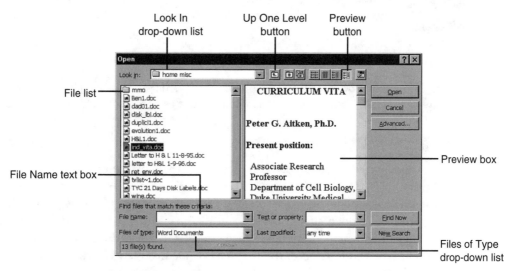

Figure 4.2 The Open dialog box.

The file list shows all of the Word documents and folders in the current folder. Each document is represented by a small page icon that appears next to its name; folders have a file folder icon next to them. The Look In list box shows the name of the current folder. You can take the following actions in the Open dialog box:

- To open a file, click its name in the file list or type its name into the **File Name** list box; then press **Enter** or click the **Open** button. Or you can simply double-click the file name.

- To preview the contents of a file, click the file name, and then click the **Preview** button. Click the **Preview** button again to turn preview off.

- To look for files other than Word documents, click the **Files of Type** drop-down arrow and select the desired document type.

- To move up one folder in your drive's hierarchy, click the **Up One Level** button.

- To move down one level to a different folder, double-click the folder name in the file list.

- To move to another folder or drive, click the **Look In** drop-down arrow and select the desired folder.

Folder   Windows uses folders to organize files on a disk. Before Windows 95, folders were called subdirectories.

TIP   **Word on the Web**   To open a Web document for editing in Word, select **HTML Document** from the **Files of Type** list. Then select the document and click **Open**.

To quickly open a document you recently worked on, you can use Word's Recently Used File List instead of the Open dialog box. To view this list, open the **File** menu. The list is displayed at the bottom of the menu just above the Exit command. To open a file on the list, press the number corresponding to the file, or click the file name with the mouse. This list displays the document files that you have saved most recently. If you have just installed Word, there will be no files displayed here, of course. If you have saved files and the list still doesn't display them, see the next paragraph.

Converting Files If you plan on exchanging Word 97 files with users who have earlier versions of Word, you might want to check out the Microsoft Word 97 Converter in the Office 97 ValuPack. See Appendix B for more information.

You can control how many files appear on the Recently Used File List *and* whether the list appears at all. Click **Tools, Options** to open the Options dialog box. Click the **General** tab if necessary. Click the **Recently Used File List** check box to turn it on or off to control the display of the list. To change the number of files displayed in the list, enter a number in the **Entries** text box or click the up/down arrows to change the existing entry. Click **OK** when you're finished.

TIP **Quick Open** You can open a Word document (and start Word if it is not already running) by double-clicking the document name or icon in the Windows Explorer or My Computer window.

In this lesson, you learned how to name your document, save it to disk, and open a document you saved earlier. The next lesson shows you how to change screen display options.

Changing Screen Display Options

*In this lesson, you learn how to control the Word screen display
to suit your working style.*

Looking at Document Display Options

Word offers several ways to display your document. Each of these views is
designed to make certain editing tasks easier. The available views include:

- **Normal**   Best for general editing tasks.
- **Page Layout**   Ideal for working with formatting and page layout.
- **Online Layout**   Optimized for viewing on-screen.
- **Outline**   Designed for working with outlines.

The view you use has no effect on the contents of your document or on the way
it will look when printed. They affect only the way the document appears on-
screen.

Normal View

Normal view is suitable for most editing tasks; it is the view you will probably
use most often. This is Word's default view. All special formatting is visible on-
screen, including different font sizes, italic, boldface, and other enhancements.
The screen display of your document is essentially identical to how the document will appear when printed. However, Word does not display certain
aspects of the page layout, which makes it easier and quicker for you to edit.
For example, you do not see headers and footers or multiple columns.

To select Normal view, select **View**, **Normal** or click the **Normal View** button at the left end of the horizontal scroll bar. Figure 5.1 shows a document in Normal view.

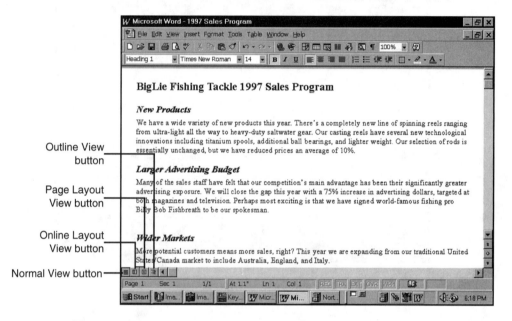

Outline View button

Page Layout View button

Online Layout View button

Normal View button

Figure 5.1 A document displayed in Normal view.

Page Layout View

Page Layout view displays your document exactly as it will print. Headers, footers, and all other details of the page layout appear on-screen. You can edit in Page Layout view; it's ideal for fine-tuning the details of page composition. Be aware, however, that the additional computer processing required makes display changes relatively slow in Page Layout view, particularly when you have a complex page layout.

 TIP **Sneak Preview** Use Page Layout view to see what your printed document will look like before you actually print. The Print Preview feature (**File**, **Print Preview**) is preferred for previewing entire pages.

 Click **View**, **Page Layout** (or click the **Page Layout View** button) to switch to Page Layout view. Figure 5.2 shows a sample document in Page Layout view.

25

Header

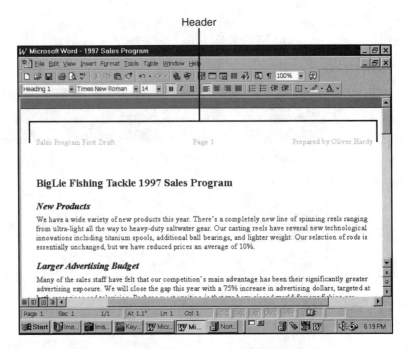

Figure 5.2 A document in Page Layout view displays the header.

Online Layout View

Online Layout view is optimal for reading and editing a document on-screen. Legibility is increased by using larger fonts; displaying shorter lines of text; hiding headers, footers, and similar elements; and basing the layout on the screen as opposed to the printed page. Also, the document map is displayed on the left side of the screen (the document map is covered later in this lesson). The screen display will not match the final printed appearance. Online Layout view is ideal for editing the document text, but is not suited for working with page layout or graphics.

TIP **Content Editing** Use Online Layout view when editing the document contents, not the appearance.

Click **View**, **Online Layout** (or click the **Online Layout View** button) to switch to Online Layout view.

When you're in Online Layout view, the horizontal scroll bar and its View buttons are hidden. You must use the **View** menu commands to switch to a different view. Figure 5.3 shows a document in Online Layout view.

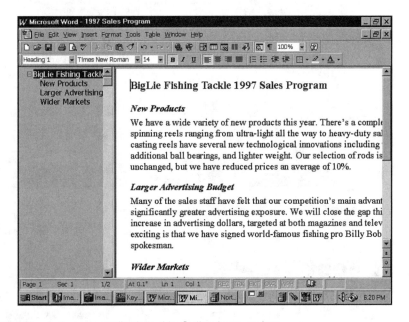

Figure 5.3 A document displayed in Online Layout view.

Outline View

Use Outline view to create outlines and to examine the structure of a document. Figure 5.4 shows a document in Outline view. In this view, you can choose to view only your document headings, thus hiding all subordinate text. You can quickly promote, demote, or move document headings along with subordinate text to a new location. For this view to be useful, you need to assign heading styles to the document headings, a technique you'll learn about in Lesson 13.

 Click **View**, **Outline** to switch to Outline view, or click the **Outline View** button at the left end of the horizontal scroll bar.

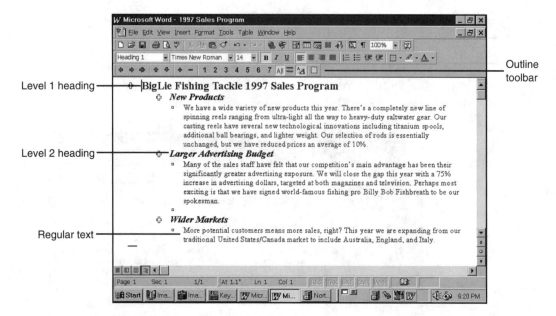

Level 1 heading

Level 2 heading

Regular text

Outline
toolbar

Figure 5.4 A document displayed in Outline view.

Draft Font View

Draft Font view is a display option you can apply in both Normal and Outline views. As you can see in Figure 5.5, Draft Font view uses a single generic font for all text; it indicates special formatting by underlining or boldface. Graphics display as empty boxes. Draft Font view provides the fastest editing and screen display, and it is particularly useful when editing the content of documents that contain a lot of fancy formatting and graphics. This view is ideal when you're concentrating on the contents of your document and not on its appearance.

Follow these steps to turn Draft Font view on or off:

1. Open the **Tools** menu and select **Options** to display the Options dialog box.

2. If necessary, click the **View** tab to display the View options.

3. Click the **Draft Font** check box to turn it on or off.

4. Click **OK**.

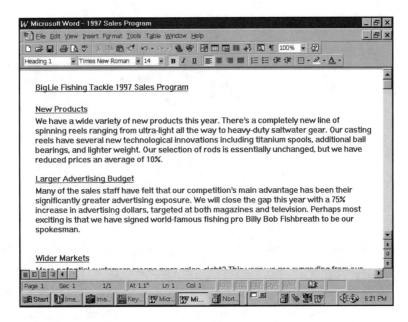

Figure 5.5   A document displayed in Draft Font view.

Full Screen View

Full Screen view provides the maximum amount of screen real estate to display your document contents. In Full Screen view, the title bar, menu, toolbars, status bar, and all other Word elements are hidden, and your document occupies the entire screen. You use Full Screen view in combination with other views. Thus you can use Full Screen view in Normal view, Page Layout view, and so on. You can enter and edit text in this view and select from the menus using the usual keyboard commands.

To turn on Full Screen view, click **View**, **Full Screen**. To turn off Full Screen view, select **View**, **Full Screen** again (using the keyboard) or click the **Close Full Screen** box that appears in the lower-right corner of the screen.

Zooming the Screen

The Zoom command lets you control the size of your document on-screen. You can enlarge it to facilitate reading small fonts, and you can decrease it to view an entire page at one time. Click **View**, **Zoom** to open the Zoom dialog box (see Figure 5.6).

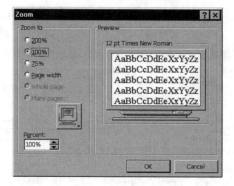

Figure 5.6   The Zoom dialog box.

The following options are available in the Zoom dialog box. As you make selections, the Preview area shows you what the selected zoom setting will look like.

- Select **200%**, **100%**, or **75%** to zoom to the indicated magnification. 200% is twice normal size, 75% is three-quarters normal size, and so on.
- Enter a custom magnification percentage of 10–200% in the **Percent** text box.
- Select **Page Width** to scale the display to fit the entire page width on-screen.
- Select **Whole Page** to scale the display to fit the entire page, vertically and horizontally, on-screen.
- Select **Many Pages** to display two or more pages at the same time. Click the **Monitor** button under the Many Pages option, and then drag to specify how many pages to display.

The Whole Page and Many Pages options are available only if you are viewing the document in Page Layout view.

TIP   **Quick Zoom**   You can quickly change the zoom setting by clicking the **Zoom** drop-down arrow on the Standard toolbar and selecting the desired zoom setting from the list.

Using the Document Map

The Document Map is a separate pane that displays your document's headings. You do not edit in the Document Map; rather, you use it to quickly move around your document. The Document Map is displayed automatically when you switch to Online Layout view. You can also display it in other views by selecting **View**, **Document Map**. Figure 5.7 shows a document with the map displayed.

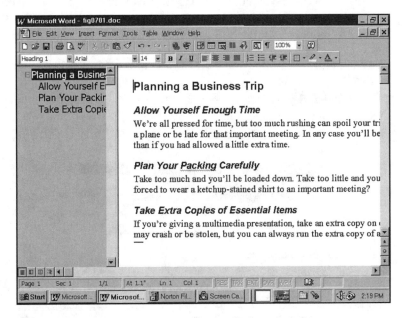

Figure 5.7   The Document Map is displayed to the left of the work area.

To use the Document Map, click the desired map heading. The main document window scrolls to that location in the document. You can control the width of the map display by dragging the border between the map and the document to the desired location. Dragging the border to the left edge of the screen has the same effect as turning the Document Map off.

Splitting the Screen

Word lets you split the work area into two panels, one above the other, so you can view different parts of one document at the same time. Each panel scrolls independently and has its own scroll bars. Figure 5.8 shows a document displayed on a split screen. Editing changes that you make in either panel affect the document.

These steps walk you through splitting the screen:

1. Open the **Window** menu and select **Split** or press **Ctrl+Alt+S**. Word displays a horizontal split line across the middle of the work area.

2. To accept two equal size panes, click with the left mouse button or press **Enter**. To create different size panes, move the mouse until the split line is in the desired location, and then click or press **Enter**.

When working with a split screen, you move the editing cursor from one pane to the other by clicking with the mouse. To change the pane sizes, point at the split line and drag it to the new location. To remove the split and return to regular view, drag the split line to either the top or the bottom of the work area, or select **Windows**, **Remove Split**.

Splitter bar ——

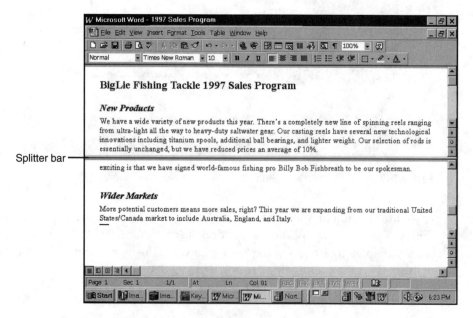

Figure 5.8 Viewing a document in Split Screen view.

TIP   **Quick Split**   You can quickly split the screen by pointing at the splitter bar, just above the up arrow on the vertical toolbar (refer to Figure 5.8), and dragging it down to the desired location.

In this lesson, you learned how to control Word's screen display. In the next lesson, you'll learn how to work with fonts, borders, and shading.

Fonts, Borders, and Shading

6

In this lesson, you learn how to use different fonts in your document and how to apply borders and shading.

Working with Fonts

Word offers you a huge assortment of fonts to use in your documents. Each font has a specific *typeface*, which determines the appearance of the characters. Typefaces are identified by names such as Arial, Courier, and Times New Roman. Each font also has a size, which is specified in *points*. There are 72 points in an inch, so a 36-point font would have its largest characters 1/2 inch tall. Most documents use font sizes in the 8- to 14-point range, but larger and smaller sizes are available for headings and other special needs.

More Fonts!   The Office 97 ValuPack has more fonts you can install and use with the various Office programs. Check out Appendix B for more information.

You can change the font of text that already has been typed by first selecting the text. To specify the font for text you are about to type, simply move the cursor to the desired location. Then follow these steps to choose a font for the selected text or the text you're about to type:

1. Open the **Format** menu and select **Font** to display the Font dialog box shown in Figure 6.1.

Select the font name ⟶ 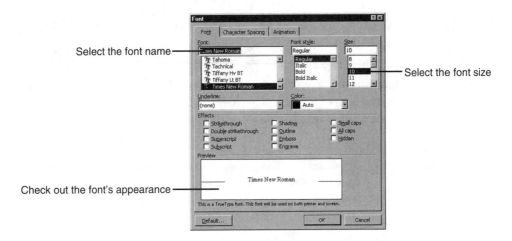 ⟵ Select the font size

Check out the font's appearance ⟶

Figure 6.1 The Font dialog box.

2. The Font text box displays the name of the current font. Scroll through the **Font** list box and select a new font name.

3. The Size text box displays the current font size. Select a new size from the **Size** list box or type a number in the text box. The Preview box shows a preview of what the selected font looked like.

4. Click **OK** to exit the dialog box and apply the new settings.

TIP **Quick Select** If you want to change the font for a whole document, remember that you can select the entire document by pressing **Ctrl+A**.

A quicker way to change fonts and sizes is to use the Formatting toolbar. The Font list box and the Font Size list box display the name and size of the current font. You can change the font by clicking the drop-down arrow of either list and making a selection. Note that in the Font list, the fonts you have used most recently appear at the top.

TIP **Keyboard Happy?** From the keyboard, you can access the Font and Font Size lists on the toolbar by pressing **Ctrl+Shift+F** or **Ctrl+Shift+P** (respectively) followed by the down-arrow key. Then use the arrow keys to select a new font or font size from the list.

Using Boldface, Italics, and Underlining

Three of the most popular formatting commands are bold, italic, and underline. You can apply these commands to any of Word's fonts. You can also use two or three of these effects in combination. As you can with other formatting, you can apply these effects to existing text by first selecting the text, or you can apply them to text you are about to type.

The quickest way to assign boldface, italics, or underlining is with the buttons on the Formatting toolbar. Click a button to turn the corresponding attribute on; click it again to turn it off. When the cursor is at a location where one of these attributes is turned on, the corresponding toolbar button appears to be pressed in.

You can also assign font attributes using the Font dialog box. (If you want to use underlining other than the default single underline, you must use this method.) Here's how to use the dialog box:

1. Open the **Format** menu and select **Font** to open the Font dialog box.
2. Under Font Style, select **Bold**, **Italic**, or **Bold Italic**. Select **Regular** to return to normal text.
3. Click the **Underline** drop-down arrow and select the desired underline style from the list; or select **None** to remove underlining.
4. Click **OK**.

TIP   **A New Default**   To change the default font used in documents based on the Normal template, open the **Font** dialog box, select the desired font and attributes, and click the **Default** button.

Applying Special Font Effects

Word has a number of special font effects that you can use. These include superscript and subscript, strikethrough, and several graphics effects (such as shadow and outline). You can also specify that text be hidden, which means it will not display on-screen or be printed.

To assign special font effects to selected text or text you are about to type, follow these steps:

1. Open the **Format** menu and select **Font** to open the Font dialog box.

2. In the Effects area, select the effects you want. To turn on an effect, click to place an X in the check box. To turn off an effect, click to remove the X from the check box. The Preview box shows you what the font will look like with the selected effects.

3. When you're satisfied with your settings, click **OK**.

CAUTION

Where's That Hidden Text? To locate hidden text, click **Tools**, **Options**, click the **View** tab, and then select the **Hidden Text** option. Word displays hidden text with a dotted underline. You can also display hidden text by clicking the **Show/Hide ¶** button.

Displaying Borders

Word's Borders command lets you improve the appearance of your documents by displaying borders around specified text. Figure 6.2 shows examples of the use of borders (and it illustrates shading, covered in the section "Applying Shading" later in this lesson).

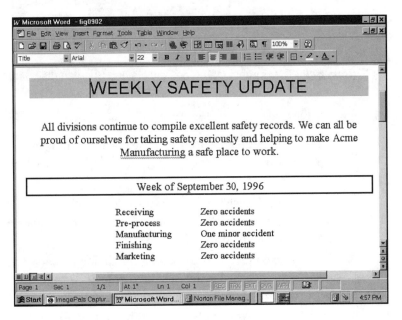

Figure 6.2 A document with borders and shading.

You can apply a border to selected text or to individual paragraphs. To put a border around text, select the text. For a paragraph, place the cursor anywhere in the paragraph. The quickest way to apply a border is to use the Border button on the Formatting toolbar. Click the **Outside Border** drop-down arrow to view a palette of available border settings, and then click the desired border diagram. Click the **No Borders** diagram to remove borders.

If you need to customize the appearance of your borders, you must use the Borders and Shading dialog box (see Figure 6.3). To open this dialog box, click **Format, Borders and Shading,** and then click the **Borders** tab, if necessary, to bring it to the front of the dialog box.

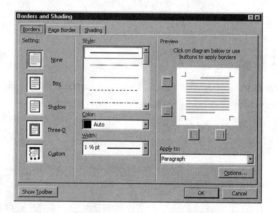

Figure 6.3 The Borders tab of the Borders and Shading dialog box.

The steps for creating a border are as follows:

1. Select the general appearance of the borders you want by clicking the corresponding icon in the Setting area (the Custom setting is explained later).

2. In the **Style** list, select the desired line style, color, and width.

3. In the Preview area, click the buttons or click directly on the page diagram to add or remove borders from the four sides of the text.

4. If you selected text before opening the dialog box, use the **Apply To** list to specify whether the border is to be displayed around the selected text or the current paragraph.

5. Click **OK,** and Word puts your settings into effect.

The normal border settings apply the same line style (solid, dotted, and so on) to all four sides of the border box. To create a custom border that combines different styles, use these steps:

1. Click the **Custom** icon.
2. In the **Style** list, select the line style, color, and width for one side of the border box.
3. In the Preview area, click the button or click directly on the page diagram to specify the side of the border box to which you want to apply the style you selected in step 2.
4. Repeat steps 2 and 3 to specify the style for the other three sides of the border box.
5. Select **OK**.

You can also place borders around entire pages in your document. To do so, click the **Page Border** tab of the Borders and Shading dialog box. This tab looks and operates just as the Borders tab does in terms of specifying the border's appearance. The only difference is specifying where the border will be applied, which is done with the options in the **Apply To** list. You have four choices:

- Whole Document
- This Section
- This Section - First Page Only
- This Section - All Except First Page

You'll learn how to divide a document into sections in Lesson 9.

Applying Shading

You can use shading to display a background color under text (such as black text on a light gray background). Figure 6.2 shows an example of shading. You can apply shading to selected text or to individual paragraphs. Shading can be made up of a fill color (a solid background color), a pattern color (a background made of a pattern instead of a solid color), or a combination of both.

Here's how to apply shading:

1. Select the text to be shaded, or position the cursor anywhere in the paragraph to shade an entire paragraph.

2. Pull down the **Format** menu, and select **Borders and Shading** to open the Borders and Shading dialog box. If necessary, click the **Shading** tab (see Figure 6.4).

3. To use a fill color, select it from the palette in the Fill area of the dialog box. To use only a pattern color, click the **None** button.

4. To use a pattern color, select its style and color from the lists in the Patterns section of the dialog box. To use only a fill color, select the **Clear** style. You can view the appearance of the selected settings in the Preview area of the dialog box.

5. If you selected text before opening the dialog box, use the **Apply To** list to specify whether the fill should apply to the selected text or the current paragraph.

6. Click **OK**.

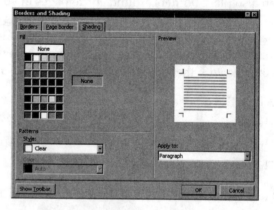

Figure 6.4 The Shading tab of the Borders and Shading dialog box.

 TIP **Printing Color?** Of course, color shading will print in color only if you have a color printer. You need to perform test printouts of pages with shading because how Word displays shading on-screen is often quite different from the final printed results.

In this lesson, you learned how to use fonts, borders, and shading in your documents. In the next lesson, you learn how to control indentation and justification of text, and how to control line breaks.

Using Indents and Justification

In this lesson, you learn how to set the indentation and alignment of text in your document, and how to control line breaks.

Working with Indentation

The distance between your text and the left and right edges of the page is controlled by two things: the left and right page margins and the text indentation. Margins (which are covered in detail in Lesson 9) are usually changed only for entire documents or large sections of a document. Indentation is used with smaller sections of text, such as individual lines and paragraphs.

Indentation The distance between a paragraph's text and the margins for the entire document. For example, if the left margin is set at 1" and a particular paragraph has a 1" indentation, that paragraph starts 2" from the edge of the paper.

The easiest way to set indents is by using the Ruler and your mouse. To display the Ruler (or hide it), click **View**, **Ruler**. The numbers on the Ruler indicate the space from the left margin in inches. Figure 7.1 shows the Ruler and identifies the various elements you use to set indents. In addition, the sample text in the figure illustrates the various indent options.

Rapid Ruler Quickly display the Ruler by positioning the mouse pointer at the top edge of the work area for a moment. When you finish using the Ruler, move the mouse pointer away, and the Ruler is automatically hidden again.

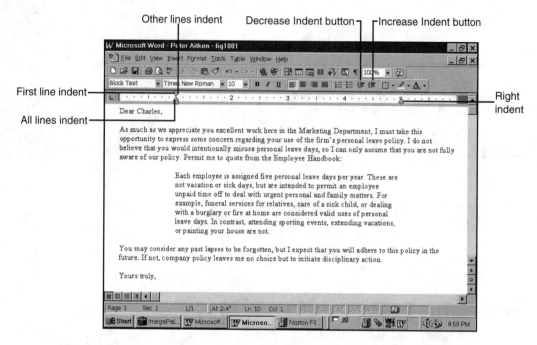

Figure 7.1   Use the Ruler to set text indentation. The second paragraph is indented one inch from both the right and left margins.

Indentation applies to individual paragraphs. To set indentation for one paragraph, position the cursor anywhere in the paragraph. For more than one paragraph, select those paragraphs. (Otherwise, the new indents will apply only to new paragraphs that you type from the insertion point forward.) Then drag the indent markers on the Ruler to the desired positions. As you drag, a dotted vertical line appears, stretching down through the document to show the new indent location. Use these guidelines when setting paragraph indentation:

- To change the indent of the first line of a paragraph, drag the **First Line Indent** marker to the desired position.

- To change the indent of all lines of a paragraph except the first one, drag the **Other Lines Indent** marker to the desired position (this is called a *hanging indent*).

- To change the indent of all lines of a paragraph, drag the **All Lines Indent** marker to the desired position.

- To change the indent of the right edge of the paragraph, drag the **Right Indent** marker to the desired position.

You can also quickly increase or decrease the left indent for the current paragraph in 1/2-inch increments by clicking the **Increase Indent** or **Decrease Indent** buttons on the Formatting toolbar. And undoubtedly, the quickest way to indent the first line of a paragraph is to position the cursor at the start of the line and press **Tab**.

Hanging Indent A paragraph in which the first line is indented less than all the other lines.

Setting Indents with the Paragraph Dialog Box

Word also gives you the option of setting indents using the Paragraph dialog box. These steps walk you through that process.

1. Open the **Format** menu and select **Paragraph** to open the Paragraph dialog box. Then click the **Indents and Spacing** tab if necessary to display the indents and spacing options (see Figure 7.2).

2. In the Indentation area, click the increment arrows for the **Left** and **Right** text boxes to increase or decrease the indentation settings. To set a first line or a hanging indent, select the indent type in the **Special** drop-down list and enter the indent amount in the **By** text box. The sample page in the dialog box illustrates how the current settings will appear.

3. Click **OK**, and Word applies the new settings to any selected paragraphs or to new text.

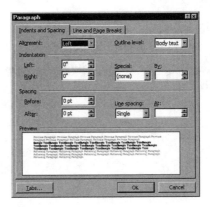

Figure 7.2   Setting indents in the Paragraph dialog box.

Setting Text Alignment

Alignment, sometimes called *justification*, refers to the manner in which the left and right ends of lines of text are aligned. Word offers four alignment options:

- *Align left* aligns the left ends of lines.
- *Align right* aligns the right ends of lines.
- *Justify* aligns both the left and right ends of lines.
- *Align center* centers lines between the left and right margins.

 TERM   **Justify**   Both the left and right edges or paragraphs are aligned. This is accomplished by inserting extra space between words and letters in the text as needed. This is a common format in books and magazines.

Figure 7.3 illustrates the alignment options. To change the alignment for one or more paragraphs, first select the paragraphs to change. Then click one of the alignment buttons on the Formatting toolbar.

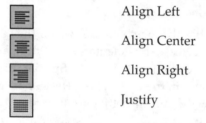

Align Left

Align Center

Align Right

Justify

If you prefer to use a dialog box to change alignment, select the paragraphs and then use these steps:

1. Pull down the **Format** menu and select **Paragraph** to open the Paragraph dialog box, and click the **Indents and Spacing** tab if necessary.

2. Click the **Alignment** drop-down arrow and select the desired alignment from the list.

3. Select **OK**.

 TIP   **How Is It Justified?**   The toolbar button corresponding to the current paragraph's alignment setting appears to be pressed in.

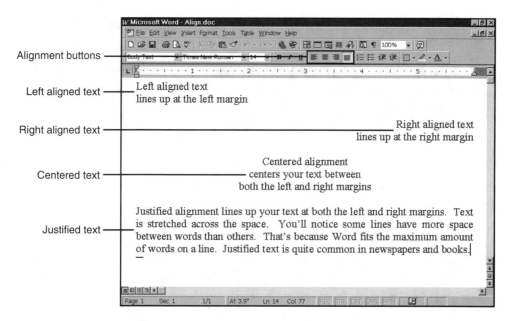

Alignment buttons

Left aligned text — Left aligned text lines up at the left margin

Right aligned text — Right aligned text lines up at the right margin

Centered text — Centered alignment centers your text between both the left and right margins

Justified text — Justified alignment lines up your text at both the left and right margins. Text is stretched across the space. You'll notice some lines have more space between words than others. That's because Word fits the maximum amount of words on a line. Justified text is quite common in newspapers and books.

Figure 7.3 Click these buttons to set text alignment.

Controlling Line Breaks

The word wrap feature automatically breaks each line in a paragraph when it reaches the right margin. Word offers a couple of methods for controlling the way lines break. You can prevent a line break from occurring between two specific words to ensure that the words always remain together on the same line. These methods can be particularly useful when you modify indents and alignment because this often changes where individual lines break.

Word's default is to break lines as needed at spaces or hyphens. To prevent a line break, you must insert a nonbreaking space or a nonbreaking hyphen instead. To insert a nonbreaking hyphen, press **Ctrl+Shift**+- (hyphen). To insert a nonbreaking space, press **Ctrl+Shift+Spacebar**.

You can also use an *optional hyphen* to specify where a word can be broken, if necessary. This is useful with long words that may fall at the end of the line; if word wrap moves the long word to the next line, there will be an unsightly gap at the end of the previous line. An optional hyphen remains hidden unless the word extends past the right margin. Then the hyphen appears, and only the part of the word after the hyphen wraps to the new line. To insert an optional hyphen, press **Ctrl+-** (hyphen).

Finally, you can insert a line break without starting a new paragraph by pressing **Shift+Enter**.

In this lesson, you learned how to set the indentation and alignment of text in your document, and how to control line breaks. The next lesson shows you how to work with tabs and line spacing.

Creating Tabs and Line Spacing

In this lesson, you learn how to use and set tab stops, and how to change line spacing.

Working with Tabs

Tabs provide another way for you to control the indentation and alignment of text in your document. When you press the **Tab** key, Word inserts a tab in the document and moves the cursor (and any text to the right of it) to the next tab stop. By default, Word has tab stops at 0.5-inch intervals across the width of the page. You can modify the location of tab stops and control the way text aligns at a tab stop.

Types of Tab Stops

Word offers four types of tab stops, each of which aligns text differently:

- **Left-aligned**   The left edge of text aligns at the tab stop. Word's default tab stops are left-aligned.
- **Right-aligned**   The right edge of text aligns at the tab stop.
- **Center-aligned**   The text is centered at the tab stop.
- **Decimal-aligned**   The decimal point (period) is aligned at the tab stop. You use this type of tab for aligning columns of numbers.

Figure 8.1 illustrates the effects of the four tab alignment options and shows the four markers that appear on the Ruler to indicate the position of tab stops.

Click here until it
shows the marker
for the type of tab
you want.

Left-aligned tab stop

Center-aligned
tab stop

Right-aligned tab stop

Decimal-aligned
tab stop

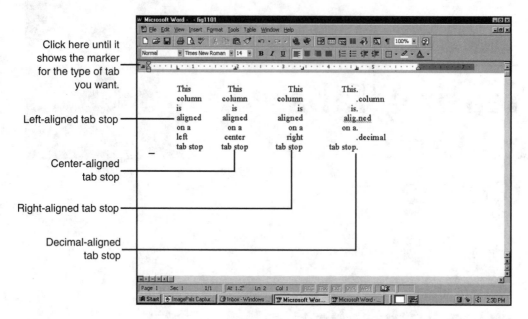

Figure 8.1   The four tab stop alignment options.

Changing the Default Tab Stops

Default tab stops affect all paragraphs for which you have not set custom tab stops (covered in the next section). You cannot delete the default tab stops, but you can change the spacing between them. The default tab stop spacing affects the entire document. Here are the steps to follow:

1. Select **Format**, **Tabs** to display the Tabs dialog box, shown in Figure 8.2.

2. In the **Default Tab Stops** box, click the increment arrows to increase or decrease the spacing between default tab stops.

3. Click **OK**.

TIP   **Good-Bye, Tab**   To effectively "delete" the default tab stops, set the spacing between them to a value larger than the page width.

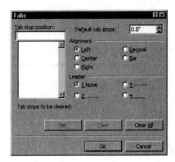

Figure 8.2 The Tabs dialog box.

Creating Custom Tab Stops

If the default tab stops are not suited to your needs, you can add custom tab stops. The number, spacing, and type of custom tab stops is totally up to you. Use these steps to set custom tab stops:

1. Select the paragraphs that will have custom tabs. If no text is selected, the new tabs will affect the paragraph containing the cursor and new text you type.
2. Click the tab symbol at the left end of the Ruler until it displays the marker for the type of tab you want to insert (refer to Figure 8.1).
3. Point at the approximate tab stop location on the Ruler, and press and hold the left mouse button. A dashed vertical line extends down through the document to show the tab stop position relative to your text.
4. Move the mouse left or right until the tab stop is at the desired location.
5. Release the mouse button.

TIP **No Ruler?** If your Ruler is not displayed, choose **View**, **Ruler** or position the mouse pointer near the top edge of the work area for a few seconds.

When you add a custom tab stop, all of the default tab stops to the left are temporarily inactivated. This ensures that the custom tab stop will take precedence. If custom tab stops have been defined for the current paragraph, the custom tabs are displayed on the Ruler; otherwise, the default tab stops are displayed.

Moving and Deleting Custom Tab Stops

Follow these steps to move a custom tab stop to a new position:

1. Point at the tab stop marker on the Ruler.
2. Press and hold the left mouse button.
3. Drag the tab stop to the new position.
4. Release the mouse button.

To delete a custom tab stop, follow the same steps, but in step 3, drag the tab stop marker off the Ruler. Then release the mouse button.

Changing Line Spacing

Line spacing controls the amount of vertical space between lines of text. Different spacing is appropriate for different kinds of documents. If you want to print your document on as few pages as possible, use single line spacing to position lines close together. In contrast, a document that will later be edited by hand should be printed with wide line spacing to provide space for the editor to write comments.

Word offers a variety of line spacing options. If you change line spacing, it affects the selected text; if there is no text selected, it affects the current paragraph and text you type at the insertion point.

Follow these steps to change line spacing:

1. Open the **Format** menu and select **Paragraph** to display the Paragraph dialog box. If necessary, click the **Indents and Spacing** tab (see Figure 8.3).
2. Click the **Line Spacing** drop-down arrow and select the desired spacing from the list. The Single, 1.5 Lines, and Double settings are self-explanatory. The other settings are:
    - **Exactly** Space between lines will be exactly the value—in points—that you enter in the **At** text box.
    - **At Least** Space between lines will be at least the value you enter in the **At** text box; Word will increase the spacing as needed if the line contains large characters.
    - **Multiple** Changes spacing by the factor you enter in the **At** text box. For example, enter **1.5** to increase spacing by one and a half times, and enter **2** to double the line spacing.

CAUTION

Underline Missing? If you set line spacing using the Exactly option at the same value as your font size, underline character formatting will display only for the last line of each paragraph.

3. To add spacing before the first line or after the last line of the paragraph, enter the desired space (in points), or click the arrows in the **Before** and **After** text boxes.

4. Click **OK**.

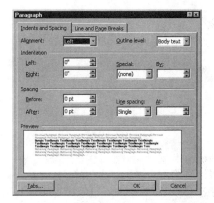

Figure 8.3 The Paragraph dialog box with the Indents and Spacing options displayed.

In this lesson, you learned how to use and set tab stops, and how to change line spacing. The next lesson shows you how to use margins, pages, and sections.

Adding Margins, Pages, and Sections

9

In this lesson, you learn how to use document sections, set page margins, work with different paper sizes, and specify the source of paper used in printing.

Using Section Breaks

Word gives you the option of breaking your document into two or more *sections*, each of which can have its own page formatting. You need to use sections only when you want some aspect of page layout, such as page margins (covered later in this lesson) or columns (covered in Lesson 18), to apply to only part of the document. The default is for page layout settings such as these to apply to the entire document.

Word offers three types of section breaks. They have the same effect in terms of controlling page layout, but differ as to where the text that comes after the break is placed:

- **Next Page**   The new section begins at the top of the next page. This is useful for section breaks that coincide with major breaks in a document, such as a new chapter starting.

- **Continuous**   The new section begins on the same page as the preceding section. This is useful for a section that has a different number of columns from the preceding one but is still part of the same page. An example would be a newsletter: the title runs across the top of the page in one column, and then after a section break, the body of the newsletter appears below the title in three columns.

- **Odd Page or Even Page** The new section begins on the next even- or odd-numbered page. This is useful when a section break coincides with a major break (like a chapter) in a document where each chapter must start on an odd page (or an even page).

In Normal view, Word marks the location of section breaks by displaying a double horizontal line with the label **Section Break** followed by the type of break. These markers do not appear in Page Layout view or on the printed document.

To insert a section break, follow these steps:

1. Click **Insert**, **Break** to open the Break dialog box.
2. Select the desired type of section break (as described in the previous list).
3. Click **OK**.

A section break mark is just like any character in your document. To delete a section break, place the cursor right before it and press **Delete,** or place the cursor right after it and press **Backspace**. Each section break marker holds the settings for the text that comes before it, so when you delete a section break, text in the section before the break becomes part of the section that was after the break, and it assumes the page layout formatting of that section.

Inserting Manual Page Breaks

When text reaches the bottom margin of a page, Word automatically starts a new page and continues the text at the top of that page. However, you can manually insert page breaks to start a new page at any desired location. Here's how:

1. Open the **Insert** menu and choose **Break** to open the Break dialog box.
2. Select **Page Break**.
3. Click **OK**.

TIP **Quick Breaks** You can enter a page break by pressing **Ctrl+Enter**. To start a new line without starting a new paragraph, press **Shift+Enter**.

A page break appears in the document as a single horizontal line. Like section break markers, page break markers do not appear in Page Layout view or in printouts. To delete a page break, move the cursor to the line containing the break and press **Delete**.

Setting Page Margins

The page margins control the amount of white space between your text and the edges of the page. Each page has four margins: left, right, top, and bottom. When you change page margins, the new settings will affect the entire document or, if you have inserted one or more section breaks, the current section.

The easiest way to set page margins is with your mouse and the Ruler. You can work visually instead of thinking in terms of inches or centimeters. To display the Ruler, click **View**, **Ruler** or position the mouse pointer near the top edge of the work area.

You can use the Ruler to change margins only while working in Page Layout view (select **View**, **Page Layout**). In Page Layout view, Word displays both a horizontal ruler at the top of the page and a vertical ruler on the left edge of the page. This permits you to set both the left/right and the top/bottom margins using a Ruler.

On each ruler, the white bar shows the current margin settings, as shown in Figure 9.1. To change the left or right margin, point at the margin marker on the horizontal ruler, at the left or right end of the white bar; the mouse pointer will change to a two-headed arrow. Then, drag the margin to the new position. For the top or bottom margin, follow the same procedure using the vertical ruler.

 Margins   The distances between the text and the edges of the page.

Note that the margin symbols—not the small triangular buttons—on the horizontal ruler are the vertical edges of the white margin bar. The small triangular buttons are the indent markers, which you learned about in Lesson 7. If your mouse pointer has changed to a two-headed arrow, you know you have found the margin symbol.

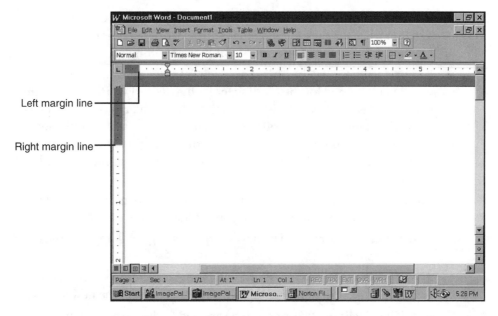

Left margin line

Right margin line

Figure 9.1 The Ruler displays a white bar showing the current margin settings.

TIP **Changing Margins** Margins apply to the entire section, unlike indents (which apply to individual paragraphs). To change the margins for only a portion of a document, insert a section break as described previously in this lesson. You can then specify different margins for each section.

CAUTION

Can't Change Margins? Be sure you're in Page Layout view or the rulers won't work for changing margins. (You can, however, drag the indent markers on the ruler in Normal view, as you learned in Lesson 7.)

You can also set the page margins using a dialog box. Use this method when you don't want to use the mouse or need to enter precise margin values. (You also don't have to switch to Page Layout view to do it.) It gives you more control over where in the document the new margins are applied. Here's how:

1. Open the **File** menu and select **Page Setup** to open the Page Setup dialog box.

2. If necessary, click the **Margins** tab to display the margins options shown in Figure 9.2.

3. In the **Top**, **Bottom**, **Left**, and **Right** text boxes, enter the desired margin size (in inches) or click the increment arrows to set the desired value. The Preview shows you the effects of your margin settings.

4. If your document will be bound and you want to leave an extra large margin on one side for the binding, enter the desired width in the **Gutter** text box. This extra space will be added to the left margin of every page or, if you select the **Mirror Margins** check box, it will be added to the left margin of odd-numbered pages and the right margin of even-numbered pages (which is useful for binding a document that is printed on both sides of the paper).

5. Click the **Apply To** drop-down arrow and select where the new margins will apply from the list. These are your options:

   - **Whole Document**   The new margin settings will apply to the entire document.

   - **This Point Forward**   Word will insert a continuous section break at the cursor location and apply the new margins to the new section.

   - **This Section**   Margins will be applied to the current document section. This option is not available if you have not broken your document into sections.

6. Click **OK**.

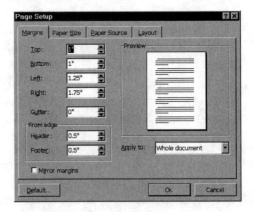

Figure 9.2 Setting margins in the Page Setup dialog box.

Controlling Paper Size and Orientation

Word's default is to format documents to fit on standard 8 1/2×11-inch letter size paper and to print in portrait orientation, which means the lines of text run parallel to the short edge of the paper. You can specify a different paper size, selecting from several standard paper and envelope sizes or defining a custom paper size. You can also print in landscape orientation, in which the lines of text are parallel to the long edge of the paper.

Follow these steps to specify paper size and orientation:

1. Open the **File** menu and choose **Page Setup** to display the Page Setup dialog box.

2. If it isn't already on top, click the **Paper Size** tab (see Figure 9.3).

3. Click the **Paper Size** drop-down arrow and select a predefined paper size from the list. Or, enter a custom height and width in the text boxes provided.

4. Select **Portrait** or **Landscape** orientation.

5. Click the **Apply To** drop-down arrow and select the portion of the document to which the new paper setting is to apply:

   - **Whole Document**   The new paper setting will be used for the entire document.

   - **This Point Forward**   Word will insert a continuous section break at the cursor location and apply the new paper settings to the new section.

   - **This Section**   Paper settings will be applied to the current document section. This option is not available if your document has not been broken into sections.

6. Select **OK**.

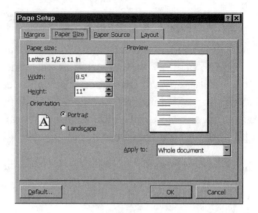

Figure 9.3   Setting paper size and orientation.

Specifying a Paper Source

Some documents require printing on different kinds of paper. For example, with a multipage business letter you may want to print the first page on company letterhead and the other pages on plain paper. Within the limitations of your printer, you can tell Word where it should get the paper for each section of the document. Most laser printers give you two choices: the regular paper tray or manual feed. Advanced printers will have more options, such as two or more paper trays and an envelope feeder.

Use these steps to specify the paper source:

1. Select **File**, **Page Setup** to open the Page Setup dialog box.

2. If it's not on top, click the **Paper Source** tab (see Figure 9.4).

3. In the **First Page** list box, specify the paper source for the first page. The choices available here will depend on your printer model.

4. In the **Other Pages** list box, specify the paper source for the second and subsequent pages.

5. Click the **Apply To** drop-down arrow and select which part of the document the paper source settings are to apply.

6. Select **OK**.

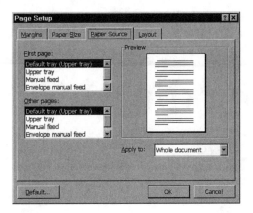

Figure 9.4 Specifying the paper source.

In this lesson, you learned how to use document sections, how to set page margins, how to work with different paper sizes, and how to specify the source of paper used in printing. In the next lesson, you will learn how to use styles.

Making the Most of Styles

In this lesson, you learn how to use styles in your documents.

Understanding Styles

Word's styles provide a great deal of power and flexibility when it comes to formatting your document. A *style* is a collection of formatting specifications that has been assigned a name and saved. For example, a given style could specify 14-point Arial font, 1-inch indent, double line spacing, and full justification. After you define a style, you can quickly apply it to any text in your document.

Applying a style is a lot faster than manually applying individual formatting elements, and it has the added advantage of assuring consistency. If you later modify a style definition, all of the text in the document to which that style has been assigned will automatically change to reflect the new style formatting. Word has several predefined styles, and you can create your own.

 What Is a Style? A style is a named grouping of paragraph or character formatting that can be reused.

Word has two types of styles:

Paragraph styles apply to entire paragraphs and can include all aspects of formatting that affect a paragraph's appearance: font, line spacing, indents, tab stops, borders, and so on. Every paragraph has a style; the default paragraph style is called Normal.

Character styles apply to any section of text and can include any formatting that applies to individual characters: font name and size, underlining, boldface, and so on (in other words, any of the formats that you can assign by clicking Format, Font). There is no default character style.

When you apply a character style, the formatting is applied in addition to whatever formatting the text already possesses. For example, if you apply the bold character style to a sentence that is already formatted as italic, the sentence appears in both bold and italic. The uses of styles are covered in this lesson and the next one.

Assigning a Style to Text

To assign a paragraph style to multiple paragraphs, select the paragraphs. To assign a paragraph style to a single paragraph, place the cursor anywhere in the paragraph. To assign a character style, select the text you want the style to affect. Then follow these steps to apply the desired formatting:

1. Click the **Style** drop-down arrow on the Formatting toolbar to see a list of available styles, with each style name displayed in the style's font. Symbols in the list also indicate whether a style is a paragraph or character style, as well as its font size and justification (see Figure 10.1).

2. Select the desired style by clicking its name. The style is applied to the specified text.

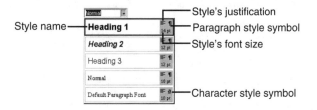

Figure 10.1   Select a style from the Style list on the Formatting toolbar.

TIP   **Paragraph or Character Style?**   In the Style list, paragraph styles are listed with the paragraph symbol next to them, and character styles are listed with an underlined letter "a" next to them.

To remove a character style from text, select the text and apply the character style **Default Paragraph Font**. This is not really a style; instead it specifies that the formatting defined in the current paragraph style should be used for the text.

Viewing Style Names

The Style list box displays the name of the style assigned to the text where the insertion point is located. If there is text selected or if the insertion point is in text that has a character style applied, the Style list box displays the character style name. Otherwise, it displays the paragraph style of the current paragraph.

Word can also display the name of the paragraph and character styles assigned to specific text in your document. Follow these steps to see how:

1. Press **Shift+F1** or click **Help, What's This?** to activate What's This Help. The mouse cursor displays a question mark.
2. Click the text of interest, and Word displays information about the text's assigned style in a balloon (see Figure 10.2).
3. Repeat step 2 as needed for other text.
4. Press **Esc** when you are done.

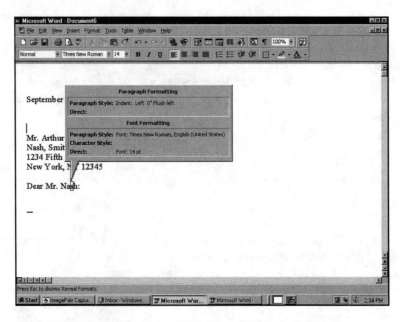

Figure 10.2 Displaying text's style information with What's This Help.

Creating a New Style

You are not limited to using Word's predefined styles. In fact, creating your own styles is an essential part of getting the most out of Word's style capabilities. One way to create a new style is "by example," as described in these steps:

1. Place the insertion point in a paragraph to which you want to apply the new style.

2. Format the paragraph as desired. In other words, apply the formatting you want included in the new style definition.

3. With the insertion point anywhere in the paragraph, click the **Style** list box or press **Ctrl+Shift+S** (both activate the Style list box).

4. Type a name for the new style and press **Enter**.

In step 4, make sure you do not enter the name of an existing style. If you do, that style's formatting will be applied to the paragraph, and the formatting changes you made will be lost. If this happens, you can recover the formatting by clicking **Edit**, **Undo**. Then repeat steps 3 and 4 and give the style a new and unique name.

You can also create a new style by making formatting entries in dialog boxes. You *must* use this method to create a character style; it is optional for paragraph styles. You can create a new style from scratch, or you can base it on an existing style. If you choose the latter method, the new style will have all of the formatting of the base style plus any additions and changes you make while defining the style. Here are the required steps:

1. Select **Format**, **Style** to open the Style dialog box.

2. Click the **New** button. The New Style dialog box appears (see Figure 10.3).

Figure 10.3   The New Style dialog box.

3. Click the **Style Type** drop-down arrow and select **Character** or **Paragraph** from the list to indicate the type of style you're creating.

4. Click the **Name** text box and type the name for the new style.

5. If you want to base the new style on an existing style, click the **Based On** drop-down arrow and select the desired base style from the list.

6. If you want the new style to be part of the template that the current document is based on, select the **Add to Template** check box. If you do not select this check box, the new style will be available only in the current document.

7. (Optional) Select the **Automatically Update** check box if you want Word to add to the style definition all manual formatting changes you make to paragraphs with this style assigned. (This option is available only for paragraph styles.)

8. Click the **Format** button and select **Font** or **Border** to specify the font or border of the new style. As you make formatting changes, the Preview box displays an image of what the style will look like, and the Description area provides a description of the style elements.

9. For paragraph styles only, click the **Format** button and select **Paragraph** to set the style's indents and line spacing. Then select **Tabs** to set the new style's tab stops.

10. Click **OK** to return to the Style dialog box.

11. Click **Apply** to assign the new style to the current text or paragraph. Click **Close** to save the new style definition without assigning it to any text.

Modifying a Style

You can change the formatting associated with any paragraph or character style, whether it is a style you define or one of Word's predefined styles. When you do so, all text in the document that has the style assigned will be modified. Follow these steps to change a style throughout a document:

1. Open the **Format** menu and select **Style**. This opens the Style dialog box (see Figure 10.4).

2. Click the **List** drop-down arrow and select which styles should be displayed in the Styles list:

    • **All Styles**   All styles defined in the current document.

    • **Styles in Use**   Styles that have been assigned to text in the current document.

- **User Defined Styles** All user-defined styles in the current document.

3. In the **Styles** list, click the name of the style you want to modify.

4. Click the **Modify** button. The Modify Style dialog box appears; it looks the same as the New Style dialog box (refer to Figure 10.3). Specify the style's new format specifications.

5. Click **OK** to return to the Style dialog box. Then click **Close**.

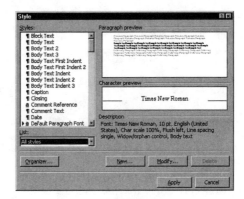

Figure 10.4 The Style dialog box.

In this lesson, you learned what styles are, how to apply styles to text, and how to create and modify styles. The next lesson shows you how to apply automatic formatting to text.

Applying Automatic Formatting

In this lesson, you learn how to use Word's automatic formatting capability.

What AutoFormatting Can Do

Automatic formatting is a feature that lets Word analyze the parts of a document, recognize certain elements (such as body text, headings, bulleted lists, and quotations), and then apply appropriate styles to the various text elements to create an attractively formatted document. (You learned about styles in Lesson 10.) You can accept or reject the automatically applied format in part or in whole, and you can later make desired modifications to the document.

In addition to applying styles, automatic formatting removes extra returns between paragraphs; automatically formats Internet, network, and e-mail addresses as hyperlinks; applies bold or underline character formatting to text surrounded by asterisks (*) or underscores (_); replaces two hyphens (--) with an em dash (—)and more.

 TIP **Word on the Web** If you format Internet and e-mail addresses as hyperlinks, users will be able to access them over the Internet simply by clicking the link in the document.

There are two ways to use automatic formatting: Word can format items as you type them, or you can create an unformatted document and then apply automatic formatting to the entire document.

Is automatic formatting right for you? The only way to find out is to try it yourself. Take a document that's typical of documents you usually work on, save it under a new name (so the original is not changed), and then experiment. You'll soon find out if you like automatic formatting—or if you prefer to format your documents manually.

Applying Formatting as You Type

Word can apply a variety of formatting to text as you type it. Some examples include:

- **Tables**   If you type a line of plus signs and hyphens (such as +----+----+) and then press Enter, Word creates a table with one column for each plus sign. Initially, the table will have one row, and the cursor will be positioned in the first cell.

- **Borders**   If you type three or more hyphens, underscores, or equal signs, Word will insert a thin, thick, or double border, respectively.

- **Bulleted Lists**   If you start a paragraph with an asterisk, a lowercase "o," or a hyphen, followed by a space or tab, Word automatically creates a bulleted list.

To set your preferences for which types of formatting are applied as you type, follow these steps:

1. Select **Format**, **AutoFormat** to display the AutoFormat dialog box.

2. Click the **Options** button to open the AutoCorrect dialog box.

3. If necessary, click the **AutoFormat As You Type** tab to see the options shown in Figure 11.1.

4. Select or deselect the check boxes as desired.

What Does That Do?   Remember, you can get Help information on any option by clicking the **AutoHelp** button (the question mark) in a dialog box's title bar and then clicking the option in question.

CAUTION

5. Click **OK**.

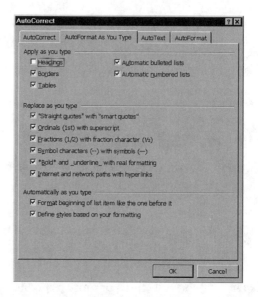

Figure 11.1   Setting the AutoFormat As You Type options.

Changing options in this dialog box does not affect text that has already been formatted. It affects only text that is typed after the options are changed.

Applying AutoFormatting to Your Document

Here are the steps required to apply automatic formatting to the entire document after you've typed it:

1. Select **Format**, **AutoFormat** to open the AutoFormat dialog box.

2. Select **AutoFormat Now** to apply AutoFormatting without reviewing individual changes. Select **AutoFormat and Review Each Change** if you want to be able to accept or reject each format change.

3. (Optional) Click the **Document Type** drop-down arrow and select the type of document you are working on from the list.

4. Click **OK**.

If you selected **AutoFormat Now** in step 2, Word analyzes your document and applies formatting based on the document contents. You cannot reverse individual formatting changes, but you can undo the entire AutoFormat effect by selecting **Edit**, **Undo AutoFormat**.

If you selected **AutoFormat and Review Each Change** in step 2, Word formats your document and displays the AutoFormat dialog box shown in Figure 11.2. You can scroll around in your document while this dialog box is displayed to view the changes that Word made. Then click one of the following command buttons to proceed:

- **Accept All**   Accepts all formatting changes.
- **Reject All**   Rejects all formatting changes.
- **Review Changes**   Lets you view each formatting change and accept or reject it (see the next paragraph).
- **Style Gallery**   Displays the Style Gallery, from which you can select an overall "look" for your document. After you select a style, you return to the AutoFormat dialog box.

Figure 11.2   The AutoFormat dialog box.

If you decide to review changes, the Review AutoFormat Changes dialog box appears (see Figure 11.3). You use the commands in this dialog box to examine the format changes one at a time, accepting or rejecting each one. Font changes are not reviewed, but all other formatting changes are. While you are working in this dialog box, Word displays the document with marks indicating the changes made. Table 11.1 lists the types of changes you can make and the marks Word displays in your document.

Table 11.1   Marks Displayed to Indicate AutoFormat Changes

Change Made	Mark Displayed
New style applied to the paragraph	Blue paragraph mark
Paragraph mark deleted	Red paragraph mark
Text or spaces deleted	Strikethrough
Characters added	Underline
Text or formatting changed	Vertical bar in left margin

Formatted text—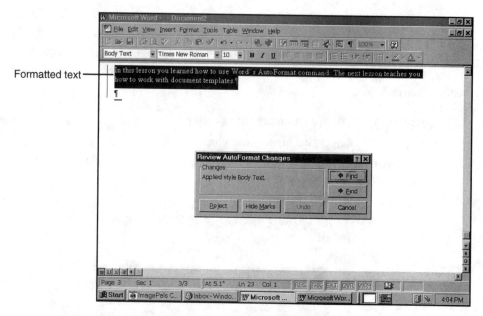

Figure 11.3   The Review AutoFormat Changes dialog box.

Word searches for the AutoFormatting changes that were made and highlights each one in the document. Use the command buttons in the dialog box to tell Word what to do with each AutoFormatting change:

← **Find** tells Word to locate and highlight the previous change.

→ **Find** tells Word to locate and highlight the next change.

Reject tells Word to undo the highlighted formatting change.

Hide Marks tells Word to hide the indicator marks in the document to make it easier to evaluate its appearance. Click **Show Marks** to redisplay the marks.

Undo tells Word to reinstate the previous rejected change.

Cancel returns you to the AutoFormat dialog box.

Note that you do not need to take any action to accept a change. If you do not explicitly reject a change, Word automatically accepts it.

Oops! To be sure you can recover from unwanted AutoFormat changes, first save your document under a different name.

CAUTION

Setting AutoFormat Options

The AutoFormat feature has a number of settings that control which document elements it will modify. You can change these options to suit your preferences:

1. Select **Format**, **AutoFormat** to open the AutoCorrect dialog box.

2. Click the **AutoFormat** tab to display the AutoFormat options (see Figure 11.4).

3. Select or deselect the various AutoFormat check boxes as desired. Use **AutoHelp** as needed to get information on individual options. (Click the question mark in the dialog box's title bar, and then click the element you need help with.)

4. When you're finished making changes, click **OK**.

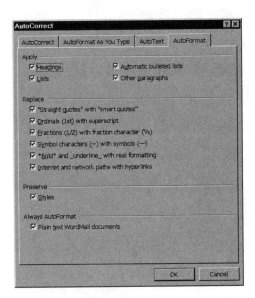

Figure 11.4 Setting AutoFormat options.

Changes you make to AutoFormat options will not affect a previously formatted document, but they will apply to future uses of the AutoFormat command.

In this lesson, you learned how to use Word's AutoFormat command. The next lesson teaches you how to work with document templates.

Working with Templates

In this lesson, you learn how to create new document templates and modify existing templates.

Creating a New Template

You learned in Lesson 2 that every Word document is based on a template, and that Word comes with a variety of predefined templates. You can also create your own templates or modify existing templates to suit your individual needs.

You can create a new template based on an existing template, and the new template will contain all the elements of the base template plus any text or formatting you add. To create a new template from scratch, base it on the Blank Document template. Here are the steps to follow:

1. Select **File**, **New** to open the New dialog box (see Figure 12.1).

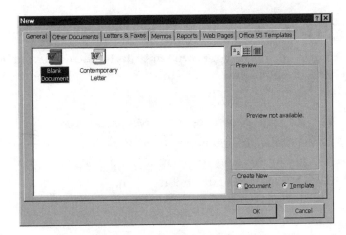

Figure 12.1 Creating a new template based on the Blank Document template.

2. Click the **Template** option button (in the lower-right corner).

3. If you want the new template based on an existing template, select that template icon in the dialog box. Otherwise, select the **Blank Document** icon.

4. Click **OK**. A blank document-editing screen appears with a default name, such as TEMPLATE1.

5. Enter the boilerplate text and other items that you want to include in the new template, and then apply formatting to the text as desired. You should also create any styles that you want in the template.

 TERM   **Boilerplate**   This is text that you want to appear in every document based on the new template.

6. Select **File**, **Save** or click the **Save** button on the Standard toolbar. The Save As dialog box appears.

7. If necessary, select the folder you want the new template saved in by double-clicking its name. For example, if it is a template for a letter, you would probably save it in the Letters & Faxes folder.

8. In the **File Name** text box, enter a descriptive name for the template, using up to 256 characters. Be sure to use a different name than the template you selected in step 3, or the new template will replace the original one.

9. Select **Save**. Word saves the template under the specified name. It is now available for use each time you start a new document.

Modifying an Existing Template

Suppose you create your own template, but then you find out that you need to change the boilerplate text slightly. You can retrieve any existing template from disk and modify it. Here's how:

1. Select **File**, **New** to open the New dialog box.

2. Select the tab containing the template you want to modify, and then select the template icon you want to modify.

3. Select the **Template** option button.

4. Click **OK**.

5. Make the desired modifications and additions to the template's text and styles.

6. Select **File**, **Save** or click the **Save** button on the Standard toolbar, and Word saves the modified template to disk.

When you modify a template, changes you make are not reflected in documents that were created based on the template before it was changed. Only new documents will be affected.

Instead of modifying a template, it's often better to create a new template based on it. This way, the original template will still be available should you want to use it again.

More Templates You'll find additional Word templates you can use in the Office 97 ValuPack. Refer to Appendix B for more information.

TIP Recycle Old Templates? You can use old templates from earlier versions of Word (Word for Windows 95 and Word for Windows 6.0) to create new documents in Word.

Creating a Template from a Document

Sometimes you will find it useful to create a template based on an existing Word document. Here are the steps to follow:

1. Open the document that you want to base the new template on.

2. Use Word's editing commands to delete any document text and formatting that you do not want to include in the template.

3. Select **File**, **Save As** to open the Save As dialog box (see Figure 12.2).

4. Click the **Save As Type** drop-down arrow and choose **Document Template** from the list. The Save In box automatically changes to indicate the Templates folder.

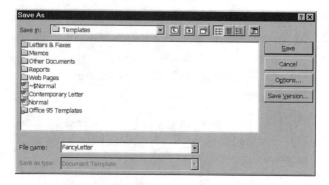

Figure 12.2 Saving a document as a template.

5. If appropriate, double-click the name of the folder in which you want to save the template.

6. Type a descriptive name for the template in the **File Name** text box.

7. Click **Save**.

In step 5, it's important to select the proper template folder. When you select Document Template in step 4, Word automatically switches to the Templates folder (which is different from where documents are saved). Templates saved in this folder will appear on the General tab in the New dialog box. Because Word organizes templates by category, you may want to place your new template in the appropriate folder because if you don't, you may have trouble finding it later. For example, if you create a template for a memo, save it in the Memos folder so it will appear on the Memos tab in the New dialog box.

Updating a Document When the Template Changes

If you modify a template, only new documents based on that template will reflect the changes. Existing documents that were based on the old version of the template will not be affected. You can, however, import new styles from a modified template to an existing document. Here's how:

1. Open the document.

2. Select **Tools**, **Templates and Add-ins**.

3. Select the **Automatically Update Document Styles** check box.

4. Select **OK**.

With this check box selected, the document styles will automatically be updated to reflect the styles in its attached template each time the document is loaded. Other elements of a template, such as boilerplate text, will not be affected.

In this lesson, you learned how to create and modify document templates. The next lesson shows you how to use page numbers, headers, and footers in your documents.

Inserting Page Numbers, Headers, and Footers

In this lesson, you learn how to add page numbers, headers, and footers to your documents.

Adding Page Numbers

Many documents—particularly long ones—require that the pages be numbered. Word offers many choices as to the placement and appearance of page numbers. Page numbers are always part of a header or footer. You can place a page number by itself in a header or footer, as covered in this section. You can also include additional information in the header or footer, as covered later in this lesson.

To add page numbers to your document, follow these steps:

1. Open the **Insert** menu and select **Page Numbers**. The Page Numbers dialog box appears, as shown in Figure 13.1.

Figure 13.1 The Page Numbers dialog box.

2. Click the **Position** drop-down arrow and select the desired position on the page: **Top of Page (Header)** or **Bottom of Page (Footer)**.

3. Click the **Alignment** drop-down arrow and select **Left**, **Center**, or **Right**. You can also select **Inside** or **Outside** if you're printing two-sided pages and want the page numbers positioned near to (Inside) or away from (Outside) the binding.

4. The default number format consists of Arabic numerals (1, 2, 3, and so on). To select a different format (such as, i, ii, iii), click **Format** and select the desired format.

5. Click **OK**.

When you add a page number using this procedure, Word makes the page number part of the document's header or footer. The next section describes headers and footers.

TIP **Can I Print Both Sides?** Two-sided printing is an option on certain printers. Lesson 9 shows you how to set margins for two-sided printing.

CAUTION

No Page Numbers Command? When you're in Online Layout view or Outline view, the Page Numbers option is not available on the Insert menu. In Normal view, you can add page numbers, but you cannot see them.

What Are Headers and Footers?

A *header* or *footer* is text that prints at the top (header) or bottom (footer) of every page of a document. Headers and footers can show the page number; they are also useful for displaying chapter titles, authors' names, and similar information. Word offers several header/footer options, including the following:

- The same header/footer on every page of the document.
- One header/footer on the first page of the document and a different header/footer on all other pages.

- One header/footer on odd-numbered pages and a different header/footer on even-numbered pages.
- If your document is divided into sections, you can have a different header/ footer for each section.

 Headers and Footers Text that is displayed at the top (header) or bottom (footer) of every page.

Adding or Editing a Header or Footer

To add a header or footer to your document, or to edit an existing header or footer, follow these steps:

1. If your document is divided into sections, move the cursor to any location in the section where you want the header or footer placed.

2. Select **View**, **Header and Footer**. Word switches to Page Layout view and displays the current page's header enclosed in a nonprinting dashed line (see Figure 13.2). Regular document text is dimmed, and the Header and Footer toolbar is displayed. On the toolbar, click the **Switch** button to switch between the current page's header and footer.

3. Enter the header or footer text and formatting using the normal Word editing techniques. Use the **Alignment** buttons on the Formatting toolbar to control the placement of items in the header/footer.

4. Use the other toolbar buttons, which are described in Table 13.1, however you want in order to customize your header/footer.

5. When finished, click the **Close** button on the Header and Footer toolbar to return to the document.

Table 13.1 Header and Footer Toolbar Buttons

Button	Description
Insert AutoText ▾	Inserts an AutoText entry
[#]	Inserts a page number code

Button	Description
	Inserts the total number of pages
	Formats the page number
	Inserts a date code
	Inserts a time code
	Opens the Page Setup dialog box so you can set margins (Lesson 9)
	Shows or hides document text
	Makes the header/footer the same as the previous one
	Switches between header and footer
	Shows the previous header or footer
	Shows the next header or footer
Close	Closes the Header and Footer toolbar and returns to the document

 TIP **Good-Bye, Header!** To delete the contents of a header or footer, follow the previous steps for editing the header or footer. Select all of the text in the header or footer and press **Delete**.

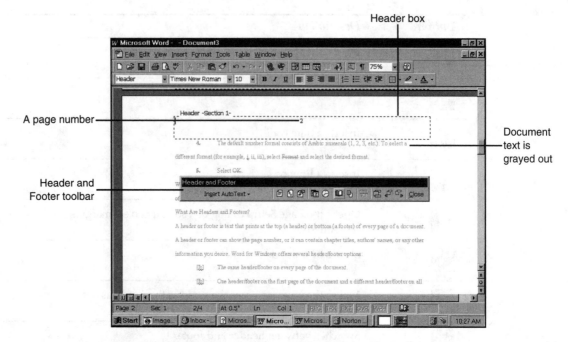

Header box

A page number

Document text is grayed out

Header and Footer toolbar

Figure 13.2   The Header and Footer toolbar.

Creating Different Headers and Footers for Different Pages

Word's default is to display the same header/footer on all the pages in a section or document. One way to have different headers/footers in different parts of the document is to break the document into two or more sections, as explained in Lesson 9. Then you can use the techniques described earlier in the lesson to add a different header/footer to each section.

In addition to using sections, you have the following options:

- One header/footer on the first page with a different header/footer on all other pages.
- One header/footer on odd-numbered pages with another header/footer on even-numbered pages.

To activate one or both of these options:

1. Select **View, Header and Footer**.
2. Click the **Page Setup** button on the Header and Footer toolbar. Word displays the Layout tab of the Page Setup dialog box (see Figure 13.3).
3. Select the **Different Odd and Even** check box and the **Different First Page** check box.
4. Click **OK** to close the Page Setup dialog box.

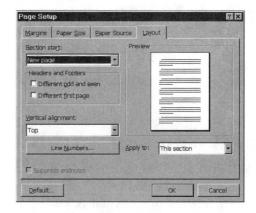

Figure 13.3 Setting header/footer options in the Page Setup dialog box.

After selecting one of these header/footer options, you use the techniques described earlier in this lesson (in the section "Adding or Editing a Header or Footer") to add and edit the header/footer text. For example, say you specified Different Odd and Even. If the cursor is on an even-numbered page and you select the View, Headers and Footers command, Word displays the header/footer text that will display on even-numbered pages so you can edit it. If you click the Show Next button on the Header/Footer toolbar, Word moves to the header/footer for odd-numbered pages.

In this lesson, you learned to add page numbers, headers, and footers to a document. In the next lesson, you will learn how to create numbered and bulleted lists.

Creating Numbered and Bulleted Lists

This lesson shows you how to add numbered and bulleted lists to your documents.

Why Use Numbered and Bulleted Lists?

Numbered and bulleted lists are useful formatting tools for setting off lists of information in a document—you've seen plenty of both in this book! Word can automatically create both types of lists. Use bulleted lists for items that consist of related information that does not have to be listed in any particular order. Use numbered lists for items that must fall in a specific order. When you create a numbered or bulleted list, each paragraph is considered a separate list item and receives its own number or bullet.

Creating a Numbered or Bulleted List

You can create a list from existing text or create the list as you type. To create a numbered or bulleted list from existing text, follow these steps:

1. Select the paragraphs you want in the list.
2. Select **Format**, **Bullets and Numbering** to open the Bullets and Numbering dialog box.
3. Depending on the type of list you want, click the **Bulleted** tab or the **Numbered** tab. Figure 14.1 shows the Numbered tab options, and Figure 14.2 shows the Bulleted tab options.

4. Click the bullet or number style you want.

5. Click **OK**.

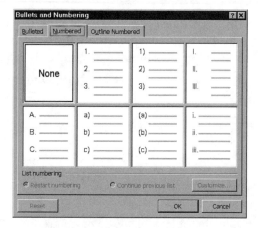

Figure 14.1 Numbered list style options in the Numbered tab.

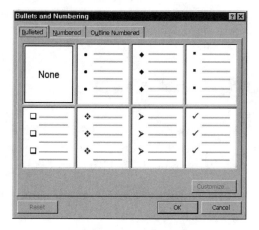

Figure 14.2 Bulleted list style options in the Bulleted tab.

Follow these steps to create a numbered or bulleted list as you type:

1. Move the insertion point to the location for the list, and press **Enter**, if necessary, to start a new paragraph.

2. Select **Format, Bullets and Numbering** to open the Bullets and Numbering dialog box.

3. Depending on the type of list you want, click the **Bulleted** tab or the **Numbered** tab.

4. Click the bullet or number style you want.

5. Click **OK**.

6. Type the list elements, pressing **Enter** at the end of each paragraph. Word automatically places a bullet or number in front of each new paragraph.

7. At the end of the last paragraph, press **Enter** twice.

 TIP   **Quick Lists**   Quickly create a numbered or bulleted list in the default list style by clicking the **Numbering** or **Bullets** button on the Formatting toolbar before typing or after selecting the list text.

 TIP   **Automatic Lists**   If the corresponding AutoFormat options are on, Word automatically starts a numbered or bulleted list anytime you start a paragraph with a number and period or an asterisk followed by a space or tab. To turn these options on or off, select **Format**, **AutoFormat**, **Options** and click the **Lists** and the **Automatic Bulleted Lists** check boxes to turn them on or off.

Using Multilevel Lists

A multilevel list contains two or more levels of bullets or numbering within a single list. For example, a numbered list could contain a lettered list under each numbered item, or each level could be numbered separately, as in an outline. Here's how to create a multilevel list:

1. Select **Format**, **Bullets and Numbering** to open the Bullets and Numbering dialog box.

2. Click the **Outline Numbered** tab to display the multilevel options, as shown in Figure 14.3.

3. Click the list style you want, and then click **OK**.

4. Start typing the list, pressing **Enter** after each item.

5. (Optional) After pressing **Enter**, press **Tab** to demote the new item one level, or press **Shift+Tab** to promote it one level. If you don't do either, the new item will be at the same level as the previous item.

 6. After typing the last item, press **Enter**, and then click the **Numbering** button on the Formatting toolbar to end the list.

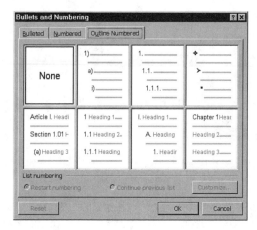

Figure 14.3 Use the Outline Numbered tab of the Bullets and Numbering dialog box to create a multilevel list.

You can convert regular text or a one-level numbered or bulleted list to a multilevel list. You can also change the style of an existing multilevel list. Here are the steps to follow:

1. Select all the paragraphs you want to include in the new list or whose format you want to modify.

2. Select **Format**, **Bullets and Numbering**, and then click the **Outline Numbered** tab.

3. Click the desired list style and click **OK**.

4. Move the insertion point to an item in the list whose level you want to change.

 5. Click the **Decrease Indent** or the **Increase Indent** button on the Formatting toolbar to change the item's level.

 6. Repeat steps 4 and 5 as needed to change other items.

Removing a Numbered or Bulleted List

Follow these steps to remove bullets or numbers from a list but keep the text and convert it to normal paragraphs:

1. Select the paragraphs from which you want the bullets or numbering removed. This can be the entire list or just part of it. The corresponding

button (Bullets or Numbering) on the Formatting toolbar appears to be pressed in.

2. Click the **Bullets** or **Numbering** button to turn the formatting style off.

Changing the Format of a Numbered or Bulleted List

You can also change the format of an existing bulleted or numbered list, to change the bullet symbol or the numbering style. Here's how:

1. Select the paragraphs from which you want the bullets or numbering removed. (This can be the entire list or just part of it.)

2. Select **Format, Bullets and Numbering** to open the Bullets and Numbering dialog box.

3. For a bulleted list, click the **Bulleted** tab and select the desired style. Select **None** to remove bullets.

4. For a numbered list, click the **Numbered** tab and select the desired numbering style, or click **None** to remove numbering from the list.

5. Click **OK** to put your changes into effect.

Adding Items to Numbered and Bulleted Lists

You can add new items to a numbered or bulleted list using the steps here:

1. Move the insertion point to the location in the list where you want the new item.

2. Press **Enter** to start a new paragraph. Word automatically inserts a new bullet or number and renumbers the list items if necessary.

3. Type the new text.

4. (Optional) If it's a multilevel list, click the **Decrease Indent** or the **Increase Indent** button on the Formatting toolbar to change the item's level.

5. Repeat these steps as many times as needed.

This lesson showed you how to create numbered and bulleted lists. The next lesson shows you how to add symbols and other special characters to your document.

Using Symbols and Special Characters

15

In this lesson, you learn how to use symbols and special characters.

What Are Symbols and Special Characters?

Symbols and *special characters* are not part of the standard character set and, therefore, will not be found on your keyboard. Accented letters (such as è), the Greek letter mu (μ), and the copyright symbol (©) are examples. Even though these characters are not on your keyboard, Word can still insert them in your documents.

Inserting a Symbol

To insert a symbol in your document, place the insertion point where you want the symbol, and then follow these steps:

1. Select **Insert**, **Symbol** to open the Symbol dialog box (see Figure 15.1). Click the **Symbols** tab if it is not already displayed.

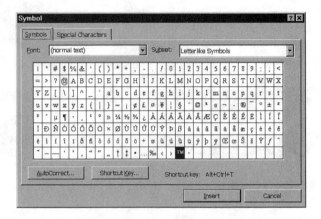

Figure 15.1 The Symbols dialog box.

2. Click the **Font** drop-down arrow and select the desired symbol set from the list. Those you will use most often include:

- **Symbol** Greek letters, mathematical symbols, arrows, trademark and copyright symbols, and more.
- **Normal Text** Letters with accents and other special marks, currency symbols, the paragraph symbol, and more.
- **WingDings** Icons for clocks, envelopes, telephones, and so on.

3. Look through the grid of symbols for the one you want. To see an enlarged view of a symbol, click it.

4. To insert a selected symbol, click **Insert**. To insert any symbol (that's not selected), double-click the symbol.

5. Click **Close** to close the dialog box after you insert one or more symbols. (Or click the **Cancel** button to close the dialog box without inserting a symbol.)

Inserting a Special Character

The distinction between "special characters" and "symbols" is not a clear one. In fact, there is some overlap between the two. Symbols include letters with accents and other diacritical marks used in some languages, Greek letters, arrows, and mathematical symbols (such as ±). Special characters include the copyright symbol (©), the ellipsis (...), and typographic symbols such as em spaces (a wider than normal space). You'll see that Word provides many more symbols than it does special characters.

To insert a special character in your document, place the insertion point where you want the character, and then follow these steps:

1. Select **Insert**, **Symbol** to open the Symbol dialog box.

2. Click the **Special Characters** tab to display the list of available special characters (see Figure 15.2).

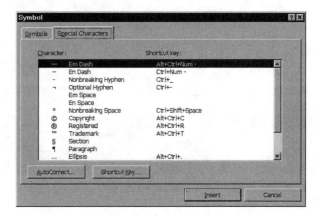

Figure 15.2 The Special Characters list.

3. Look through the list of special characters for the one you want.

4. To insert a selected character, click **Insert**. To insert any character in the list that's not selected, double-click it.

5. Click **Close** to close the dialog box after you insert a character. Or click the **Cancel** button to close the dialog box without inserting a character.

Assigning Shortcut Keys to Symbols

You may want to assign a shortcut key to any symbol you use frequently. Then you can insert it quickly by pressing that key combination. Most of the special characters already have shortcut keys assigned to them; these key assignments are listed on the Special Characters tab in the Symbol dialog box.

Follow these steps to assign a shortcut key to a symbol:

1. Select **Insert**, **Symbol** and click the **Symbols** tab (refer to Figure 15.1).

2. Click the desired symbol. (If necessary, first select the proper font from the **Font** list.)

3. If the selected symbol already has a shortcut key assigned to it, the key combination appears in the lower-right corner of the dialog box.

4. Click the **Shortcut Key** button to display the Customize Keyboard dialog box (see Figure 15.3).

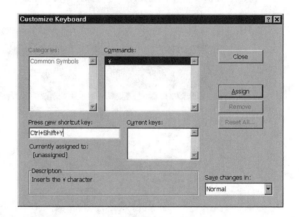

Figure 15.3   Assigning a shortcut key to a symbol.

5. Press **Alt+N** to move to the **Press New Shortcut Key** text box (or click in that box).

6. Press the shortcut key combination you want to assign. Its description appears in the Press New Shortcut Key text box. A list of permitted key combinations follows these steps.

7. If the specified key combination is unassigned, Word displays (unas-signed) under the Press New Shortcut Key text box. If it has already been assigned, Word displays the name of the symbol, macro, or command to which the selected shortcut key is assigned.

8. If the shortcut key is unassigned, click **Assign** to assign it to the symbol. If it is already assigned, press **Backspace** to delete the shortcut key display and return to step 6 to try another key combination.

9. When you're done, click **Close** to return to the Symbols dialog box, and then click **Close** again to return to your document.

The shortcut keys are really key combinations. You can select from the following key combinations, where *key* is a letter key, number key, function key, or cursor movement key:

Shift+*key*   Alt+Shift+*key*

Ctrl+*key*   Ctrl+Shift+*key*

Alt+*key*   Ctrl+Shift+Alt+*key*

Alt+Ctrl+*key*

Understanding Special Characters

Some of the special characters that Word offers may seem unfamiliar to you, but they can be quite useful in certain documents. The following are brief descriptions of the less well-known ones:

- **En dash**   A dash that is the same as the standard dash (inserted with the key above the P key on your keyboard). The en dash is properly used in combinations of figures and/or capital letters, as in "Please refer to part 1–A."

- **Em dash**   Slightly longer than an en dash, the em dash has a variety of purposes, the most common of which is to mark a sudden change of thought. For example, "She said—and no one dared disagree—that the meeting was over."

- **En space**   A space slightly longer than the standard space. This space is an en space.

- **Em space**   A space slightly longer than the en space. This space   is an em space.

- **Non-breaking space**   A space that will not be broken at the end of the line. The words separated by a non-breaking space always stay on the same line.

- **Non-breaking hyphen**   Similar to a non-breaking space. That is to say, two words separated by a non-breaking hyphen will always stay on the same line.

- **Optional hyphen**   A hyphen that will not be displayed unless the word it is in needs to be broken at the end of a line.

In this lesson, you learned how to use symbols and special characters in your Word documents. In the next lesson, you will learn how to proof your document.

Proofing Your Document

This lesson shows you how to use Word's spelling and grammar checker, thesaurus, and Print Preview window to proof your document.

Using the Spelling Checker

Word's spelling checker lets you verify and correct the spelling of words in your document. Words are checked against a standard dictionary and unknown words are flagged. You can then ignore the word, correct it, or add it to the dictionary.

To check spelling in a portion of a document, select the text to check. Otherwise, Word will check the entire document starting at the location of the cursor. If you want to check starting at the beginning of the document, move the insertion point to the start of the document by pressing **Ctrl+Home**. Then follow these steps:

1. Select **Tools, Spelling and Grammar**, or press **F7**, or click the **Spelling and Grammar** button on the Standard toolbar. The Spelling and Grammar dialog box appears (see Figure 16.1). If you want to check spelling only, deselect the **Check Grammar** check box. The remainder of these steps assume that you are checking spelling only. (If you tell Word to check grammar, it flags suspected grammar errors; how you deal with these is described later in this lesson.)

2. When Word locates a word in the document that is not in the dictionary, it displays the word and its surrounding text in the **Not in Dictionary** list box with the word highlighted in red. In Figure 16.1, for example, the word **checcker** is highlighted. Suggested replacements for the word appear in

the Suggestions list box (if Word has no suggestions, this box will be empty). For each word that Word stops on, take action in one of these ways:

- To correct the word manually, edit it in the **Not in Dictionary** list box and click **Change**.
- To use one of the suggested replacements, highlight the desired replacement word in the **Suggestions** list box and click **Change**.
- To replace all instances of the word in the document with either the manual corrections you made or the word selected in the Suggestions box, click **Change All**.
- To ignore this instance of the word, click **Ignore**.
- To ignore this and all other instances of the word in the document, click **Ignore All**.
- To add the word to the dictionary, click **Add**.

3. Repeat as needed. When the entire document has been checked, Word displays a message to that effect. (Or, you can click **Cancel** at any time to end spell checking early.)

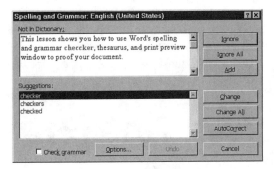

Figure 16.1 Checking spelling in the Spelling and Grammar dialog box.

 TIP **Use AutoCorrect** To add a misspelled word and its correction to the AutoCorrect list, select **AutoCorrect** in the Spelling and Grammar dialog box. Future misspellings will then be corrected automatically as you type them.

Checking Your Grammar

Word can check the grammar of the text in your document, flagging possible problems so you can correct them if needed. To check your grammar while checking spelling, follow the previous steps listed, and make sure the **Check Grammar** check box is selected in the Spelling and Grammar dialog box (refer to Figure 16.1). When Word locates a word or phrase with a suspected grammatical error, it displays the word or phrase and its surrounding text in the dialog box with the word highlighted in green and a description of the suspected problem above the text. Suggested fixes, if any, are listed in the Suggestions list box. For each potential mistake that Word stops on, take action in one of these ways:

- To manually correct the error, edit the text and click **Change**.
- To use one of the suggested replacements, select it in the **Suggestions** list box and click **Change**.
- To ignore this instance of the problem, click **Ignore**.
- To ignore this instance and all other instances of the problem in the document, click **Ignore All**.

CAUTION

Don't Rely on Word   Word's grammar checker is a useful tool, but don't rely on it to catch everything. It is no substitute for careful writing and editing.

Checking Spelling and Grammar as You Type

In addition to checking your document's spelling and grammar all at once, Word can check text as you type it. Words not found in the dictionary will be underlined with a wavy red line, and suspected grammatical errors will be marked with a wavy green line. You can deal with the errors immediately or whenever you choose. To turn automatic spell/grammar checking on or off:

1. Select **Tools**, **Options** to open the Options dialog box.
2. If necessary, click the **Spelling and Grammar** tab.
3. Select or deselect the **Check Spelling As You Type** and the **Check Grammar As You Type** check boxes.
4. Click **OK**.

To deal with a word that has been underlined by automatic spell checking or grammar checking, right-click the word. A pop-up menu appears, containing suggested replacements for the word (if any are found) as well as several commands. Figure 16.2 shows the pop-up menu that appears when you right-click a misspelled word.

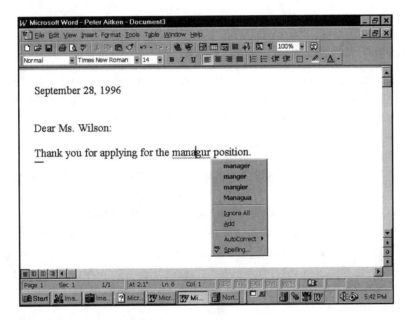

Figure 16.2 Correcting spelling as you type.

For a spelling error, you have the following choices:

- To replace the word with one of the suggestions, click the replacement word.
- To ignore all occurrences of the word in the document, click **Ignore All**.
- To add the word to the dictionary, click **Add**.
- To add the misspelling to the AutoCorrect list, select **AutoCorrect**, and then select the proper replacement spelling.
- To start a regular spelling check, click **Spelling**.

When you right-click a grammatical error, you are offered the following choices:

- Select a suggested replacement to insert it in the document.
- Select **Ignore Sentence** to ignore the possible error.
- Select **Grammar** to start a regular grammar check.

97

TIP   **Hide Spelling/Grammar Marks**   If your document contains words underlined by the automatic spelling or grammar checker and you want to hide the underlines, select **Tools**, **Options**, click the **Spelling and Grammar** tab, and select the **Hide Spelling Errors in This Document** check box or the **Hide Grammatical Errors in This Document** check box. Deselect these check boxes to redisplay the underlines.

Using the Thesaurus

A thesaurus provides you with synonyms and antonyms for words in your document. Using the thesaurus can help you avoid repetition in your writing (and improve your vocabulary).

To use the thesaurus:

1. Place the insertion point on the word of interest in your document.

2. Press **Shift+F7** or select **Tools**, **Thesaurus**. The Thesaurus dialog box opens. This dialog box has several components:

- The **Looked Up** list box displays the word of interest.

- The **Meanings** list box lists alternate meanings for the word. If the word is not found, Word displays an **Alphabetical List** box instead; this list contains a list of words with spellings similar to the selected word.

- If the thesaurus finds one or more meanings for the word, the dialog box displays the **Replace with Synonym** list showing synonyms for the currently highlighted meaning of the word. If meanings are not found, the dialog box displays a **Replace with Related Word** list.

3. While the Thesaurus dialog box is displayed, take one of these actions:

- To find synonyms for the highlighted word in the Replace with Synonym list or the Replace with Related Words list (depending on which one is displayed), click **Look Up**.

- To find synonyms for a word in the Meanings list, select the word and then click **Look Up**.

- For some words, the thesaurus displays the term **Antonyms** in the **Meanings** list. To display antonyms for the selected word, highlight the term **Antonyms** and then click **Look Up**.

4. To replace the word in the document with the highlighted word in the Replace with Synonym list or the Replace with Related Word list, click **Replace**.

5. To close the thesaurus without making any changes to the document, click **Cancel**.

Finding and Replacing Text

Word's Replace command lets you search for instances of text and replace them with new text. This can be very helpful if, for example, you misspelled the same word multiple times in the same document. To replace text, follow these steps:

1. Open the **Edit** menu and choose **Replace** or press **Ctrl+H**. The Replace dialog box appears (see Figure 16.3).

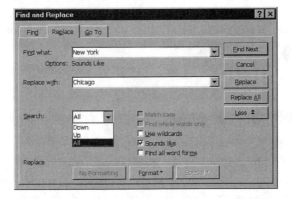

Figure 16.3 The Replace tab in the Find and Replace dialog box.

 TIP **Find or Replace** You can access the Find dialog box from the Replace dialog box (and vice versa) by clicking the corresponding tab.

2. In the **Find What** text box, enter the text you want to replace.

3. In the **Replace With** text box, enter the replacement text.

4. (Optional) Click the **More** button and specify search options as explained in the previous section.

5. Click **Find Next** to locate and highlight the first instance of the target text.

6. For each occurrence Word finds, respond using one of these buttons:

- Click **Replace** to replace the highlighted instance of the target text and then locate the next instance of it.

- Click **Find Next** to leave the highlighted instance of the target text unchanged and to locate the next instance.

- Click **Replace All** to replace all instances of the target text in the entire document.

TIP   **Deleting Text**   To delete the target text, follow the previous steps but leave the **Replace With** text box empty.

Recovery!   If you make a mistake replacing text, you can recover by clicking **Edit, Undo Replace**.

CAUTION

Using Print Preview

 Word's Print Preview feature lets you view your document on the screen exactly as it will be printed. While Page Layout view also displays your document in its final form, Print Preview offers some additional features that you may find useful. To use Print Preview, select **File, Print Preview** or click the **Print Preview** button on the Standard toolbar. The current page appears in the Preview window (see Figure 16.4).

These guidelines outline your available options in the Preview window:

- Press **Page Up** or **Page Down** or use the vertical scroll bar to view other pages.

- Click the **Multiple Pages** button and drag over the page icons to preview more than one page at once. Click the **One Page** button to preview a single page.

- Click the **Zoom Control** drop-down arrow and select a magnification to preview the document at different magnifications.

Print

Magnifier

One Page

Multiple Pages

Zoom Control list

View Rulers

Shrink to Fit

Full Screen View

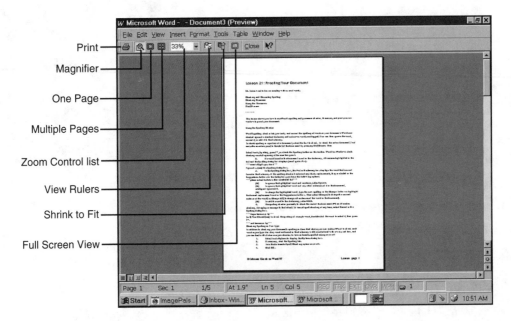

Figure 16.4 The Print Preview screen.

- Click the **View Ruler** button to display the Ruler. You can then use the Ruler to set page margins and indents as described in Lessons 7 and 9.
- Click the **Magnifier** button and click in the document to enlarge that part of the document.
- Click the **Shrink to Fit** button to prevent a small amount of text from spilling onto the document's last page. Word will attempt to adjust formatting to reduce the page count by one.
- Click the **Print** button to print the document. Click again to return to the original view.
- Click **Close** or press **Esc** to end Print Preview display.

In this lesson, you learned how to use Word's proofing tools to check your document's spelling and grammar, and how to use the thesaurus and Print Preview. The next lesson shows you how to use tables.

Working with Tables

*In this lesson, you learn how to add tables to your document,
and how to edit and format tables.*

What's a Table?

A *table* lets you organize information in a row and column format. Each entry in a table, called a *cell,* is independent of all other entries. You can have almost any number of rows and columns in a table. You also have a great deal of control over the size and formatting of each cell. A table cell can contain text, graphics, and just about anything that a Word document can contain. The one exception is that a table cannot contain another table.

 TIP   **On the Table**   Use tables for columns of numbers, lists, and anything else that requires a row and column arrangement.

Inserting a Table

To insert a new empty table at any location within your document, follow these steps:

1. Move the cursor to the document location where you want the table.
2. Select **Table**, **Insert Table**. The Insert Table dialog box appears (see Figure 17.1).

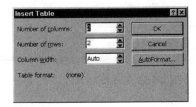

Figure 17.1 The Insert Table dialog box.

3. In the **Number of Columns** and **Number of Rows** text boxes, click the arrows or enter the number of rows and columns the table should have. (You can adjust these numbers later.)

4. To apply one of Word's automatic table formats to the table, click the **AutoFormat** button, select the desired format, and click **OK**. (AutoFormat is covered in more detail later in this lesson.)

5. In the **Column Width** text box, select the desired width for each column (in inches). Select **Auto** in this box to have the page width evenly divided among the specified number of columns.

6. Select **OK**. Word creates a blank table with the cursor in the first cell.

TIP **Quick Tables** To quickly insert a table, click the **Insert Table** button on the Standard toolbar and drag over the desired number of rows and columns.

Working in a Table

When the cursor is in a table cell, you can enter and edit text as you would in the rest of the document. Text entered in a cell automatically wraps to the next line within the column width. You can move the cursor to any cell by clicking it. You can also navigate in a table using the following special key combinations:

Press This	To Move Here
Tab	The next cell in a row
Shift+Tab	The previous cell in a row

continues

continued

Press This	To Move Here
Alt+Home	The first cell in the current row
Alt+Page Up	The top cell in the current column
Alt+End	The last cell in the current row
Alt+Page Down	The last cell in the current column

If the cursor is at the edge of a cell, you can also use the arrow keys to move between cells. To insert a Tab in a table cell, press **Ctrl+Tab**.

Editing and Formatting a Table

After you create a table and enter some information, you can edit its contents and format its appearance to suit your needs. The following sections explain common editing and formatting tasks you might want to perform.

Deleting and Inserting Cells, Rows, and Columns

You can clear individual cells in a table, erasing their contents and leaving the cells blank. To clear the contents of a cell, simply select the cell and press **Delete**.

TIP   **Fast Select!**   You can select the text in the cell or the entire cell itself. To select an entire cell, click in the left margin of the cell, between the text and the cell border. The mouse pointer changes to an arrow when it's in this area.

You can also remove entire rows and columns. When you do so, columns to the right or rows below move to fill in for the deleted row or column. To completely remove a row or column from the table, follow these steps:

1. Move the cursor to any cell in the row or column to be deleted.
2. Select **Table, Delete Cells**. The Delete Cells dialog box appears (see Figure 17.2).
3. Select **Delete Entire Row** or **Delete Entire Column**.
4. Click **OK**, and Word deletes the row or column.

Recovery Remember that you can undo table editing actions with the **Edit**, **Undo** command or just click the **Undo** button on the Standard toolbar.

CAUTION

Figure 17.2 The Delete Cells dialog box.

Follow these steps to insert a single row or column into a table:

1. Move the cursor to a cell to the right of where you want the new column or below where you want the new row.

2. Select **Table**, **Insert Columns** to insert a new blank column to the left of the selected column. Select **Table**, **Insert Rows** to insert a new blank row above the selected row.

Changing Commands? The commands on the Table menu change according to circumstances. For example, if you select a column in a table, the Insert Columns command is displayed but the Insert Rows command is not.

CAUTION

Use these steps to insert more than one row or column into a table:

1. Select cells that span the number of rows or columns you want to insert. For example, to insert three new rows between rows 2 and 3, select cells in rows 3, 4, and 5 (in any column).

2. Select **Table**, **Select Row** (if inserting rows) or **Table**, **Select Column** (if inserting columns).

3. Select **Table**, **Insert Rows** or **Table**, **Insert Columns** as appropriate.

TIP **Add a Row** To insert a new row at the bottom of the table, move the cursor to the last cell in the table and press **Tab**.

105

To insert a new column at the right edge of the table, follow these steps:

1. Click just outside the table's right border.
2. Select **Table, Select Column**.
3. Select **Table, Insert Columns**.

Moving or Copying Columns and Rows

Here's how to copy or move an entire column or row from one location in a table to another:

1. Select the column or row by dragging over the cells, or by clicking in the column or row and selecting **Table, Select Row** or **Table, Select Column**.

2. To copy, press **Ctrl+C** or click the **Copy** button on the Standard toolbar. To move, press **Ctrl+X** or click the **Cut** button.
3. Move the cursor to the new location for the column or row. (It will be inserted above or to the left of the location of the cursor.)
4. Press **Ctrl+V** or click the **Paste** button on the Standard toolbar.

Changing Column Width

You can quickly change the width of a column with the mouse.

1. Point at the right border of the column whose width you want to change. The mouse pointer changes to a pair of thin vertical lines with arrowheads pointing left and right.
2. Drag the column border to the desired width.

You can also use a dialog box to change column widths. Follow these steps to learn how:

1. Move the cursor to any cell in the column you want to change.
2. Select **Table, Cell Height and Width**. The Cell Height and Width dialog box appears (see Figure 17.3). If necessary, click the **Column** tab to display the column options.
3. In the **Width of Column** text box, enter the desired column width, or click the up and down arrows to change the setting. Note that the label identifies which column you are working on by number. To automatically adjust the column width to fit the widest cell entry, click the **Autofit** button.

Figure 17.3 Changing column width.

4. Change the value in the **Space Between Columns** text box to modify spacing between columns. Changing this setting increases or decreases the amount of space between the text in each cell and the cell's left and right borders.

5. Click **Next Column** or **Previous Column** to change the settings for other columns in the table.

6. Click **OK**. The table changes to reflect the new column settings.

Table Borders

Word's default is to place a single, thin border around each cell in a table. However, you can modify the borders or remove them altogether. The techniques for working with table borders are essentially the same as for adding borders to other text (see Lesson 6). Briefly, here are the steps involved:

1. Select the table cells whose borders you want to modify.

2. Select **Format, Borders and Shading** to display the Borders and Shading dialog box. Click the **Borders** tab if necessary (refer to Figure 6.3).

3. Select the desired border settings, using the Preview box to see how your settings will appear.

4. Click **OK**.

In a table with no borders, you can display non-printing gridlines on-screen to make it easier to work with the table. Select **Table, Show Gridline** to display gridlines. When you finish working with the table, select **Table, Hide Gridlines** to turn them off.

Automatic Table Formatting

Word provides a variety of predefined table formats. Using these formats makes it easy to apply attractive formatting to any table. These steps show you how to use a predefined table format:

1. Place the cursor anywhere in the table.

2. Select **Table**, **Table AutoFormat**. The Table AutoFormat dialog box appears (see Figure 17.4). This is the same dialog box you would see if you selected AutoFormat in the Insert Table dialog box when first creating a table (as covered earlier in this lesson).

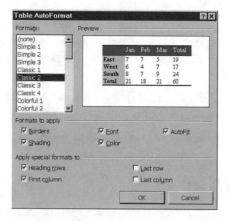

Figure 17.4   The Table AutoFormat dialog box.

3. The **Formats** list names the available table formats. As you scroll through the list, the Preview box shows the appearance of the highlighted format.

4. Select and deselect the formatting check boxes as needed until the Preview shows the table appearance you want.

5. When you're satisfied with what you see in the Preview area, click **OK**. Word applies the selected formatting to the table.

In this lesson, you learned how to add tables to your document, and how to edit and format tables. The next lesson shows you how to use columns in your documents.

Using Columns in Your Document

In this lesson, you learn how to format your document text in two or more columns per page.

Why Use Columns?

Columns are commonly used in newsletters, brochures, and similar documents. The shorter lines of text provided by columns are easier to read, and they provide greater flexibility in formatting a document with graphics, tables, and so on. Word makes it easy to use columns in your documents. Figure 18.1 shows a document formatted with two columns.

The columns you create in Word are *newspaper* style columns, in which the text flows to the bottom of one column and then continues at the top of the next column on the page. For side-by-side paragraphs, such as you would need in a résumé or a script, use Word's table feature, which is covered in Lesson 17.

When you define columns with text selected, the column definition will apply to the selected text. Word will insert section breaks before and after the selection. If you do not select text first, the column definitions will apply to the entire document unless you divided the document into two or more sections, in which case the columns will apply only to the current section. See Lesson 9 for more information about document sections.

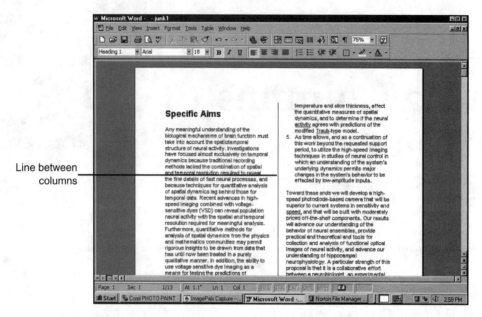

Line between columns

Figure 18.1 A document formatted with two columns.

Creating Columns

Word has four predefined column layouts:

- Two equal width columns
- Three equal width columns
- Two unequal width columns with the wider column on the left
- Two unequal width columns with the wider column on the right

You can apply any of these column formats to an entire document, to one section of a document, to selected text, or from the insertion point onward. Follow these steps to learn how:

1. If you want only a part of the document in columns, select the text you want in columns, or move the insertion point to the location where you want columns to begin. Word will insert section breaks before or after the text, as appropriate.

2. Select **Format**, **Columns** to open the Columns dialog box (see Figure 18.2).

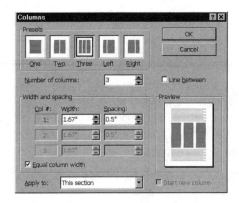

Figure 18.2 The Columns dialog box.

3. Under Presets, click the column format you want.

4. Click the **Apply To** drop-down arrow and specify the extent to which the columns should apply. The following options are available:

- **Whole Document** This is available only if the document has not been broken into sections.

- **This Section** Available only if you have broken the document into sections.

- **This Point Forward** Word will insert a section break at the current cursor location and apply the new column setting to the latter of the two sections.

5. Select the **Line Between** check box to display a vertical line between columns (like in a newspaper).

6. Click **OK**.

TIP   **Quick Columns** To display selected text, the current section, or the entire document in one to four equal width columns, click the Columns button on the Standard toolbar and then drag over the desired number of columns.

CAUTION   **No Columns?** Columns display on-screen only in Page Layout view. In Normal view, Word displays only a single column at a time (although your multiple columns will look fine when printed, even from Normal view). To switch to Page Layout view, select **View**, **Page Layout**.

Modifying Columns

You can modify existing columns, change the number of columns, change column widths, and change the spacing between columns. Here's how:

1. Move the cursor to the columns you want to modify.

2. Select **Format**, **Columns** to open the Columns dialog box (refer to Figure 18.2). The options in the dialog box will reflect the current settings for the columns you selected.

3. To apply a different predefined column format, click the desired format in the Presets area of the dialog box.

4. To change the width or spacing of a specific column, enter the desired width and spacing values (or click the arrows) in the column's **Width** and **Spacing** text boxes. The Preview box shows you what the settings will look like.

5. When you're satisfied with what you see in the Preview area, click **OK**.

Turning Columns Off

To convert multiple-column text back to normal text (which is really just one column), follow these steps:

1. Select the text that you want to change from multiple columns to a single column.

2. Select **Format**, **Columns** to open the Columns dialog box (refer to Figure 18.2).

3. Under Presets, select the **One** option.

4. Click **OK**.

 TIP A Quicker Way To quickly convert text in columns back to normal single-column text, select the text, click the **Columns** button on the Standard toolbar, and drag to select a single column.

This lesson showed you how to arrange text in columns. The next lesson shows you how to work with graphics in your document.

Adding Graphics

In this lesson, you learn how to add graphics to your documents and how to create your own drawings.

Adding a Graphic Image

A *graphic image* is a picture that is stored on disk in a graphics file. Word can utilize graphics files created by a variety of applications, including PC Paintbrush, Windows' own Paint program, Lotus 1-2-3, Micrografx Designer, and AutoCAD. Additionally, your Word installation includes a small library of clip art images that you can use in your documents. Figure 19.1 shows a document with a graphic image.

To add a graphic image to a Word document, follow these steps:

1. Move the insertion point to the location for the graphic.

2. Select **Insert, Picture, From File**. The Insert Picture dialog box appears (see Figure 19.2).

3. If necessary, click the **Look In** drop-down arrow to specify the folder where the graphic file is located.

4. The large box in the center of the dialog box normally lists all graphics files in the specified directory. To have the list restricted to certain types of graphics files, click the **Files of Type** drop-down arrow and select the desired file type from the list.

5. In the **File Name** text box, type the name of the file to insert, or select the file name from the list.

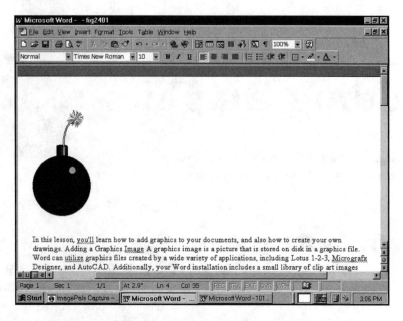

Figure 19.1 A document with a graphic.

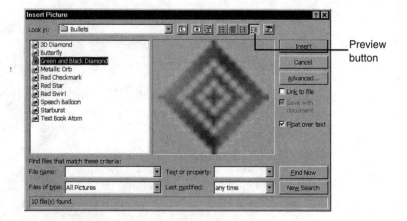

Figure 19.2 The Insert Picture dialog box.

6. To preview the picture in the Preview box, click the **Preview** button.

7. Choose from the following options:

- Select **Link to File** if you want the graphic in your document updated if the graphics file on disk changes.

- If you selected **Link to File**, you can select **Save with Document** to save a copy of the picture with the document. Although this increases the document's file size, it makes it possible for the picture to be displayed even if the original file is no longer available.

- Select **Float over Text** to enable the picture to be displayed "behind" or "over" text and other objects. (Otherwise, the image will be displayed inline with text.)

8. Click **OK**, and Word inserts the graphic into your document.

Adding Clip Art

Clip art is a special category of pictures that consists of generally small, simple images that you use to add visual appeal and interest to your documents. Word comes with an extensive gallery of clip art that you can use freely. Here's how to add a clip art image to a document:

1. Move the cursor to the document location where you want the image.

2. Select **Insert**, **Picture**, **Clip Art** to open the Microsoft Clip Gallery dialog box (see Figure 19.3).

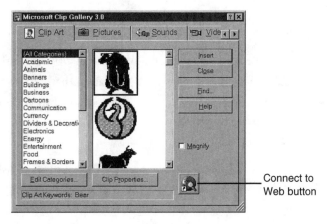

Figure 19.3 Selecting clip art from the Microsoft Clip Gallery.

3. In the list on the left, select the desired category of images. Or, select **(All Categories)** to view all clip art images.

4. Scroll through the image list until you find the image you want. Then click it to select it.

5. Click **Insert** to add the image to your document.

115

TIP **Word on the Web** If you have Internet access, you can click the **Connect to Web** button in the Microsoft Clip Gallery dialog box to connect to Microsoft's Web site and access additional clip art images.

Displaying Graphics

The screen display of graphics images can slow down screen scrolling. If you're working on the document text in Page Layout or Online Layout view and don't need to see the images, you can speed up screen display by displaying empty rectangles called *placeholders* in place of the images (images are automatically hidden in Normal and Outline view). In addition, if you selected the Link to File option when inserting the graphic file, Word inserts a field code in the document. The screen will display this code instead of the picture when field codes are displayed.

 TERM **Field Code** A code in a document that tells Word to display a certain item, such as a graphic.

Here's how to control the display of graphics:

1. Select **Tools**, **Options** to open the Options dialog box.
2. If necessary, click the **View** tab to display the View options.
3. In the Show section, select or deselect the **Picture Placeholders** and **Field Codes** check boxes as desired.
4. Click **OK**.

The screen display of placeholders or field codes does not affect printing; the actual graphics are always printed in the document.

 TIP **Speed It Up!** When working on a document that contains a lot of graphics, you can speed up screen display and scrolling by displaying placeholders for the graphics.

Cropping and Resizing a Graphic

Before you can work with a graphic in your document, you must select it. There are two ways to do this:

- Click the graphic.
- Using the keyboard, position the insertion point immediately to the left of the graphic, and then press **Shift+→**.

A selected graphic is surrounded by eight small black squares called *sizing handles*. Figure 19.4 shows sizing handles around a selected clip art image.

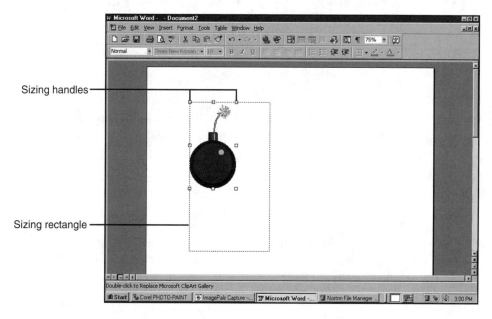

Figure 19.4 Resizing a selected graphic.

You can resize a graphic in your document to display the entire picture at a different size. You can also *crop* a graphic to hide portions of the picture that you don't want to display. To resize or crop a graphic, follow these steps:

1. Select the graphic.

2. Point at one of the resizing handles. The mouse pointer changes to a double-headed arrow.

117

3. Do either or both of the following, depending on how you want to modify the image:

- To *resize* the graphic, press the left mouse button and drag the handle until the outline of the graphic reaches the desired size. You can either enlarge or shrink the graphic.
- To *crop* the graphic, press and hold **Shift**, and then press the left mouse button and drag a handle toward the center of the graphic.

4. Release the mouse button.

Deleting, Moving, and Copying Graphics

To delete a graphic, select it and press **Delete**. To move or copy a graphic to a new location, follow these steps:

1. Select the graphic.

2. To copy the graphic, press **Ctrl+C**, or select **Edit**, **Copy**, or click the **Copy** button on the Standard toolbar. To move the graphic, press **Ctrl+X**, or select **Edit**, **Cut**, or click the **Cut** button on the Standard toolbar.

3. Move the cursor to the new location for the graphic.

4. Press **Ctrl+V**, or select **Edit**, **Paste**, or click the **Paste** button on the Standard toolbar.

TIP   **Drag That Image**   If the image and its destination are both in view, you can move it by dragging it to the new location. To copy instead of moving, hold down **Ctrl** while dragging.

Drawing in Your Document

In addition to adding existing graphics to a document, Word lets you create your own drawings. The drawing tools that are available let even the complete non-artist create professional-looking drawings. To draw, you must display the Drawing toolbar. Select **View**, **Toolbars**, **Drawing**. Figure 19.5 shows the Drawing toolbar and identifies the buttons on it.

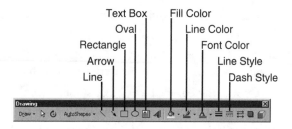

Figure 19.5 The Drawing toolbar.

 No Microsoft Draw? If you didn't install Draw 97 when you installed Word, you can return to the Setup program and do so, or you'll find a copy of the applet in the Office 97 ValuPack. Check out Appendix B for more information.

The process of drawing consists of the following general actions:

- Adding drawing objects to the document. The available objects include lines, arrows, shapes, and text. Most of Word's drawing objects are called *AutoShapes*.

- Moving drawing objects to new locations and changing their size and proportions.

- Modifying drawing objects. For example, you might change the thickness of a line, the color of text, or the type of arrowhead on an arrow.

The Drawing toolbar displays buttons for the most commonly needed drawing objects: lines, arrows, 3-D shapes, and so on. (You access the less common drawing objects via menus or dialog boxes associated with the Drawing toolbar.) The following list explains the most frequently used drawing procedures:

- To draw an object, click its button on the Drawing toolbar. Or, click the **AutoShapes** button and select the shape from the list. Then draw in the document to insert the object. Hold down **Shift** while drawing to draw an object with a 1:1 aspect ratio (for example, to draw a square or circle instead of a rectangle or ellipse).

- To select an object you have already drawn, click it. The object will display small rectangles called *resizing handles*. Hold down **Shift** and click to select more than one object. Press **Delete** to delete the selected object(s).

- To move a selected object, point at it (but not at a handle) and drag to the new location.
- To change a selected object's size or shape, point at one of its resizing handles and drag to the desired size and shape.
- To change the color of an object's line, click the **Line Color** button on the Drawing toolbar and select the desired color.
- To change the interior color of a solid object, click the **Fill Color** button and select the desired color.
- To change the thickness or style of the lines used for an object, select the object and click the **Line Style** or **Dash Style** button.
- To add a text label, click the **Text Box** button, drag in the document to add the text box, and then type the text. Click outside the text box when you're done.

Word's drawing capabilities go much further than what is described here. You should experiment on your own to discover their full capabilities.

In this lesson, you learned how to add graphics and drawings to your documents. The next lesson teaches you how to print, e-mail, and fax your Word documents.

Printing, Mailing, and Faxing Your Document

20

In this lesson, you learn how to print your document, and how to send a document via e-mail or fax.

Printing Using the Default Settings

It's very simple to print using Word's default settings. This means to print a single copy of the entire document on the default Windows printer. Follow these steps:

1. Open the **File** menu and select **Print** or click the **Print** button on the Standard toolbar. The Print dialog box appears (see Figure 20.1).

2. Click **OK**, and Word prints the document.

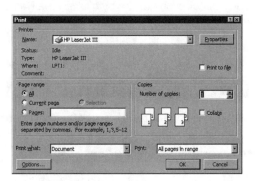

Figure 20.1 The Print dialog box.

TIP **Another Way to Print** You can also press **Ctrl+P** to print using the defaults without going to the Print dialog box.

Printer Not Working? Refer to your Microsoft Windows and printer documentation for help. If you're using a network printer, see your network administrator.

CAUTION

Printing Multiple Copies

With the options in the Print dialog box, you can print more than one copy of a document, and you can specify that the copies be collated. To do either of those, follow these steps:

1. Open the **File** menu and select **Print** or click the **Print** button on the Standard toolbar. The Print dialog box appears.
2. In the **Number of Copies** box (refer to Figure 20.1), enter the desired number of copies. Or, click the increment arrows to set the desired value.
3. Click the **Collate** check box to turn that feature on or off.
4. Click **OK**.

More than One Printer? If you have two or more printers installed, you can select the one to use by clicking the **Name** drop-down arrow at the top of the Print dialog box and selecting the desired printer from the list.

CAUTION

Printing Part of a Document

Most often you will want to print all of a document. You can, however, print just part of a document, ranging from a single sentence to a range of pages. Follow these steps to print a smaller portion:

1. To print a section of text, select the text. To print a single page, move the cursor to that page.
2. Open the **File** menu and select **Print** or click the **Print** button on the Standard toolbar. The Print dialog box appears.

3. In the Page Range area, specify what you want printed:

- Choose **Selection** to print the selected text.
- Choose **Current Page** to print the page containing the cursor.
- Choose **Pages** to print specified pages, and then enter the page numbers in the text box. For example, enter **1–3** to print pages 1 through 3, or enter **2,4** to print pages 2 and 4.

4. Click **OK**.

 TIP **Printing Properties** To print a document's properties instead of its text, click the **Print What** drop-down arrow in the Print dialog box and select **Document Properties** from the list.

Changing Your Print Options

Word offers a number of printing options that you may need to use at times. You can print only the odd-numbered pages or the even-numbered pages. This option is useful to create two-sided output on a standard one-sided printer: print the odd-numbered pages, flip the printed pages over and place them back in the printer's paper tray, and then print the even-numbered pages. You select which pages to print by clicking the **Print** drop-down arrow in the Print dialog box and selecting **Odd Pages** or **Even Pages** from the list. Select **All Pages in Range** to return to printing all pages.

You can set other print options in the Print Options dialog box (shown in Figure 20.2). To display this dialog box, open the Print dialog box as described previously and click the **Options** button.

The following list outlines the options you will use most often:

- **Draft Output** Produces draft output that prints faster, but may lack some graphics and formatting (depending on your specific printer).
- **Reverse Print Order** Prints pages in last-to-first order. This setting produces collated output on printers that have face-up output.
- **Background Printing** Permits you to continue working on the document while printing is in progress. This setting uses additional memory and usually results in slower printing.
- **Update Fields** Updates the contents of all document fields before printing.

- **Document Properties** Prints the document's properties in addition to its contents.

- **Comments** Includes document comments in the printout.

Figure 20.2 The Print Options dialog box.

After setting the desired printing options, click **OK** to return to the Print dialog box.

TIP **Save Paper!** Use Page Layout view or Print Preview to check the appearance of your document before you print it.

Printing Labels? If your small business uses Avery Dennison labels, you'll find a helpful Avery Wizard in the Office 97 ValuPack. Refer to Appendix B for more information.

Faxing a Document

If your system is set up for faxing, you can fax a document directly to one or more recipients without having to print a paper copy and feed it into a standard fax machine. This capability saves both time and paper. Follow these steps to fax the current document:

1. Pull down the **File** menu, select **Send To**, **Fax Recipient**. Word starts the Fax Wizard.

2. The Fax Wizard takes you through the steps of preparing the fax, choosing a cover page, and selecting recipients. For each step, enter the requested information and click **Next**.

3. After the final step, click **Finish**.

4. If you requested a cover sheet, Word displays it. You can make any additions or changes to the cover sheet at this time.

5. Click the **Send Fax Now** button to send the fax.

CAUTION

No Fax Option? If the Fax Recipient option is not available on your Send To submenu, it means that your system has not been set up for faxing.

TIP **Another Way to Fax** You can also fax a document by selecting **Microsoft Fax** (or the name of whatever fax program you use) as the destination printer in the Print dialog box and then printing in the usual fashion.

Mailing a Document

If you have Microsoft Messaging or another e-mail program installed on your system, you can send a document directly to a mail recipient. Here are the steps to take:

1. Open the **File** menu, select **Send To**, **Mail Recipient**.

2. Depending on the specifics of your system, Word may ask you to select a profile setting. Generally, the default setting is the one you should select.

3. Next you will see your usual New Message window. The appearance of this window will vary depending on the mail system you are using, but it will be the same mail form that you use for other e-mail messages. Figure 20.3 shows the New Message window used by the Windows Messaging system. The document will already be inserted in the message as an icon. Add text to the message if desired.

4. Fill in the **To...** line of the message with the recipient's address.

5. When the message is complete, click the **Send** button.

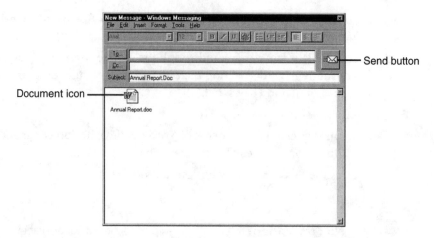

Document icon ⎯⎯⎯⎯⎯

Send button

Figure 20.3 A new message with the document inserted as an icon.

When the recipient receives your message, he or she will be able to double-click the document icon to open the document in Word for printing, editing, and so on.

TIP **E-Mailing with Outlook** You can also use Microsoft Outlook as your e-mail client. Turn to Part III to learn all about using Outlook.

In this lesson, you learned how to print your document and how to send it as a fax or as an e-mail message. The next lesson shows you how to work with multiple documents.

Working with Multiple Documents

This lesson shows you how to simultaneously edit multiple documents in Word.

Starting or Opening a Second Document

Working on one document at a time is often all you need, but in some situations the capability to work on multiple documents at once can be very useful. For example, you can refer to one document while working on another, and you can copy and move text between documents. Word lets you have as many documents as you need open simultaneously.

While you're working on one document, you can start a new document or open another existing document at any time. To do so, follow the procedure you learned in Lesson 2 for creating a new document or in Lesson 4 for opening a document. Briefly:

- To create a new document based on the Normal template, click the **New** button on the Standard toolbar.

- To create a document based on another template or one of Word's Wizards, select **File**, **New**.

- To open an existing document, select **File**, **Open** or click the **Open** button on the Standard toolbar.

A new window opens and displays the document you created or opened. Both the newly created and the original documents are in memory and can be edited, printed, and so on. You can continue opening additional documents until all of the files you need to work with are open.

TIP   **Opening Multiple Documents at Once**   In the Open dialog box, you can select multiple documents by holding **Shift** and clicking the document names. Then click **Open** to open all of the selected documents.

Switching Between Documents

When you have multiple documents open at one time, only one of them can be *active* at a given moment. The active document is displayed on-screen (although inactive documents may be displayed as well). The title bar of the active document is displayed in a darker color, and if documents are overlapping each other the active one will be on top. The important thing you need to remember, though, is that the active document is the only one affected by editing commands.

To switch between open documents, follow these steps:

1. Open the **Window** menu. At the bottom is a list of all open documents with a check mark next to the name of the currently active document (see Figure 21.1).

2. Select the name of the document you want to make active. (You can click the document name or press the corresponding number key.)

The selected document becomes active and appears on-screen.

TIP   **Next, Please!**   To cycle to the next open document, press **Ctrl+F6**.

128

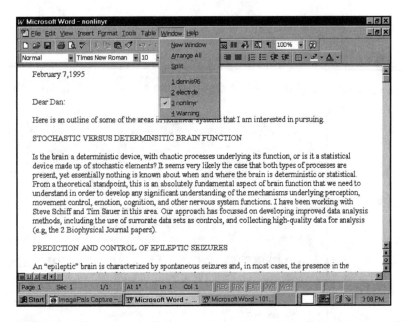

Figure 21.1 The Window menu lists open documents and indicates the currently active document.

Controlling Multiple Document View

Word gives you a great deal of flexibility in displaying multiple documents. You can have the active document occupy the entire screen, with other open documents temporarily hidden. You can also have several documents displayed at the same time, each in its own window. A document window can be in one of three states:

- **Maximized**   The window occupies the entire work area, and no other open documents are visible. When the active document is maximized, its title appears in Word's title bar at the top of the screen. Figure 21.2 shows a maximized document.

- **Minimized**   The window is reduced to a small icon displayed at the bottom of the Word screen. The document title is displayed on the icon.

- **Restored**   The document window assumes an intermediate size, and the document title is displayed in the title bar of its own window instead of Word's title bar.

Figure 21.3 shows both a restored and a minimized document.

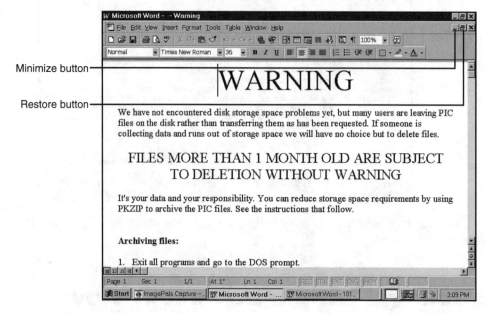

Figure 21.2   A maximized document window.

You can control the display of multiple documents in the following ways:

- To restore or minimize a maximized window, click its **Restore** or **Minimize** button.

- To maximize or minimize a restored window, click its **Maximize** or **Minimize** button.

- To display a minimized window, click its icon. Then either click its **Restore** or **Maximize** button or select from the pop-up menu that appears.

When a document is in the restored state, you can control the size and position of its window. To move the window, click its title bar and drag it to the new position. To change window size, point at a border or corner of the window (the mouse pointer changes to a two-headed arrow), and then click and drag the window to the desired size.

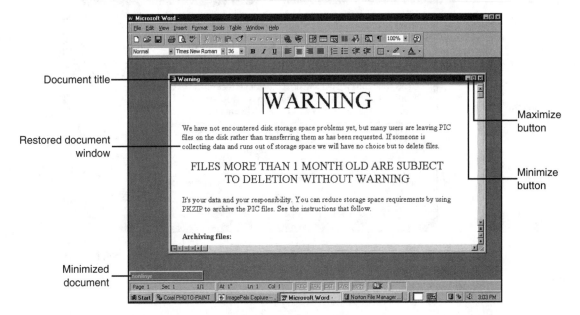

Document title

Restored document window

Maximize button

Minimize button

Minimized document

Figure 21.3   Restored and minimized document windows.

Viewing All Open Documents

Word has a command that displays all of your open documents. Select **Window**, **Arrange All** to tile all document windows. When you tile your documents, every open document is displayed in a small window, and none of the windows overlap. If you have more than a few documents open, these windows will be quite small and won't be very useful for editing. They are useful, however, for seeing exactly which documents you have open and finding the one you need to work in at the moment. Figure 21.4 shows the result of the Window, Arrange All command with four documents open.

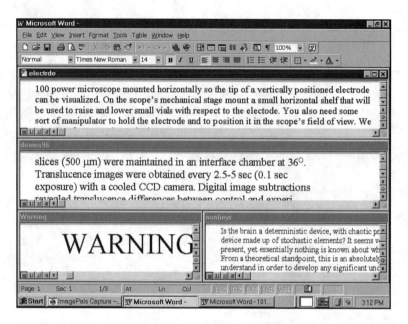

Figure 21.4 The Arrange All command displays all open documents, each in its own window.

Moving and Copying Text Between Documents

When you have more than one document open, you can move and copy text and graphics between documents. Follow these procedures to learn how:

1. Make the source document active, and then select the text or graphic you want to move or copy.

2. Press **Ctrl+X**, or select **Edit**, **Cut**, or click the **Cut** button on the Standard toolbar if you want to move the text. Press **Ctrl+C**, or select **Edit**, **Copy**, or click the **Copy** button on the Standard toolbar to copy the text.

3. Make the destination document active. Move the insertion point to the location for the text.

4. Press **Ctrl+V**, or select **Edit**, **Paste**, or click the **Paste** button on the Standard toolbar.

If both documents are visible, you can copy or move text from one to the other with drag-and-drop, as described here:

1. Select the text to be copied or moved.

2. Point at the selected text. To move the text, press and hold the left mouse button. To copy the text, press **Ctrl** and the left mouse button.

3. Drag to the new location for the text and release the mouse button (and the Ctrl key, if you were copying).

Saving Multiple Documents

When you're working with multiple documents, you save individual documents with the **File**, **Save** and **File**, **Save As** commands you learned about in Lesson 4. These commands save the active document only. There is no command to save all open documents in one step. If you attempt to close a document that has not been saved, you will be prompted to save it. If you try to quit Word with one or more documents unsaved, you will be prompted one-by-one to save each document.

TIP   **No Save All**   The Save All command that was available in earlier versions of Word is not present in Word 97.

Closing a Document

You can close an open document when you finish working with it. These steps teach you how to close a document:

1. Make the document active.

2. Select **File**, **Close** or click the **Close** button at the right end of the document's title bar. (Be sure not to click the Close button in Word's main title bar.)

3. If the document contains unsaved changes, Word prompts you to save the document. Click **Yes** and save the file, or click **No**. Either way, Word closes the document.

This lesson showed you how to simultaneously edit multiple documents in Word.

Excel 97

Starting and Exiting Excel

In this lesson, you learn how to start and end a typical Excel work session, and take a look at Excel's screen elements.

Introducing Excel

When it comes to managing finances or handling accounting tasks, there's no better program to use than Microsoft Excel. Excel is a powerful tool for number-juggling tasks of any kind, and the new and improved Excel 97 makes spreadsheet projects even easier. You can perform complex calculations, organize data so it's easy to find, build business reports and databases, and more.

In addition to the great tools and templates found in Excel, Office 97 Small Business Edition also comes with the Small Business Financial Manager, a collection of useful templates and wizards designed specifically for the small business user. You can even plug in data from other accounting packages and create professional reports and analysis using Excel 97. Lessons 21 through 26 will show you how to tap into Financial Manager and put Excel's features to work for you.

Starting Excel

To start Excel from the Windows 95 desktop, follow these steps:

1. Click the **Start** button, and the Start menu appears.
2. Choose **Programs**, and the Programs menu appears.
3. Choose the **Microsoft Excel** program item to start the program.

The Excel opening screen appears (see Figure 1.1), displaying a blank *workbook* labeled Book1. Excel is now ready for you to begin creating a document.

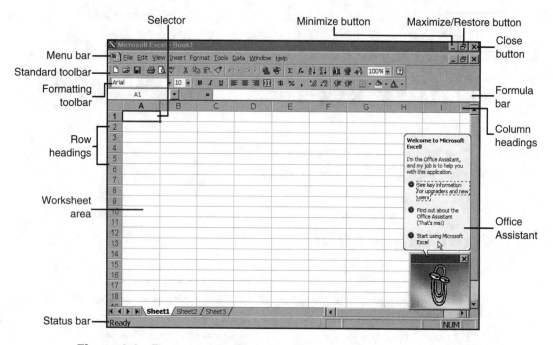

Figure 1.1 Elements of the Excel window.

Workbook   An Excel file is called a *workbook*. Each workbook consists of three worksheets (although you can add or remove worksheets as needed). Each worksheet consists of columns and rows that intersect to form boxes called *cells* into which you enter text. The tabs at the bottom of the workbook (labeled Sheet1, Sheet2, and so on) let you flip through the worksheets by clicking them with the mouse.

TIP   **What's the Office Assistant?**   When you first start Excel, you're greeted by an animated icon called the Office Assistant. He's there to offer help, and he'll pop up from time to time whenever you encounter new features. Close the Assistant by clicking **Start Using Microsoft Excel**.

Parts of the Excel Window

As you can see in Figure 1.1, the Excel window contains many common Windows elements, including a menu bar (from which you can select commands), a Status bar (which displays the status of the current activity), and toolbars (which contain buttons and drop-down lists that provide quick access to common commands and features). You also see the Minimize, Maximize/Restore, and Close buttons in the upper-right corner of the window (use these buttons to control the window's size on-screen or close the program).

CAUTION

Missing Status Bar?   By default, Excel does not display the status bar. To display it, open the **Tools** menu, select **Options**, and click the **View** tab. In the Show area, select **Status Bar** and click **OK**.

In addition, the window contains some elements that are unique to Excel, including:

Formula bar   When you enter information into a *cell*, anything you type appears in the Formula bar. The cell's location also appears in the Formula bar.

Cell   Each worksheet contains a grid consisting of alphabetized columns and numbered rows. Where a row and column intersect, they form a box called a *cell*. Each cell has an *address* that consists of the column letter and row number (A1, B3, C4, and so on). You enter data and formulas in the cells to create your worksheets. You'll learn more about cells in Lessons 4 and 5.

Workbook window   Each Excel file is a workbook that consists of one or more worksheets. You can open several files (workbooks) at a time, each in its own window.

Column headings   The letters across the top of the worksheet, which identify the columns in the worksheet.

Row headings   The numbers down the side of the worksheet, which identify the rows in the worksheet.

Selector   The outline that indicates the active cell (the one in which you are working).

Exiting Excel

To exit Excel and return to the Windows 95 desktop, use any of these steps:

- Open the **File** menu and select **Exit**.
- Click the **Close** (X) button in the Excel window.
- Press **Alt+F4** on the keyboard.
- Click the **Control-menu icon** and select **Close**.

If you changed the workbook in any way without saving the file, Excel displays a prompt asking if you want to save the file before exiting. Select the desired option. See Lesson 6 for help in saving your workbook.

In this lesson, you learned how to start and exit Excel. In the next lesson, you'll learn about moving around the Excel workbook window.

Moving Around the Excel Window

2

In this lesson, you'll learn the basics of moving around in the Excel window and in the workbook window.

Moving from Worksheet to Worksheet

An Excel file is called a *workbook*. Each workbook has *worksheets* which consist of columns and rows that intersect to form *cells*—where you enter data and formulas. Workbooks, worksheets, and cells are the building blocks of Excel spreadsheets.

By default, each workbook starts off with three worksheets. You can add worksheets to or delete worksheets from the workbook as needed. Because each workbook consists of one or more worksheets, you need a way of moving from worksheet to worksheet easily. Use one of the following methods:

- Press **Ctrl+PgDn** to move to the next worksheet or **Ctrl+PgUp** to move to a previous one.
- Click the tab of the worksheet you want to go to (see Figure 2.1). If the tab is not shown, use the tab scroll buttons to bring the tab into view, and then click the tab.

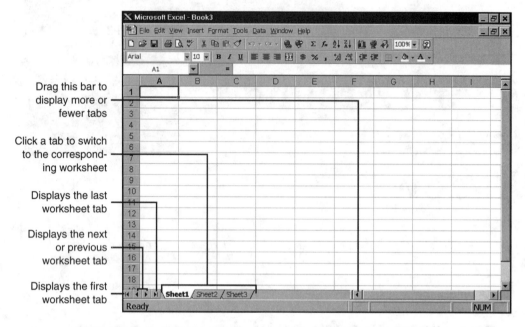

Drag this bar to display more or fewer tabs

Click a tab to switch to the corresponding worksheet

Displays the last worksheet tab

Displays the next or previous worksheet tab

Displays the first worksheet tab

Figure 2.1 You can move from worksheet to worksheet with tabs.

Moving Within a Worksheet

Once the worksheet you want to work on is displayed, you'll need some way of moving to the various cells within the worksheet. Keep in mind that the part of the worksheet displayed on-screen is only a small part of the actual worksheet. To move around the worksheet with your keyboard, use the keys listed in Table 2.1.

Table 2.1 Moving Around a Worksheet with the Keyboard

Press This	To Move...
↑ ↓ ← →	One cell in the direction of the arrow.
Ctrl+↑ or Ctrl+↓	To the top or bottom of a data region (the area of a worksheet that contains data).

Press This	*To Move...*
Ctrl+← or Ctrl+→	To the leftmost or rightmost cell in a data region.
PgUp	Up one screen.
PgDn	Down one screen.
Home	Leftmost cell in a row.
Ctrl+Home	Upper-left corner of a worksheet.
Ctrl+End	Lower-right corner of a worksheet.
End+↑, End+↓, End+←, End+→	If the active cell is blank, moves in the direction of the arrow to the *first* cell that contains data. If the active cell contains an entry, moves in the direction of the arrow to the *last* cell that has an entry.

If you have a mouse, you can use the scroll bars to scroll to the area of the screen that contains the cell you want to work with. Then click the cell to make it the active cell.

Keep in mind that as you scroll, the scroll box moves within the scroll bar to tell you where you are within the file. In addition, the size of the scroll box changes to represent the amount of the total worksheet that is currently visible. If the scroll box is large, you know you're seeing most of the current worksheet in the window. If the scroll box is small, most of the worksheet is currently hidden from view.

TIP **Fast Scrolling**   If you want to scroll to a specific row within a large worksheet, press and hold the **Shift** key while you drag the scroll box. The current row is displayed as you move the scroll box.

TIP **Move to a Specific Cell**   To move quickly to a specific cell on a worksheet, type the cell's address in the **Name** box at the left end of the Formula bar and press **Enter**. A cell address consists of the column letter and row number that define the location of the cell (for example **C25**). To go to a cell on a specific worksheet, type the worksheet's name, an exclamation point, and the cell address (such as **sheet3!C25**) and press **Enter.**

Changing the View of Your Worksheet

There are many ways to change how your worksheet appears within the Excel window. Changing the view has no effect on how your worksheets will look when printed, but changing the view and getting a different perspective often helps you see your data more clearly. For example, you can enlarge or reduce the size of its text in order to view more or less of the worksheet at one time. You can also "freeze" row or column headings so you won't lose your place as you scroll through a large worksheet.

Magnifying and Reducing the Worksheet View

`100% ▼` To enlarge or reduce your view of the current worksheet, use the Zoom feature. Simply click the **Zoom** button (on the Standard toolbar) and select the zoom percentage you want to use, such as **25%** or **200%**. You can enlarge a specific area of the worksheet if you'd like by selecting it first, opening the **Zoom** menu, and choosing **Selection**.

If you want, you can display your worksheet so that it takes up the full screen—eliminating toolbars, Formula bar, Status bar, and so on—as shown in Figure 2.2. To do so, open the **View** menu and select **Full Screen**. To return to Normal view, click **Close Full Screen**.

Freezing Column and Row Headings

As you scroll through a large worksheet, it's often helpful to freeze your headings so that you can view them with related data. For example, as you can see in Figure 2.3, you need to be able to view the column and row headings in order to understand the data in the cells.

To freeze row or column headings (or both), follow these steps:

1. Click the cell to the right of the row headings or below any column headings you want to freeze. This highlights the cell.
2. Open the **Window** menu and select **Freeze Panes**.

Play around a little, moving the cursor all around the document. As you do, the row and column headings remain locked in their positions. This enables you to view data in other parts of the worksheet without losing track of what that data represents. To unlock headings, open the **Window** menu again and select **Unfreeze Panes**.

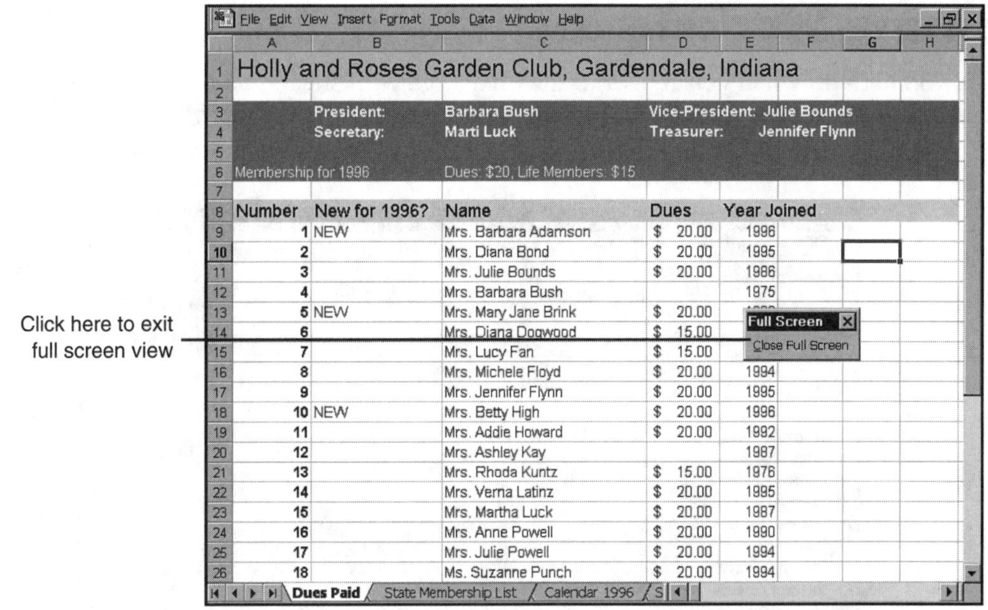

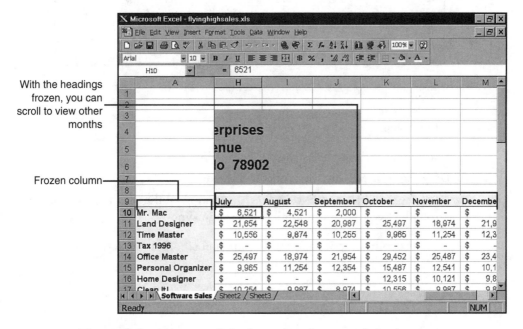

Click here to exit
full screen view

Figure 2.2 View your worksheet in a full window.

With the headings
frozen, you can
scroll to view other
months

Frozen column

Figure 2.3 As you scroll, the frozen headings remain in place.

Splitting Worksheets

Sometimes when you're working with a large worksheet, you find yourself wanting to view two parts of it at one time in order to compare data. To view two parts of a worksheet, you *split* it. Figure 2.4 shows a split worksheet.

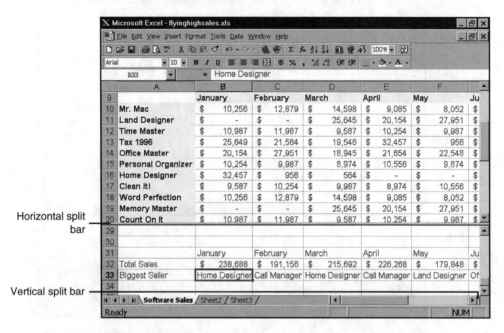

Figure 2.4   Split a worksheet to view two parts at one time.

Follow these steps to split a worksheet:

1. Click either the vertical or the horizontal split bar.

2. Drag the split bar into the worksheet window.

3. Drop the split bar, and Excel splits the window at that location. When you scroll, the two panes automatically scroll in sync.

To remove the split, drag it back to its original position on the scroll bar.

Hiding Workbooks, Worksheets, Columns, and Rows

For those times when you're working on high priority or top secret information, you can hide workbooks, worksheets, columns or rows from prying eyes. For example, if you have confidential data stored in one particular worksheet, you can hide that worksheet, yet still be able to view the other worksheets in that workbook. You can also hide particular columns (see Figure 2.5) or rows within a worksheet—or even an entire workbook if you want.

Columns D and E, which contain addresses and phone numbers, are hidden from view

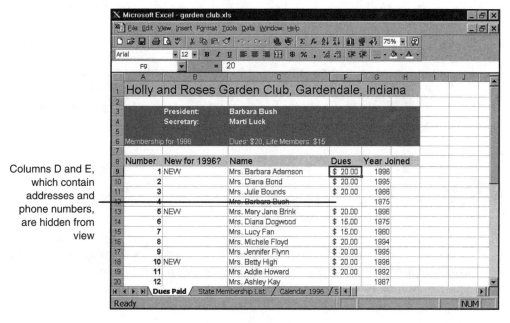

Figure 2.5 Hide data to prevent it from being viewed, printed, or changed.

In addition to hiding data in order to prevent it from appearing on a report, you might hide it to prevent it from accidentally being changed. When data is hidden, it cannot be viewed, printed, or changed. This is *unlike* other changes you might make to the view (such as changing the Zoom), which do not affect your worksheet when printed. Hiding data *does* prevent that data from being printed.

Use these methods to hide data:

- To hide a *workbook*, open the **Window** menu and select **Hide**.
- To hide a *worksheet*, click its tab to select it. Then open the **Format** menu, select **Sheet**, and select **Hide**.
- To hide *rows* or *columns*, click a row or column heading to select it. Then open the **Format** menu, select **Row** or **Column**, and select **Hide**.

 TIP **Hide More than One** To select several worksheets, press and hold **Ctrl** while you click each tab. To select several rows or columns, press and hold **Ctrl** while you click each heading.

Of course, whenever you need to, you can redisplay the hidden data easily. To redisplay hidden data, select the hidden area first. For example, select the rows, columns, or sheets adjacent to the hidden ones. Then repeat the previous steps, selecting **Unhide** from the appropriate menus.

 You Can't Hide It Completely! It's easy to undo the command to hide data, so you can't really hide data completely as a means of security. If you give the workbook file to someone else, for example, he or she can easily

CAUTION unhide and view the data you hid.

In this lesson, you learned how to move around within workbooks and worksheets. You also learned how to change the view of your worksheet, freeze column and row headings, and hide data. In the next lesson, you will learn how to use Excel's toolbars.

Using Excel's Toolbars

In this lesson, you learn how to use Excel's toolbars to save time when you work. You also learn how to arrange them for maximum performance.

Using the Toolbars

Unless you tell it otherwise, Excel displays the Standard and Formatting toolbars as shown in Figure 3.1. To select a tool from a toolbar, simply click the tool.

CAUTION

Off Duty   If a tool appears grayed, it is currently unavailable. Tools become unavailable when they are not applicable to your current activity.

TERM

Toolbar   A collection of tools or icons displayed in a long bar that you can move and reshape for your convenience. Each icon represents a common command or task.

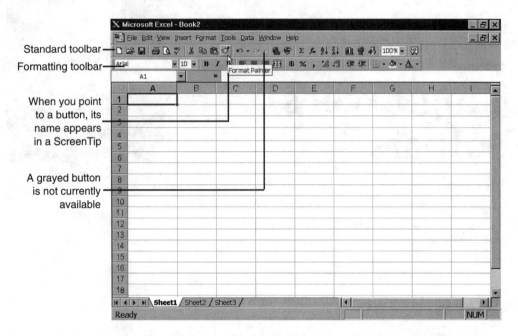

Standard toolbar

Formatting toolbar

When you point
to a button, its
name appears
in a ScreenTip

A grayed button
is not currently
available

Figure 3.1   The Standard and Formatting toolbars contain buttons for Excel's most commonly used features.

Here are some easy ways to learn about the available toolbar buttons:

- To view the name of a button, position the mouse pointer over it. Excel displays a ScreenTip, which displays the name of the button (as shown in Figure 3.1).

- To get help with the command associated with a particular button, press **Shift+F1**. The mouse pointer changes to a question mark. Move the question mark pointer over a button and click it. A description box appears on-screen detailing the feature you clicked (click **Esc** to close the box after reading).

Turning Toolbars On and Off

By default, Excel initially displays the Standard and Formatting toolbars. If you find that you don't use these toolbars, you can turn one or both of them off to free up some screen space. In addition, you can turn on other toolbars (although some toolbars appear on their own when you perform a related activity).

Follow these steps to turn a toolbar on or off:

1. Open the **View** menu and choose **Toolbars**. A submenu appears.

2. A check mark next to a toolbar's name indicates that the toolbar is currently displayed. To turn a toolbar on or off, simply click its name in the list to add or remove the check mark.

TIP   **Quick View**   To display a hidden toolbar quickly, right-click an existing toolbar and select the toolbar you want to display from the shortcut menu.

Moving Toolbars

After you have displayed the toolbars you need, you can position them in your work area where they are most convenient. Figure 3.2 shows an Excel screen with three toolbars in various positions on the screen.

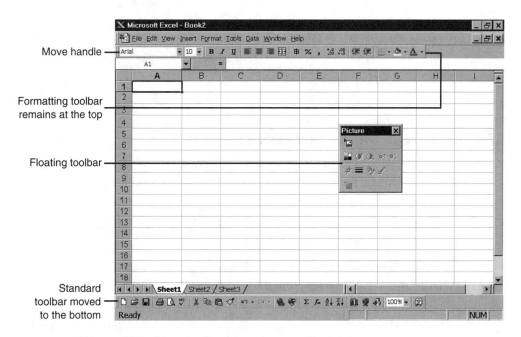

Figure 3.2 Three toolbars in various positions.

Here's what you do to move a toolbar:

1. Click a toolbar's move handle. (If the toolbar is floating in the middle of the window, click its title bar instead.)

2. Hold down the mouse button and drag the toolbar to where you want it. You can drag it to a side of the window (to a "dock") or let it "float" anywhere in the window.

Although you can drag a toolbar anywhere, if you drag one that contains drop-down lists (such as the Standard or Formatting toolbar) to the left or right side of the window, the drop-down list buttons disappear. If you move the toolbar back to the top or bottom of the window (or let it float) the drop-down lists reappear.

 Floating Toolbar   Acts just like a window; you can drag a floating toolbar title bar to move it or drag a border to size it. If you drag a floating toolbar to the top or bottom of the screen, it turns back into a horizontal toolbar.

 TIP   **Quickly Moving a Toolbar**   To quickly move a floating toolbar to the top of the screen, double-click its title bar. To move a docked toolbar into the middle of the window, double-click its move handle.

Customizing the Toolbars

If Excel's toolbars provide too few (or too many) options for you, you can create your own toolbars or customize existing toolbars. To customize a toolbar, follow these steps:

1. Right-click any toolbar and choose **Customize** from the shortcut menu, or open the **Tools** menu and select **Customize**.

2. If the toolbar you want to customize is not currently visible, click the **Toolbars** tab and select it from the list. The toolbar appears.

3. To change the size of the toolbar icons, to turn on or off ScreenTips, or to change the animation of your menus, click the **Options** tab. On the Options tab, select the options you want to apply. For example, to make the toolbar icons larger, click the **Large Icons** option.

4. To add or remove buttons from a toolbar, click the **Commands** tab.

5. To add a button to a toolbar, select its category. (For example, to add the Clear Contents button to a toolbar, select the Edit category.) You can add menus to a toolbar as well; you'll find them listed at the bottom of the Categories list. Once you select the proper category, click the command you want and drag it onto the toolbar, as shown in Figure 3.3.

Drag a button to a bar to add it

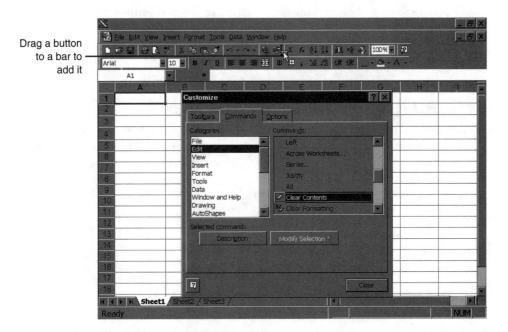

Figure 3.3 To add a button to a toolbar, drag it there.

TIP **Don't Know What an Option Is For?** Simply select the command and then click **Description** to learn what that command does.

6. To remove a button from a toolbar, drag it off the toolbar.

7. To rearrange the buttons on a toolbar, drag them around within the bar.

8. To change a button so that it displays text or an icon with text, right-click the button to display a shortcut menu. Select **Text Only (Always)**, **Text Only (in Menus)**, or **Image and Text**.

TIP **Play to Your Heart's Content** On the shortcut menu, you can find other commands of interest, such as **Change Button Image** (which allows you to select a different icon) and **Edit Button Image** (which allows you to make changes to the current icon).

9. Click the **Close** button when you're done.

If you mess up a toolbar, you can return to its default settings (the way it was before you or someone else changed it). From within the Customize dialog box, click **Toolbars**, highlight the name of the toolbar you want to reset, and then click the **Reset** button.

Creating Your Own Toolbar

Instead of changing any of the standard Excel toolbars, you can create one of your own and fill it with the tools you use most often. Follow these steps to learn how:

1. Open the **Tools** menu and select **Customize.**

2. Click the **Toolbars** tab.

3. Click the **New** button.

4. Type a name for your new toolbar (such as Jen's Favorites) and click **OK.** Excel creates a new floating toolbar.

5. Click the **Commands** tab, select the proper category for a desired button, and then drag it onto the toolbar.

6. Repeat step 5 to add more buttons to your new toolbar. When you finish, click **Close.**

If you want to delete a custom toolbar, open the **Tools** menu and select **Customize**. In the Toolbars list, click the custom toolbar you want to delete. Then click the **Delete** button in the Customize dialog box.

In this lesson, you learned how to use Excel's toolbars and to customize them for your own unique needs. In the next lesson, you'll learn how to enter different types of data.

Entering Different Kinds of Data

In this lesson, you learn how to enter different types of data in an Excel worksheet.

The Data Types

To create a worksheet that does something, you must enter data into the cells that make up the worksheet. There are many types of data that you can enter, including:

- Text
- Numbers
- Dates
- Times
- Formulas
- Functions

In this lesson, you learn how to enter text, numbers, dates, and times. In Lessons 12, 13, and 14, you learn how to enter formulas and functions.

Entering Text

Text is any combination of letters, numbers, and spaces. By default, text is automatically left-aligned in a cell.

To enter text into a cell:

1. Click in the cell in which you want to enter text.

2. Type the text. As you type, your text appears in the cell and in the Formula bar, as shown in Figure 4.1.

3. Press **Enter**. Your text appears in the cell, left-aligned. (You can also press **Tab** or an **arrow key** to enter the text and move to another cell.) And if you make a mistake and you want to abandon your entry, press **Esc** instead.

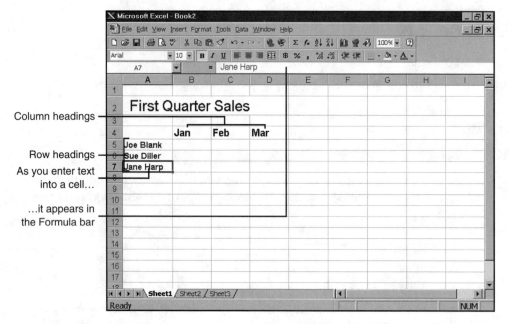

Column headings

Row headings

As you enter text
into a cell...

...it appears in
the Formula bar

Figure 4.1 Data that you enter also appears in the Formula bar as you type it.

CAUTION

But It Doesn't Fit! To widen a column to display all of its data, move to the column headings bar at the top of the worksheet. Then double-click the right border of the column you want to autofit to hold your data. See Lesson 18 for more help.

> **TIP** **Numbers as Text** You might want to enter a number that will be treated as text (such as a ZIP code). To do so, precede the entry with a single quotation mark ('), as in '**46220**. The single quotation mark is an alignment prefix that tells Excel to treat the following characters as text and left-align them in the cell.

Entering Column and Row Headings

Column and row headings identify your data. Column headings appear across the top of the worksheet beneath the title. Row headings are entered on the left side of the worksheet, usually in Column A.

Column headings describe what the numbers in a column represent. Typically, column headings specify time periods such as years, months, days, dates, and so on. Row headings describe what the numbers in each row represent. Typically, row headings specify data categories, such as product names, employee names, or income and expense items in a budget.

When entering column headings, press the **Tab** key to move from one cell to the next instead of pressing **Enter**. When entering row headings, use the **down arrow** key.

> **TIP** **Entering Similar Data as Headings** When you need to enter similar data (such as a series of months or years) as column or row headings, there's a trick for entering them quickly. See the section, "Entering a Series with AutoFill," later in this lesson for help.

Adding Comments to Cells

You can use cell comments to provide detailed information about data in a worksheet. For example, you can create a comment to help remind you of the purpose behind a particular formula or data that should be updated. Once you create a comment, you can display it at any time.

To add a comment to a cell, do the following:

1. Select the cell to which you want to add a comment.

2. Open the **Insert** menu and choose **Comment,** or click the **New Comment** button on the Audit toolbar.

3. Type your comment, as shown in Figure 4.2.

4. Click outside the cell. A red dot appears in the upper-right corner of the cell to show that it contains a comment.

Type your comment here

Click outside the cell to add the comment

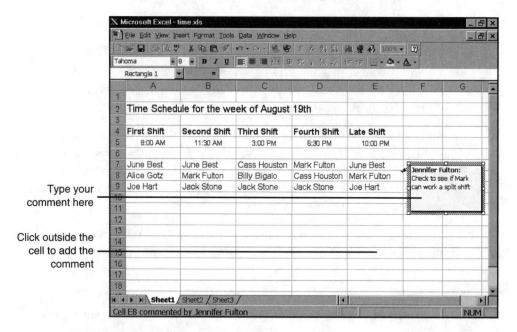

Figure 4.2 Adding a cell comment.

To view comments later, point to any cell that contains a red dot in its upper-right corner. Excel displays the comment.

To edit a comment, select the cell that contains the note and choose **Insert**, **Edit Comment**. Make your changes, and then click outside the cell to save them. To delete a comment, click the cell, select **Edit**, **Clear**, and then select **Comments**.

Entering Numbers

Valid numbers can include the numeric characters 0–9 and any of these special characters: + − / . , ( ) $ % . This means that you can include commas, decimal points, dollar signs, percent signs, and parentheses in the values that you enter.

Although you can include punctuation when you type your entries, you may not want to. For example, instead of typing a column of dollar amounts including dollar signs, commas, and decimal points, you can type numbers such as 700 and 81295, and then format the column with currency formatting. Excel then changes your entries to $700.00 and $81,295.00 or to $700 and $81295, depending on the number of decimal points you specify. See Lesson 15 for more information.

To enter a number:

1. Click the cell into which you want to enter a number.
2. Type the number. To enter a negative number, precede it with a minus sign or surround it with parentheses. To enter a fraction, precede it with a 0, as in 0 1/2.
3. Press **Enter**, and the number appears in the cell, right-aligned.

CAUTION

#######   If you enter a number and it appears in the cell as all pound signs (#######) or in scientific notation (such as 7.78E+06), don't worry—the number is okay. The cell just isn't wide enough to display the entire number. To fix it, move to the column headings at the top of the worksheet and double-click the right border of the column. The column expands to fit the largest entry. See Lesson 18 for more help.

Entering Dates and Times

You can enter dates and times in a variety of formats. When you enter a date using a format shown in Table 4.1, Excel converts the date into a number that reflects the number of days between January 1, 1900, and that date. Even though you won't see this number (Excel displays your entry as a normal date), the number is used whenever you use this date in a calculation. By the way, the feature that automatically formats your data based on the way you enter it is called AutoFormat.

Table 4.1   Valid Formats for Dates and Times

Format	Example
M/D	4/8
M-YY	4-58

continues

Table 4.1 Continued

Format	Example
MM/DD/YY	4/8/58 or 04/08/58
MMM-YY	Jan-92
MMMMMMMM-YY	September-93
MMMMMMMM DD, YYYY	September 3, 1993
DD-MMM-YY	28-Oct-91
DD-MMM	6-Sep
HH:MM	16:50
HH:MM:SS	8:22:59
HH:MM AM/PM	7:45 PM
HH:MM:SS AM/PM	11:45:16 AM
MM/DD/YY HH:MM	11/8/80 4:20
HH:MM MM/DD/YY	4:20 11/18/80

Follow these steps to learn how to enter a date or time:

1. Click the cell into which you want to enter a date or time.
2. Type the date or time in the format in which you want it displayed. You can use hyphens (-) or slashes (/) when typing dates.
3. Press **Enter**. As long as Excel recognizes the entry as a date or time, it appears right-aligned in the cell. If Excel doesn't recognize the entry, it's treated as text and left-aligned.

If you're entering a column of dates, you can specify the date format you want first. Then as you type your dates, Excel will automatically adapt them to fit that format. For example, suppose you like the MMMMMMMM DD, YYYY format. Instead of typing each date in full, you can select that format for the column and then type 9/3/93, and Excel changes it to display September 3, 1993. To format a column, click the column header to select the column. Then open the **Format** menu and select **Cells**. On the **Numbers** tab, select the date format you want. (See Lesson 5 for more help.)

Not Wide Enough?   If you enter a long date and it appears in the cell as all number signs (######), Excel is trying to tell you that the column is not wide enough to display it.

CAUTION

CAUTION

Day or Night? Unless you type AM or PM after your time entry, Excel assumes that you are using a 24-hour military clock. Therefore, 8:20 is assumed to be AM, not PM. So if you mean PM, type the entry as 8:20 PM, or 8:20 p (if you want to use a shortcut). Note that you must type a space between the time and the AM or PM notation.

Copying Entries Quickly

You can copy an existing entry into surrounding cells by performing the following steps:

1. Click the fill handle of the cell whose contents you want to copy.

2. Drag the fill handle down or to the right to copy the data to adjacent cells (see Figure 4.3). A bubble appears to let you know *exactly* what data is being copied to the other cells.

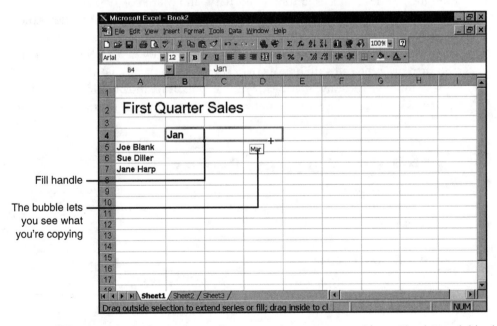

Fill handle

The bubble lets you see what you're copying

Figure 4.3 Drag the fill handle to copy the contents and formatting into neighboring cells.

If you're copying a number, a month, or other item that might be interpreted as a series (such as January, February, and so on), but you *don't* want to create a series—you just want to copy the contents of the cell exactly—press and hold the **Ctrl** key as you drag the fill handle.

 TIP **Copying Across Worksheets** You can copy the contents of cells from one worksheet to one or more worksheets in the workbook. First, select the worksheet(s) you want to copy to by clicking the sheet tabs while holding down the **Ctrl** key. Then select the cells you want to copy (see Lesson 5). Open the **Edit** menu, select **Fill**, and select **Across Worksheets**. Then select **All** (to copy both the cells' contents and their formatting), **Contents**, or **Formats**, and click **OK**.

Entering a Series with AutoFill

Entering a series (such as January, February, and March or 1994, 1995, 1996, and 1997) is similar to copying a cell's contents. As you drag the fill handle of the original cell, AutoFill does all the work for you, interpreting the first entry and creating a series of entries based on it. For example, if you type Monday in a cell, and then drag the cell's fill handle over some adjacent cells, you'll create the series Monday, Tuesday, Wednesday.... As you drag, the bubble lets you know exactly what you're copying so that you can stop at the appropriate cell to create exactly the series you want.

Entering a Custom Series

Although AutoFill is good for a brief series of entries, you may encounter situations in which you need more control. Excel can handle several different types of series, as shown in Table 4.2.

Table 4.2 Data Series

Series	Initial Entries	Resulting Series
Linear	1,2	1, 2, 3, 4
	100,99	100, 99, 98, 97
	1,3	1, 3, 5, 7
Growth	10, 20	10, 20, 40, 80
	10, 50	10, 50, 250, 1250

Series	Initial Entries	Resulting Series
Date	Mon, Wed	Mon, Wed, Fri
	Feb, May	Feb, May, Aug
	Qtr1, Qtr3	Qtr1, Qtr3, Qtr1
	1992, 1995	1992, 1995, 1998

Basically, you make two sample entries for your series in adjacent cells, and Excel uses them to calculate the rest of the series. Here's what you do:

1. Enter the first value in one cell and press **Enter**.

2. Move to the second cell and enter the next value in the series.

3. Select both cells by dragging over them. (See Lesson 6 for more information.) Excel highlights the cells.

4. Drag the fill handle over as many adjacent cells as necessary. Excel computes your series and fills the selected cells with the appropriate values, as shown in Figure 4.4.

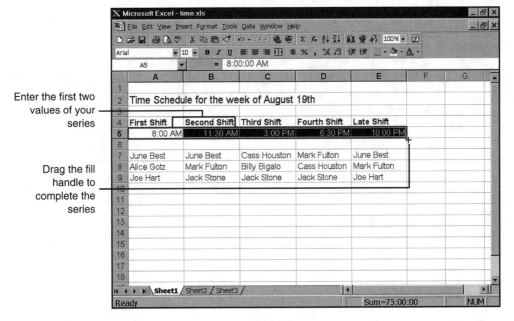

Figure 4.4 Drag to create your series.

Entering the Same Data Over and Over with AutoComplete

When you type the first few letters of an entry, AutoComplete intelligently completes the entry for you based on the entries you've already made in that particular column. AutoComplete works with data entered in columns only, not rows. For example, suppose you want to enter the countries of origin for a series of packages. You type the name of a country once, and the next time you start to type that entry, AutoComplete inserts it for you.

By default, AutoComplete is always turned on, so you don't have to worry about that. However, if it drives you crazy, you can turn it off with the **Tools**, **Options** command. Click the **Edit** tab and change the settings for the AutoComplete options you find there.

Follow these steps to try out AutoFormat:

1. Type **England** into a cell, and press the **down arrow** key to move to the next cell down. Type **Spain** and press the down arrow key again. Then type **Italy** and press the down arrow key.

2. Type **e** again, and England appears in the cell. Press **Enter** to accept the entry. (Likewise, the next time you type **i** or **s**, Italy or Spain will appear.)

3. To see a list of AutoComplete entries, right-click a cell and select **Pick From List** from the shortcut menu. Excel shows you a PickList of entries (in alphabetical order) that it has automatically created from the words you've typed in the column.

4. Click a word in the PickList to insert it in the selected cell.

In this lesson, you learned how to enter different types of data and how to automate data entry. In the next lesson, you will learn how to edit entries.

Editing Entries

5

In this lesson, you learn how to change data and how to undo those changes if necessary. You'll also learn how to copy, move, and delete data.

Editing Data

After you enter data into a cell, you can edit it in either the Formula bar or in the cell itself.

To edit an entry in Excel:

1. Click the cell in which you want to edit data.
2. To begin editing, click the **Formula** bar, press **F2**, or double-click the cell. This puts you in Edit mode; the word Edit appears in the status bar.
3. Press ← or → to move the insertion point within the entry. Press the **Backspace** key to delete characters to the left of the insertion point; press the **Delete** key to delete characters to the right. Then type any characters you want to add.

4. Click the **Enter** button on the Formula bar or press **Enter** on the keyboard to accept your changes.

Or, if you change your mind and you no longer want to edit your entry, click the **Cancel** button or press **Esc**.

Checking Your Spelling

Excel offers a spelling checker feature that rapidly finds and highlights misspellings in a worksheet.

To run the spelling checker, follow these steps:

1. Click the **Spelling** button on the Standard toolbar. Excel finds the first misspelled word and displays it at the top of the Spelling dialog box. A suggested correction then appears in the Change To box (see Figure 5.1).

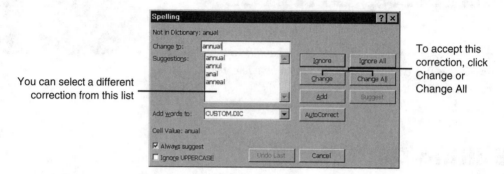

Figure 5.1 Correct spelling mistakes with the options in the Spelling dialog box.

2. To accept the suggestion and change the misspelled word, click **Change**. Or, click **Change All** to change all occurrences of the misspelled word.

3. If the suggestion in the Change To box is not correct, you can do any of the following:

   • Select a different suggestion from the Suggestions box, and then click **Change** or **Change All**. (You can display additional words in the Suggestions list by clicking **Suggest**.)

   • Type your own correction in the Change To box, and then click **Change** or **Change All**.

   • Click **Ignore** to leave the word unchanged.

   • Click **Ignore All** to leave all occurrences of the word unchanged.

   • Click **Add** to add the "mistake" to the dictionary so Excel won't ever flag it as misspelled again.

4. When the spelling checker can't find any more misspelled words, it displays a prompt telling you that the spelling check is complete. Click **OK** to confirm that the spelling checking is finished.

Choose the Wrong Option? If you mistakenly select the wrong option, you can click the **Undo Last** button in the Spelling dialog box to undo the last selection you made.

CAUTION

Using AutoCorrect to Correct Spelling Mistakes

Excel's AutoCorrect feature automatically corrects common typing mistakes as you type. If you type a mistake (such as **teh** instead of **the**) and press **Enter**, Excel enters the corrected text in the cell.

AutoCorrect also corrects two initial capitals. For example, if you type **MAine** and press **Enter**, Excel will enter **Maine** in the cell. In addition, AutoCorrect capitalizes the first letter of a sentence and the names of days.

You can teach AutoCorrect the errors you normally make, and have it correct them for you as you type. For example, if you always type **breif** instead of **brief**, you can add it to the AutoCorrect list. You can also use AutoCorrect to replace an abbreviation, such as **ndiv**, with the words it represents: **Northern Division**. Here's how:

1. Open the **Tools** menu and select **AutoCorrect**. The AutoCorrect dialog box appears.
2. Type your error in the **Replace** text box.
3. Type the correction in the **With** text box.
4. Click **Add** to add the entry to the AutoCorrect list.
5. If you want to delete an entry from the AutoCorrect list, select it from the list and click the **Delete** button.

Too Quick! If you want to turn AutoCorrect off because it's "correcting" your entries before you get a chance to stop it, turn off the **Replace Text As You Type** option in the AutoCorrect dialog box.

CAUTION

Undoing an Action

 You can undo almost anything you do while working in Excel, including any change you enter into a cell. To undo a change, click the **Undo** button on the Standard toolbar.

 To undo an Undo (reinstate a change), click the **Redo** button in the Standard toolbar.

 TIP **Undoing/Redoing More than One Thing** Normally, when you click the Undo or Redo button, Excel undoes or redoes only the most recent action. To undo (or redo) an action prior to the most recent, click the drop-down arrow on the button and select the action you want from the list. Also new in Excel 97, you can click the **Undo** button multiple times to undo multiple previous actions.

Selecting Cells

In order to copy, move, or delete the data in several cells at one time, you must select those cells first. Then you can perform the appropriate action:

- To select a single cell, click it.
- To select adjacent cells (a *range*), click the upper-left cell in the group and drag down to the lower-right cell to select additional cells. (If you want more help in selecting ranges of various sizes, see Lesson 9.)
- To select nonadjacent cells, press and hold the **Ctrl** key as you click individual cells.
- To select an entire row or column of cells, click the row or column header. To select adjacent rows or columns, drag over their headers. To select nonadjacent rows or columns, press **Ctrl** and click each header you want to select.

 Range A selection of adjacent cells.

Copying Data

When you copy or move data, Excel places a copy of that data in a temporary storage area called the *Clipboard*. You can copy data to other sections of your worksheet or to other worksheets or workbooks. When you copy, the original data remains in its place and a copy of it is placed where you indicate.

What Is the Clipboard? An area of memory that is accessible to all Windows programs. Use the Clipboard to copy or move data from place to place within a program or between programs. The techniques that you learn here are the same ones used in all Windows programs.

Follow these steps to copy data:

1. Select the cell(s) that you want to copy.

2. Click the **Copy** button on the Standard toolbar. Excel copies the contents of the selected cell(s) to the Clipboard.

3. Select the first cell in the area where you want the copy to appear. (To copy the data to another worksheet or workbook, change to that worksheet or workbook first.)

4. Click the **Paste** button. Excel inserts the contents of the Clipboard in the location of the insertion point.

Watch Out! When copying or moving data, be careful not to paste the data over existing data (unless, of course, you intend to).

CAUTION

You can copy the same data to several places by repeating the Paste command. Data copied to the Clipboard remains there until you copy or cut (move) something else.

Using Drag-and-Drop

The fastest way to copy something is to drag and drop it. Select the cells you want to copy, hold down the **Ctrl** key, and drag the border of the range you selected (see Figure 5.2). When you release the mouse button, the contents appear at the new location. (If you forget to hold down the Ctrl key, Excel moves the data instead of copying it.) To insert the data *between* existing cells, press **Ctrl+Shift** as you drag.

To drag a copy to a different sheet, press **Ctrl+Alt** as you drag the selection to the sheet's tab. Excel switches you to that sheet, where you can drop your selection in the appropriate location.

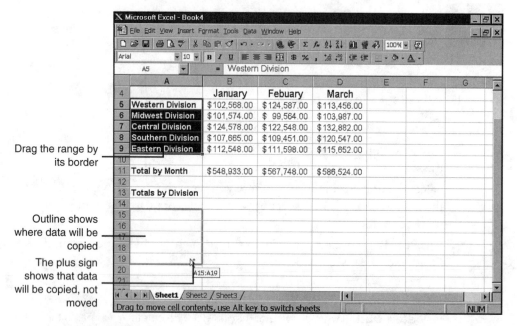

Drag the range by its border

Outline shows where data will be copied

The plus sign shows that data will be copied, not moved

Figure 5.2 To copy data, hold down the Ctrl key while dragging the cell selector border.

Moving Data

Moving data is similar to copying except that Excel removes the data from its original place and places it in the new location.

To move data, follow these steps:

1. Select the cells you want to move.

 2. Click the **Cut** button.

3. Select the first cell in the area where you want to place the data. To move the data to another worksheet, change to that worksheet.

4. Click **Paste**.

To move data quickly, use the drag-and-drop feature. Select the data you want to move, and then drag the border of the selected cells to its new location. To insert the data between existing cells, press **Shift** while you drag. To move the data to a different worksheet, press the **Alt** key and drag the selection to the worksheet's tab. You're switched to that sheet, where you can drop your selection at the appropriate point.

TIP **Shortcut Menu** When cutting, copying, and pasting data, don't forget the shortcut menu. Simply select the cells you want to cut or copy, *right-click*, and choose the appropriate command from the shortcut menu that appears.

Deleting Data

To delete the data in a cell or cells, you can just select them and press **Delete**. However, Excel offers additional options for deleting cells:

- With the Edit, Clear command, you can delete just the formatting of a cell (or an attached comment), instead of deleting its contents. The formatting of a cell includes the cell's color, border style, numeric format, font size, and so on. You'll learn more about this option in a moment.

- With the Edit, Delete command, you can remove cells and everything in them. This option is covered in Lesson 13.

To use the Clear command to remove the formatting of a cell or a note, follow these steps:

1. Select the cells you want to clear.

2. Open the **Edit** menu and select **Clear**. The Clear submenu appears.

3. Select the desired clear option: **All** (which clears the cells of its contents, formatting, and notes), **Formats**, **Contents**, or **Notes**.

Finding and Replacing Data

With Excel's Find and Replace features, you can locate certain data and replace it with new data. When you have a label, a value, or formula that is entered incorrectly throughout the worksheet, you can use the **Edit**, **Replace** command to search and replace all occurrences of the incorrect information with the correct data.

To find and replace data, follow these steps:

1. Open the **Edit** menu and select **Replace**. The Replace dialog box appears, as shown in Figure 5.3.

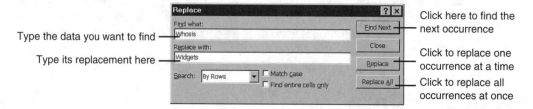

Figure 5.3 Finding and replacing data with the Replace dialog box.

2. Type the text you want to find in the **Find What** text box.

3. Click in the **Replace With** text box and type the text you want to use as replacement text.

4. If you want to match the exact case of your entry, click **Match Case**. If you want to locate cells that contain exactly what you entered (and no additional data), click **Find Entire Cells Only**.

5. Click **Find Next** to find the first occurrence of your specified text. Then click **Replace** to replace only this occurrence or **Replace All** to replace all occurrences of the data you specified.

In this lesson, you learned how to edit cell data and undo changes. In addition, you learned how to copy, move, and delete data. In the next lesson, you learn how to work with workbook files.

Creating and Saving Workbook Files

In this lesson, you will learn how to create new workbooks and save workbook files.

Creating a New Workbook

You can create a new blank workbook, or you can use a template to create a more complete workbook. A *template* is a predesigned workbook that you can modify to suit your needs. Excel contains templates for creating invoices, expense reports, and other common worksheets.

Here's how you create a new workbook:

1. Pull down the **File** menu and select **New**. The New dialog box appears. As you can see in Figure 6.1, this dialog box contains two tabs: General and Spreadsheet Solutions.

2. To create a blank workbook, click the **General** tab and click the **Workbook** icon.

   To create a workbook from a template, click the **Spreadsheet Solutions** tab. You'll see icons for several common worksheet types. Click the icon for the type of worksheet you want to create.

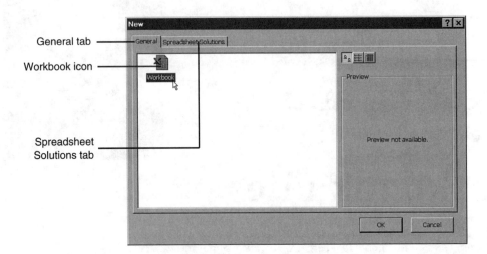

Figure 6.1 Click the icon for the type of worksheet you want to create.

3. Once you've made your selection, click **OK** or press **Enter**. A new work-book opens on-screen with a default name in the title bar. Excel numbers its files sequentially. For example, if you already have Book1 open, the Workbook title bar will read **Book2**.

 TIP **Instant Workbook** If you want to create a blank workbook (instead of creating one from a template), you can bypass the New dialog box by simply clicking the **New** button on the Standard toolbar. Excel opens a new workbook window without displaying the New dialog box.

 TIP **Fast Start** When you start Excel, you're normally given a blank worksheet to begin with. However, you can select a template instead. Just click the **Start** button and select **New Office Document**. Excel displays the New dialog box. Click the **Spreadsheet Solutions** tab, select the type of worksheet you want to create, and then click **OK**.

Saving and Naming a Workbook

Whatever you type into a workbook is stored only in your computer's tempo-rary memory. If you exit Excel, that data will be lost. Therefore, it is important to save your workbook files to a disk regularly.

The first time you save a workbook to a disk, you have to name it. Follow these steps to name your workbook:

1. Open the **File** menu and select **Save**, or click the **Save** button on the Standard toolbar. The Save As dialog box appears (see Figure 6.2).

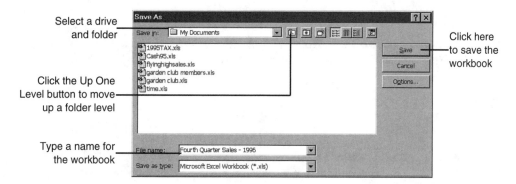

Figure 6.2 The Save As dialog box.

2. Type the name you want to give the workbook in the **File Name** text box. You can use up to 218 characters, including any combination of letters, numbers, and spaces (as in **Fourth Quarter Sales - 1996**).

3. Normally, Excel saves your workbooks in the My Documents folder. To save the file to a different folder, select it from the **Save In** list. You can move up a folder level by clicking the **Up One Level** button on the Save toolbar at the top of the dialog box. You can change to a different drive by selecting a drive in the Save In box. When you save a file to any of the places listed in the Save In box, here's what happens:

- **Desktop** Saves the file as an icon on the Windows desktop. Double-click the icon on your desktop to quickly start Excel and open the workbook file at the same time. If you're working on a project in Excel on a daily basis, you might want to have the file icon on the desktop for your convenience.

- **My Computer** Saves the file to Windows' My Computer folder. Open the My Computer window and double-click the file icon to start Excel and open the workbook file. If you are working in My Computer regularly, it might be convenient to save the file to My Computer. You can also save your file to your hard drive, floppy drive, or CD in My Computer.

- **Network Neighborhood**   Saves the file to Windows' Network Neighborhood. Open Network Neighborhood and double-click the file icon to start Excel and open the workbook file. If you work in Network Neighborhood regularly, it might be convenient to save the file to Network Neighborhood.

 TIP   Excel on the Web   You can save your worksheet in HTML format and add it to your company's intranet (or Internet) Web site. See Lesson 21 for help.

4. Click the **Save** button or press **Enter**.

 TIP   Default Directory   Normally, files are saved to the My Documents directory. You can change the default to your own private directory if you want. Open the **Tools** menu, select **Options**, and click the **General** tab. Click in the **Default File Location** text box and type a complete path for the drive and directory you want to use (the directory must be an existing one). Click **OK**.

 To save a file you have saved previously (and named), all you do is click the **Save** button. (Or you can press **Ctrl+S** or use the **File, Save** command.) Excel automatically saves the workbook and any changes you entered without displaying the Save As dialog box.

Saving a Workbook Under a New Name

Sometimes you might want to change a workbook but keep a copy of the original workbook, or you may want to create a new workbook by modifying an existing one. You can do this by saving the workbook under another name or in another folder. The following steps show how you do that:

1. Open the **File** menu and select **Save As**. You'll see the Save As dialog box, just as if you were saving the workbook for the first time.

2. To save the workbook under a new name, type the new file name over the existing name in the **File Name** text box.

3. To save the file on a different drive or in a different folder, select the drive letter or the folder from the **Save In** list.

4. To save the file in a different format (such as Lotus 1-2-3 or Quattro Pro), click the **Save As Type** drop-down arrow and select the desired format.

5. Click the **Save** button or press **Enter**.

TIP **Backup Files** You can have Excel create a backup copy of each work-book file you save. That way, if anything happens to the original file, you can use the backup copy. To turn the backup feature on, click the **Options** button in the Save As dialog box, select **Always Create Backup**, and click **OK**. To use the backup file, choose **File**, **Open** to display the Open dialog box, and then select **Backup Files** from the **Files of Type** list. Double-click the backup file in the files and folders list to open the file.

In this lesson, you learned how to create new workbooks and save workbooks. In the next lesson, you'll learn how to open and close workbook files.

Opening and Closing Workbook Files

In this lesson, you learn how to open and close workbook files. You also learn how to locate misplaced files.

Opening an Existing Workbook

If you have closed a workbook and then later you want to use it again, you must reopen it. Follow these steps to open an existing workbook:

1. Open the **File** menu and select **Open**, or click the **Open** button on the Standard toolbar. The Open dialog box shown in Figure 7.1 appears.

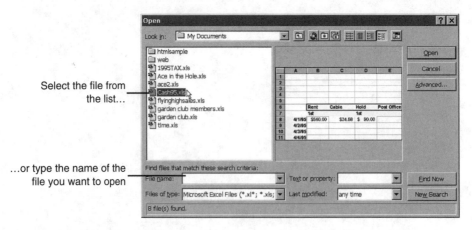

Select the file from the list...

...or type the name of the file you want to open

Figure 7.1 The Open dialog box.

2. If the file is not located in the current folder, open the **Look In** box and select the correct drive and folder.

3. Click the file you want to open in the files and folders list. Or, type the name of the file in the **File Name** box. (As you type, Excel highlights the first file name in the list that matches your entry; this is a quick way to move through the list.)

 TIP **Save Your Favorites** You can save the worksheets you use most often in the Favorites folder by selecting them and clicking the **Add to Favorites** button. Whenever you need to, you can open one of those worksheets by clicking the **Look in Favorites** button at the top of the Open dialog box.

4. To see a preview of the workbook before you open it, click the **Preview** button at the top of the dialog box. Excel displays the contents of the workbook in a window to the right of the dialog box.

5. Click **Open** or press **Enter**.

 TIP **Recently Used Workbooks** If you've recently used the workbook you want to open, you'll find it listed at the bottom of the File menu. Just open the **File** menu and select it from the list.

 TIP **Excel on the Web** You can browse the Web for a worksheet with the **Search the Web** button at the top of the Open dialog box. But if you know the exact address of the worksheet you want to open—whether it's on the Web or on a local intranet—just type its address (such as **http://www.worldnews.com/ facts.xls**) in the **File Name** text box. (You must connect to the Internet before you click **Open**.)

You can also open a specific workbook when you first start Excel. Just click the **Start** button and select **Open Office Document**. Select the workbook you want to open and click **Open**. Excel starts with the workbook you selected open and ready to edit.

Finding a Workbook File

If you forget where you saved a file, Excel can help you. You can use the **Find Now** option in the Open dialog box. Follow these steps to have Excel hunt for a file for you:

179

1. Open the **File** menu and select **Open**, or click the **Open** button in the Standard toolbar. The Open dialog box appears (see Figure 7.2).

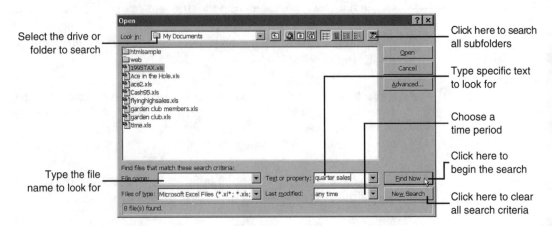

Select the drive or folder to search

Click here to search all subfolders

Type specific text to look for

Choose a time period

Click here to begin the search

Type the file name to look for

Click here to clear all search criteria

Figure 7.2 The Search options in the Open dialog box enable you to specify what you want to search for.

2. Open the **Look In** box and select the drive or folder you want to search. For example, if you select C:, Excel will search the entire C drive. If you select C: and then select the Excel folder, Excel searches only the EXCEL directory on drive C. You can select My Computer to search all the drives on your computer.

3. Narrow your search using any of the following methods:

If you want to search for a particular file, type its name in the **File Name** text box. You can use wild-card characters in place of characters you can't remember. Use an asterisk (*) in place of a group of characters; use a question mark (?) in place of a single character. (For example, if you enter **sales??**, Excel finds all files whose file names begin with the word "sales" followed by two characters, such as SALES01, SALES02, and so on.)

You can search the contents of your workbooks for a particular phrase by typing it in the **Text Or Property** box. For example, type **brook trout** to find a workbook that contains the words brook trout.

To specify a time period for the files you want to search, choose an option from the **Last Modified** box.

 To have Excel search all subfolders of the drive you specify, click the **Commands and Settings** button and choose **Search Subfolders** from the pop-up menu that appears.

TIP **Do Over** You can clear your search selections by clicking the **New Search** button.

4. When you finish entering your search criteria, click the **Find Now** button. Excel finds the files that match the search instructions you entered and displays them in the files and folders list.

5. Look through the list, highlight the file you want, and click the **Open** button.

CAUTION

File Not Found? If the file you want is not listed in the files and folders list, you can specify more detailed search criteria by using the Advanced Find feature. Click the **Advanced** button in the Open dialog box. Enter search criteria such as property, condition, or value, and then click the **Find Now** button to search for the file using these additional criteria.

Moving Among Open Workbooks

Sometimes you may have more than one workbook open at a time. If so, you can switch back and forth as necessary to view or edit their contents. There are several ways to move among open workbooks:

- If part of the desired workbook window is visible, click it.
- Open the **Window** menu and select the name of the workbook to which you want to switch.
- Press **Ctrl+F6** to move from one workbook window to another.

TERM

The Active Window If you have more than one workbook open, only the one where the cell selector is located is considered active. The title bar of the active workbook will be darker than the title bars of other open workbooks.

Closing Workbooks

When you close a workbook, Excel removes its workbook window from the screen. You should close workbooks when you finish working on them to free up your computer's resources so it can respond to your commands more quickly. To close a workbook, follow these steps:

1. If the window you want to close isn't currently active, make it active by selecting the workbook from the list of workbooks at the bottom of the **Window** menu.

2. Click the **Close** (X) button in the upper-right corner of the workbook.

TIP   **Close All**   In Excel 97, if you have more than one workbook open, you can close all workbooks at once by holding down the **Shift** key, opening the **File** menu, and selecting **Close All**.

In this lesson, you learned how to open and close workbooks, as well as how to find misplaced workbook files. The next lesson teaches you how to work with the worksheets in a workbook.

Working with Worksheets

In this lesson, you learn how to add and delete worksheets with workbooks. You also learn how to copy, move, and rename worksheets.

Selecting Worksheets

By default, each workbook consists of three worksheet pages whose names appear on tabs near the bottom of the screen. You can insert new worksheet pages or delete worksheet pages as desired. One advantage to having multiple worksheet pages is to organize your data into logical chunks. Another advantage to having separate worksheets for your data is that you can reorganize the worksheets in a workbook easily.

Before we get into the details of inserting, deleting, and copying worksheets, you should know how to select one or more worksheets. For example, you may want to select two worksheets to copy to another file. Here's what you need to know about selecting worksheets:

- To select a single worksheet, click its tab. The tab becomes highlighted to show that the worksheet is selected.
- To select several neighboring worksheets, click the tab of the first worksheet in the group, and then hold down the **Shift** key and click the tab of the last worksheet in the group.
- To select several non-neighboring worksheets, hold down the **Ctrl** key and click each worksheet's tab.

If you select two or more worksheets, they remain selected until you ungroup them. To ungroup worksheets, do one of the following:

- Right-click one of the selected worksheets and choose **Ungroup Sheets**.
- Hold down the **Shift** key and click the active tab.
- Click any tab outside the group.

Inserting Worksheets

When you create a new workbook, it contains three worksheets. You can easily add additional worksheets to a workbook.

TIP **Start with More** You can change the number of worksheets Excel places in a new workbook by opening the **Tools** menu, selecting **Options**, clicking the **General** tab, and then changing the number under the **Sheets in New Work-book** option. Click **OK** to save your changes.

Follow these steps to add a worksheet to a workbook:

1. Select the worksheet *before* which you want the new worksheet inserted. For example, if you select Sheet2, the new worksheet (which will be called Sheet4 because the workbook already contains 3 worksheets) will be inserted before Sheet2.

2. Open the **Insert** menu.

3. Select **Worksheet**. Excel inserts the new worksheet, as shown in Figure 8.1.

TIP **Shortcut Menu** A faster way to work with worksheets is to right-click the worksheet tab. This brings up a shortcut menu that lets you insert, delete, rename, move, copy, or select all worksheets. When you choose **Insert** from the shortcut menu, Excel displays the Insert dialog box. Click the **Worksheet** icon and click **OK** to insert a new worksheet.

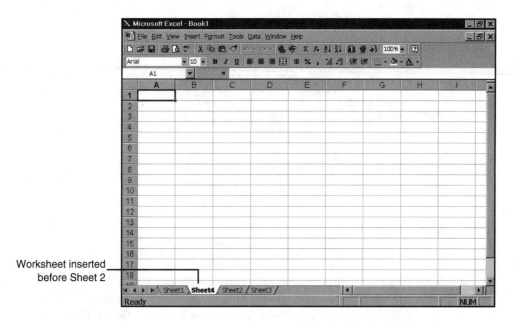

Worksheet inserted before Sheet 2

Figure 8.1 Excel inserts the new worksheet before the worksheet you selected.

Deleting Worksheets

If you plan to use only one worksheet, you can remove the two other worksheets to free up memory. Here's how you remove a worksheet:

1. Select the worksheet(s) you want to delete.

2. Open the **Edit** menu and select **Delete Sheet**. A dialog box appears, asking you to confirm the deletion.

3. Click the **OK** button. The worksheets are deleted.

Moving and Copying Worksheets

You can move or copy worksheets within a workbook or from one workbook to another. Here's how:

1. Select the worksheet(s) you want to move or copy. If you want to move or copy worksheets from one workbook to another, be sure to open the target workbook.

2. Open the **Edit** menu and choose **Move or Copy Sheet**. The Move or Copy dialog box appears, as shown in Figure 8.2.

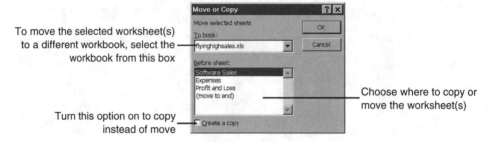

To move the selected worksheet(s) to a different workbook, select the workbook from this box

Choose where to copy or move the worksheet(s)

Turn this option on to copy instead of move

Figure 8.2 The Move or Copy dialog box asks you where you want to copy or move a worksheet.

3. To move the worksheet(s) to a different workbook, select that workbook's name from the **To Book** drop-down list. If you want to move or copy the worksheet(s) to a new workbook, select **(new book)** in the **To Book** drop-down list. Excel creates a new workbook and then copies or moves the worksheet(s) to it.

4. In the **Before Sheet** list box, choose the worksheet *before* which you want the selected worksheet(s) to be moved.

5. To copy the selected worksheet(s) instead of moving them, select **Create a Copy** to put a check mark in the check box.

6. Select **OK**. The selected worksheet(s) are copied or moved as specified.

Moving a Worksheet Within a Workbook by Dragging and Dropping

An easier way to copy or move worksheets within a workbook is to use the drag-and-drop feature. First, select the tab of the worksheet(s) you want to copy or move. Move the mouse pointer over one of the selected tabs, click and hold the mouse button, and drag the tab where you want it moved. To copy the worksheet, hold down the **Ctrl** key while dragging. When you release the mouse button, the worksheet is copied or moved.

Moving a Worksheet Between Workbooks by Dragging and Dropping

You can also use the drag-and-drop feature to quickly copy or move worksheets between workbooks. First, open the workbooks you want to copy or move. Choose **Window**, **Arrange** and select the **Tiled** option. Click **OK** to arrange the windows so that a small portion of each one appears on-screen. Select the tab of the worksheet(s) you want to copy or move. Move the mouse pointer over one of the selected tabs, click and hold the mouse button, and drag the tab where you want it moved. To copy the worksheet, hold down the **Ctrl** key while dragging. When you release the mouse button, the worksheet is copied or moved.

Changing Worksheet Tab Names

By default, all worksheets are named "Sheet$X$," where X is a number starting with the number 1. So that you'll have a better idea of the information each sheet contains, you can change the names that appear on the tabs. Here's how you do it:

1. Double-click the tab of the worksheet you want to rename. The current name is highlighted. (You can also right-click and select **Rename**.)

2. Type a new name for the worksheet and press **Enter**. Excel replaces the default name with the name you typed.

In this lesson, you learned how to insert, delete, move, copy, and rename worksheets. In the next lesson, you'll learn how to print worksheets and workbooks.

Printing Your Workbook

In this lesson, you will learn how to print a workbook or a portion of one, and how to enhance your printout with headers and footers.

Changing the Page Setup

As mentioned in previous lessons, a workbook is a collection of many worksheets, which are like pages in a notebook. You can print the whole workbook at once, or just one or more pages at a time.

Before you print a worksheet, you should make sure that the page is set up correctly for printing. To do this, open the **File** menu and choose **Page Setup**. You'll see the Page Setup dialog box shown in Figure 9.1.

 TIP **Right-Click the Workbook Title Bar** For quick access to commands that affect a workbook, right-click the workbook's title bar. If the workbook is maximized to a full screen (and the title bar is therefore not visible), right-click the Control-menu box to access the shortcut menu. For example, to check the page setup, right-click the title bar or the **Control-menu** box and choose **Page Setup**.

The Margins tab   The Header/Footer tab

The Page tab—

—The Sheet tab

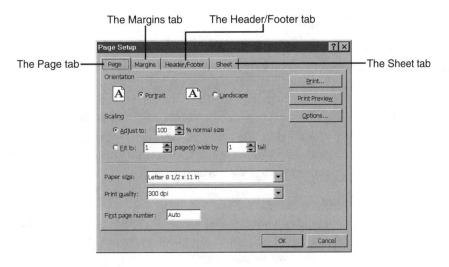

Figure 9.1 The Page Setup dialog box.

The following list outlines the page setup settings, grouped according to the tab on which they appear:

- **Page tab**

    Orientation   Select **Portrait** to print across the short edge of a page; select **Landscape** to print across the long edge of a page. (Landscape makes the page wider than it is tall.)

    Scaling   You can reduce and enlarge your workbook or force it to fit within a specific page size.

    Paper Size   This is 8 1/2 by 11 inches by default, but you can choose a different size from the list.

    Print Quality   You can print your spreadsheet in draft quality to print quickly and save wear and tear on your printer, or you can print in high quality for a final copy. Print quality is measured in *dpi* (dots per inch); the higher the number, the better the print.

    First Page Number   You can set the starting page number to something other than 1. The Auto option (default) tells Excel to set the starting page number to 1 if it is the first page in the print job, or to set the first page number at the next sequential number if it is not the first page in the print job.

- **Margins tab**

  Top, Bottom, Left, Right You can adjust the size of the top, bottom, left, and right margins.

  Header, Footer You can specify how far you want a Header or Footer printed from the edge of the page. (You use the Header/Footer tab to add a header or footer to your workbook.)

  Center on Page You can center your workbook data between the left and right margins (**Horizontally**) and between the top and bottom margins (**Vertically**).

- **Header/Footer tab**

  Header, Footer You can add a header (such as a title) that repeats at the top of each page, or a footer (such as page numbers) that repeats at the bottom of each page.

  Custom Header, Custom Footer You can use the Custom Header or Custom Footer button to create headers and footers that insert the time, date, worksheet tab name, and workbook file name.

- **Sheet tab**

  Print Area You can print a portion of a workbook or worksheet by entering the range of cells you want to print. You can type the range, or click the **Collapse Dialog Box** icon at the right of the text box to move the Page Setup dialog box out of the way and drag the mouse pointer over the desired cells. If you do not select a print area, Excel will print either the sheet or the workbook, depending on the options set in the Page tab.

TIP **Don't Print That!** Ordinarily, if there's a portion of your worksheet that you don't want to print, you can avoid it by selecting the area you want to print and printing only that selection. However, if the data you want to hide is located *within* the area you want to print, what do you do? In that case, you can hide the columns, rows, or cells to prevent them from being printed. (See Lesson 2 for help.)

Print Titles If you have a row or column of entries that you want repeated as titles on every page, type the range for this row or column, or drag over the cells with the mouse pointer (see Lesson 10).

Print You can tell Excel exactly how to print some aspects of the workbook. For example, you can have the gridlines (the lines that define the cells) printed. You can also have a color spreadsheet printed in black-and-white.

Page Order You can indicate how data in the worksheet should be read and printed: in sections from top to bottom or in sections from left to right. This is the way Excel handles printing the areas outside of the printable area. For example, if some columns to the right don't fit on the first page and some rows don't fit at the bottom of the first page, you can specify which area will print next.

When you finish entering your settings, click the **OK** button.

Previewing a Print Job

 After you've determined your page setup and print area, you should preview what the printed page will look like before you print. To preview a print job, open the **File** menu and select **Print Preview** or click the **Print Preview** button in the Standard toolbar. Your workbook appears as it will when printed, as shown in Figure 9.2.

 TIP **Page Setup Print Preview** You can also preview a print job when you are setting up a page or while you are in the Print dialog box. When the Page Setup dialog box is displayed, click the **Print Preview** button. In the Print dialog box, click the **Preview** button.

 TIP **A Close-Up View** Zoom in on any area of the preview by clicking it with the mouse pointer (which looks like a magnifying glass). You can also use the **Zoom** button at the top of the Print Preview screen.

191

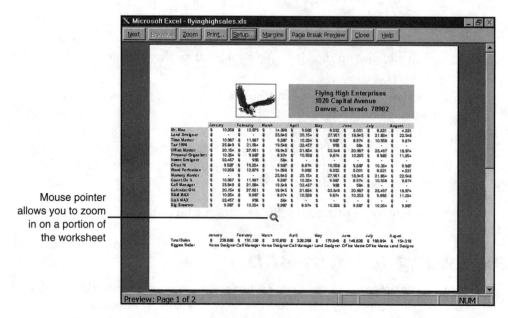

Mouse pointer
allows you to zoom
in on a portion of
the worksheet

Figure 9.2   You can preview your workbook before printing it.

Printing Your Workbook

After setting the page setup and previewing your data, it is time to print. You can print selected data, selected sheets, or the entire workbook.

To print your workbook, follow these steps:

1. If you want to print a portion of the worksheet, select the range you want to print (see Lesson 10 for help). If you want to print one or more sheets within the workbook, select the sheet tabs (see Lesson 8). To print the entire workbook, skip this step.

2. Open the **File** menu and select **Print** (or press **Ctrl+P**). The Print dialog box appears, as shown in Figure 9.3.

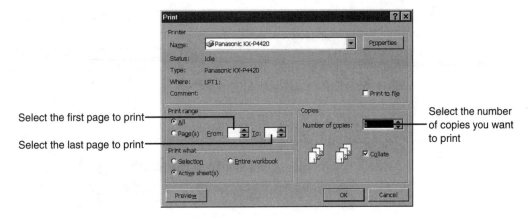

Select the first page to print ——
Select the last page to print ——

Select the number of copies you want to print

Figure 9.3 The Print dialog box.

CAUTION

Too Quick to Print   If you click the Print button instead of using the File, Print command, Excel prints your current worksheet without letting you make any selections.

3. Select the options you would like to use:

> **Print range** lets you print one or more pages. For example, if the selected print area will take up 15 pages and you want to print only pages 5–10, select **Page(s)**, and then type the numbers of the first and last page you want to print in the **From** and **To** boxes.

> **Print What** allows you to print the currently selected cells, the selected worksheets, or the entire workbook.

> **Copies** allows you to print more than one copy of the selection, worksheet, or workbook.

> **Collate** allows you to print a complete copy of the selection, worksheet, or workbook before the first page of the next copy is printed. This option is available when you print multiple copies.

4. Click **OK** or press **Enter**.

While your job is printing, you can continue working in Excel. If the printer is working on another job that you (or someone else, in the case of a network printer) sent, Windows holds the job until the printer is ready for it.

Sometimes, you might want to delete a job while it is printing or before it prints. For example, suppose you think of other numbers to add to the worksheet or realize you forgot to format some text; you'll want to fix these things before you print the file. In such a case, deleting the print job is easy. To display the print queue and delete a print job, follow these steps:

1. Double-click the **Printer** icon on the Windows taskbar, as shown in Figure 9.4. The print queue appears.

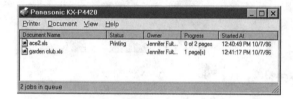

Figure 9.4   To stop a document from printing, use the print queue.

2. Click the job you want to delete.

3. Open the **Document** menu and select **Cancel Printing**.

 TIP   **Clear the Queue!**   To delete all the files from the print queue, open the **Printer** menu and select **Purge Print Jobs**. This cancels the print jobs, but doesn't delete the files from your computer.

 TIP   **E-Mail Your Worksheet**   With Excel 97, you get a newly expanded ability to send your worksheet directly to the people who need it, instead of printing it. Open the **File** menu, select **Send To**, and then select the appropriate option: **Mail Recipient** (to send an e-mail), **Routing Recipient** (to send an e-mail to several people), or **Exchange Folder** (to send an e-mail through Microsoft Exchange).

Selecting a Print Area

You can tell Excel what part of the worksheet you want to print using the Print Area option. This option lets you single out an area as a separate page and then print that page. If the area is too large to fit on one page, Excel breaks it into multiple pages. If you do not select a print area, Excel prints either the entire worksheet or the entire workbook, depending on the options set in the Page tab of the Page Setup dialog box.

CAUTION

To Include or Not to Include? When deciding which cells to select for your print area, make sure you do *not* include the title, the subtitle, and the column and row headings in the print area. If you do, Excel may print the labels twice. Instead, print your titles and headings on each page of your printout by following the steps in the upcoming section, "Printing Column and Row Headings."

To select a print area and print your worksheet at the same time, follow these steps:

1. Open the **File** menu and choose **Page Setup**. The Page Setup dialog box appears.

2. Click the **Sheet** tab to display the Sheet options.

3. Click the **Collapse Dialog** icon to the right of the Print Area text box. Excel reduces the Page Setup dialog box in size.

4. Drag over the cells you want to print (see Lesson 9). As you can see in Figure 9.5, a dashed line border surrounds the selected area, and the absolute cell references for those cells appear with dollar signs ($) in the Print Area text box. (If you want to type the range, you don't have to include the $ in the cell references. See Lesson 13 for more information about absolute cell references.)

5. Click the **Collapse Dialog** icon to return to the Page Setup dialog box.

6. Click **Print** in the Page Setup dialog box to display the Print dialog box. Then click **OK** to print your worksheet.

TIP **Set Your Area** To set the print area without printing, select the cells you want to print later, open the **File** menu, select **Print Area**, and select **Set Print Area**.

TIP **Remove the Print Area** To remove the print area, open the **File** menu, select **Print Area**, and select **Clear Print Area**.

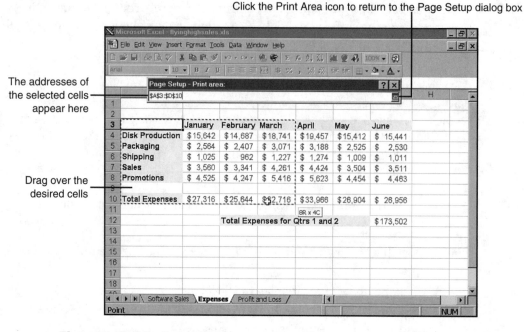

Figure 9.5 Selecting a print area.

Adjusting Page Breaks

When you print a workbook, Excel determines the page breaks based on the paper size and margins and the selected print area. To make the pages look better and break things in logical places, you may want to override the automatic page breaks with your own breaks. However, before you add page breaks, try these options:

- Adjust the widths of individual columns to make the best use of space (see Lesson 18).
- Consider printing the workbook sideways (using Landscape orientation).
- Change the left, right, top, and bottom margins to smaller values.

If after trying these options you still want to insert page breaks, Excel 97 offers you an option of previewing exactly where the page breaks appear and then adjusting them. Follow these steps:

1. Open the **View** menu and select **Page Break Preview**.

2. If a message appears, click **OK**. Your worksheet is displayed with page breaks, as shown in Figure 9.6.

Drag a page
break to move it

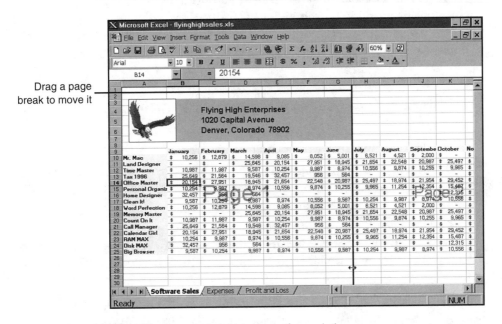

Figure 9.6 Check your page breaks before printing.

3. To move a page break, drag the dashed line to the desired location.

   To delete a page break, drag it off the screen.

   To insert a page break, move to the first cell in the column to the *right* of where you want the page break inserted, or move to the row *below* where you want the break inserted. For example, to insert a page break between columns G and H, move to cell H1. To insert a page break between rows 24 and 25, move to cell A25. Then open the **Insert** menu and select **Page Break**. A dashed line appears to the left of the selected column or above the selected row.

4. To exit Page Break Preview and return to your normal worksheet view, open the **View** menu and select **Normal**.

Printing Column and Row Headings

Excel provides a way for you to select labels and titles that are located on the top edge and left side of a large worksheet, and print them on every page of the printout. This option is useful when a worksheet is too wide to print on a single page. If you don't use this option, the extra columns or rows will be printed on subsequent pages without any descriptive labels.

Follow these steps to print column or row headings on every page:

1. Open the **File** menu and choose **Page Setup**. The Page Setup dialog box appears.

2. Click the **Sheet** tab to display the Sheet options.

3. To repeat column labels and a worksheet title, click the **Collapse Dialog** icon to the right of the Rows to Repeat at Top text box. Excel reduces the Page Setup dialog box in size.

4. Drag over the rows you want to print on every page, as shown in Figure 9.7. A dashed line border surrounds the selected area, and absolute cell references with dollar signs ($) appear in the Rows to Repeat at Top text box.

5. Click the **Collapse Dialog** icon to return to the Page Setup dialog box.

6. To repeat row labels that appear on the left of the worksheet, click the **Collapse Dialog** icon to the right of the Columns to Repeat at Left text box. Again, Excel reduces the Page Setup dialog box.

7. Select the row labels you want to repeat.

8. Click the **Collapse Dialog** icon to return once again to the Page Setup dialog box.

9. To print your worksheet, click **Print** to display the Print dialog box. Then click **OK**.

CAUTION

Select Your Print Area Carefully   If you select rows or columns to repeat, and those rows or columns are part of your print area, the selected rows or columns will print twice. To fix this, select your print area again, leaving out the rows or columns you're repeating. See "Selecting a Print Area" earlier in this lesson for help.

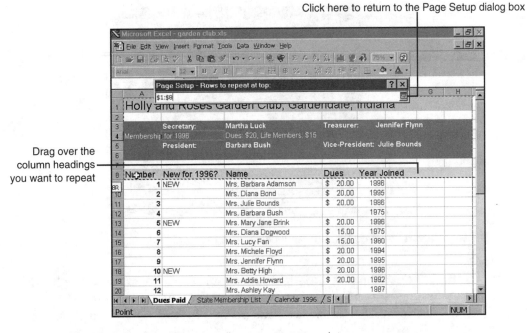

Click here to return to the Page Setup dialog box

Drag over the column headings you want to repeat

Figure 9.7 Specifying headings you want to print on every page.

Adding Headers and Footers

Excel lets you add headers and footers to print information at the top and bottom of every page of the printout. The information can include any text, as well as page numbers, the current date and time, the workbook file name, and the worksheet tab name.

You can choose the headers and footers suggested by Excel, or you can include any text plus special commands to control the appearance of the header or footer. For example, you can apply bold, italic, or underline to the header or footer text. You can also left-align, center, or right-align your text in a header or footer (see Lesson 18).

To add headers and footers, follow these steps:

1. Open the **View** menu and choose **Header and Footer**. The Page Setup dialog box appears (see Figure 9.8). Click the **Header and Footer** tab in the Page Setup dialog box.

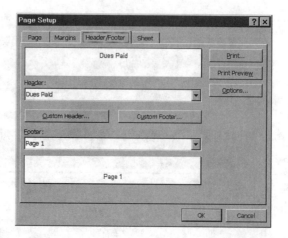

Figure 9.8   Adding headers and footers with Header/Footer options.

2. To select a header, click the **Header** drop-down arrow. Excel displays a list of suggested header information. Scroll through the list and click a header you want. The sample header appears at the top of the Header/Footer tab.

TIP   **Don't See What You Like?**   If none of the suggested headers or footers suits you, click the **Custom Header** or **Custom Footer** button and enter your exact specifications.

3. To select a footer, click the **Footer** drop-down arrow. Excel displays a list of suggested footer information. Scroll through the list and click a footer you want. The sample footer appears at the bottom of the Header/Footer tab.

4. Click **OK** to close the Page Setup dialog box and return to your worksheet. Or, click the **Print** button to display the Print dialog box, and click **OK** to print your worksheet.

Don't Want Any Headers or Footers?   To remove the header or footer, choose **None** in the Header or Footer suggestion lists.

CAUTION

Scaling a Worksheet to Fit on a Page

If your worksheet is too large to print on one page even after you change the orientation and margins, you might consider using the Fit To option. This option shrinks the worksheet to make it fit on the specified number of pages. You can specify the document's width and height.

Follow these steps to scale a worksheet to fit on a page:

1. Open the **File** menu and choose **Page Setup**. The Page Setup dialog box appears.
2. Click the **Page** tab to display the Page options.
3. In the **Fit to XX Page(s) Wide By** and the **Tall** text boxes, enter the number of pages in which you want Excel to fit your data.
4. Click **OK** to close the Page Setup dialog box and return to your worksheet. Or, click the **Print** button in the Page Setup dialog box to display the Print dialog box, and then click **OK** to print your worksheet.

In this lesson, you learned how to print a worksheet. In the next lesson, you will learn how to work with ranges.

Working with Ranges

In this lesson, you will learn how to select and name cell ranges.

What Is a Range?

A *range* is a rectangular group of connected cells. The cells in a range may all be in one column, or one row, or any combination of columns and rows, as long as the range forms a rectangle, as shown in Figure 10.1.

Learning how to use ranges can save you time. For example, you can select a range and use it to format a group of cells with one step. You can use a range to print only a selected group of cells. You can also use ranges in formulas.

Ranges are referred to by their anchor points (the upper-left corner and the lower-right corner). For example, the ranges shown in Figure 10.1 are B4:G8, A10:G10, and G12.

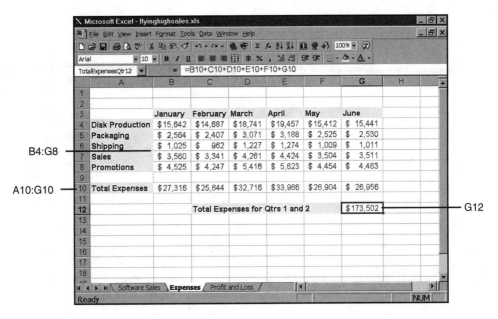

Figure 10.1 A range is any combination of cells that forms a rectangle.

Selecting a Range

To select a range by using the mouse, follow these steps:

1. To select the same range of cells on more than one worksheet, select the worksheets (see Lesson 8).

2. Move the mouse pointer to the upper-left corner of a range.

3. Click and hold the left mouse button.

4. Drag the mouse to the lower-right corner of the range and release the mouse button. The selected range is highlighted.

There are some techniques that you can use to quickly select a row, a column, an entire worksheet, or several ranges, as shown in Table 10.1.

203

Table 10.1 Selection Techniques

To Select This	Do This
Several ranges	Select the first range, hold down the **Ctrl** key, and select the next range. Do this for each range you want to select.
Row	Click the row heading number at the left edge of the worksheet. You also can press **Shift+Spacebar**.
Column	Click the column heading letter at the top edge of the worksheet. You also can press **Ctrl+Spacebar**.
Entire worksheet	Click the **Select All** button (the blank rectangle in the upper-left corner of the worksheet, above row 1 and left of column A). You also can press **Ctrl+A**.
Range that is out of view	Press **Ctrl+G** (Goto) and type the address of the range you want to select in the **Reference** text box. For example, to select the range R100 to T250, type **R100:T250** and press **Enter**.

Deselecting a Selection   To remove the range selection, click any cell in the worksheet.

CAUTION

Naming Cells and Cell Ranges

Up to this point, you have used cell addresses to refer to cells. Although that works, it is often more convenient to name cells with more recognizable names. For example, say you want to determine your net income by subtracting expenses from income (see Lesson 12). You can name the cell that contains your total income **INCOME**, and name the cell that contains your total expenses **EXPENSES**. You can then determine your net income by using the formula:

= INCOME – EXPENSES

Giving the cells memorable names will make the formula more logical and easier to manage. Naming cells and ranges also makes it easier to cut, copy, and move blocks of cells, as explained in Lesson 5.

Follow these steps to name a cell range:

1. Select the range of cells you want to name. Make sure all the cells are on the same worksheet. (You cannot name cells and cell ranges that are located on more than one sheet.)

2. Click in the **Name** box on the left side of the Formula bar (see Figure 10.2).

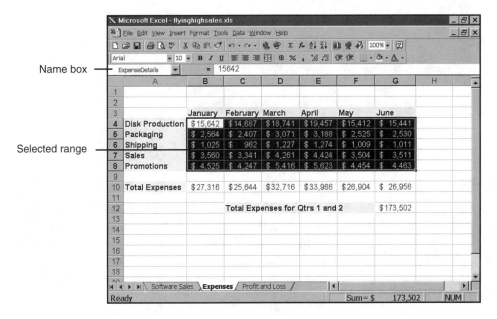

Figure 10.2   Type a name in the Name box.

3. Type a range name using up to 255 characters. Valid names can include letters, numbers, periods, and underlines, but *no* spaces. In addition, a number cannot be used as the first character in the range name.

4. Press **Enter**.

5. To see the list of range names, click the **Name** box's drop-down arrow (on the Formula bar).

Another way to name a range is to select it, open the **Insert** menu, select **Name**, and choose **Define**. This displays the Define Name dialog box shown in Figure 10.3. Type a name in the **Names in Workbook** text box and click **OK**.

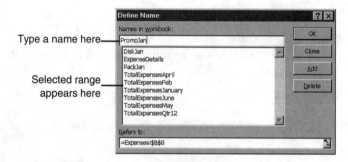

Type a name here

Selected range
appears here

Figure 10.3   The Define Name dialog box.

The Define Name dialog box enables you to see what range a range name contains. Click a range name in the Names in Workbook list, and you'll see the cell address(es) assigned to the range name in the Refers To text box. You can edit the range or type a new one.

The dollar signs in the cell addresses indicate absolute cell references, which always refer to the same cell. An absolute cell reference will not be adjusted if changes are made to those cells in the worksheet (see Lesson 13). You don't have to type the dollar signs in the cell address. When you select cells with the mouse, Excel inserts the dollar signs automatically.

This dialog box also lets you delete names. To delete a range name, click a name in the **Names in Workbook** list and click the **Delete** button.

In this lesson, you learned how to select and name ranges. In the next lesson, you will learn how to insert and delete cells, rows, and columns.

Inserting and Removing Cells, Rows, and Columns

11

In this lesson, you learn how to rearrange your worksheet by adding and removing cells, rows, and columns.

Inserting Cells

Sometimes, you will need to insert information into a worksheet, right in the middle of existing data. With the Insert command, you can insert one or more cells, or entire rows or columns.

CAUTION

Shifting Cells Inserting cells in the middle of existing data will cause the data in existing cells to shift down a row or over a column. If your worksheet contains formulas that rely on the contents of the shifting cells, this could throw off the calculations (see Lessons 12 and 13). However, formulas adjust automatically when you insert entire rows or entire columns.

To insert a single cell or a group of cells, follow these steps:

1. Select the cell(s) where you want the new cell(s) inserted. Excel will insert the same number of cells as you select.

2. Open the **Insert** menu and choose **Cells**. The Insert dialog box shown in Figure 11.1 appears.

3. Select **Shift Cells Right** or **Shift Cells Down**.

4. Click **OK**. Excel inserts the cell(s) and shifts the data in the other cells in the specified direction.

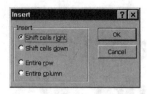

Figure 11.1   The Insert dialog box.

 TIP   **Drag Insert**   A quick way to insert cells is to hold down the **Shift** key and then drag the fill handle (the little box in the lower-right corner of the selected cell or cells—see Figure 11.2). Drag the fill handle up, down, left, or right to set the position of the new cells.

Merging Cells

In Excel 97, you can merge the data in one cell with other cells to form a big cell that is easier to work with. Merging cells is especially handy when creating a decorative title for the top of your worksheet (see Figure 11.2 for an example). Within a single merged cell, you can quickly change the font, point size, color, and border style of your title. (See Lessons 15, 16, and 17 to learn more about formatting cells.)

To create a title with merged cells, follow these steps:

1. Type your title in the upper-left cell of the range you want to use for your heading. If you have a multiline title, like the one in Figure 11.2, press **Alt+Enter** to insert each new line.

2. Select the range in which you want to place your title.

3. Open the **Format** menu and select **Cells**. The Format Cells dialog box appears.

4. Click the **Alignment** tab.

5. Click **Merge Cells**. You may also want to make adjustments to the text within the merged cells. For example, you may want to select **Center** in the **Vertical** drop-down list to center the text vertically within the cell.

6. Click **OK** when you're done. The selected cells are merged into a single cell, which you can format as needed.

 You can merge selected cells and center the data in the leftmost cell by clicking the **Merge and Center** button on the Formatting toolbar.

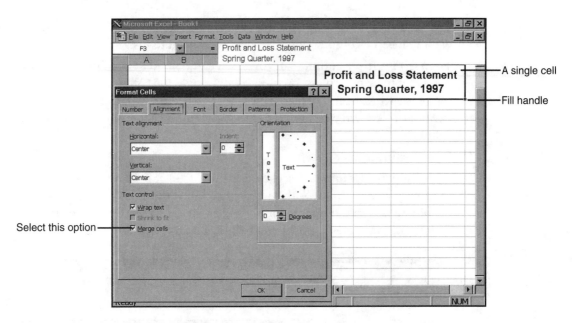

Figure 11.2 Merge cells to form a single cell.

Removing Cells

In Lesson 5, you learned how to clear the contents and formatting of selected cells. That merely removed what was inside the cells. But sometimes you will want to eliminate the cells completely. When you do, Excel removes the cells and adjusts the data in surrounding cells to fill the gap.

If you want to remove the cells completely, perform the following steps:

1. Select the range of cells you want to remove.
2. Open the **Edit** menu and choose **Delete**. The Delete dialog box appears.
3. Select the desired Delete option: **Shift Cells Left** or **Shift Cells Up**.
4. Click **OK**.

Inserting Rows and Columns

Inserting entire rows and columns in your worksheet is easy. Here's what you do:

1. **To insert a single row or column,** select the cell to the *left* of which you want to insert a column, or *above* which you want to insert a row.

  To insert multiple columns or rows, select the number of columns or rows you want to insert. To insert columns, drag over the column letters at the top of the worksheet. To insert rows, drag over the row numbers. For example, select three column letters or row numbers to insert three rows or columns.

2. Open the **Insert** menu.

3. Select **Rows** or **Columns**. Excel inserts the row(s) or column(s) and shifts the adjacent rows down or the adjacent columns right. The inserted rows or columns contain the same formatting as the cells you selected in step 1. Figure 11.3 simulates a worksheet before and after two rows were inserted.

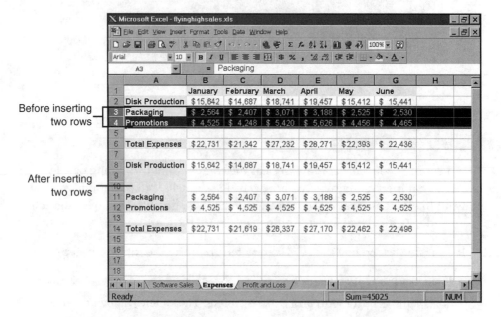

Figure 11.3   Inserting two rows in a worksheet.

TIP   **Shortcut Insert**   To quickly insert rows or columns, select one or more rows or columns. Then right-click one of them and choose **Insert** from the shortcut menu.

Removing Rows and Columns

Deleting rows and columns is similar to deleting cells. When you delete a row, the rows below the deleted row move up to fill the space. When you delete a column, the columns to the right shift left.

Follow these steps to delete a row or column:

1. Click the row number or column letter of the row or column you want to delete. You can select more than one row or column by dragging over the row numbers or column letters.

2. Open the **Edit** menu and choose **Delete**. Excel deletes the row(s) or column(s) and renumbers the remaining rows and columns sequentially. All cell references in formulas and names in formulas are updated appropriately, unless they are absolute ($) values (see Lesson 13).

In this lesson, you learned how to insert and delete cells, rows, and columns. In the next lesson, you will learn how to use formulas.

Performing Calculations with Formulas

In this lesson, you will learn how to use formulas to calculate results in your worksheets.

What Is a Formula?

Worksheets use formulas to perform calculations on the data you enter. With formulas, you can perform addition, subtraction, multiplication, and division using the values contained in various cells.

Formulas typically consist of one or more cell addresses or values and a mathematical operator, such as + (addition), – (subtraction), * (multiplication), or / (division). For example, if you want to determine the average of the three values contained in cells A1, B1, and C1, you would type the following formula in the cell where you want the result to appear:

=(A1+B1+C1)/3

Start Right   Every formula must begin with an equal sign (=).

CAUTION

Figure 12.1 shows several formulas in action. Study the formulas and their results. Table 12.1 lists the mathematical operators you can use to create formulas.

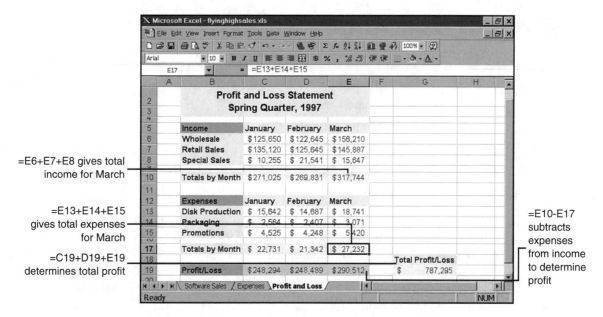

Figure 12.1 Type a formula in the cell where you want the resulting value to appear.

Table 12.1 Excel's Mathematical Operators

Operator	Performs	Sample Formula	Result
^	Exponentiation	=A1^3	Enters the result of raising the value in cell A1 to the third power.
+	Addition	=A1+A2	Enters the total of the values in cells A1 and A2.
−	Subtraction	=A1−A2	Subtracts the value in cell A2 from the value in cell A1.
*	Multiplication	=A2*3	Multiplies the value in cell A2 by 3.
/	Division	=A1/50	Divides the value in cell A1 by 50.
	Combination	=(A1+A2+A3)/3	Determines the average of the values in cells A1 through A3.

Order of Operations

Excel performs the operations within a formula in the following order:

1st   Exponential and equations within parentheses

2nd   Multiplication and division

3rd   Addition and subtraction

For example, given the formula =C2+B8*4+D10, Excel computes the value of B8*4, then adds that to C2, and then adds D10. Keep this order of operations in mind when you are creating equations because it determines the result.

If you don't take this order into consideration, you could run into problems when entering your formulas. For example, if you want to determine the average of the values in cells A1, B1, and C1, and you enter =A1+B1+C1/3, you'll get the wrong answer. The value in C1 will be divided by 3, and that result will be added to A1+B1. To determine the total of A1 through C1 first, you must enclose that group of values in parentheses, as in =(A1+B1+C1)/3.

Entering Formulas

You can enter formulas in either of two ways: by typing the formula or by selecting cell references. To type a formula, perform the following steps:

1. Select the cell in which you want the formula's calculation to appear.
2. Type the equal sign (=).
3. Type the formula. The formula appears in the Formula bar.

4. Press **Enter** or click the **Enter** button (the check mark), and Excel calculates the result.

CAUTION

 Unwanted Formula If you start to enter a formula and then decide you don't want to use it, you can skip entering the formula by pressing **Esc** or clicking the **Cancel** button.

TIP **Name That Cell** If you plan to use a particular cell in several formulas, you can give it a name, such as **Income**. Then you can use the name in the formula, as in =Income+$12.50. To name a cell, use the **Insert**, **Name**, **Define** command.

To enter a formula by selecting cell references, take the following steps:

1. Select the cell in which you want the formula's result to appear.

2. Type the equal sign (=).

3. Click the cell whose address you want to appear first in the formula. The cell address appears in the Formula bar.

 TIP **Can I Use a Cell Reference from Another Worksheet?** You can refer to a cell in a different worksheet by switching to that sheet and clicking the cell. To refer to a cell in a different workbook, open the workbook and click the cell. In Excel 97, you can even refer to a workbook located on the Internet or an intranet, if you want.

4. Type a mathematical operator after the value to indicate the next operation you want to perform. The operator appears in the Formula bar.

5. Continue clicking cells and typing operators until the formula is complete.

6. Press **Enter** to accept the formula or **Esc** to cancel the operation.

 Error! If ERR appears in a cell, make sure that you did not commit one of these common errors: try to divide by zero, use a blank cell as a divisor, refer to a blank cell, delete a cell used in a formula, or include a reference to the cell in which the answer appears.

CAUTION

 TIP **Natural Language Formulas** Excel 97 now lets you refer to row and column headings (labels) when entering a formula. For example, if you had a worksheet with row headings "Revenues," "Expenses," and "Profit," and you had column headings for each month, you could enter a formula such as =Jan Profit+Feb Profit or =Revenues–Expenses.

Calculating Results Without Entering a Formula

You can view the sum of a range of cells simply by selecting the cells and looking at the status bar, as shown in Figure 12.2. You can also view the average, minimum, maximum, and the count of a range of cells. To do so, right-click the status bar and select the option you want from the shortcut menu that appears.

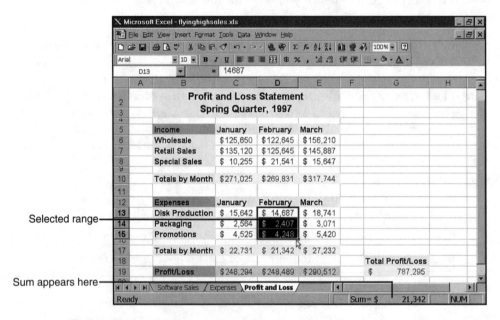

Selected range—

Sum appears here—

Figure 12.2 View a sum without entering a formula.

CAUTION

Where's the Status Bar? By default, Excel does not display the status bar. To display it, open the **Tools** menu, select **Options**, and click the **View** tab. Select the **Status Bar** option in the Show section and click **OK**.

Displaying Formulas

Normally, Excel does not display the actual formula in a cell. Instead, it displays the result of the calculation. You can view the formula by selecting the cell and looking in the Formula bar. However, if you're trying to review the formulas in a large worksheet, it might be easier if you could see them all at once (or print them). If you want to view formulas in a worksheet, follow these steps:

1. Open the **Tools** menu and choose **Options**.
2. Click the **View** tab.
3. In the Window Options area, click to select the **Formulas** check box.
4. Click **OK**.

TIP **Display Formulas Quickly** You can use a keyboard shortcut to toggle between viewing formulas and viewing values. To do so, hold down the **Ctrl** key and press ` (the accent key to the left of the 1 key; it has the tilde (~) on it). When you no longer want to view the formulas, press **Ctrl+`** again.

Editing Formulas

Editing a formula is the same as editing any entry in Excel. Here's how you do it:

1. Select the cell that contains the formula you want to edit.
2. Click in the Formula bar or press **F2** to enter Edit mode.

TIP **Quick In-Cell Editing** To quickly edit the contents of a cell, double-click the cell. The insertion point appears inside the cell, and you can make any necessary changes.

3. Press the left-arrow key (←) or right-arrow key (→) to move the insertion point. Then use the **Backspace** key to delete characters to the left, or use the **Delete** key to delete characters to the right. Type any additional characters.

4. When you finish editing the data, click the **Enter** button (the check mark) on the Formula bar or press **Enter** to accept your changes.

Another way to edit a formula is to click the **Edit Formula** button (the = sign) on the Formula bar. When you do, the Formula bar expands to provide you with help. Make your changes to the formula and then click **OK**.

In this lesson, you learned how to enter and edit formulas. In the next lesson, you learn how to copy formulas, when to use relative and absolute cell addresses, and how to change Excel's settings for calculating formulas in the worksheet.

Copying Formulas and Recalculating

In this lesson, you learn how to copy formulas, use relative and absolute cell references, and change calculation settings.

Copying Formulas

When you copy a formula, the formula is adjusted to fit the location of the cell to which it is copied. For example, if you copy the formula =C2+C3 from cell C4 to cell D4, the formula is adjusted for column D: It becomes =D2+D3. This allows you to copy similar formulas (such as the totals for a range of sales items) into a range of cells.

You can copy formulas using the Copy and Paste buttons (see Lesson 5), but there's a faster way.

1. Click the cell that contains the formula you want to copy.
2. Press **Ctrl** and drag the cell's border to the cell to which you want to copy your formula.
3. Release the mouse button, and Excel copies the formula to the new location.

If you want to copy a formula to a neighboring range of cells, follow these steps:

1. Click the cell that contains the formula you want to copy.
2. Move the mouse pointer over the fill handle.
3. Drag the fill handle across the cells into which you want to copy the formula.

TIP **Fast Copy** If you want to enter the same formula into a range of cells, select the range first. Then type the formula for the first cell in the range and press **Ctrl+Enter**.

Get an Error? If you get an error after copying a formula, verify the cell references in the copied formula. See the next section, "Using Relative and Absolute Cell Addresses," for more details.

CAUTION

Using Relative and Absolute Cell Addresses

When you copy a formula from one place in the worksheet to another, Excel adjusts the cell references in the formulas relative to their new positions in the worksheet. For example, in Figure 13.1, cell B8 contains the formula =B2+B3+B4+B5+B6, which computes the total expenses for January. If you copy that formula to cell C8 (to determine the total expenses for February), Excel automatically changes the formula to =C2+C3+C4+C5+C6. This is how relative cell addresses work.

Sometimes you may not want the cell references to be adjusted when you copy formulas. That's when absolute cell references become important.

TERM

Absolute versus Relative An *absolute reference* is a cell reference in a formula that does not change when copied to a new location. A *relative reference* is a cell reference in a formula that is adjusted when the formula is copied.

In the example shown in Figure 13.1, the formulas in cells B12, C12, D12, E12, F12, and G12 contain an absolute reference to cell B10, which holds the total expenses for quarters 1 and 2. (The formulas in B12, C12, D12, E12, F12, and G12 divide the sums from row 8 of each column by the contents of cell B10.) If you didn't use an absolute reference when you copied the formula from B10 to C10, the cell reference would be incorrect, and you would get an error message.

Cell references are adjusted for column C —

	A	B	C	D	E	F	G
		January	February	March	April	May	June
1							
2	Disk Production	$ 15,642	$ 14,687	$18,741	$19,457	$15,412	$ 15,44
3	Shipping	$ 1,564	$ 1,469	$ 1,874	$ 1,946	$ 1,541	$ 1,54
4	Handling	$ 1,125	$ 1,056	$ 1,347	$ 1,398	$ 1,107	$ 1,10
5	Packaging	$ 2,564	$ 2,407	$ 3,071	$ 3,188	$ 2,525	$ 2,53
6	Promotions	$ 4,525	$ 4,248	$ 5,420	$ 5,626	$ 4,456	$ 4,46
7							
8	Total Expenses for the Month	$ 25,420	$ 23,867	$30,453	$31,615	$25,041	$ 25,08
9							
10	Total Expenses Qtrs 1 and 2	$161,485					
11							
12	Percentage of Total Expenses	16%	15%	19%	20%	16%	16
13							
14							
15							
16							
17							
18							

Cell reference / formula bar: =C2+C3+C4+C5+C6 (TotalExpensesFeb)

Figure 13.1 Excel adjusts cell references when you copy formulas to different cells.

To make a cell reference in a formula absolute, you add a $ (dollar sign) before the letter and number that make up the cell address. For example, the formula in B12 would read as follows:

=B8/B10

You can type the dollar signs yourself, or you can press **F4** after typing the cell address.

Some formulas use mixed references. For example, the column letter might be an absolute reference, and the row number might be a relative reference, as in the formula $A2/2. If you entered this formula in cell C2 and then copied it to cell D10, the result would be the formula $A10/2. The row reference (row number) would be adjusted, but the column reference (the letter A) would not be.

Mixed References A reference that is only partially absolute, such as A$2 or $A2. When a formula that uses a mixed reference is copied to another cell, part of the cell reference (the relative part) is adjusted.

Changing the Calculation Setting

Excel recalculates the formulas in a worksheet every time you edit a value in a cell. However, on a large worksheet, you may not want Excel to recalculate until you have entered all of your changes. For example, if you are entering a lot of changes to a worksheet that contains many formulas, you can speed up the response time by changing from automatic to manual recalculation. To change the recalculation setting, take the following steps:

1. Open the **Tools** menu and choose **Options**.

2. Click the **Calculation** tab to see the options shown in Figure 13.2.

3. Select one of the following Calculation options:

Automatic   This is the default setting. It recalculates the entire workbook each time you edit or enter a formula.

Automatic Except Tables   This automatically recalculates everything except formulas in a data table.

Manual   This option tells Excel to recalculate only when you say so. To recalculate, you press **F9** or choose the **Tools**, **Options**, **Calculation** command and click the **Calc Now** button. When this option is selected, you can turn the **Recalculate Before Save** option off or on.

4. Click **OK**.

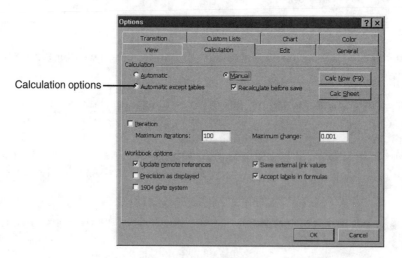

Calculation options

Figure 13.2   Change your calculation setting in the Options dialog box.

In this lesson, you learned how to copy formulas. You also learned when to use relative and absolute cell addresses and how to change calculation settings. In the next lesson, you learn how to use Excel's Function Wizard to insert another type of formula, called a *function*.

Performing Calculations with Functions

In this lesson, you learn how to perform calculations with functions and how to use Excel's Function Wizard to quickly insert functions in cells.

What Are Functions?

Functions are complex ready-made formulas that perform a series of operations on a specified range of values. For example, to determine the sum of a series of numbers in cells A1 through H1, you can enter the function =SUM(A1:H1) instead of entering =A1+B1+C1 and so on. Functions can use range references (such as B1:B3), range names (such as SALES), and numerical values (such as 585.86).

Every function consists of the following three elements:

- The = sign indicates that what follows is a function (formula).
- The function name, such as SUM, indicates which operation will be performed.
- The argument, such as (A1:H1), indicates the cell addresses of the values that the function will act on. The argument is often a range of cells, but it can be much more complex.

You can enter functions either by typing them in cells or by using the Function Wizard, as you'll see later in this lesson.

Table 14.1 shows Excel's most common functions that you'll use in your worksheets.

Table 14.1   Excel's Most Common Functions

Function	Example	Description
AVERAGE	=AVERAGE(B4:B9)	Calculates the mean or average of a group of numbers.
COUNT	=COUNT(A3:A7)	Counts the numeric values in a range. For example, if a range contains some cells with text and other cells with numbers, you can count how many numbers are in that range.
COUNTA	=COUNTA(B4:B10)	Counts all cells in a range that are not blank. For example, if a range contains some cells with text and other cells with numbers, you can count how many cells in that range contain text.
IF	=IF(A3>=100,A3*2,A2*2)	Allows you to place a condition on a formula. In this example, if A3 is greater than or equal to 100, the formula A3*2 is used. If A3 is less than 100, the formula A2*2 is used instead.
MAX	=MAX(B4:B10)	Returns the maximum value in a range of cells.
MIN	=MIN(B4:B10)	Returns the minimum value in a range of cells.
PMT	=PMT(rate,nper,pv)	Calculates the periodic payment on a loan when you enter the interest rate, number of periods, and principal as arguments. Example: =PMT(.0825/12,360,180000) for 30-year loan at 8.25% for $180,000.
PMT	=PMT(rate,nper,,fv)	Calculates the deposit needed each period to reach some future value. Example: =PMT(.07/12,60,,10000) calculates the deposit needed to accumulate $10,000 at an annual rate of 7%, making monthly payments for 5 years (60 months).
SUM	=SUM(A1:A10)	Calculates the total in a range of cells.

continues

225

Table 14.1 Continued

Function	Example	Description
SUMIF	=SUMIF(rg,criteria,sumrg)	Calculates the total of the range *rg* for each corresponding cell in *sumrg* that matches the specified criteria. For example, =SUMIF (A2:A4,>100,B2:B4) adds the cells in the range A2:A4 whose corresponding cell in column B is greater than 100.

TIP   **Excel on the Web**   A new function, =HYPERLINK(), is used to create links to Web sites right in your worksheet. For example, =HYPERLINK(http://www.microsoft.com,"Visit Microsoft") will display the words "Visit Microsoft" in a cell. When the user clicks the cell, he or she is connected to the Microsoft home page. You can also use this feature to link to worksheets on your company's intranet.

Enter Text Correctly   When entering text into a formula, be sure to surround it in quotation marks, as in "Seattle."

CAUTION

Using AutoSum

Because SUM is one of the most commonly used functions, Excel provides a fast way to enter it—you simply click the AutoSum button in the Standard toolbar. Based on the currently selected cell, AutoSum guesses which cells you want summed. If AutoSum selects an incorrect range of cells, you can edit the selection.

To use AutoSum, follow these steps:

1. Select the cell in which you want the sum inserted. Try to choose a cell at the end of a row or column of data; doing do will help AutoSum guess which cells you want added together.

2. Click the **AutoSum** button in the Standard toolbar. AutoSum inserts =SUM and the range address of the cells to the left of or above the selected cell (see Figure 14.1).

3. If the range Excel selected is incorrect, drag over the range you want to use, or click in the Formula bar and edit the formula.

4. Click the **Enter** button in the Formula bar or press **Enter**. Excel calculates the total for the selected range.

SUM function appears in the selected cell and in the Formula bar

AutoSum selects a range of cells above or to the left of the selected cell

The selected range becomes the function's argument

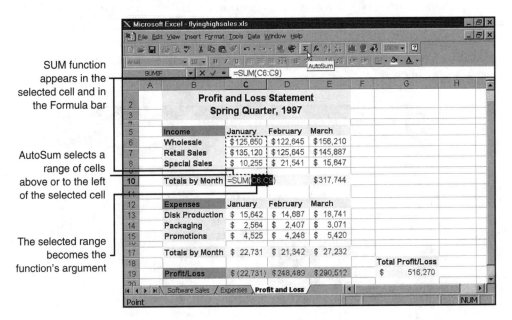

Figure 14.1 AutoSum inserts the SUM function and selects the cells it plans to total.

TIP **Quickie AutoSum** To quickly insert the sum function, select the cell in which you want the sum inserted and double-click the **AutoSum** tool on the Standard toolbar. When you double-click the AutoSum button instead of single-clicking, you bypass the step where Excel displays the SUM formula and its arguments in the cell. Instead, you see the total in the cell and the SUM formula in the Formula bar. Of course, the problem with using this method is that you're not given a chance to "second-guess" the range of cells AutoSum decides to add.

Using AutoCalculate

When you wanted to quickly check a total in earlier versions of Excel, did you ever use a calculator or enter temporary formulas on a worksheet? If you did, you might find Excel's AutoCalculate feature very handy. AutoCalculate lets you quickly check a total or an average, count entries or numbers, and find the maximum or minimum number in a range.

Here's how AutoCalculate works. To check a total, select the range you want to sum. Excel automatically displays the answer in the AutoCalculate area (as shown in Figure 14.2). If you want to perform a different function on a range of numbers, select the range and right-click in the AutoCalculate area to display the shortcut menu. Then choose a function from the menu. For example, choose Count to count the numeric values in the range. The answer appears in the AutoCalculate area.

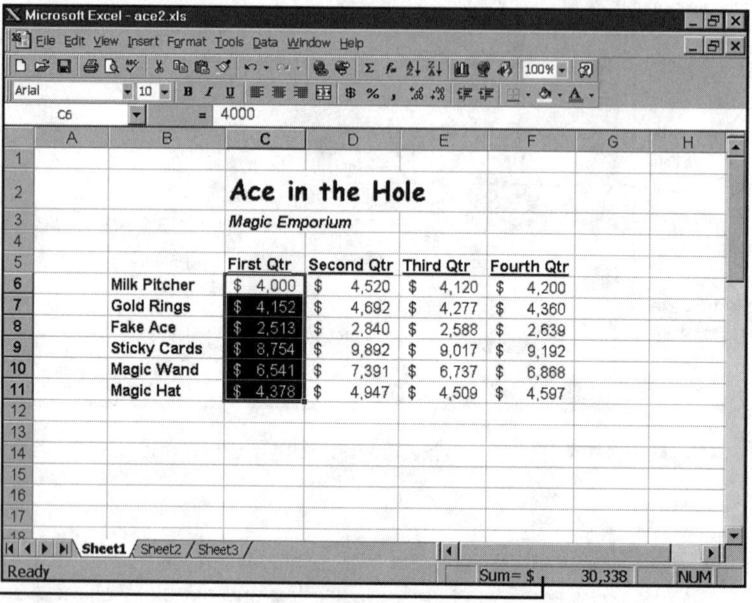

AutoCalculate area

Figure 14.2 AutoCalculate lets you quickly view a sum.

Where's My Status Bar? If the status bar is not displayed, open the **Tools** menu, select **Options**, and click the **View** tab. Then select the **Status Bar** option and click **OK**.

Using the Function Wizard

Although you can type a function directly into a cell just as you can type formulas, you may find it easier to use the Function Wizard. The Function Wizard leads you through the process of inserting a function. The following steps walk you through using the Function Wizard:

1. Select the cell in which you want to insert the function. (You can insert a function by itself or as part of a formula.)

2. Type = or click the **Edit Formula (=)** button on the Formula bar. The Formula Palette appears, as shown in Figure 14.3.

Functions button —

Edit Formula button

Formula Palette

Collapse Dialog button

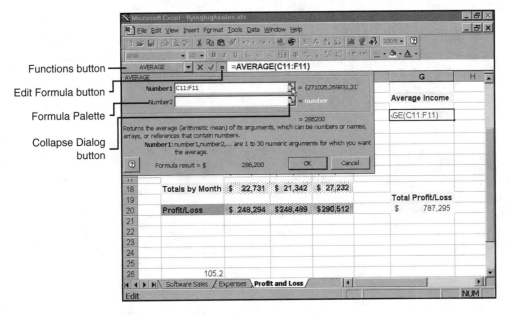

Figure 14.3 The Function Wizard helps you enter functions.

3. Select the function you want to insert from the **Functions** list by clicking the **Functions** button (see Figure 14.3). If you don't see your function listed, select **More Functions** at the bottom of the list.

CAUTION

What's This Function? If you don't know a lot about a particular function and you'd like to know more, click the **Help** button in the Formula Palette. When the Office Assistant appears, click **Help with the Feature**. Then click **Help on Selected Function**.

4. Enter the arguments for the formula. If you want to select a range of cells as an argument, click the **Collapse Dialog** button shown in Figure 14.3.

5. After selecting a range, click the **Collapse Dialog** button again to return to the Formula Palette.

6. Click **OK**. Excel inserts the function and argument in the selected cell and displays the result.

To edit a function, click the **Edit Formula** button. The Formula Palette appears. Change the arguments as needed and click **OK**.

In this lesson, you learned the basics of dealing with functions, and you learned how to use Excel's Function Wizard to quickly enter functions. You also learned how to quickly total a series of numbers with the AutoSum tool and how to check the sum of numbers with AutoCalculate. In the next lesson, you learn how to format values in your worksheet.

Changing How Numbers Look

In this lesson, you learn how to customize the appearance of numbers in your worksheet.

Formatting Values

Numeric values are usually more than just numbers. They represent a dollar value, a date, a percent, or some other value. Excel offers a wide range of number formats, which are listed in Table 15.1.

Table 15.1   Excel's Number Formats

Number Format	Examples	Description
General	10.6 $456,908.00	Excel displays your value as you enter it. In other words, this format displays currency or percent signs only if you enter them yourself.
Number	3,400.50 (120.39)	The default Number format has two decimal places and a comma for a thousand separator. Negative numbers appear in red and in parentheses, preceded by a minus sign.
Currency	$3,400.50 ($3,400.50)	The default Currency format has two decimal places and a dollar sign. Negative numbers appear in red and in parentheses.

continues

Table 15.1 Continued

Number Format	Examples	Description
Accounting	$ 3,400.00 $ 978.21	Use this format to align dollar signs and decimal points in a column. The default Accounting format has two decimal places and a dollar sign.
Date	11/7	The default Date format is the month and day separated by a slash; however, you can select from numerous other formats.
Time	10:00	The default Time format is the hour and minutes separated by a colon; however, you can opt to display seconds, AM, or PM.
Percentage	99.50%	The default Percentage format has two decimal places. Excel multiplies the value in a cell by 100 and displays the result with a percent sign.
Fraction	1/2	The default Fraction format is up to one digit on each side of the slash. Use this format to display the number of digits you want on each side of the slash and the fraction type (such as halves, quarters, eighths, and so on).
Scientific	3.40E+03	The default Scientific format has two decimal places. Use this format to display numbers in scientific notation.
Text	135RV90	Use Text format to display both text and numbers in a cell as text. Excel displays the entry exactly as you type it.
Special	02110	This format is specifically designed to display ZIP codes, phone numbers, and Social Security numbers correctly, so

Number Format	Examples	Description
		that you don't have to enter any special characters, such as hyphens.
Custom	00.0%	Use Custom format to create your own number format. You can use any of the format codes in the Type list and then make changes to those codes. The # symbol represents a number placeholder, and 0 represents a zero placeholder.

After deciding on a suitable numeric format, follow these steps:

1. Select the cell or range that contains the values you want to format.

2. Open the **Format** menu and select **Cells**. The Format Cells dialog box appears, as shown in Figure 15.1.

3. Click the **Number** tab.

4. In the **Category** list, select the numeric format category you want to use. The sample box displays the default format for that category.

5. Make changes to the format as needed.

6. Click **OK** or press **Enter**. Excel reformats the selected cells based on your selections.

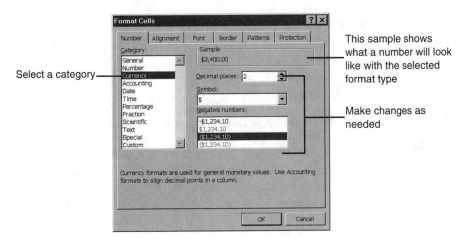

Figure 15.1 The Format Cells dialog box with the Number tab displayed.

CAUTION

Removing Formatting If you want to remove a number format from a cell (and return it to General format), select the cells whose formatting you want to remove, open the **Edit** menu, select **Clear**, and then select **Formats**.

Using the Style Buttons to Format Numbers

The Formatting toolbar (just below the Standard toolbar) contains several buttons for selecting a number format, including the following:

Button	Name	Example/Description
$	Currency Style	$1200.90
%	Percent Style	20.90%
,	Comma Style	1,200.90
+.0 .00	Increase Decimal	Adds one decimal place
.00 +.0	Decrease Decimal	Deletes one decimal place

To use one of these buttons, select the cell you want to format and then click the desired button. You can also change the Number format of a cell by using the shortcut menu. Select the cell, right-click to display the shortcut menu, and choose **Format Cells**.

CAUTION

That's Not the Date I Entered! If you enter a date in a cell that is formatted with the Number format, the date will appear as a number. With the Number format, Excel converts the date to a value that represents the number of days between January 1, 1900, and that date. For example, 01/01/1900 equals 1, and 12/31/1900 equals 365. To fix your problem, change the cell's formatting from Number format to Date format and select a date type.

TIP **Conditioned Cells** If you want to highlight cells that meet certain conditions, such as all values that are larger than 1,000, use conditional formatting. See Lesson 16 for more information.

Creating Your Own Custom Format

If you need to enter special numbers, such as account numbers, you may want to create your own number format and use it to format your account numbers. For example, suppose your account numbers look like this:

10-20190-109

You could create a format like this:

##-#####-###

Then when you enter the number, 9089212098, for example, Excel formats it for you, adding the hyphens where needed:

90-89212-098

Mixed Metaphors Unfortunately, you can't create a format for a value that includes both text and numbers combined.

CAUTION

To create your own format, follow these steps:

1. Open the **Format** menu and select **Cells**.
2. Click the **Number** tab.
3. In the **Category** list, select **Custom**.
4. Type your custom format in the **Type** box and click **OK**.

When entering your format, use the following codes:

#	Displays the number, unless it's an insignificant zero
0	Adds zeroes where needed to fill out the number
?	Adds spaces where needed to align decimal points

Table 15.2 shows some sample formats.

Table 15.2   Sample Custom Formats

Value Entered	Custom Format	Value Displayed in Cell
3124.789	####.##	3124.79
120.5	###.#00	120.500
.6345	0.##	0.63
21456.25	##,###.00	21,456.000
120.54	$##,###.#0	$120.50

You can enter formats for how you want positive and negative numbers displayed, along with zero values and text. Simply separate the formats with a semicolon (;) like this:

##.#0;[MAGENTA]–##.#0;[GREEN]0.00;@

In this example format, positive numbers entered into the cell are displayed with two decimal places (a zero is added to fill two decimal places if needed). Negative numbers are displayed with a preceding minus sign (-) in magenta. Zero values are displayed as 0.00 in green. Text is permitted in these cells, as indicated by the final format (@). If you do not include the text format, any text you type into the cell simply will not be displayed at all. If you want to add a particular word or words in front of all text entered into a cell, include the word(s) in double quotation marks, as in "Acct. Code:"@.

In this lesson, you learned how to format numbers and create custom formats. In the next lesson, you learn how to format text.

Giving Your Text a New Look

In this lesson, you learn how to change the appearance of the text in the cells.

How to Give Text a Different Look

When you type text or numbers, Excel automatically formats it in the Arial font, which doesn't look very fancy. You can change the following text attributes to improve the appearance of your text or set it apart from other text:

Font A typeface—for example, Algerian, Desdemona, or Wide Latin.

Font Style For example, Bold, Italic, Underline, or Strikethrough.

CAUTION

Text Underline versus Cell Border You can add underlining to important information in one of two ways. With the underline format explained in this lesson, a line (or lines, depending on which underline format you choose) is placed under the cell's contents. This is different from adding a line to the bottom of a cell's border, which is explained in the next lesson.

Size For example, 10-point, 12-point, or 20-point. (The higher the point size, the bigger the text is; there are approximately 72 points in an inch.)

Color For example, Red, Magenta, or Cyan.

Alignment For example, centered, left-aligned, or right-aligned within the cell.

TERM   **Font**   A set of characters that have the same typeface, which means they are of a single design (such as Times New Roman). When you select a font, Excel also allows you to change the font's size; add optional *attributes* to the font, such as bold or italic; underline the text; change its color; and add special effects such as strikethrough, superscript, subscript, and small caps.

Figure 16.1 shows a worksheet after some attributes have been changed for selected text.

This text is centered across columns and set in 16-point bold type

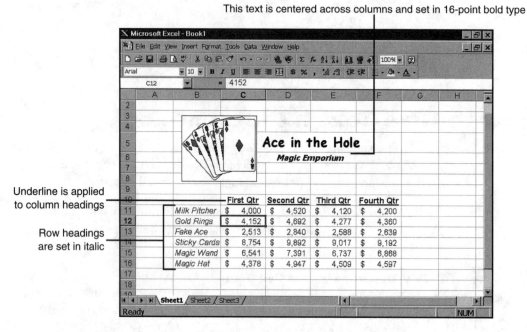

Underline is applied to column headings

Row headings are set in italic

Figure 16.1   A sampling of several text attributes.

Using the Format Cells Dialog Box

You can change the look of your text by using the Format Cells dialog box. Just follow these steps:

1. Select the cell or range that contains the text you want to format.

2. Open the **Format** menu and choose **Cells**, or press **Ctrl+1**. (You can also right-click the selected cells and choose **Format Cells** from the shortcut menu.)

3. Click the **Font** tab. The Font options jump to the front, as shown in Figure 16.2.

4. Select the options you want.

5. Click **OK** or press **Enter**.

Excel uses a default font to style your text as you type it. To change the default font, enter your font preferences in the Font tab and click the **Normal Font** option. When you click the **OK** button, Excel makes your preferences the default font.

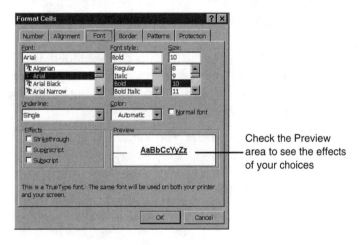

Check the Preview area to see the effects of your choices

Figure 16.2   The Format Cells dialog box with the Font tab up front.

TIP   **Font Shortcuts**   You can apply certain attributes quickly by using keyboard shortcuts. First select the cell(s), and then press **Ctrl+B** for bold, **Ctrl+I** for Italic, **Ctrl+U** for Single Underline (Accounting style), or **Ctrl+5** for Strikethrough.

Changing Text Attributes with Toolbar Buttons

A faster way to enter font changes is to use the Formatting toolbar shown in Figure 16.3.

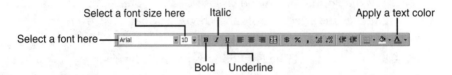

Select a font size here   Italic   Apply a text color

Select a font here

Bold   Underline

Figure 16.3   Use the Formatting toolbar to quickly make font changes.

To use a tool to change text attributes, follow these steps:

1. Select the cell or range that contains the text whose look you want to change.

2. To change the font or font size, pull down the appropriate drop-down list and click the font or size you want. You can also type the point size in the **Font Size** box.

3. To add an attribute (such as bold or underlining), click the desired button. When selected, a button looks like it has been pressed in. You can add more than one attribute to text, making it bold and italic, for example.

TIP   **Change Before You Type**   You can activate the attributes you want *before* you type text. For example, if you want a title in Bold 12-point Desdemona type, select the cells for which you want to change the attributes, and then set the attributes before you start typing. Unlike in a word processor where you must turn attributes on and off, in Excel, selecting formats for cells in advance of typing your data has no effect on the unselected cells; data in unselected cells will be the default Arial 10-point type.

Aligning Text in Cells

When you enter data into an Excel worksheet, that data is aligned automatically. Text is aligned on the left, and numbers are aligned on the right. Both text and numbers are initially set at the bottom of the cells. However, you can change both the vertical and the horizontal alignment of data in your cells.

Follow these steps to change the alignment:

1. Select the cell or range you want to align. If you want to center a title or other text over a range of cells, select the entire range of blank cells in which you want the text centered, including the cell that contains the text you want to center.

2. Pull down the **Format** menu and select **Cells,** or press **Ctrl+1.** The Format Cells dialog box appears.

3. Click the **Alignment** tab. The alignment options appear in front (see Figure 16.4).

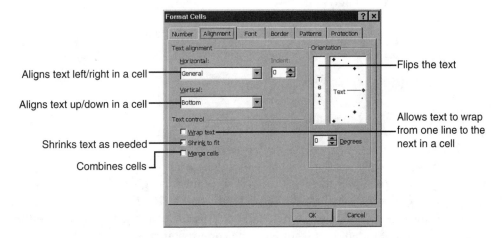

Aligns text left/right in a cell

Aligns text up/down in a cell

Shrinks text as needed

Combines cells

Flips the text

Allows text to wrap from one line to the next in a cell

Figure 16.4 The Alignment options.

4. Choose from the following options and option groups to set the alignment:

   Horizontal lets you specify a left/right alignment in the cell(s). (The Center Across selection centers a title or other text within a range of cells.)

   Vertical lets you specify how you want the text aligned in relation to the top and bottom of the cell(s).

   Orientation lets you flip the text sideways or print it from top to bottom (instead of left to right).

   Wrap text tells Excel to wrap long lines of text within a cell without changing the width of cell. (Normally, Excel displays all text in a cell on one line.)

   Shrink to fit shrinks the text to fit within the cell's current width. If the cell's width is adjusted, the text increases or decreases in size accordingly.

Merge cells combines several cells into a single cell. All data is overlaid, except for the cell in the upper-left corner of the selected cells.

5. Click **OK** or press **Enter**.

 TIP   Alignment Buttons   A quick way to align text and numbers is to use the alignment buttons in the Formatting toolbar. The following buttons allow you to align the text:

   Align Left

   Center

   Align Right

   Merge and Center

New to Excel 97 is the capability to indent your text within a cell. If you're typing a paragraph worth of information into a single cell, you can indent that paragraph by selecting left alignment from the **Horizontal** list box in the Font Cells dialog box (as explained earlier). After selecting left alignment, set the amount of indent you want with the **Indent** spin box.

In addition, you can add an indent quickly by clicking the following buttons on the Formatting toolbar:

- Decrease Indent   Removes an indent or creates a negative indent.
- Increase Indent   Adds an indent.

In this lesson, you learned how to customize your text formatting to achieve the look you want. In the next lesson, you learn how to add borders and shading to your worksheet.

Adding Cell Borders and Shading

In this lesson, you will learn how to add pizzazz to your worksheets by adding borders and shading.

Adding Borders to Cells

As you work with your worksheet on-screen, you'll notice that each cell is identified by gridlines that surround the cell. Normally, these gridlines do not print; even if you choose to print them, they may appear washed out. To have more well-defined lines appear on the printout (or on-screen, for that matter), you can add borders to selected cells or entire cell ranges. A border can appear on all four sides of a cell or only on selected sides, whichever you prefer.

CAUTION

The Gridlines Don't Print? In Excel 97, as in Excel 95, the gridlines do not print by default. But if you want to try printing your worksheet with gridlines first just to see what it looks like, open the **File** menu, select **Page Setup**, click the **Sheet** tab, select **Gridlines**, and click **OK**.

To add borders to a cell or range, perform the following steps:

1. Select the cell(s) around which you want a border to appear.
2. Open the **Format** menu and choose **Cells**. The Format Cells dialog box appears.
3. Click the **Border** tab to see the Border options shown in Figure 17.1.

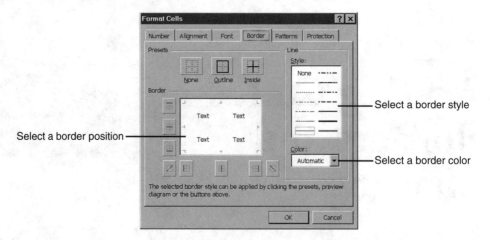

Select a border position ———

Select a border style

Select a border color

Figure 17.1   Choose border options from the Format Cells dialog box.

4. Select the desired position, style (thickness), and color for the border. You can click inside the Border box itself, or you can click a preset border pattern button to add your border.

5. Click **OK** or press **Enter**.

TIP   **Hiding Gridlines**   When adding borders to a worksheet, you might need to hide the gridlines to get a better idea of how the borders will look when printed. Open the **Tools** menu, select **Options**, click the **View** tab, and select **Gridlines** to remove the check mark from the check box. Of course, selecting this option has no effect on whether or not the gridlines actually print, only on whether or not they are displayed on-screen.

 To add borders quickly, select the cells around which you want the border to appear, and then click the **Borders** drop-down arrow in the Formatting toolbar. Click the desired border. If you click the **Borders** button itself (instead of the arrow), Excel automatically adds the border line you last chose to the selected cells.

Adding Shading to Cells

For a simple but dramatic effect, you can add shading to your worksheets. With shading, you can add a color or gray shading to a cell. You can add colors at full strength or partial strength to create the exact effect you want. To lessen the strength of the cell color you select, you add your shading with a pattern, such as a diagonal. Figure 17.2 illustrates some of the effects you can create with shading.

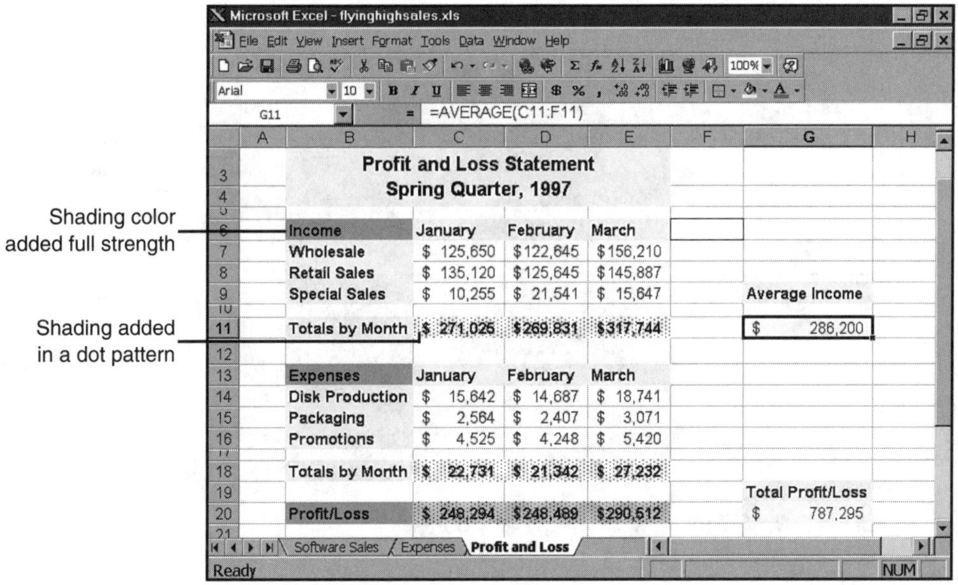

Figure 17.2 A worksheet with added shading.

Follow these steps to add shading to a cell or range. As you make your selections, keep in mind that if you plan to print your worksheet with a black-and-white printer, your pretty colors may not be different enough to create the effect you want. Select colors that contrast well in value (intensity), and use the Print Preview command (as explained in Lesson 10) to view your results in black-and-white before you print.

1. Select the cell(s) you want to shade.
2. Open the **Format** menu and choose **Cells**.
3. Click the **Patterns** tab. Excel displays the shading options (see Figure 17.3).
4. Click the **Pattern** drop-down arrow, and you will see a grid that contains all the colors from the color palette, as well as patterns. Select the shading color and pattern you want to use. The Color options let you choose a color

for the overall shading. The Pattern options let you select a black-and-white or colored pattern that lies on top of the overall shading. A preview of the result appears in the Sample box.

5. When you like the results you see, click **OK** or press **Enter**.

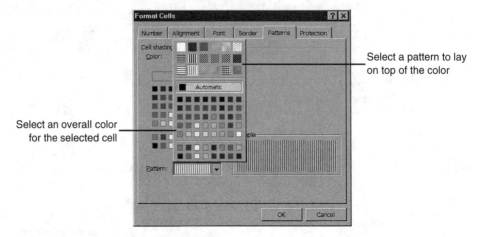

Select a pattern to lay on top of the color

Select an overall color for the selected cell

Figure 17.3 Selecting a shading and a pattern.

A quick way to add cell shading (without a pattern) is to select the cells you want to shade, click the **Fill Color** drop-down arrow, and click the color you want to use.

TIP **Quick Color** To add the color shown in the bucket of the Fill Color button, simply click the button itself—do not bother to click the arrow to the right of the button.

If the shading is too dark, consider using the **Font Color** button (just to the right of the Color button) to select a lighter color for the text.

Using AutoFormat

Excel offers the AutoFormat feature, which takes some of the pain out of formatting. AutoFormat provides you with 16 predesigned table formats that you can apply to a worksheet.

To use predesigned formats, perform the following steps:

1. Select the worksheet(s) and cell(s) that contain the data you want to format.

2. Open the **Format** menu and choose **AutoFormat**. The AutoFormat dialog box appears, as shown in Figure 17.4.

3. In the **Table Format** list, choose the predesigned format you want to use. When you select a format, Excel shows you what it will look like in the Sample area.

4. To exclude certain elements from AutoFormat, click the **Options** button and choose the formats you want to turn off.

5. Click **OK**, and Excel formats your table to make it look like the one in the preview area.

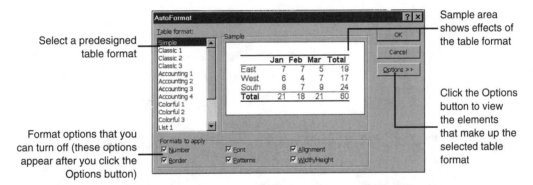

Select a predesigned table format

Format options that you can turn off (these options appear after you click the Options button)

Sample area shows effects of the table format

Click the Options button to view the elements that make up the selected table format

Figure 17.4 Use the AutoFormat dialog box to select a prefab format.

CAUTION **Deformatting an AutoFormat** If you don't like what AutoFormat did to your worksheet, select the table, open the **Format** menu, and choose **AutoFormat**. From the **Table Format** list, choose **None** to remove the AutoFormat.

Copying Formats with Format Painter

Excel gives you two ways to copy and paste formatting:

- You can use the **Edit, Copy** command and then the **Edit Paste Special** command and select **Formats** from the **Paste** options in the Paste Special dialog box.
- You can use the **Format Painter** button in the Standard toolbar.

The Format Painter lets you quickly copy and paste formats that you have already used in a workbook. Because the Format Painter button is faster, I'll give you the steps you need to paint formats.

1. Select the cell(s) that contain the formatting you want to copy and paste.

2. Click the **Format Painter** button on the Standard toolbar. Excel copies the formatting. The mouse pointer changes into a paintbrush with a plus sign next to it.

3. Click and drag over the cells to which you want to apply the copied formatting.

4. Release the mouse button, and Excel copies the formatting and applies it to the selected cells.

TIP   **Faster Painter**   To paint several areas at one time, double-click the **Format Painter** button. Then drag over the first section you want to paint. The cursor remains as a paintbrush, meaning that you can continue to drag over other cells to paint them, too. When you're through, press **Esc** to return to a normal cursor.

Applying Conditional Formatting

If you want to highlight particular values in your worksheet, you can use conditional formatting. For example, if you want to highlight all sales figures under a particular mark, you could apply a conditional red shading.

To apply conditional formatting, follow these steps:

1. Select the cells you want to format.

2. Open the **Format** menu and select **Conditional Formatting**. The Conditional Formatting dialog box appears, as shown in Figure 17.5.

3. To apply a format based on the value found in a selected cell, choose **Cell Value Is** from the **Condition 1** list.

   To apply a format based on the value found in a cell outside the selected range, select **Formula Is** from the **Condition 1** list.

Figure 17.5 Apply formats conditionally to highlight certain values.

4. Enter the value or formula you want to use as the *condition* that determines when Excel can apply the formatting you select. If you choose to use a formula, be sure to include the beginning equal (=) sign.

CAUTION

Using a Formula If you choose Formula Is in step 3, the formula you enter must result in a true or false value (so use the IF statement). For example, if you wanted to format some cells based on whether or not a corresponding value in column A is less than 20% of projected sales (cell D12), you could use this formula:

=IF(A1<20%*D12,TRUE,FALSE)

5. Click the **Format** button and select the format you want to apply when the condition is true. Click **OK** to return to the Conditional Formatting dialog box.

6. (Optional) If you want to add more than one condition, click **Add**. Then repeat steps 3 and 4 to add the condition.

7. When you finish adding conditions, click **OK**.

 You can copy the conditional formatting from one cell to other cells using the Format Painter button. Simply click the cell whose formatting you want to copy and click the **Format Painter** button. Then drag over the cells to which you want to copy the formatting.

In this lesson, you learned some ways to enhance the appearance of your worksheets. In the next lesson, you learn how to change the sizes of rows and columns.

Changing Column Width and Row Height

In this lesson, you learn how to adjust the column width and row height to make the best use of the worksheet space. You can set these manually or let Excel make the adjustments for you with its AutoFit feature.

Adjusting Column Width and Row Height with a Mouse

You can adjust the width of a column or the height of a row by using a dialog box or by dragging with the mouse.

Why Bother? You might not want to bother adjusting the row height because it's automatically adjusted as you change font size. However, if a column's width is not as large as its data, that data may not be displayed and may appear as ########. In such a case, you must adjust the width of the column in order for the data to be displayed at all.

Here's how you adjust the row height or column width with the mouse:

1. To change the row height or column width for a single row or column, skip to step 2. To change the height or width for two or more rows or columns, select them first by dragging over the row or column headings.

2. Position the mouse pointer over one of the row heading or column heading borders as shown in Figure 18.1. (Use the right border of the column heading to adjust column width; use the bottom border of the row heading to adjust the row height.)

3. Drag the border to the size you want.

4. Release the mouse button, and Excel adjusts the row height or column width.

Dragging the right border of column A changes its width

	A	B	C	D	E	F	G
1		January	February	March	April	May	June	To
2	Disk Production	$ 15,642	$ 14,687	$18,741	$19,457	$15,412	$ 15,441	$
3	Shipping	$ 1,564	$ 1,469	$ 1,874	$ 1,946	$ 1,541	$ 1,544	$
4	Handling	$ 1,125	$ 1,056	$ 1,347	$ 1,398	$ 1,107	$ 1,109	$
5	Packaging	$ 2,564	$ 2,407	$ 3,071	$ 3,188	$ 2,525	$ 2,530	$
6	Promotions	$ 4,525	$ 4,248	$ 5,420	$ 5,626	$ 4,456	$ 4,465	$
7								
8	Total Expenses for the M	$ 25,420	$ 23,867	$30,453	$31,615	$25,041	$ 25,089	$
9								
10	Total Expenses Qtrs 1 ar	$161,485						
11								
12	Percentage of Total Expe	16%	15%	19%	20%	16%	16%	

Figure 18.1 The mouse pointer changes to a double-headed arrow when you move it over a border in the row or column heading.

TIP **AutoFit Cells** To quickly make a column as wide as its widest entry using Excel's AutoFit feature, double-click the right border of the column heading. To make a row as tall as its tallest entry, double-click the bottom border of the row heading. To change more than one column or row at a time, drag over the desired row or column headings, and then double-click the bottom most or right most heading border.

Using the Format Menu for Precise Control

You can change a row or column's size by dragging the border of a row or column. However, you cannot control the size as precisely as you can by providing specific sizes with the Format, Row Height and Format, Column Width commands.

These steps show you how to use the Format menu to change the column width:

1. Select the column(s) whose width you want to change. To change the width of a single column, select any cell in that column.

2. Open the **Format** menu, select **Column**, and select **Width**. The Column Width dialog box appears (see Figure 18.2).

3. Type the number of characters you would like as the width. The default width is 8.43.

4. Click **OK** or press **Enter** to put your changes into effect.

Figure 18.2 Changing the column width.

By default, Excel makes a row a bit taller than the tallest text in the row. For example, if the tallest text is 10 points tall, Excel makes the row itself 13.2 points tall. You can use the Format menu to change the row height manually:

1. Select the row(s) whose height you want to change. (To change the height of a single row, select any cell in that row.)

2. Open the **Format** menu, select **Row**, and select **Height**. The Row Height dialog box shown in Figure 18.3 appears.

3. Type the desired height (in points).

4. Click **OK** or press **Enter** to implement the change in your worksheet.

Figure 18.3 Changing the row height.

In this lesson, you learned how to change the row height and column width. In the next lesson, you learn how to create charts.

Creating Charts

In this lesson, you will learn to create charts to represent your workbook data as a picture.

19

Chart Types

With Excel, you can create various types of charts. Some common chart types are shown in Figure 19.1. The chart type you choose depends on your data and on how you want to present that data. These are the major chart types and their purposes:

- **Pie** Use this chart to show the relationship among parts of a whole.
- **Bar** Use this chart to compare values at a given point in time.
- **Column** Similar to the Bar chart; use this chart to emphasize the difference between items.
- **Line** Use this chart to emphasize trends and the change of values over time.
- **Scatter** Similar to a Line chart; use this chart to emphasize the difference between two sets of values.
- **Area** Similar to the Line chart; use this chart to emphasize the amount of change in values over time.

Most of these basic chart types also come in three-dimensional varieties. In addition to looking more professional than the standard flat charts, 3-D charts can often help your audience distinguish between different sets of data.

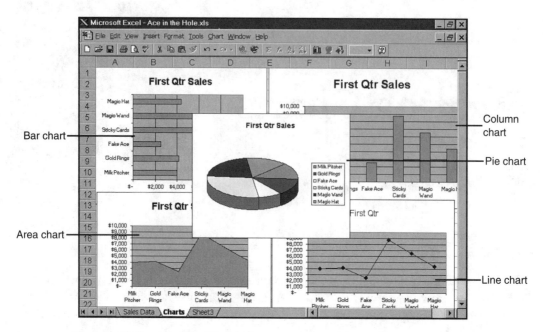

Figure 19.1   Common Excel chart types.

   Embedded Charts   A chart that is placed on the same worksheet that contains the data used to create the chart. A chart can also be placed on a chart sheet in the workbook so that the worksheet and chart are separate. Embedded charts are useful for showing the actual data and its graphic representation side-by-side.

Charting Terminology

Before you start creating charts, familiarize yourself with the following terminology:

- **Data Series**   The bars, pie wedges, lines, or other elements that represent plotted values in a chart. For example, a chart might show a set of similar bars that reflects a series of values for the same item. The bars in the series would all have the same pattern. If you have more than one pattern of bars, each pattern would represent a separate data series. For instance, charting the sales for Territory 1 versus Territory 2 would require two data series—one for each territory. Often, data series correspond to rows of data in your worksheet.

- **Categories** Categories reflect the number of elements in a series. You might have two data series to compare the sales of two different territories and four categories to compare these sales over four quarters. Some charts have only one category, and others have several. Categories normally correspond to the columns that you have in your chart data, and the category labels coming from the column headings.

- **Axis** One side of a chart. A two-dimensional chart has an x-axis (horizontal) and a y-axis (vertical). The x-axis contains all the data series and categories in the chart. If you have more than one category, the x-axis often contains labels that define what each category represents. The y-axis reflects the values of the bars, lines, or plot points. In a three-dimensional chart, the z-axis represents the vertical plane, and the x-axis (distance) and y-axis (width) represent the two sides on the floor of the chart.

- **Legend** Defines the separate series of a chart. For example, the legend for a pie chart will show what each piece of the pie represents.

- **Gridlines** Emphasize the y-axis or x-axis scale of the data series. For example, major gridlines for the y-axis will help you follow a point from the x- or y-axis to identify a data point's exact value.

Creating a Chart

You can create charts as part of a worksheet (an embedded chart) or as a chart on a separate worksheet. If you create an embedded chart, it will print side-by-side with your worksheet data. If you create a chart on a separate worksheet, you can print it independently. Both types of charts are linked to the worksheet data that they represent, so when you change the data, the chart is automatically updated.

The Chart Wizard button in the Standard toolbar allows you to quickly create a chart. To use the Chart Wizard, follow these steps:

1. Select the data you want to chart. If you typed names or other labels (such as Qtr 1, Qtr 2, and so on) and you want them included in the chart, make sure you select them.

2. Click the **Chart Wizard** button on the Standard toolbar.

3. The Chart Wizard Step 1 of 4 dialog box appears, as shown in Figure 19.2. Select a **Chart Type** and select a **Chart Sub-Type** (a variation on the selected chart type). Click **Next**.

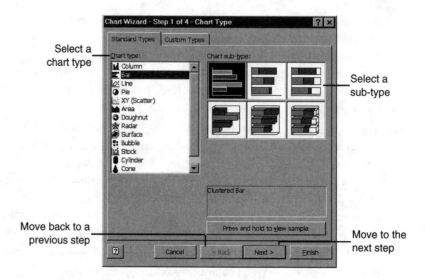

Select a chart type

Select a sub-type

Move back to a previous step

Move to the next step

Figure 19.2 Chart Wizard asks you to choose the chart type you want.

4. Next you're asked if the selected range is correct. You can correct the range by typing a new range or by clicking the **Collapse Dialog** button (located at the right end of the Data Range text box) and selecting the range you want to use.

5. By default, Excel assumes that your different data series are stored in rows. You can change this to columns if necessary by clicking the **Series in Columns** option. When you're through, click **Next**.

6. Click the various tabs to change options for your chart (see Figure 19.3). For example, you can delete the legend by clicking the **Legend** tab and deselecting **Show Legend**. You can add a chart title on the **Title** tab. Add data labels (labels which display the actual value being represented by each bar, line, and so on) by clicking the **Data Labels** tab.

7. Finally, you're asked if you want to embed the chart (as an object) in the current worksheet, or if you want to create a new worksheet for it. Make your selection and click the **Finish** button. Your completed chart appears.

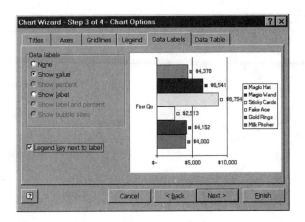

Figure 19.3 Select from various chart appearance options.

TIP **Moving and Resizing a Chart** To move an embedded chart, click anywhere in the chart area and drag it to the new location. To change the size of a chart, select the chart, and then drag one of its *handles* (the black squares that border the chart). Drag a corner handle to change the height and width, or drag a side handle to change only the width. (Note that you can't really resize a chart that is on a sheet by itself.)

TIP **Create a Chart Fast!** To create a chart quickly, select the data you want to use and press **F11**. Excel creates a column chart (the default chart type) on its own sheet. You can switch to that sheet, select the chart, and customize it as needed.

Customizing Your Chart with the Chart Toolbar

You can use the Chart toolbar to change how your chart looks. If the Chart toolbar is not displayed, you can turn it on by opening the **View** menu, selecting **Toolbars**, and then selecting **Chart**.

Table 19.1 shows each button on the Chart toolbar and explains its purpose.

Table 19.1 Buttons on the Chart Toolbar

Button	Name	Use
	Chart Objects	Click here to select the part of the chart you want to change. Optionally, you can simply click the part you want to select.
	Format Object	Click here to change the formatting of the object whose name appears in the Chart Objects text box.
	Chart Type	Click the arrow to change the chart type, from bar to line, for example. If you click the button itself, the displayed chart type will be applied.
	Legend	Click this to display or hide the legend.
	Data Table	Click here to add a data table, a grid which displays the data from which the chart was created.
	By Row	Click here if your data series are stored in rows.
	By Column	Click here if your data series are stored in columns.
	Angle Text Downward	Click here to angle text in selected area downward.
	Angle Text Upward	Click here to angle text in selected area upward.

Saving Charts

The charts you create are part of the current workbook. To save a chart, simply save the workbook that contains the chart. For more details, refer to Lesson 6, "Creating and Saving Workbook Files."

Printing a Chart

If a chart is embedded, it will print when you print the worksheet that contains the chart. If you want to print just the embedded chart, click it to select it, and then open the **File** menu and select **Print**. Make sure that the **Selected Chart** option is turned on. Then click **OK** to print the chart.

If you created a chart on a separate worksheet, you can print the chart separately by printing only that worksheet. For more information about printing, refer to Lesson 9, "Printing Your Workbook."

In this lesson, you learned about the different chart types and how to create them. You also learned how to save and print charts. In the next lesson, you learn how to create a database in Excel.

Learning
Database Basics

In this lesson, you will learn about database basics and how to create your own database.

Database Basics

A *database* is a tool used for storing, organizing, and retrieving information. For example, if you want to save the names and addresses of all the people on your holiday card list, you can create a database and then save the following information for each person: first name, last name, street number, and so on. Each piece of information is entered into a separate *field* (cell) in the list. All of the fields for one person in the list make a *record*.

In Excel, a cell is a field, and a row of field entries makes a record. The column headings in the list are called *field names* in the database. Figure 20.1 shows a database and its component parts.

 Database or Data List? Excel has simplified the database operations by treating the database as a simple *list* of data. You enter the database information just like you would enter data into a worksheet. When you select a command from the Data menu, Excel recognizes the list as a database.

Field names
are used
as column
headings

Each row is
a record

Each cell
contains a
single field
entry

Figure 20.1   The parts of a database.

You must observe the following rules when you enter information into your
database:

- **Field Names**   You must enter field names in the first row of the database.
  For example, you might type **First Name** for the column that will hold first
  names, and you might type **Last Name** for the column that will hold last
  names. Do *not* skip a row between the field names row and the first record.

- **Records**   Each record must be in a separate row, and there cannot be any
  empty rows between records.

- **Same Stuff**   The cells in a given column must contain information of the
  same type. For example, if you have a ZIP code column, all cells in that
  column must contain a ZIP code, and not some other kind of data. A cell
  can be left blank if a particular column does not apply to that record.

- **Calculations**   You can create a *calculated field*, which uses information
  from another field of the same record and produces a result. For example,
  if you have a column called "Sales Amount," you could use a formula to
  create the values in a column called "Sales Commission." (To do so, enter
  a formula, as explained in Lesson 12.)

261

TIP **Record Numbering** You might want to add a column that numbers the records. The record number is likely to be the only thing about the record that won't be repeated in another record, and having a unique field could come in handy in advanced databases. Also, if the records are sorted incorrectly, you can use the numbered column to restore the records to their original order.

Planning a Database

Before you create your database, you should ask yourself these questions:

- What are the fields that make up an individual record? If you are creating the database to take the place of an existing form (a Rolodex card, information sheet, or address list), use that form to determine which fields you need.

- Which types of data might you want to sort by? If you want to sort by last name, make sure that the last name is stored in its own field, and not combined with the first name in a single field. If you want to sort by city, phone number, or ZIP code, make sure that each of these is stored in its own field.

- Which types of data might you want to search for? If you want to search for all contacts who work in a particular sales area, make sure you place sales areas in their own field.

- What is the most often referenced field in the database? (This field should be placed in the first column.)

- What is the longest entry in each column? Use this information to set the column widths. (Or you can make your entries and then use **Format Column AutoFit Selection** to have Excel adjust the column widths.)

Creating a Database

To create a database, you don't have to use any special commands. All you do is enter data into the cells as you would enter data on any worksheet. However, as you enter data, you must follow these guidelines:

- You must enter field names in the top row of the database. Enter the first record just below this field names row.

- Type field entries into each cell in a single row to create a record. (You can leave a field blank, but you may run into problems later when you sort the database—that is, if you sort the database by that particular field.)

- Do *not* leave an empty row between the field names and the records or between any records.

- If you want to enter street numbers with the street names at the beginning of the field (such as 155 State Street), start the entry with an apostrophe so that Excel interprets the entry as text instead of as a numeric value. However, note that if you want to enter, for example, One Washington Square Suite 600, you don't need the apostrophe because it begins with text.

- Keep the records on one worksheet. You cannot have a database that spans several worksheets.

CAUTION

Forget Someone?   To add records to a database, either add the rows above the last row in the database (see Lesson 11, "Inserting and Removing Cells, Rows, and Columns") or select the **Data**, **Form** command and enter the additional records using the data form.

Using Data Forms to Add, Edit, or Delete Records

Data forms are like index cards: there is one data form for each record in the database, as shown in Figure 20.2. You may find it easier to flip through these data form "cards" and edit entries than to edit them as worksheet data. To edit your database using a data form, perform the following steps:

1. Open the **Data** menu and select **Form**. You will see a data form that contains the first record in the database (see Figure 20.2).

2. The number of the current record appears in the upper-right corner of the form. Flip to the form you want to edit by using the scroll bar, pressing the up or down arrow key, or clicking **Find Prev** or **Find Next**.

3. To edit an entry in a record, tab to the text box that contains the entry and type your correction.

4. To delete the current record, click **Delete**.

5. Repeat steps 2–4 to change as many records as needed.

6. Click the **Close** button when you're done using the data form.

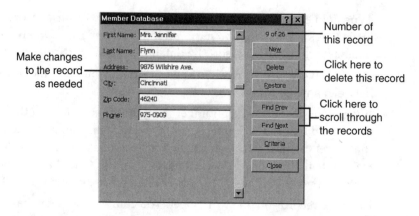

Figure 20.2   The data form.

CAUTION

Come Back!   You can restore field data to what it was before you changed it—provided you haven't changed to a different record. To do so, click the **Restore** button. After you move on to a different record, you'll just have to retype the field data.

You can also use the data form to add records to the database, as described here:

1. Open the **Data** menu and choose **Form** to display the data form.

2. Click the **New** button.

3. Type an entry into each of the text boxes.

4. Repeat steps 2 and 3 to add additional records.

5. When you finish adding records, click **Close**.

TIP   **Template Wizard**   Use the Template Wizard to create a worksheet template into which you can enter some of the data that you later want to save in a database. For example, you could create a sales worksheet and then link it to a client database so you can save information on the items each client purchases. Just open the **Data** menu and select **Template Wizard**. The Template Wizard walks you step by step through linking cells in the template to fields in a database.

In this lesson, you learned about database basics and how to create a database. In the remaining lessons in this section, you'll learn how to use the Small Business Financial Manager with Excel.

Working with the Financial Manager

In this lesson, you'll learn how to start and exit the Small Business Financial Manager, and learn about the program's features.

What Is the Small Business Financial Manager?

The Microsoft Small Business Financial Manager works alongside Excel 97 to help you analyze, manipulate, and summarize your company's bookkeeping and financial records. Financial Manager is a great tool for helping you examine your business data and making better financial decisions. For example, use the Report Wizard to keep track of sales, inventory levels, and expenditures. You can view your entire company's financial data, or simply track an individual account. Then use the What If Wizard to create "what-if" analyses on the data, such as what happens when you increase product prices or increase service costs.

The Small Business Financial Manager offers three key tools to help you examine, manipulate, and analyze accounting data:

Import Wizard   If you use another accounting package, such as Peachtree or Quickbooks, you can import the data into Excel for analysis. Learn more about using this feature in Lesson 22.

Report Wizard   Use the Report Wizard to create comprehensive, detailed reports for viewing your data more clearly. Learn more about using this Wizard in Lesson 23.

What-If Wizard Use this feature to see how your decisions impact your data. Create and save scenarios that show you how a few important changes in your data can affect your bottom line. Find out how to use this Wizard in Lesson 24.

TIP **Installation Help** If you've not yet installed the Small Business Financial Manager, stop and do so now. Turn to Appendix D for installation instructions.

Starting the Small Business Financial Manager

You can start the Small Business Financial Manager from the Excel window, if you have Excel open. When you install Financial Manager, a new Accounting menu is added to Excel's menu bar (see Figure 21.1). If you display the Help menu, you'll also notice new commands for accessing Financial Manager help topics. To start any of the Small Business Financial Manager tools, simply click the **Accounting** menu, as shown in Figure 21.1, and select the appropriate Wizard you want to use.

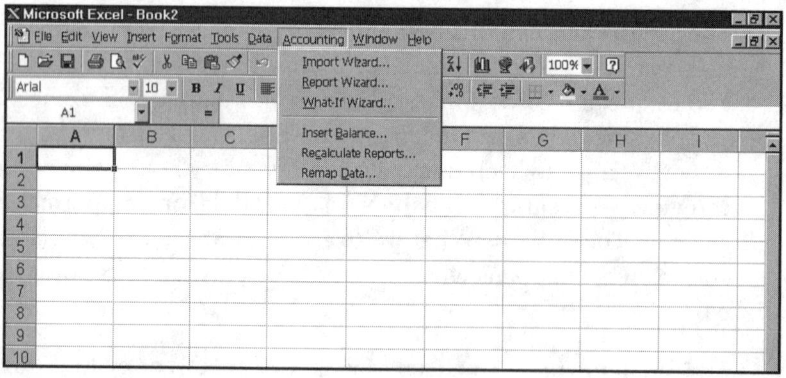

Figure 21.1 An extra menu is added to Excel's menu bar when you install the Small Business Financial Manager.

After choosing a Wizard, the Small Business Financial Manager startup screen appears and the appropriate Wizard dialog box displays.

You can also start the Small Business Financial Manager by clicking its shortcut icon on the Windows 95 desktop. This shortcut icon, shown in Figure 21.2, is automatically added when you install Financial Manager.

Double-click the shortcut icon to open the Excel program and display the Small Business Financial Manager startup screen. If you choose this startup route, you may first encounter a warning box, as shown in Figure 21.3, that cautions you about using macros. Recently, viruses have been showing up attached to macros; click the **Tell Me More** button to learn more about this topic. Or, click the **Enable Macros** button to display the Small Business Financial Manager startup screen.

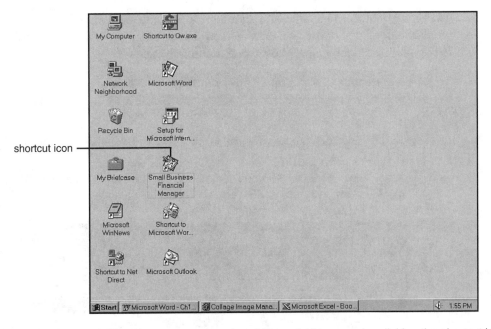

shortcut icon —

Figure 21.2 You can start Excel and Financial Manager by clicking the shortcut icon.

 Macros A record of commonly used keystrokes or computer tasks that you can save and use again and again. Macros can be as simple as turning text bold and italic or complex steps for entering or formatting data.

 Virus A computer program designed to vandalize or harm your system. Some viruses can be very destructive; some are just minor annoyances. Viruses are usually attached to computer files and are passed along by floppy disks or through downloaded files from the Internet. To avoid viruses, use a virus protection program.

CAUTION

Watch Out for Viruses   Macro viruses are computer viruses stored in a workbook's macro when you save the file. When you open a workbook containing a macro virus and activate the macro, the virus can spread. Excel 97 displays a warning box every time you open a workbook that uses macros. If you're sure the file is from a trusted source, select **Enable Macros**. If you're not sure, select **Disable Macros**, which lets you view the macros but not activate them. It's a good idea to run a virus protection program.

The Small Business Financial Manager startup screen (see Figure 21.3) lets you choose to open one of the three Financial Manager Wizards—the same three Wizards found on the new Accounting menu in Excel.

To start a particular Wizard, move your mouse pointer over the area of the screen listing the Wizard, then click. This opens the appropriate Wizard dialog box.

TIP   **It Works with Excel**   Remember, the Small Business Financial Manager works alongside Excel, so when you double-click the **Small Business Financial Manager** shortcut icon, Excel opens onto your screen.

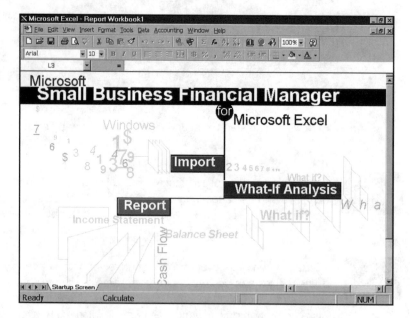

Figure 21.3   The Small Business Financial Manager startup screen.

Exiting the Small Business Financial Manager

To exit Excel and the Small Business Financial Manager, simply close the program using any of the following methods:

- Click the **Close** button in the upper-right corner of the program window.
- Open the **File** menu and select **Exit**.
- Press **Alt+F4** on the keyboard.
- Click the **Control-menu icon** and select **Close**.

If you worked on a file, you'll be prompted to save the file before exiting. For more information about saving Excel files, turn to Lesson 6 in this section of the book.

In this lesson, you learned about Microsoft's Small Business Financial Manager program and how it works alongside Excel. You also learned how to start and exit the program. In the next lesson, you learn how to use the Import Wizard.

Using the Import Wizard

In this lesson, you learn how to use the Import Wizard to import data from other accounting software packages.

Working with the Import Wizard

If you use another accounting software package to keep track of your company's financial data, you can easily import the data into Excel and use Excel's features to view, summarize, and manipulate your data. The Small Business Financial Manager supports the following accounting packages:

BusinessWorks for DOS and Windows (State of the Art, version 9.0)

Simply Accounting for Windows (Computer Associates, version 3.0)

ACCPAC Plus Accounting for DOS (Computer Associates, version 6.1)

DacEasy Accounting for DOS (DacEasy, Inc., version 6.0)

Great Plains Accounting for DOS (Great Plains Software, version 8.0, 8.1, 8.2)

Quickbooks (Intuit, version 3.1, 4.0, Pro 4.0)

M-A-S 90 Evolution/2 (State of the Art, version 1.51)

One-Write Plus Accounting with Payroll for DOS (ADP Company, version 4.03)

Peachtree for Windows (Peachtree Software, Inc., version 3.0, 3.5, 4.0)

Peachtree Complete Accounting for DOS (Peachtree Software, Inc., version 8.0)

Platinum Series for DOS and Windows (Platinum, version 4.1, 4.4)

MV Server/MetaView (Timeline, Inc., version 2.3, 2.4, 2.5)

TIP **Accounting Package Not Listed?** Visit Microsoft's Web site (**http://www.microsoft.com/**) for new filters or call Microsoft Customer Support at 1-800-426-9400 and ask what's available for your software package.

When you import accounting data from another program into Excel, you don't necessarily have to have the accounting package installed on your computer, just the data files you use. If you use QuickBooks, however, it does need to be installed in order for the import to work.

What Data Is Imported with the Import Wizard?

The more detailed your data from the accounting package you use to import from, the more detailed your analysis, reports, and scenarios can be with Small Business Financial Manager. Depending on your existing package, and the way it's set up, you may be limited in the kinds of analysis you can perform. For example, if you're keeping a general ledger on your accounting package and an accounts receivable subsystem, but don't update sales or invoicing data from the subsystem into the general ledger, then you won't be able to create an analysis on individual customers. Table 22.1 describes types of data that can be imported.

Table 22.1 Types of Data that Can Be Imported

Data Type	Imported Information
System information	Includes company name, fiscal year, and accounting periods.
Account information	Includes charts of accounts, posted transactions, product lists, sales force, services, customer/client information, and so on.
Balance sheet information	Beginning year balances for each account, including assets, liabilities, and equity.
General ledger information	Posted general ledger transactions.
Sales information	Includes sales invoice information, such as customers, services/products, quantities sold, and so on.
Product information	Includes inventory balances for stock items.

As you can see from the table above, budget information from your accounting package will not import into Small Business Financial Manager. Also keep in mind that you need to use a 12-period account in order to import into Financial Manager, plus the accounting system should be set up using accrual basis accounting, not cash basis accounting.

Don't Close Out Your Fiscal Year!   Be sure to import your accounting data into Financial Manager before using your accounting software to close out fiscal periods. If you don't, Financial Manager won't be able to import all your transaction details.

CAUTION

In addition to data types, Small Business Financial Manager recognizes various account categories, listed in Table 22.2.

Table 22.2   Account Categories Recognized by Financial Manager

Account Category	Credit or Debit	FSIC	Category Description
1110 Cash	D	CA	Cash accounts and other assets that can be turned into cash
1111 Credit card receipts	D	CCE	Posted credit card receipts
1121 Accounts receivable	D	AR	Trade AR accounts
1122 Allowance for bad debts	D	ABD	Noncollectible trade AR accounts
1130 Inventory	D	INV	Inventory accounts
1190 Other current assets	D	OCA	Current assets from other categories
1211 Property, plant, equipment	D	PPE	Cost of assets
1212 Accumulated depreciation	D	AD	Accumulated depreciation of property, plant, equipment
1290 Other non-current assets	D	ONCA	Other non-current assets aside from property, plant, equipment

Account Category	Credit or Debit	FSIC	Category Description
2110 Accounts payable	C	AP	Payable trade accounts
2120 Short-term debt	C	STD	Debts that are paid off within the current year
2130 Credit cards payable	C	CCP	Recorded credit card purchases
2190 Other current liabilities	C	OCL	Current current liabilities (except accounts payable and short-term debt)
2210 Long-term debt	C	LTD	Debts recorded more than one year in duration
2240 Other non-current liabilities	C	ONCL	All other non-current liabilities
3100 Equity	C	EQ	Accumulated dividends, capital stock, other paid-in capital
3200 Retained savings	C	RS	All prior retained earnings
3999 Revenue/expense clearing	C	RE	Year-end closing account for revenue and expenses
4000 Net sales	C	NS	All sales accounts
5000 Cost of sales	D	COS	All direct costs of sales
6100 Amortization and depreciation	D	ADE	Depreciation and amortization costs
6200 Bad debt expense	D	BDE	All bad debt expense
6300 Officer compensation	D	OC	Expenses for compensation of company officers
6400 Interest expense	D	INT	Recorded interest expense

continues

Table 22.2 Continued

Account Category	Credit or Debit	FSIC	Category Description
6500 Operating expense	D	OOE	All other expenses not recorded elsewhere
7100 Non-operating income	C	ONOI	All revenue not classified as net sales
7200 Non-operating expense	D	ONOE	Other non-operating expenses
8000 Income taxes	D	IT	State and federal taxes paid

Importing with the Import Wizard

The Import Wizard walks you through the necessary steps to import accounting data or use an existing database. A series of four dialog boxes will help you with each step. Simply enter the appropriate information, then click **Next** to continue. To return to a previous step at any time, click the **Back** button. To exit the procedure without completing the import, click the **Cancel** button.

 TIP **I Need Help!** If at any time during the import procedure you need some help, click the **Help** button to open Financial Manager's help system.

1. To import accounting data from another software package into Excel's Small Business Financial Manager, follow these steps:

   From the Excel window, open the Accounting menu and select Import Wizard.

   Or, from the Financial Manager startup screen, click the **Import** button (see Figure 22.1).

2. The Import Wizard dialog box appears, as shown in Figure 22.2. Choose one of the following options:

   • Select the **Import** option to import accounting data, then click **Next** to continue.

   • If you're updating from an existing database, click the **Update** option, and then click **Next**.

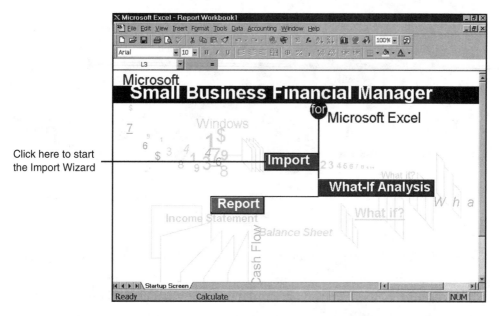

Click here to start
the Import Wizard

Figure 22.1   The Small Business Financial Manager startup screen.

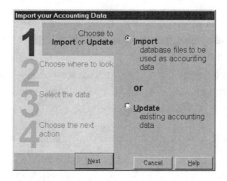

Figure 22.2   The Import Wizard dialog box.

3. In the next Import Wizard screen (see Figure 22.3), select the **Look On** option to search all of your drives for accounting data. To look only in specific folders, click the **In Specific Folders** option, and then select the folders you want to search. Click the folder from the list, and then click the **Add Folder to List** button.

275

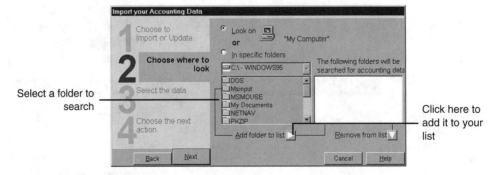

Select a folder to
search

Click here to
add it to your
list

Figure 22.3   Specify where you want to look for accounting data on your system.

4. Click **Next** to continue.

5. The third box lets you select the accounting data for importing. Click the data you want, and then click the **Next** button to continue.

6. The next box prompts you about the amount of time the import will take; click **Yes** to continue.

7. When the import is complete, click **Finish**.

After importing the accounting data, it's a good idea to see how Small Business Financial Manager mapped the data into its account categories. Financial Manager may not be able to match the right account categories, which in turn affects any reports or scenarios you might generate. For that reason, take a moment and check. If any categories need correcting, you can do so now. Follow these steps:

1. Open the **Accounting** menu and select **Remap Data**.

2. The Select a Company for Remapping Accounts box appears. Select the company you want to remap and click **OK**.

3. The Map Your Accounts box appears. Use the + or - symbols in front of the account categories to expand or collapse the subcategories.

4. To move an account to another category, select the account, and click **Cut**.

5. Locate the category you want it moved to, and then click **Paste**.

6. Continue following steps 3 through 5 to rearrange the categories as needed. Click **OK** when finished.

CAUTION

Caution!   It's better to remap your data before creating reports or scenarios. If you don't, then any reports and scenarios won't reflect the remapping changes you make using the preceding steps.

After importing your accounting data, you're ready to create reports and what-if scenarios. You'll learn how to use these features in the remaining lessons in this part of the book.

In this lesson, you learned how to use the Import Wizard to import data from other accounting packages into Excel 97. In the next lesson, you learn how to work with the Report Wizard.

Using the Report Wizard

23

In this lesson, you learn how to use the Report Wizard to generate detailed financial reports.

Working with the Report Wizard

There are dozens of different reports you can create with Small Business Financial Manager and your financial data. The Report Wizard can walk you through each step for generating a report. There are seven basic financial reports you can create, plus many variations of each one. Here's a rundown of the basic reports you can create:

Balance Sheet   Use this type of report to reflect a snapshot of your company's financial status, such as assets, equity, and liabilities.

Trial Balance   Trace your account's audit trail of balance and net change for your company for a particular accounting period. The balance includes opening account balance, current period activity of debits and credits, and a closing balance.

Income Statement   Detail your company's performance over a specific amount of time, including profit or loss, with a report that summarizes revenues and expenses.

Cash Flow   Show your company's cash flow, in and out, and spot potential problems.

Changes in Stockholders Equity   Use this report to analyze how much stock ownership is controlled by you and your investors and your creditors.

Sales Analysis Find out sales, expense, and gross profit using a PivotTable for each area of your business.

Ratios Use this type of report to calculate ratios and quickly examine your company's financial status.

CAUTION

Remember! In order to generate reports, accounting information must be imported from an accounting package or created in Excel. A report will only be as detailed as your accounting data.

For each of these report categories, you'll find specific types of reports you can use. For example, if you create a report based on your company's balance sheet, the Report Wizard lets you choose from a regular balance sheet (showing your company's financial condition at the end of a certain period of time), a balance sheet with scenarios (showing projected conditions based on what-if scenarios), or a balance sheet with prior year comparisons (showing your financial condition that includes a look at previous year's figures). The different types of reports you create allow you to look at different parts of your financial data.

TIP **What-If Scenarios?** Learn more about using what-if scenarios to project new conditions on your financial data in Lesson 24.

TIP **Financial Examples** Small Business Financial Manager comes with several examples you can refer to based on a fictitious company called Volcano Coffee. Be sure to check them out.

Creating a Report with the Report Wizard

To build a report using Report Wizard, follow these steps:

1. From the Excel window, open the **Accounting** menu and select **Report Wizard**.

   Or, from the Small Business Financial Manager startup screen, click the Report button.

2. The Report Wizard dialog box appears on-screen, as shown in Figure 23.1. From the **Financial Reports** list box, select the type of report you want to use.

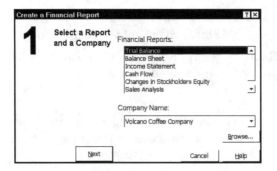

Figure 23.1   The Report Wizard helps you create a financial report.

3. From the **Company Name** drop-down list, select the financial database you want to use. If your company's database isn't listed, click the **Browse** button and locate the appropriate folder and file.

TIP   **What Database Do I Use?**   You can use a database you just imported or use one from another folder or network server. Use the **Browse** button to help locate the database folder and file.

4. To continue, click the **Next** button.

5. The second step in the Report Wizard, shown in Figure 23.2, lets you select a specific report type from the **Report Types** list box. Simply click the one you want to use.

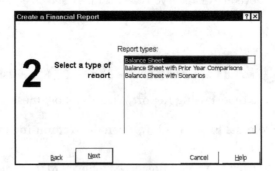

Figure 23.2   Select the type of report you want to use.

6. Click **Next** to continue.

7. The third step in the Report Wizard lets you choose the end date for your report (see Figure 23.3). Click the end date you want to use.

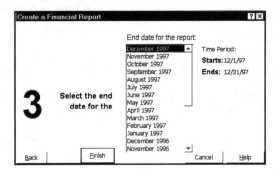

Figure 23.3 Select an end date for your report.

8. (Optional) If you want to use scenarios with the report, click the **Next** button and select the scenario.

9. After making selections for all three Report Wizard steps, click the **Finish** button.

10. The report is displayed on your screen, as shown in Figure 23.4.

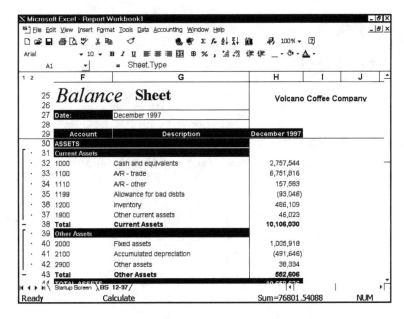

Figure 23.4 The new report appears in the Excel window.

You can now manipulate the data in your report, perform scenarios with the What-If Wizard (see Lesson 24), print your reports, and more, using Excel's spreadsheet tools. To save the report, use the steps described in Lesson 6 of this part.

Creating a Custom Report

If you prefer to create your own kind of accounting data report, you can easily do so from the Report Wizard dialog box. Follow these steps:

1. Open Excel's **Insert** menu and select **Worksheet**.
2. Open the **Accounting** menu and select **Insert Balance**. This opens the Insert Account Balance dialog box, similar to the one shown in Figure 23.5.

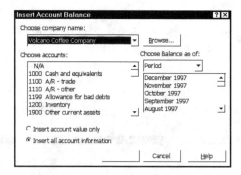

Figure 23.5 The Insert Account Balance dialog box.

3. In the **Choose Company Name** drop-down list box, select the database you want to base your report on. (If your database isn't listed, use the **Browse** button to locate it.)
4. In the **Choose Accounts** list box, click the accounts to be included. To select multiple accounts, simply hold down the **Ctrl** key and click account names.
5. In the **Choose Balance as Of** drop-down list box, select **Period**, **Quarter**, or **Year;** then choose the date for the time period you want to use.
6. Select the **Insert All Account Information** option.
7. Click **OK** and you have a customized report.

Showing or Hiding Financial Report Data

If you plan on sharing the report with others, you can choose to hide or show transaction details. The following methods can be used to show or hide details in your report:

- To show a detailed list of accounts for any account category, double-click the account category cell.
- To show details behind a particular calculated column, click the + button at the top of the column.
- To show a separate Drill Down report revealing transaction details for a particular value, double-click any cell bordered by a thick gray line on the bottom and right sides.
- To hide a detailed list for an account category, click the – button at the far left end of the row.
- To hide a column (collapse), click the – button at the top of the column.

Take a look at Figure 23.6 to locate the hide/show controls.

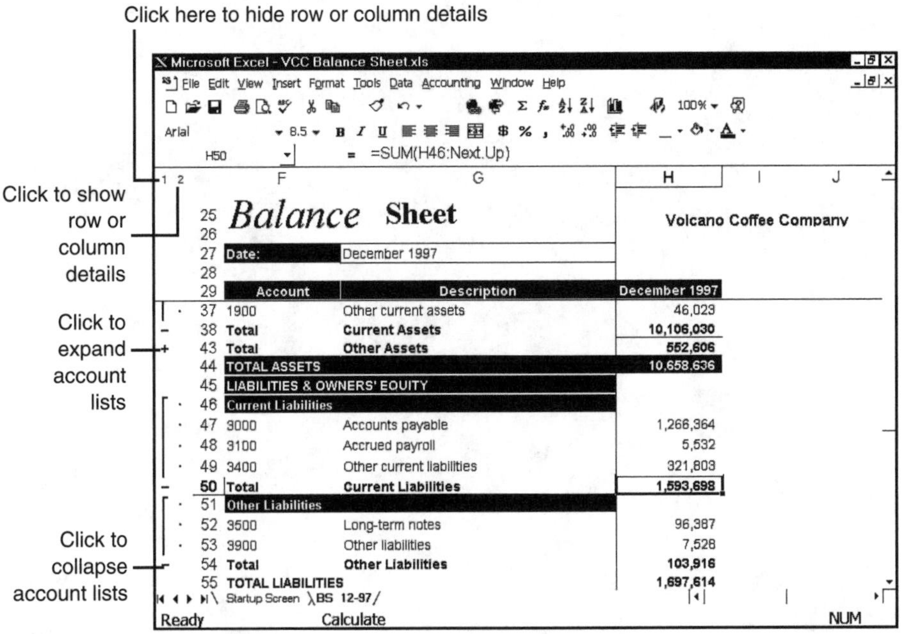

Figure 23.6 You can use the Show/Hide buttons to expand or collapse account details.

TIP **Need to Print Your Report?** Refer to Lesson 9 in this section for more information.

TIP **Integrating Tips** To learn more about integrating other parts of the Office 97 programs into Excel report worksheets, check out Part 6 of this book for more details.

In this lesson, you learned how to use the Report Wizard to create professional reports using Small Business Financial Manager. In the next lesson, you learn how to work with what-if scenarios.

Working with What-If Scenarios

24

In this lesson, you learn how to use the What-If Wizard to create what-if projections based on your financial data.

What Are What-Ifs?

What-if scenarios are simply speculations you can make on your financial and accounting data to determine different outcomes. Just like the name implies, what-if scenarios involve playing with future projections, such as "what if you increased product prices," "what if you dropped shipping charges," "what if you purchased more office equipment." With what-if scenarios, you can plug different values into a copy of your existing spreadsheet data and find out how the changes will affect your financial data and your overall bottom line.

For example, perhaps you're purchasing a new company car and need a general idea of how much your monthly car payment will be. If you've already got a spreadsheet detailing your current loan payment for a $20,000 car at 3.9% interest, but want to find out what the payment might be for a $25,000 or $30,000 car using different interest rates, a what-if scenario can help you out.

The Small Business Financial Manager has a what-if tool designed specifically for creating what-if analysis on your company's financial data. It's called the *What-If Wizard*. You can use the Wizard to create a What-If Overview worksheet. You can quickly manipulate values, select analysis topics, and see what happens to your financial data. There's no limit to the scenarios you can create:

- Analyze your current pricing and what would happen if you increase product prices.

- Analyze your sales revenue, and see what happens if you increase your sales revenues by 10%.

- Find out the effects of changing your inventory stocking levels, or see a breakdown of products or services.

- Examine the effects of taking out another loan or paying off an existing one.

- What would happen to your numbers if you sell your property or used equipment?

These are just a scant few of the types of analysis you can perform using the What-If Wizard. You can designate the types of analysis you want to see, and let Financial Manager help you with the steps needed to perform them.

Using the What-If Wizard

To use the Small Business Financial Manager What-If Wizard, follow the steps below:

1. From the Excel window, open the **Accounting** menu and select **What-If Wizard**.

Or, from the Small Business Financial Manager startup screen, click the **What-If Analysis** button.

2. The What-If Wizard dialog box appears on-screen, as shown in Figure 24.1. Choose a company financial database to use. If yours isn't listed, click the **Browse** button and locate the database.

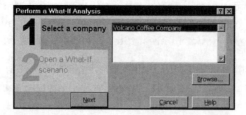

Figure 24.1 The dialog boxes will walk you through the steps for building a what-if scenario.

3. To continue, click the **Next** button and the box displays options for opening a new or existing scenario (see Figure 24.2).

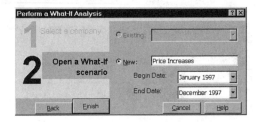

Figure 24.2 In step 2 of the What-If Wizard, you can choose to open a new or existing scenario.

4. To create a new scenario, click the **New** option and type in a name for the scenario. To use an existing scenario, click the **Existing** option and select a previously saved scenario from the drop-down list.

TIP **How Lengthy Is Your Name?** The scenario name you type in can be up to 50 characters long.

5. Next, select a starting date for the scenario in the **Begin Date** box and an ending date in the **End Date** box.

6. Click **Finish** to continue.

7. The Save Scenario Workbook As box appears, as shown in Figure 24.3. Save your scenario by clicking the **Save** button.

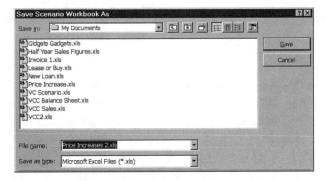

Figure 24.3 The Financial Manager prompts you to save your scenario.

8. The What-If Overview page appears on-screen, as shown in Figure 24.4. From here, you can use the various worksheet tools to specify analysis topics and build your what-if scenario.

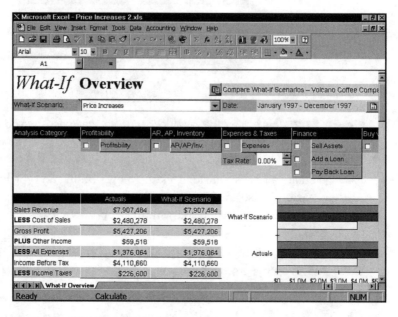

Figure 24.4 The What-If Overview worksheet.

Working with the What-If Overview Worksheet

Ready to perform a what-if analysis? The What-If Overview worksheet has three areas to work in, as detailed in Figure 24.5:

- The top rows have buttons for saving, opening, and deleting scenarios.
- The middle area of the worksheet contains analysis categories: Profitability; AR, AP, Inventory; Expenses & Taxes; Finanace; Buy vs. Lease. The topic buttons open other worksheets and wizards for changing what-if values.
- The bottom of the worksheet displays a miniature of your income statement and a graph that lets you see comparisons between the scenario you create and your actual data.

The top rows have buttons for saving,
opening, and deleting scenarios

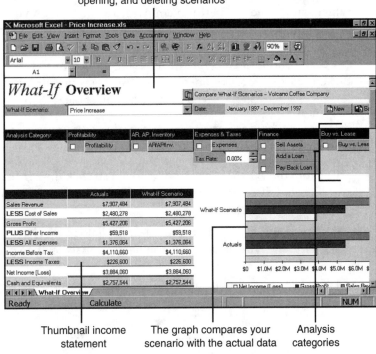

Thumbnail income   The graph compares your   Analysis
statement   scenario with the actual data   categories

Figure 24.5 The What-If Overview has three areas to work in.

Table 24.1 shows what the What-If Overview buttons do.

Table 24.1 What-If Overview Button Functions

Button	Function
	Use this button to compare what-if scenarios on a Summary Page worksheet.
New	Click this button to start a new scenario based on the values in the current scenario.
Save	Saves the current scenario.
Delete	Deletes the current what-if scenario.
?	Opens the Financial Manager Help window.

Using Analysis Categories

When you're ready to perform a nitty-gritty analysis on your what-if scenario, the middle of the Overview worksheet is the place to be. You'll notice five columns in Figure 24.5 that each represent a particular analysis category. The category buttons (located below the category headings for each column), when clicked, start Wizards or open other worksheets pertaining to the selected category. Some categories have more button choices than others.

To show you how to use a what-if scenario and a specific analysis category, the following steps tell you how to analyze your pricing:

1. From the What-If Overview worksheet, click the **Profitability** button (located directly below the Profitability category heading in the middle of the worksheet).

2. This opens the Profitability Analysis dialog box, shown in Figure 24.6. Select the type of category you want to analyze, then click **OK**.

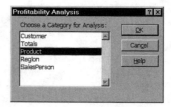

Figure 24.6   The Profitability Analysis dialog box.

3. The Profitability Analysis worksheet opens on-screen, similar to the one shown in Figure 24.7. From here, you can change values and view their effects on your data. For example, at the top of the worksheet, click the **View** drop-down button and select **Price View**.

4. In the **Unit Price** column, adjust the pricing for your products; type in new values for each item you want to change. In this particular scenario, you can find out what a difference pricing makes to your financial data.

5. To see a graph of your changes, scroll to the right of the worksheet to the **Graphical View** column, click the drop-down list, and select **Unit Price** to reflect the price changes in the graph.

Click here to display the drop-down list

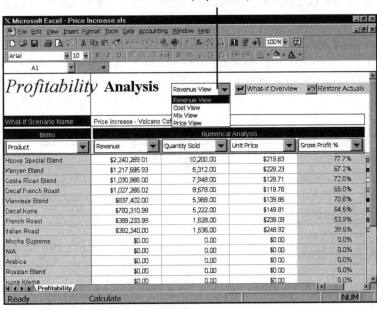

Figure 24.7 The Profitability Analysis worksheet.

TIP **Can I Add a New Item to the Sheet?** To add a new item to your database, click the **Add** selection below the **Items** column heading, and type in the appropriate information for the item as prompted. When finished, the item is added to the worksheet.

After creating a what-if scenario, you can save it or print it out. It's a good idea to save the scenario under a unique name so you can easily find it and use it again. You can save a scenario just like you save a worksheet. Click the **Save** button and give it a name. Click the **What-if Overview** button to return to the What-If Overview sheet. You can then examine the graphs to compare the what-if scenario to your actual data.

TIP **Do a Little Comparison** Use the Summary Page worksheet to compare your actual income statement to the scenarios you create. Be sure to save your scenarios first, then return to the What-If Overview sheet and select the Summary Page button.

Other What-If Scenarios You Can Use

There are five analysis categories you can use to perform what-if scenarios on your data. The previous steps showed you how to use the Profitability scenario. Each of the five categories lets you create a scenario; the Finance category lets you create three different what-if scenarios. Table 24.2 gives a description of each of the what-if scenarios you can create using the analysis category buttons:

Table 24.2 What-If Scenarios

Scenario	Description
Profitability	Creates a Profitability Analysis worksheet to view changes in your product mix pricing. You can choose to view revenue, total costs of sales or unit costs, product mix, and changes in unit prices.
AR/AP/Inv.	Opens the AR/AP/Inventory Analysis worksheet which you can use to adjust accounts receivable, accounts payable, and inventory dollar amounts or number of days. For example, find out what would happen if you reduced inventory to stock your product for 30 days of sales rather than 60.
Expenses	Creates an Expense Analysis worksheet that lets you adjust general expenses and see how the changes affect your profits. For example, what would happen if you gave your employees a raise or pared down your marketing costs?
Sell Assets	Opens the Sell Assests Wizard and creates a Finance Analysis worksheet which shows you a balance sheet summary of the effects of the sale of an asset, such as selling a computer or office copier machine.
Add a Loan	Opens the Add New Loan Wizard and creates a Finance Analysis worksheet that shows the effects of adding a new loan to your account. The worksheet details the effect on your company's cash position and you can even view a payment schedule to see what monthly payments would be like.
Pay Back Loan	Opens the Pay Back Loan Wizard and creates a Finance Analysis worksheet to show what a loan payoff will do to your finances.
Buy vs. Lease	Opens the Buy versus Lease Wizard and creates a Lease Analysis worksheet you can use to compare costs of leasing, buying with a loan, or paying cash.

TIP **Using the Wizards** Learn how to use the Buy versus Lease Wizard in Lesson 25 and the Add a Loan Wizard in Lesson 26.

In this lesson, you learned how to use the What-If Wizard to create what-if scenarios. In the next lesson, you'll learn how to use the Lease Wizard.

Analyzing a Lease Option with the Lease Wizard

In this lesson, you learn how to use the Buy Versus Lease Wizard to determine the differences in buying or leasing an asset.

Using the Analyze Buy Versus Lease Wizard

In the previous lesson, you learned how to use the What-If Wizard to speculate how changes you make to values in your accounting database will affect your bottom line. In this lesson, you continue building on those skills, by learning how to analyze a common decision among business owners—whether to lease or buy.

The Small Business Financial Manager, in addition to all the other report and analysis tools, comes with the Analyze Buy Versus Lease Wizard. With this Wizard, you can carefully evaluate various financing options for accumulating assets of any kind; for example, if your company needs new office equipment or perhaps a new delivery truck. The Buy Versus Lease Wizard can help you determine which course to take, whether it's buy new, used, lease, or pay cash (in full and up front).

Starting the Analyze Buy Versus Lease Wizard

The first step to using the Buy Versus Lease Wizard is to start a What-If Scenario or open an existing scenario. Next, you must start the Buy Versus Lease Wizard and enter the appropriate data. The last phase of the procedure will open the Lease Analysis worksheet where you can manipulate the data and see the results of making different decisions about buying and leasing.

The following steps will walk you through the entire procedure:

1. From the Excel window, open the **Accounting** menu and select **What-If Wizard**.

   Or, from the Small Business Financial Manager startup screen, click the **What-If Analysis** button.

2. The What-If Wizard dialog box appears on-screen. Choose a company financial database to use. If yours isn't listed, click the **Browse** button and locate the database.

 TIP **Using the What-If Wizard** Turn back to Lesson 24 in this section to learn more about using the What-If Wizard to create financial scenarios.

3. To continue, click the **Next** button and the box displays options for opening a new or existing scenario.

4. To create a new scenario, click the **New** option and type in a name for the scenario. To use an existing scenario, click the **Existing** option and select a previously saved scenario from the drop-down list.

5. Next, select a starting date for accessing any particular portion of your financial data in the **Begin Date** box and an ending date in the **End Date** box.

6. Click **Finish** to continue.

7. The Save Scenario Workbook As box appears. Save your scenario by clicking the **Save** button.

8. The What-If Overview page appears on-screen, as shown in Figure 25.1. Scroll to the right of the worksheet to locate the Buy vs. Lease category and click the Buy Vs. Lease button.

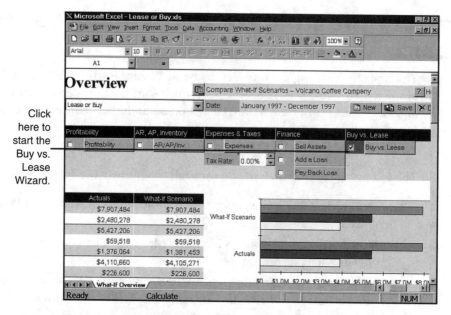

Click here to start the Buy vs. Lease Wizard.

Figure 25.1   The What-If Overview worksheet.

TIP   **Entering the Marginal Income Tax Rate**   If you want to calculate tax benefits in your scenario, be sure to enter a tax rate in the Tax Rate cell before selecting the Buy vs. Lease button.

9. The Analyze Buy Versus Lease Wizard appears, as shown in Figure 25.2. Fill out the fields for each of the following options. You don't have to add dollar signs, percent signs, or commas to the entries. You must fill out all fields before continuing.

Name of Asset   Type in a name of the asset, such as Car or Computer.

Purchase Price   Enter the original price you expect to pay, including registration or license fees.

Date of Purchase   Use the drop-down list to select a time period for the scenario.

Sales Tax Rate   Enter sales tax that applies.

Number of Months Asset Held   Type in how long you plan to hold the asset.

Estimated Resale Value   Enter the amount you can get for selling the asset.

Opportunity Cost of Capital   Enter the opportunity cost of spending money for this asset—the money you'd lose by making this purchase instead of investing the money. (If necessary, use a Ratio report to help you with this number. Create a yearly rate Ratio report for a 12-month span of return on net worth ratios.)

Depreciation Life in Years   Estimate the depreciation life of the asset.

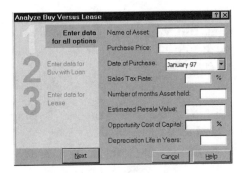

Figure 25.2   Fill out the first Wizard dialog box.

10. Click the **Next** button to continue and the second Wizard dialog box appears, as shown in Figure 25.3.

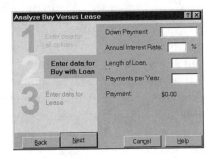

Figure 25.3   The second Wizard dialog box.

11. In the second Wizard box, enter the data for purchasing the asset through a loan. You must fill in each field, and then click **Next** to continue.

Down Payment Enter the amount of your down payment if buying the asset.

Annual Interest Rate Enter an interest rate for the loan.

Length of Loan Type in the number of years for the loan.

Payments per Year Type in the number of payments you will make per year.

TIP **Check Out Your Payments** After entering all the pertinent information about buying the asset, the bottom of the dialog box shows the monthly payment amount.

12. The third Wizard box lets you enter leasing data. Fill out each field listed below, and then click **Finish**.

Initial Payment Enter the amount needed to begin the lease, including first payment and registration fees.

Security Deposit Enter the amount of a possible security deposit you may be required to make.

Monthly Payment Type in the amount you expect to pay each month, plus taxes.

Residual Value Enter the amount it would cost you to buy the asset at the end of the lease. Don't forget to include extra charges and fees (such as excess mileage) that might inflate the residual value.

Other Outflows/Inflows Enter any payments (outflow) or returns (inflow) you may encounter at the end of the lease, such as return of security deposit. *Outflow* includes any additional costs involved at the end of the lease or loan (such as appraisal fees), inflow includes money you receive (such as the resale amount if you sell the asset). (Net inflow should be entered as a negative number.)

13. The Lease Analysis worksheet now appears on-screen, as shown in Figure 25.4. From here, you can experiment with different costs, interest rates, and other values to determine their effect on your finances.

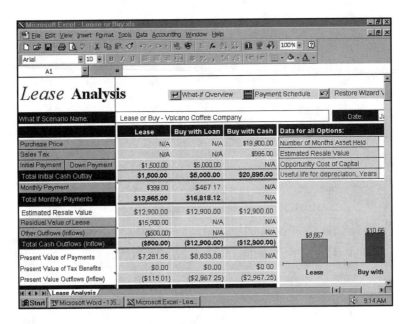

Figure 25.4 The Lease Analysis worksheet.

Working with the Lease Analysis Worksheet

The Lease Analysis worksheet shows you cost comparisons of leasing, buying with a loan, or purchasing the asset with cash. You can change the values in this worksheet to see what different options may do to your costs. Notice the amounts are divided into three sections (rows) on the worksheet:

Total Initial Cash Outlay This section summarizes up-front costs involved with starting the purchase or lease of the asset.

Total Monthly Payments This section totals all the monthly payments involved for the loan or lease for the life of the loan or lease.

Total Cash Outflows (Inflow) This row summarizes the costs involved at the end of the loan or lease, including any amount you may receive back. For example, if you sell the asset at its fully depreciated value, or if you're leasing and receive your security deposit back, the value is an inflow. Any additional costs tacked on at the end of your lease are considered outflows.

299

You can change a value by clicking the appropriate button for the value in the left column of the worksheet. For example, to change the monthly payment, click the **Monthly Payment** button. This opens the Wizard box where you can change the values you entered.

The graph located at the far right of the worksheet shows comparisons of total costs for each option. Table 25.1 explains how to use the buttons at the top of the worksheet.

Table 25.1 Lease Analysis Worksheet Buttons

Button	Function
↵	Returns you to the Overview worksheet.
▦	Creates an amortization table of loan payments.
↩	Restores the original analysis values.
▦	Opens the Windows calculator.

TIP **Need Help?** Click the **Help** button at the top, right side of the worksheet to access Financial Manager's Help window.

In this lesson, you learned how to use the Buy Versus Lease Wizard to make a what-if scenario comparing the costs of buying or leasing an asset. In the next lesson, you learn how to use the Add New Loan Wizard.

Analyzing a New Loan with the New Loan Wizard

In this lesson, you learn how to use the New Loan Wizard to speculate how a new loan will affect your financial data.

Working with the Add New Loan Wizard

In previous lessons, you learned how to use the What-If Wizard to create different kinds of scenarios. Depending on the type of scenario you're creating, various Wizards come into play. For example, in Lesson 25 you learned to use the Buy Versus Lease Wizard to make a Lease Analysis worksheet. In this lesson, you learn how to use the Add New Loan Wizard to create a Finance Analysis worksheet that you can use to see how a new loan will affect your company's finances.

Keep in mind that the Small Business Financial Manager has lots of different Wizards and worksheets you can use to help you clearly see the impact changes make on your financial data. Step-by-step, Wizards help you pinpoint the data you want to examine; then it's up to you to manipulate the data and see what happens when you change things. For more information about working with scenarios, revisit Lesson 24 in this section of the book.

Using the Add New Loan Wizard

The first step in using the Add New Loan Wizard is to start a What-If Scenario or open an existing scenario. Next, you must start the Add New Loan Wizard and enter the appropriate data. The last phase of the procedure will open the

Finance Analysis worksheet, where you can manipulate the data and see the results of taking out a new loan.

Follow these steps to walk through the entire procedure:

1. From the Excel window, open the **Accounting** menu and select **What-If Wizard**.

   Or, from the Small Business Financial Manager startup screen, click the **What-If Analysis** button.

2. The What-If Wizard dialog box appears on-screen. Choose a company financial database to use. If yours isn't listed, click the **Browse** button and locate the database.

3. To continue, click the **Next** button and the box displays options for opening a new or existing scenario.

4. To create a new scenario, click the **New** option and type in a name for the scenario. To use an existing scenario, click the **Existing** option and select a previously saved scenario from the drop-down list.

5. Next, select a starting date for accessing any particular portion of your financial data in the **Begin Date** box and an ending date in the **End Date** box.

6. Click **Finish** to continue.

7. The Save Scenario Workbook As box appears. Save your scenario by clicking the **Save** button.

8. The What-If Overview page appears on-screen, as shown in Figure 26.1. Scroll to the right of the worksheet to locate the **Finance** category and click the **Add a Loan** button.

9. The Add New Loan Wizard appears, as shown in Figure 26.2. Fill out the fields for each of the options, as described below. You don't have to add dollar signs, percent signs, or commas to the entries. You must fill out all fields before continuing.

   Loan or Lender Name   Enter the lender name or a name for the loan.

   Account Number   Select an account to place the loan in; use the drop-down arrow to display a list of your loan accounts.

   First Payment Date   Use the drop-down list to select a date for the first payment on this loan.

   Amount of Loan   Enter the total amount of the loan.

   Annual Interest Rate   Type in the interest rate you hope to use.

Length of Loan Enter the number of years for the loan.

Payments per Year Enter the number of payments you expect to make each year.

Click here to start the Add New Loan Wizard

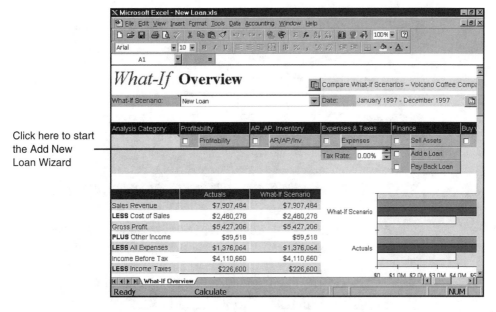

Figure 26.1 The What-If Overview worksheet.

 TIP **Check Out Your Payments** After entering in all the pertinent information about the loan, the bottom of the dialog box shows the monthly payment amount.

Figure 26.2 Fill out each field in the dialog box.

10. Click the **Finish** button. The Finance Analysis worksheet now appears on-screen, as shown in Figure 26.3. From here, you can experiment with different values involved with the loan and determine their effect on your finances.

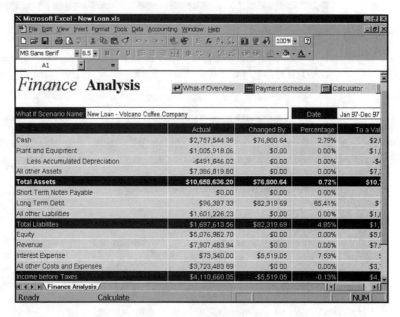

Figure 26.3 The Finance Analysis worksheet.

The Finance Analysis worksheet shows you how your data changes when introducing a new loan. You can change the values in this worksheet to see what different options may do to your costs. Table 26.1 explains how to use the buttons at the top of the worksheet.

Table 26.1 Add New Loan Worksheet Buttons

Button	Function
	Returns you to the Overview worksheet.
	Creates an amortization table of loan payments.

Button	Function
	Opens the Windows calculator.
?	Opens the Financial Manager Help window.

In this lesson, you learned how to use the Add New Loan Wizard to speculate about adding a new loan to your accounts. This completes the lessons for Part II of this book.

Outlook

Starting and
Exiting Outlook

In this lesson, you learn to start Outlook, learn about the various screen elements, and exit the program.

Introducing Outlook

Microsoft's newest Office 97 program, Outlook, is the perfect tool for organizing your daily business tasks. With Outlook, you can create appointments, manage e-mail messages, plan your calendar, generate to-do lists, keep a journal, organize notes, schedule meetings, and more. Previous versions of Microsoft Office used a similar tool called Schedule+, but the new and greatly expanded Outlook picks up where Schedule+ left off. Outlook 97 is a personal management tool that can help you keep track of your everyday business tasks and communication.

In this section of the book, you learn all the basic steps needed to utilize Outlook's many features and put them to work for your small business. In Part VI, you find ideas and suggestions for using Outlook along with the other applications to get the most out of the Office 97 suite of programs.

TIP **Outlook Enhancements** Microsoft is also adding enhancements on their Web site that you can download and install to use with Outlook. For example, you can add an enhancement that turns electronic business cards you find on the Internet (called vCards) into Outlook contacts. For more information about Outlook enhancements, and any other Office 97 enhancements, refer to Appendix D at the back of this book.

Starting Outlook

You start Outlook from the Windows desktop. After starting the program, you can leave it open on your screen, or you can minimize it. Either way, you can access it at any time during your workday.

To start Microsoft Outlook, follow these steps:

1. From the Windows desktop, click the **Start** button and choose **Programs**, **Microsoft Outlook**. The Choose Profile dialog box appears.

Profile Information about you and your communications services that is created automatically when you install Outlook.

2. Click **OK** to accept the default profile and open Microsoft Outlook. Figure 1.1 shows the Outlook screen that appears. (In Windows NT, Outlook cannot detect an existing e-mail provider. The user is prompted to set up the profile. If you need help, see your system administrator.)

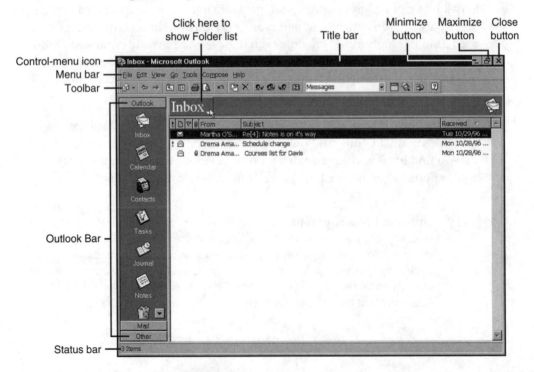

Figure 1.1   The Outlook screen includes many icons and items you'll use in your daily routine.

Understanding the Screen

The Outlook screen includes items you can use to navigate and operate the program. If you do not see some of the items listed below on your screen, open the **View** menu and select the command for the appropriate element (such as Toolbars, Status Bar, Folder List, or Outlook Bar). A check mark in front of an item means the item is currently showing.

Table 1.1 describes the elements you see in the opening screen.

Table 1.1 Elements of the Outlook Window

Element	Description
Title bar	Includes the name of the application and current folder, plus the Window's Minimize, Maximize, and Close buttons.
Control-menu button	Provides such commands as Move, Size, Minimize, and Close, with which you control the Outlook window.
Minimize button	Reduces the Outlook window to a button on the taskbar; to restore the window to its original size, click the button on the taskbar.
Maximize button	Enlarges the Outlook window to cover the Windows desktop. When the window is maximized, the Maximize button changes to a Restore button that you can click to return the window to its previous size.
Close (X) button	Closes the Outlook program.
Menu bar	Contains menus of commands you can use to perform tasks in the program.
Toolbar	Includes icons that serve as shortcuts for common commands, such as creating a new message or printing a message.
Show Folder list	Displays the current folder. Click this to display a list of Personal Folders you can open.
Outlook Bar	Displays icons representing folders: Inbox, Calendar, Contacts, and so on. Click an icon to change to the folder it names.
Information Viewer	Displays the contents of the selected folder.
Status bar	Displays information about what's in the Information Viewer.

continues

Table 1.1 Continued

Element	Description
Office Assistant	Displays help for specific topics, and enables you to view tips or select the help you need.

TIP **Finding a Toolbar Button's Purpose** If you're ever in doubt about what a particular toolbar button does, you can hold the mouse pointer over the button to view a description of the tool's function.

Exiting Outlook

When you're finished with Outlook, you can close the program in a couple of different ways. To close Outlook, do one of the following:

- Choose **File**, **Exit** (to remain connected to the mail program).
- Choose **File**, **Exit** and **Log Off** (to disconnect from the mail program, if necessary).
- Double-click the application's **Control-menu** icon.
- Click the application's **Control-menu** icon and choose **Close** from the menu.
- Press **Alt+F4**.
- Click the **Close** (X) button at the right end of Outlook's title bar.

Do I Need to Log Off or Not? You will eventually need to log off; however, you may want to remain attached to the mail server to receive mail during your workday.

CAUTION

In this lesson, you learned to start and exit Outlook. In the next lesson, you learn about Outlook's tools and controls.

Using Outlook Tools

In this lesson, you learn to change views in Outlook, use the Outlook Bar, and use the folder list.

Using the Outlook Bar

Outlook's components are organized by folder. There is a folder for e-mail, a folder for the calendar, and so on. The Outlook Bar is a tool you can use to quickly change folders in Outlook. The icons in the Outlook Bar represent all of the folders available to you and provide shortcuts to getting to the contents of those folders. Figure 2.1 shows the Outlook Bar.

There are three groups within the Outlook Bar: Outlook, Mail, and Other. Each group contains related folders in which you can work.

- The **Outlook** group contains folders for working with different features in Outlook, such as the Inbox, Calendar, Tasks, and so on.
- The **Mail** group contains folders for organizing and managing your mail.
- The **Other** group contains folders on your computer for working outside of Outlook.

To switch from one group to another, click the **Outlook**, **Mail**, or **Other** button in the Outlook Bar. The Outlook group is displayed by default.

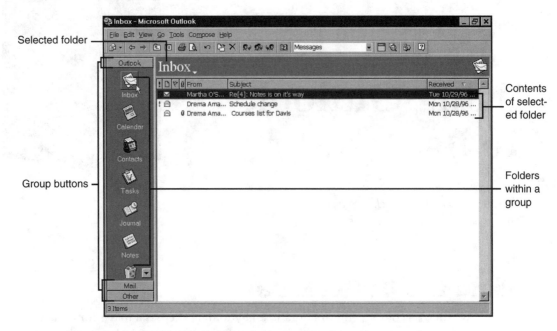

Selected folder

Group buttons

Contents of select-ed folder

Folders within a group

Figure 2.1   Use the Outlook Bar to view various items in your work.

The Outlook Group Folders

The Outlook group's folders in the Outlook Bar enable you to access your work in Outlook. That includes your mail messages, appointments, address list, and so on. Table 2.1 describes each of the folders within the Outlook group.

Table 2.1   Outlook Group Folders

Folder	Description
Inbox	Includes messages you've received via e-mail.
Calendar	Contains your appointments, events, scheduled meetings, and so on.
Contacts	Lists names and addresses of the people with whom you commu-nicate.
Tasks	Includes any tasks you have on your to-do list.
Journal	Contains all journal entries, such as phone logs, meeting notes, and so on.
Notes	Lists notes you write to yourself or others.
Deleted Items	Includes any items you've deleted from other folders.

The Mail Group Folders

The Mail group folders provide a method of organizing your incoming and outgoing e-mail messages. Table 2.2 describes each folder in the Mail group.

Table 2.2   Mail Group Folders

Folder	Description
Inbox	Contains all received messages.
Sent Items	Stores all messages you've sent.
Outbox	Contains messages to be sent.
Deleted Items	Holds any deleted mail messages.

TIP   **Outlook Enhancement Tip**   When you install the Rules Wizard enhancement (available from Microsoft's Web site), a Rules folder is added to the Mail Group folder. Rules are mini-programs you create to perform specialized tasks in Outlook. For example, you can create a rule that automatically files your incoming mail in a special folder or sends an automatic answer to certain people when you receive mail from them. Refer to Appendix D to learn more about finding and installing Outlook enhancements.

The Other Group Folders

The Other group contains folders that are on your computer but not within Outlook: My Computer, My Documents, and Favorites. This enables you to access a document or information in any of those areas so that you can attach it to a message, add notes to it, or otherwise use it in Outlook.

For example, with My Computer, you can view the contents of both hard and floppy disks, CD-ROM drives, and so on (see Figure 2.2). Double-click a drive in the window to view its folders and files. Double-click a folder to view its contents as well. Then you can attach files to messages or otherwise use the files on your hard drive with the Outlook features.

TIP   **Folders—Not Programs**   The Other group folder can only contain folders from other areas of your computer, not actual programs.

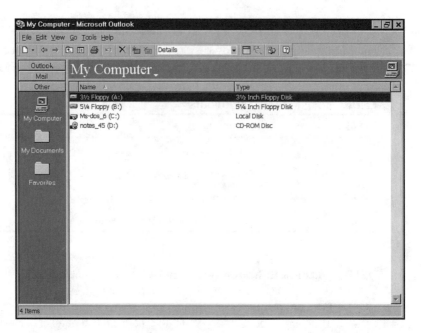

Figure 2.2 View your entire system through the My Computer folder in Outlook.

 TIP **Moving On Up** Use the **Up One Level** toolbar button to return to a folder or drive after you've double-clicked to expand it and view its contents.

Using the Folder List

Outlook provides another method of viewing the folders within Outlook and your system: The Folder List. The Folder List displays the folders within any of the three groups (Outlook, Mail, or Other). From the list, you can select the folder you want to view.

To use the Folder List, first select the group you want to view from the Outlook Bar. Then click the **Folder List** button to display the list (see Figure 2.3).

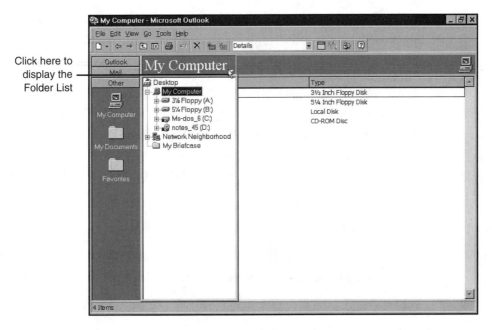

Figure 2.3 The Folder List shows all folders in the group you selected.

Choose any folder from the list, and the Information Viewer changes to reflect your selection. If you display another folder in the Information screen, double-click it to display its contents.

Changing Views

In Outlook, views give you different ways to look at the same information in a folder. Each view presents the information in a different format and organization so you can get the most from the program.

The following list outlines the general view types you can work with in Outlook and provides a brief description of each. A view type determines the basic structure of the view; within each view type, you find numerous options to change the way information is displayed within the structure of a view type.

Table view type   Presents items in a grid of sorts—in rows and columns. Use this view type to view mail messages, tasks, and details about any item.

Timeline view type   Displays items as icons arranged in chronological order from left to right on a time scale. Use this to view task entries and other items in this type of view.

Day/week/month view type   Displays items in a calendar view in blocks of time. Use this type for meetings and scheduled tasks.

Card view type   Presents items like cards in a card file. Use this to view contacts.

Icon view type   Provides graphic icons to represent tasks, notes, calendars, and so on.

TIP   **Looking at the Inbox**   The default view for your Inbox is the Table view type, in which items appear in columns and rows. Within the Table view type, you're viewing Messages.

Each folder—Inbox, Calendar, Contacts, and so on—displays its contents in a particular view type, as previously described. Additionally, within each view type, you have a choice of views that further fine-tune the presentation of the information on-screen. You can change a view by opening the **View** menu and selecting **Current View**, then selecting a particular view option. You can also change a view by clicking the **Current View** drop-down list on the standard toolbar (see Figure 2.4).

As you can see in Figure 2.4, within the Table view type of the Inbox, you can change views so that you can see all messages, messages from the last seven days, messages organized by sender, unread messages only, and so on. Similarly, the Calendar folder—which is arranged in the Day/Week/Month view type by default—enables you to view active appointments, events, recurring appointments, and so on.

As you work your way through the Outlook part of this book, you'll see examples of each view type. When you change folders in Outlook, take a quick look at the available views in the Current View drop-down list.

In this lesson, you learned to change views in Outlook, use the Outlook Bar, and use the Folder List. In the next lesson, you learn to work with incoming mail.

Views ——

Current view list ——

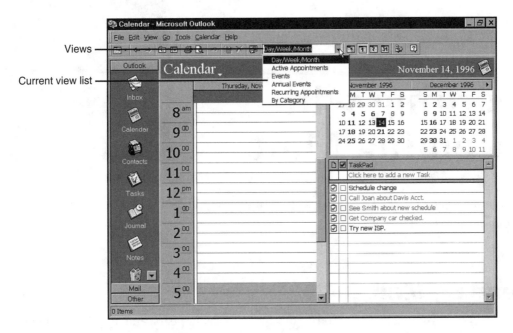

Figure 2.4   Select a view to change the format of the information.

Working with Incoming Mail

In this lesson, you learn to read your mail, save an attachment, answer mail, and close a message.

Reading Mail

When you log on to Outlook, your Inbox folder appears, and any new messages you've received are waiting for you, as shown in Figure 3.1. As you can see in this figure, the Inbox provides important information about each message. For example, two messages have been labeled as high priority, one as low priority, and one message has an attachment. You learn about priorities and attachments in Lesson 7, "Setting Mail Options." In addition, the Status bar at the bottom of the Inbox window indicates how many items the Inbox folder contains and how many of those items are unread.

TIP **Welcome!** The first time you log on, you may find a welcome message from Microsoft in your Inbox. After you read the message, you can delete it by selecting it and pressing the **Delete** key.

Are You an AOL Member? If you have an America Online account, you can use Outlook as your e-mail editor to send and receive messages. Open the Office 97 ValuPack to learn more about it (see Appendix B).

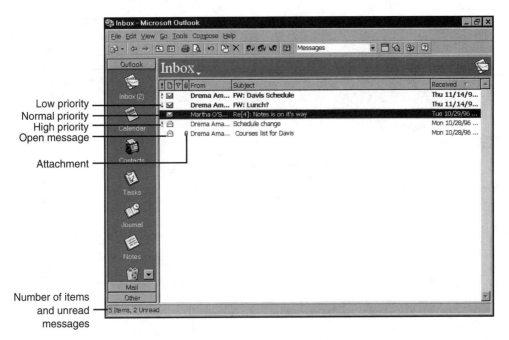

Low priority
Normal priority
High priority
Open message

Attachment

Number of items
and unread
messages

Figure 3.1 Review the sender and subject before opening your mail.

To open and read your messages, follow these steps:

1. Double-click a mail message to open it. Figure 3.2 shows an open message.

2. To read the next or previous mail message in the Inbox, click the **Previous Item** or the **Next Item** button on the toolbar. Or you can open the **View** menu, choose **Previous** or **Next**, and choose **Item**.

  Item A generic term in Outlook that describes the currently selected element. Outlook uses the word *item* to describe a mail message, an attached file, an appointment or meeting, a task, and so on.

You can mark messages as read or unread by choosing **Edit**, **Mark as Read**, or **Mark as Unread**. Outlook automatically marks messages as read when you open them. But you might want to mark messages yourself once in a while (as a reminder, for example). Additionally, you can mark all of the messages in the Inbox as read at one time by choosing **Edit**, **Mark All as Read**. You might want to mark mail messages as read so you don't read them again; you might want to mark important mail as unread so you'll be sure to open it and read it again.

Read previous
mail item

Read next
mail item

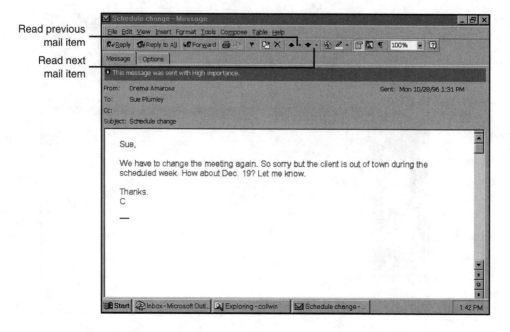

Figure 3.2 The Message window displays the message and some tools for handling this message or moving on to another.

TIP

Preview Messages For a different look at your mailbox, choose the **Messages with AutoPreview** view from the drop-down view list (near the right end of the toolbar). Unread messages display the first line or so of the message text.

CAUTION

No Mail? If you don't see any new mail in your Inbox, choose **Tools**, **Check for New Mail**, and Outlook will update your mail for you. Choose **Tools**, **Check for New Mail On** to specify a service other than the default.

Saving an Attachment

You will often receive messages that have files or other items attached. In the Inbox list of messages, an attachment is represented by a paper clip icon beside the message. You'll want to save any attachments sent to you so you can open, modify, print, or otherwise use the document. Messages can contain multiple attachments.

To save an attachment, follow these steps:

1. Open the message containing an attachment by double-clicking the message. The attachment appears as an icon in the message text (see Figure 3.3).

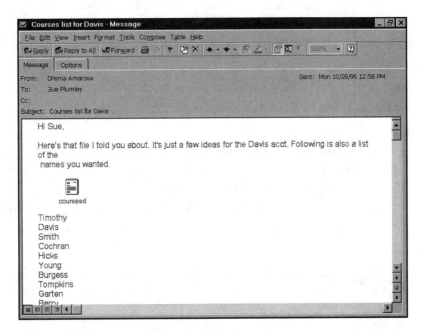

Figure 3.3 An icon represents the attached file.

2. (Optional) You can open the attachment from within the message by double-clicking the icon. The application in which the document was created—Word or Excel, for example—opens and displays the document in the window, ready for you to read. Close the application by choosing **File**, **Exit**.

3. In the message, select the attachment you want to save and choose **File**, **Save Attachments**. The Save All Attachments dialog box appears with the name of the attachment listed.

4. Click **OK**, and the Save Attachment dialog box appears (see Figure 3.4).

Figure 3.4   Save the attachment to a convenient folder.

5. Choose the folder in which you want to save the attachment and click **Save**. You can open the attachment at any time from the application in which it was created.

6. Click **Close** in the Save All Attachments dialog box to return to the message you were reading.

cc:Mail Users   If your office uses Lotus cc:mail as its e-mail system, you'll find a tool in the Office 97 ValuPack for changing your e-mail client to Outlook. Check out Appendix B for more information.

TIP   **Try the Rules Wizard!**   Advanced users may be interested in Microsoft's new Rules Wizard feature. You can use it to create and edit natural-language rules to help manage incoming and outgoing messages. To learn more about the Rules Wizard, connect to your Internet account, then open Outlook's **Help** menu, and select **Microsoft on the Web**, **Free Stuff**. This opens your Web browser to the Outlook Web page where you can learn more about downloading this tool.

Answering Mail

You might want to reply to a message after you read it. The Message window enables you to answer a message immediately, or at a later time if you prefer. To reply to any given message, open the message and follow these steps:

1. Click the **Reply** button or choose **Compose**, **Reply**. The Reply Message window appears, with the original message in the message text area and the sender of the message already filled in for you (see Figure 3.5).

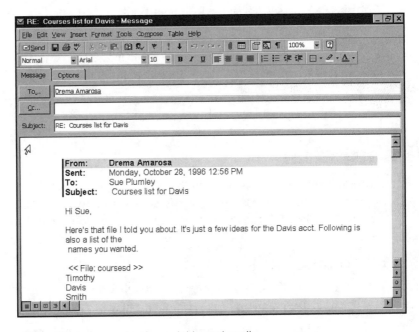

Figure 3.5 Reply to a message quickly and easily.

TIP **Reply to All** If you receive a message that has also been sent to others—as either a message or a "carbon copy" (Cc)—you can click the **Reply to All** button to send your reply to each person who received the message.

2. The insertion point is in the message text area, ready for you to enter your reply. Enter the text.

3. When you finish your reply, click the **Send** button or choose **File, Send**. Outlook either sends the message or places it to the Outbox from which you can send the message at a later time.

You also can send a reply from the Inbox without opening the message. Suppose, for example, you already read the message and closed it, but now you've decided you want to reply. Select the message in the Inbox list and click the **Reply** button. The Reply Message window appears with the original message in the text area and the sender's name in the To area. Enter your text and send the message as you learned in the previous steps.

 TIP **Reminder** The next time you open a message to which you've replied, you'll see a reminder at the top of the Message tab that tells you the date and time you sent your reply.

Printing Mail

You can print mail messages whether they're open or not. To print an unopened message, select the message in the message list of the Inbox or other folder and choose **File, Print**. If the message is already open, you can follow the steps below:

1. Open the message in Outlook.

2. Use one of the following methods to tell Outlook to print:

- Click the **Print** button on the toolbar to print using defaults.
- Choose the **File, Print** command to view the Print dialog box.
- Press **Ctrl+P**.

3. In the Print dialog box, click **OK** to print one copy of the entire message using the printer's default settings.

 TIP **More Print Info** See Lesson 16, "Printing in Outlook," for detailed information about configuring pages, setting up the printer, and so on.

Closing a Message

When you finish with a message, you can close it in any of the following ways:

- Choose **File**, **Close**.
- Click the **Control-menu icon** and click **Close**.
- Press **Alt+F4**.
- Click the **Close** (X) button in the title bar of the Message window.

 TIP **Want to Switch Between Outlook and Exchange?**   You can use the E-Mail Forms Fix Utility to configure your e-mail client so you can switch between Outlook and Microsoft Exchange on demand. You'll find this utility on Microsoft's Web site, where you can download it for free. Open your Internet connection, then open Outlook's **Help** menu, and select **Microsoft on the Web**, **Free Stuff**. Your Web browser opens and takes you to the Microsoft Outlook Web page where you'll find more information about this feature.

In this lesson, you learned to read your mail, save an attachment, answer mail, and close a message. In the next lesson, you will learn to manage your mail messages.

Managing Mail

4

In this lesson, you learn to delete and undelete messages, forward messages, and organize messages by saving them to folders.

Deleting Mail

You may want to store some important messages, but you'll definitely want to delete much of the mail you receive. Once you've answered a question or responded to a request, you probably won't have need for a reminder of that transaction. You can easily delete messages in Outlook when you're finished with them.

To delete a mail message that is open, do one of the following:

- Choose **File**, **Delete**.
- Press **Ctrl+D**.

- Click the **Delete** button on the toolbar.

If you have modified the message in any way, a confirmation message appears from the Office Assistant or as a message dialog box. Otherwise, the message is deleted without warning.

If you're in the Inbox and you want to delete one or more messages from the message list, select the single message to delete (or hold down Ctrl and click each message). Then do one of the following:

- Press the **Delete** key.

- Click the **Delete** button on the toolbar.

Undeleting Items

If you change your mind and want to get back items you've deleted, you can usually retrieve them from the Deleted Items folder. By default, when you delete an item, it doesn't disappear from your system; it merely moves to the Deleted Items folder. Items stay in the Deleted Items folder until you delete them from that folder—at which point they are unrecoverable.

To retrieve a deleted item from the Deleted Items folder, follow these steps:

1. Click the **Deleted Items** icon in the Outlook Bar to open the folder.

2. Select the items you want to retrieve and drag them to the folder from which they came on the Outlook Bar. Alternatively, you can choose **Edit, Move to Folder** and choose the folder to which you want to move the selected items.

Emptying the Deleted Items Folder

If you're really sure you want to delete the items in the Deleted Items folder, you can erase them from your system. To delete items in the Deleted Items folder, follow these steps:

1. In the Outlook Bar, choose the **Outlook** group and then select the **Deleted Items** folder. All deleted items in that folder appear in the message list, as shown in Figure 4.1.

2. To permanently delete an item, select it in the Deleted Items folder and click the **Delete** tool button or choose **Edit, Delete**.

3. Outlook displays a confirmation dialog box asking if you're sure you want to permanently delete the message. Choose **Yes** to delete the selected item.

4. To switch back to the Inbox or another folder, select the folder from either the Outlook Bar or the Folders List.

 TIP **Automatic Permanent Delete**   You can set Outlook to permanently delete the contents of the Deleted Items folder every time you exit the program. To do so, choose **Tools, Options** and click the **General** tab. In the General Settings area, select **Empty the Deleted Items Folder Upon Exiting** and click **OK**.

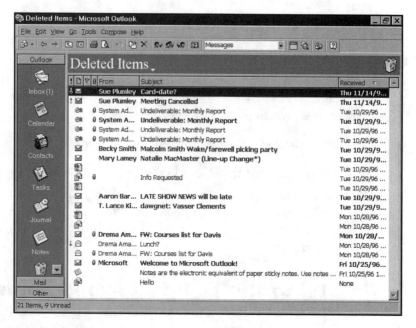

Figure 4.1   Deleted messages remain in the Deleted Items folder until you permanently delete them.

Forwarding Mail

Suppose you want to forward mail you receive from a coworker to another person who has an interest in the message. You can forward any message you receive, and you can even add comments to the message if you want.

TERM   **Forward Mail**   When you forward mail, you send a message you received to another person; you can add your own comments to the forwarded mail, if you want.

You forward an open message or a message selected in the message list in the Inbox in the same way. To forward mail, follow these steps:

1. Select or open the message you want to forward. Then click the **Forward** button or choose **Compose**, **Forward**. The FW Message dialog box appears (see Figure 4.2).

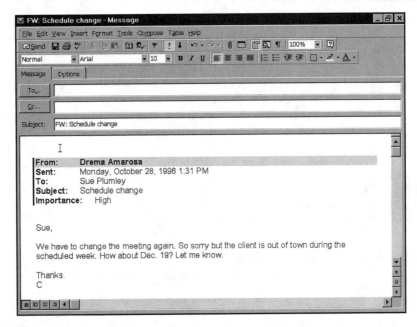

Figure 4.2 When you forward a message, the original message appears at the bottom of the message window.

2. In the **To** text box, enter the names of the people to whom you want to forward the mail. (If you want to choose a person's name from a list, click the **To...** button to display the Select Names dialog box, and then select the person's name.) Lesson 5 explains more about using the Address Book. If you enter multiple names in the To box, separate the names with a semicolon and a space.

3. (Optional) In the Cc text box, enter the names of anyone to whom you want to forward *copies* of the message (or click the **Cc...** button and choose the name from the list that appears).

4. In the message area of the window, enter any message you want to send with the forwarded text. The text you type will be a different color.

5. Click the **Send** button or choose **File**, **Send**.

Saving Mail to a Folder

Although you'll delete some mail after you read and respond to it, you'll want to save other messages for future reference. You can save a message to any folder you want, but you should use a logical filing system to ensure that you'll be able to find each message again later. Outlook offers several methods for organizing your mail.

The easiest method of saving mail to a folder is to move it to one of Outlook's built-in Mail folders (as described in Lesson 2). You can use any of the folders to store your mail, or you can create new folders. Lesson 9, "Organizing Messages," describes how to create your own folders within Outlook.

To move messages to an existing folder, follow these steps:

1. Select one message (by clicking it) or select multiple messages (by **Ctrl**+clicking).

> **TIP**   **Making Backup Copies**   You can also copy a message to another folder as a backup. To do so, choose **Edit**, **Copy to Folder**.

2. Choose **Edit**, **Move to Folder** or click the **Move to Folder** tool button on the toolbar. The Move Items dialog box appears (see Figure 4.3).

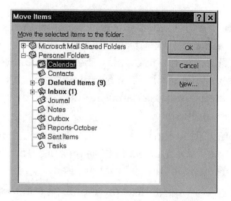

Figure 4.3   Choose the folder to which you want to move the selected message(s).

3. Select the folder you want to move the item to and click **OK**. Outlook moves the item to the folder for you.

To view the message(s) you've moved, choose the folder from the Outlook Bar or the Folders List. Then click the item you want to view.

In this lesson, you learned how to forward messages, delete messages, and organize messages by saving them to folders. In the next lesson, you will learn to work with address books.

Using the
Address Book

In this lesson, you learn to use Outlook's address book with your e-mail.

Using the Personal Address Book

The Personal Address Book contains the names and e-mail addresses of people you contact frequently. You may want to contact people from outside of your office (whom you contact via Internet addresses).

 TIP **Easier Internet E-Mail** Microsoft's Outlook Web page has an Internet Mail Enhancement Patch that improves functionality and makes it easier to send and receive e-mail over the Internet. To learn more about it, log onto your Internet connection, then open Outlook's **Help** menu, and select **Microsoft on the Web, Free Stuff**. This opens your Web browser to the Outlook Web page where you can find out more about downloading this enhancement for free.

To add names to the Personal Address Book, follow these steps:

 1. Choose **Tools, Address Book** or click the **Address Book** tool button on the toolbar. The Address Book dialog box appears (refer to Figure 5.1).

2. To view your Personal Address Book, select the **Show Names from the** drop-down list and choose **Personal Address Book**. The list changes to display those names you've added to your personal address list, but the dialog box looks the same.

 3. To add a completely new address to your Personal Address Book, click the **New Entry** button or choose **File, New Entry**. The New Entry dialog box appears (see Figure 5.2).

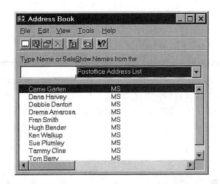

Figure 5.1 The Address Book dialog box.

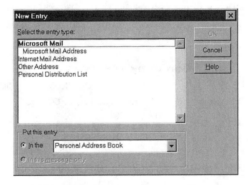

Figure 5.2 Choose a source for your new entry.

4. In the Select the Entry Type list, choose one of the following:

Personal Distribution List Use this to create one address entry for a group of recipients. When you send mail to the list name, everyone on the list receives the message. You might use this option for grouping department heads, for example.

Other Address Choose this option to add one new recipient at a time. You can enter a name, e-mail address, and e-mail type for each entry. In addition, you can enter business addresses and phone numbers, and you can add notes and comments to the entry. Use this entry for Internet addresses, for example.

5. When you're done working in your Personal Address Book, close the window by choosing **File, Close**. You're returned to the Outlook Inbox.

TIP **Working with Internet E-Mail** Make sure you have an Outlook profile that includes the Internet Mail service you use. Open the **Tools** menu, and select **Services**. If Internet Mail is not included in the list of available services, click **Add** and select **Internet Mail**, then click **OK**. Enter the pertinent Internet information where prompted in the **General** tab, and select a way to connect to the Internet in the **Connection** tab. Click **OK** twice to return to the Outlook window.

Entering an Address in a Message

You can use either address book to choose the names of recipients to whom you want to send new messages, forward messages, or send a reply. Using the address books also makes sending carbon copies and blind carbon copies easy.

Blind Carbon Copy A blind carbon copy (Bcc) of a message is a copy that's sent to someone in secret; the other recipients have no way of knowing that you're sending the message to someone via a blind carbon copy.

To address a message, follow these steps:

1. Choose **Compose**, **New Mail Message** from the Outlook Inbox window.

2. In the Message window, click the **To** button to display the Select Names dialog box.

3. Open the **Show Names From The:** drop-down list box and choose either the **Postoffice Address List** or the **Personal Address Book**.

4. From the list that appears on the left, choose the name of the intended recipient and select the **To** button or just double-click the recipient's name. Outlook copies the name to the Message Recipients list. (You can add multiple names if you want.)

5. (Optional) Select the names of anyone to whom you want to send a carbon copy and click the **Cc** button to transfer those names to the Message Recipients list.

6. (Optional) Select the names of anyone to whom you want to send a blind carbon copy and click the **Bcc** button. Figure 5.3 shows a distribution group listing as the To recipient of a message; in addition, two people are selected to receive blind carbon copies of the same message.

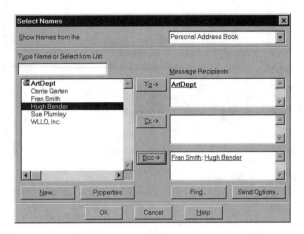

Figure 5.3   Address messages quickly with the Select Names dialog box.

7. Click **OK** to return to the Message window and complete your message. (For more information about writing messages, see Lesson 6.)

In this lesson, you learned to use the address book with your e-mail. In the next lesson, you will learn to compose a message and format it.

Creating Mail

In this lesson, you learn to compose a message, format text, check your spelling, and send mail.

Composing a Message

You can send a message to anyone for whom you have an address, whether he or she is in your address book or not. And in addition to sending a message to one or more recipients, you can send copies of a message to others on your address list. (See Lesson 5 for information about addressing a message and sending carbon copies.)

To compose a message, follow these steps:

1. In the Outlook Inbox, click the **New Mail Message** button or choose **Compose, New Mail Message**. The Untitled - Message window appears (see Figure 6.1).

2. Enter the name of the recipient in the To… text box, or click the **To…** button and select the name of the recipient from your Address Book. (See Lesson 5 for information about the Address Book.)

3. Enter the name of anyone to whom you want to send a copy of the message in the Cc text box, or click the **Cc…** button and select a name or names from the Address Book.

4. In the Subject text box, enter the subject of the message.

5. Click in the text area, and then enter the text of the message. You do not have to press the Enter key at the end of a line; Outlook automatically wraps the text at the end of a line for you. You can use the Delete and Backspace keys to edit the text you enter.

6. When you finish typing the message, you can send the message right away (see "Sending Mail" later in this lesson), or you can check the spelling and formatting as described in the following sections.

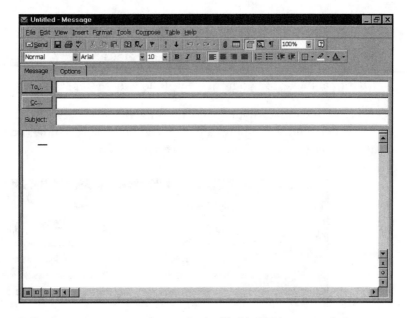

Figure 6.1 Compose a new message in the Untitled - Message window.

No Address! If you try to compose a message to someone without entering an address, Outlook displays the Check Names dialog box, in which it asks you to create an address. You can search for the name among the existing addresses, or you can create a new address for the name in much the same way you would create a new entry in the Address Book (see Lesson 5).

AOL Users You can use Outlook as your e-mail editor along with your AOL account. Turn to Appendix B to learn how.

Formatting Text

You can change the format of the text in your message to make it more attractive, or easier to read, or to add emphasis. Any formatting you add is sent to the recipient with the message if the recipient has Outlook; however, if the recipient doesn't have Outlook, formatting may not be included with the message.

There are two ways to format text. You can format the text after you type it by selecting it and then choosing a font, size, or other attribute; or you can select the font, size, or other attribute and then enter the text.

To format the text in your message, follow these steps:

1. If the Formatting toolbar is not showing, choose **View**, **Toolbars**, **Formatting**. Figure 6.2 shows a message with the Formatting Toolbar displayed. Table 6.1 explains the buttons on this toolbar.

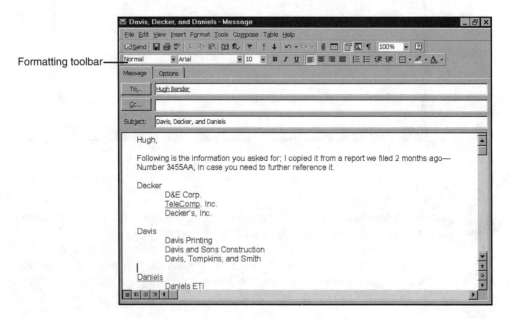

Figure 6.2   Use the Formatting toolbar to modify your message text.

Table 6.1   Formatting Toolbar Buttons

Button	Name
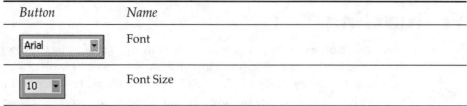 Arial	Font
10	Font Size

Button	Name
B	Bold
I	Italic
<u>U</u>	Underline
≣	Align Left
≣	Center
≣	Align Right
⦂≡	Bullets
⇤≡	Decrease Indent
⇥≡	Increase Indent

2. To apply a font to the selected or about-to-be-entered text, click the down-arrow in the Font box on the Formatting toolbar. Scroll through the font list, if necessary, to view all fonts on the system, and click the font you want to apply to the text.

 TIP **Quick Format** You can also format text by choosing **Format**, **Font** and selecting a font, size, style, and so on from the Font dialog box. You also can assign bullets and alignment to text by choosing **Format**, **Paragraph**.

3. Assign a size by clicking the down-arrow beside the Font Size drop-down list and choosing the size; alternatively, you can enter a size in the Font Size text box.

 4. To choose a color, click the **Color** tool button and select a color from the palette box that appears.

5. Choose a type style to apply to text by clicking the **Bold, Italic,** or **Underline** buttons on the Formatting toolbar.

6. Choose an alignment by selecting the **Align Left, Center,** or **Align Right** button from the Formatting toolbar.

7. Add bullets to a list by clicking the **Bullet** button on the Formatting toolbar.

8. Create text indents or remove indents in half-inch increments by clicking the **Increase Indent** or **Decrease Indent** buttons. (Each time you click the Indent button, the indent changes by half an inch.)

Checking Spelling

To make a good impression and to maintain your professional image, you should check the spelling in your mail messages before you send them. Outlook includes a spelling checker you can use for that purpose. The spelling checker, when activated, checks your spelling against words in Outlook's default dictionary. If it finds words that do not appear in the dictionary, it flags them and makes suggestions for alternate spellings when applicable. Keep in mind that the dictionary is limited and may flag words or names that are actually spelled correctly. The spelling checker is not an infallible tool, but it can help you spot check your mistakes.

To check the spelling in a message, follow these steps:

1. In the open message, choose **Tools, Spelling** or press **F7**. When the spelling checker finds a word with questionable spelling, it displays the Spelling dialog box shown in Figure 6.3.

2. You can do any of the following in response to the word Outlook questions in the Spelling dialog box:

   Change To Enter the correct spelling in this text box.

   Suggestions Select the correct spelling in this text box, and it automatically appears in the Change To text box.

   Ignore Click this button to continue the spelling check without changing this occurrence of the selected word.

   Ignore All Click this button to continue the spelling check without changing any occurrence of the word in question throughout this message.

   Change Click this button to change this particular occurrence of the word in question to the spelling in the Change To text box.

Change All Click this button to change the word in question to the spelling listed in the Change To text box every time the spelling checker finds the word in this message.

Add Click this button to add the current spelling of the word in question to the dictionary so that Outlook will not question future occurrences of this spelling.

Suggest Click this button to view Outlook's alternative spelling suggestions for the word if they are not already displayed.

Undo Last Click this button to reverse the last spelling change you made, thus returning the word to its original spelling.

Cancel Click this button to quit the spelling check.

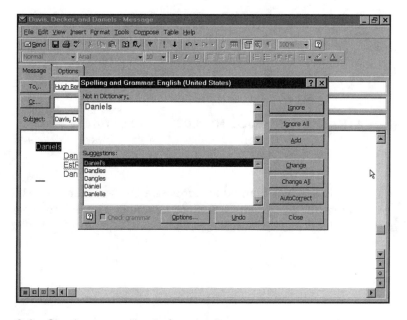

Figure 6.3 Check your spelling before sending a message.

3. When the spelling check is complete, Outlook displays a message box telling you it's done. Click **OK** to close the dialog box.

TIP **Set Your Spelling Options** Click the **Options** button in the Spelling dialog box to set options that tell Outlook to do such things as ignore words with numbers, ignore original message text in forwarded messages or replies, always check spelling before sending, and so on.

Sending Mail

When you're ready to send your mail message, do one of the following:

- Click the **Send** button.
- Choose **File**, **Send**.
- Press **Ctrl+Enter**.

Internet e-mail messages will go to the Outbox and remain there until you manually connect by choosing the **Tools**, **Check for New Mail** command from the menu, unless the Internet service profile is set to automatically poll at the specified time interval.

> **TIP** **AutoSignature** Choose **Tools**, **AutoSignature** to have Outlook automatically add a message, quotation, or other text at the end of every message you send. Additionally, after you create an AutoSignature, you can quickly add it to any message by choosing **Insert**, **AutoSignature**.

> **TIP** **Using Windows NT 4.0?** You'll need to check your rights and permissions in relation to sending e-mail within your network. Ask your system administrator for more information.

In this lesson, you learned to compose a message, format text, check your spelling, and send mail. In the next lesson, you learn how to set mail options, and tell if the recipient has received your message.

Setting Mail Options

In this lesson, you learn to set options for messages and delivery, and for tracking messages.

Customizing Options

Outlook provides options that enable you to mark any message with priority status so that the recipient knows you need a quick response, or with a sensitivity rating so your words cannot be changed by anyone after the message is sent. With other available options, you can enable the recipients of your message to vote on an issue by including voting buttons in your message and having the replies sent to a specific location.

You also can set delivery options. For example, you can schedule the delivery of a message for a specified delivery time or date if you don't want to send it right now.

To set message options, open the **Untitled - Message** window and click the **Options** tab. As you can see in Figure 7.1, the options on this tab are separated into four areas. The next four subsections discuss each of the groups of options in detail.

General Options

In the General Options area, set any of the following options for your message:

- Click the **Importance** drop-down arrow and choose a priority level of **Low**, **Normal**, or **High** from the list. (Alternatively, you could click the **Importance High** or **Importance Low** tool button on the toolbar.) When importance isn't specified, the message is given Normal Importance.

- Click the **Sensitivity** drop-down arrow and choose one of the following options:

  Normal   Use this option to indicate that the message's contents are standard or customary.

  Personal   Use this option to suggest that the message's contents are of a personal nature.

  Private   Use this option to prevent the message from being modified after you send it.

  Confidential   Use this option to denote the message's contents as restricted or private.

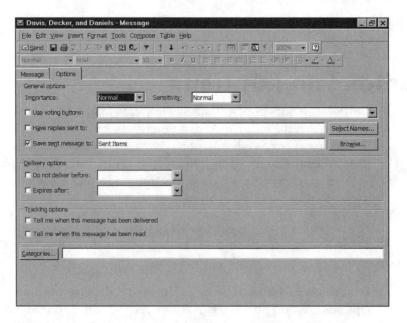

Figure 7.1   Use the Options tab to govern how your message is sent.

 TIP   **You Can Mark All Messages as Private**   You can mark all of your messages so that no one can tamper with your words by choosing **Tools**, **Options** and clicking the **Sending** tab. In the **Set Sensitivity** box, choose the level you want.

- Select the **Use Voting Buttons** check box to add the default choices (Approve and Reject) to your message. This lets the recipient choose a particular response to your message and send the response back to you. You can also add Yes and No choices or Yes, No, and Maybe choices. If you want to provide other choices, enter your own text in the text box.

- Choose the **Have Replies Sent To** check box and specify in the text box the person to whom you want the replies sent. You can use the **Select Names** button to view the Address Book and choose a name if you want.

- Select the **Save Sent Message To** check box to save your message to the Sent Items folder by default. Or specify another folder to save the message in, using the **Browse** button and the resulting dialog box if necessary to locate the folder.

Delivery Options

In addition to message options, you can set certain delivery options, such as scheduling the time of the delivery. In the Delivery Options area of the Options tab (Message window), choose one or both of the following check boxes:

Do Not Deliver Before   Check this option to specify a delivery date. Click the down-arrow in the text box beside the option to display a calendar on which you can select the day.

Expires After   Select this check box to include a day, date, and time of expiration. You can click the down-arrow in the text box to display a calendar from which you can choose a date, or you can enter the date and time yourself.

Tracking Options

If you're using Outlook with a company workgroup or internal e-mail system, you might want to set tracking options so you know when a message has been delivered or read. Tracking options are like receipts—they notify you that the message arrived safely. You set tracking options from the **Options** tab of the **Untitled - Message** window.

Choose one or both of the following Tracking Options: **Tell Me When This Message Has Been Delivered** and **Tell Me When This Message Has Been Read**.

Categories

Outlook enables you to assign messages to certain categories—such as Business, Goals/Objectives, Hot Contacts, Phone Calls, and so on. You set the category for a message in the Categories dialog box.

Categories Categories offer a way of organizing messages to make them easier to find, sort, print, and manage. For example, to find all of the items in one category, choose **Tools**, **Find Items**. Click the **More Choices** tab, choose **Categories**, and check the category for which you're searching.

To assign a category, follow these steps:

1. In the **Options** tab of the **Message** window, click the **Categories** button. The Categories dialog box appears (see Figure 7.2).

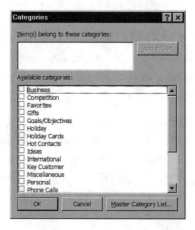

Figure 7.2 Organize your messages with categories.

2. To assign an existing category, select the category or categories that best suit your message from the Available Categories list. To assign a new category, enter a new category in the **Item(s) Belong to These Categories** text box, and then click the **Add to List** button.

3. Click **OK** to close the Categories dialog box and return to the Message window.

Using Message Flags

A message flag enables you to mark a message as important, either as a reminder for yourself or as a signal to the message's recipient. When you send a message flag, a red flag icon appears in the recipient's message list, and Outlook adds text at the top of the message telling which type of flag you are sending. In addition, you can add a due date to the flag, and that date appears at the top of the message.

The following list outlines the types of flags you can send in Outlook:

Call	No Response Necessary
Do not Forward	Read
Follow Up	Reply
For Your Information	Reply to All
Forward	Review

To use a message flag, follow these steps:

1. In the Message window, click the **Message Flag** tool or choose **Edit**, **Message Flag**. The Flag Message dialog box appears (see Figure 7.3).

Figure 7.3 Flag a message to show its importance.

2. Click the **Flag** drop-down arrow and choose the flag text you want to add to the message.

3. Click the **By** drop-down arrow and select a date from the calendar, or enter a date manually in the text box.

4. Click **OK** to return to the Message window.

TIP **View the Message Header** You can view just the header of a message to allow you more message text room, if you want to hide the Cc, Bcc, and Subject lines. Choose **View**, **Message Header** to show only the To text box and any flag text; select **View**, **Message Header** again to redisplay the Cc, Bcc, and Subject fields.

In this lesson, you learned to set options for messages and delivery, and for tracking messages. In the next lesson, you will learn to attach items to messages.

Attaching Items to a Message

In this lesson, you learn to attach a file, an object (such as an embedded file), and other items (such as an appointment or task) to a message.

Attaching a File

You can attach any type of file to an Outlook message, which makes for a convenient way of sending your files over the network to your coworkers. You might send Word documents, Excel spreadsheets, a PowerPoint presentation, or any other document you create with your Windows applications.

When you send an attached file, it appears as an icon in the message. When the recipient gets the file, he or she can open it within the message or save it for later use. However, the recipient must have the source program that you used to create the file on his or her computer. For instance, if you send a colleague a Microsoft Word file, he must have Microsoft Word in order to view the file he receives.

What If They Don't Have Word?   If you're sending an attached Word file to someone who doesn't have a copy of Word, you might want to send along a copy of Microsoft Word Viewer. It's a program that enables users to view and print Word documents without having the entire Word program installed on their computers. Microsoft Word Viewer is part of the Office 97 ValuPack. To learn more about it, refer to Appendix B.

To attach a file to a message, follow these steps:

1. In the Message window, position the insertion point in the message text, and then choose **Insert**, **File** or click the **Insert File** toolbar button. The Insert File dialog box appears (see Figure 8.1).

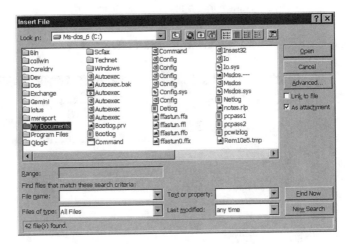

Figure 8.1   Select the file you want to attach to a message.

2. From the **Look In** drop-down list, choose the drive and folder that contains the file you want to attach.

3. Using the **Files of Type** drop-down list, choose the file type—such as Excel or Word.

4. Select the file you want to attach.

5. In the **Insert As** area of the dialog box, click one of the following option buttons:

    Text Only   Inserts the file as text into the message; if your file is not saved as an ASCII or other text-only file, do not use this option.

    Attachment   Inserts an icon representing the document. The actual file follows the message to the recipient; the recipient saves it as his or her own copy.

    Shortcut   Inserts a Windows shortcut icon into the text. This option is best used only if the file is stored on a network drive from which the recipient can easily access it through a shortcut.

6. Click **OK** to insert the attached file into the message.

351

Text Only Is Only for Text! If you try to insert a file from Word, Excel, or another application as Text Only, you end up with a lot of "garbage" characters in the text. That's because these programs' files contain special formatting codes. The only time you will use Text Only is when you export the data from its native program into a text-only file first.

Figure 8.2 shows a file inserted as an attachment.

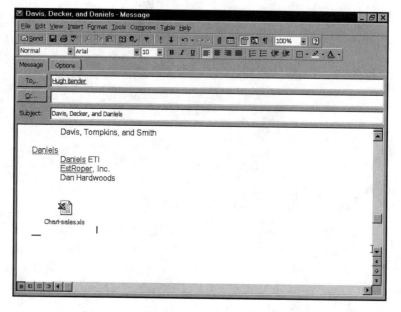

Figure 8.2 The recipient can double-click the icon to open the file.

Outlook Converters Check out the Office 97 ValuPack for Outlook import and export converters you can use to help import data from other applications into Outlook. (See Appendix B for more details.)

Attaching Outlook Items

In addition to attaching files from other programs, you can also attach an Outlook item to a message. An Outlook item can be any document saved in one of your personal folders, including a calendar, contacts, journal, notes, tasks, and so on. You can attach an Outlook item in the same manner you attach a file.

Follow these steps to attach an Outlook item:

1. In the Message window, choose **Insert**, **Item**. The Insert Item dialog box appears.

2. From the **Look In** drop-down list, choose the folder containing the item you want to include in the message.

3. Select from the items that appear in the **Items** list (see Figure 8.3). To select multiple adjacent items, hold the **Shift** key and click the first and last desired items; to select multiple nonadjacent items, hold the **Ctrl** key and click the items.

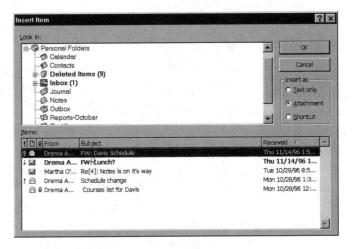

Figure 8.3 Select items from any folder in Outlook.

4. In the Insert As area, choose from the following option buttons: **Text Only**, **Attachment**, or **Shortcut**.

5. Click **OK**, and Outlook inserts the selected items in your message.

It Doesn't Work Without Outlook   If the recipient doesn't have Outlook on his computer, he will not be able to view the attached item. If you know the recipient doesn't have the program, you need to cut and paste the data into the message or simply retype it.

CAUTION

353

Inserting an Object

Just as you can insert an object—a spreadsheet, chart, drawing, presentation, media clip, clip art, WordArt, and so on—in any Windows application that supports *OLE*, you can also insert an object into an Outlook mail message.

 TERM   **OLE (Object Linking and Embedding)**   A method of exchanging and sharing data between applications; OLE is supported by most Windows applications and all Microsoft programs.

You can insert an existing object into a message, or you can create an object within a message using the source application. For example, you could create an Excel chart within your message using Excel's features through OLE.

When you send a message with an attached object, the object travels with the message to the recipient. As long as the recipient has the application on his computer, he can open the object and view it.

For more information about OLE, see Lesson 1, "Sharing Office 97 Data," in Part VI of this book.

To attach an existing object to a message, follow these steps:

1. In the Message window, position the insertion point in the message text and choose **Insert**, **Object**. The Object dialog box appears.
2. Choose the **Create from File** tab (see Figure 8.4).

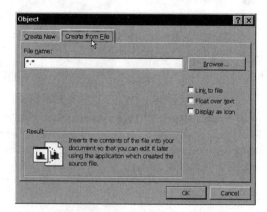

Figure 8.4   Insert an object to send with a message.

3. In the File name text box, enter the path and the name of the file you want to insert. (You can use the **Browse** button and the resulting dialog box to find the file if you want.)

4. Click **OK**. Outlook inserts the object into the message.

After you save and open an object you've received in a message, you can resize the object to suit your needs. First select it, and a frame appears with eight small black boxes (called *handles*) on the corners and along the sides. To resize the object, position the mouse pointer over one of the black handles; the mouse pointer becomes a two-headed arrow. Click and drag the handle to resize the object.

To edit an object, double-click within the frame, and the source application opens from within Outlook. Note that you still see your Outlook message and Outlook toolbars; however, you also see some tools and a menu you can use to edit the object. Figure 8.5 shows an Excel chart object within a message. Notice the Chart menu and several chart icons added for use in editing.

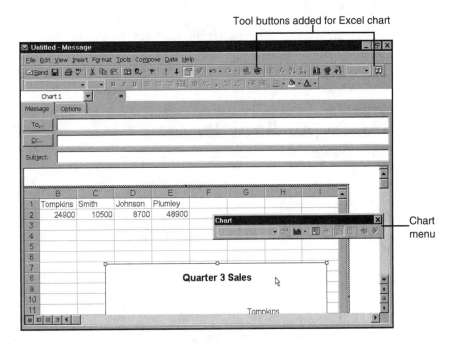

Figure 8.5 Edit the object from within your Outlook message.

In this lesson, you learned to attach a file, an object, and other items to a message. In the next lesson, you will learn to organize messages.

Organizing Messages

In this lesson, you learn to save a draft, view sent items, and create folders.

Viewing Sent Items and Changing Defaults

By default, Outlook saves a copy of all mail messages you send. It keeps these copies in the Sent Items folder, which is part of the Mail group of the Outlook Bar. You can view a list of sent items at any time, and you can open any message in that list to review its contents.

Viewing Sent Items

To view sent items, follow these steps:

1. In the Outlook Bar, choose the **Mail** group.

 TIP **Save time** You can select the **Sent Items** folder from the **Folder List** instead of following steps 1–3.

2. If necessary, scroll to the Sent Items folder.

3. Click the **Sent Items** icon, and Outlook displays a list of the contents of that folder. Figure 9.1 shows the Sent Items list. All messages you send remain in the Sent Items folder until you delete or move them.

4. (Optional) To view a sent item, double-click it to open it. When you finish with it, click the **Close** (X) button.

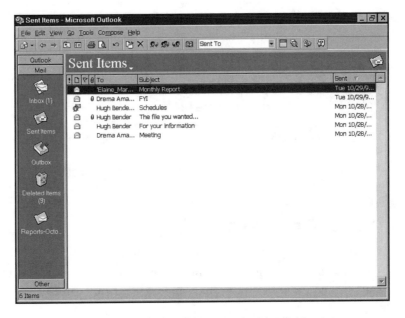

Figure 9.1   You can open any sent message by double-clicking it.

Changing Sent Items Defaults

You can control how Outlook saves copies of your sent messages. To change the default settings for the Sent Items folder, follow these steps:

1. Choose **Tools**, **Options**, and the Options dialog box appears.

2. Click the **Sending** tab.

3. Choose one or all of the following options (located near the bottom of the dialog box):

   Save Copies of Messages in "Sent Items" Folder   When this is checked, Outlook saves copies of all sent messages to the specified folder. (When the check box is empty, no copies of messages are saved automatically.)

   In Folders Other Than the Inbox, Save Replies with Original Messages   When this is checked, Outlook saves replies to messages in the same folder in which you store the original message. (When the check box is empty, it saves replies to the Sent Items folder as long as you've checked the previous check box.)

Save Forwarded Messages   When this is checked, Outlook saves a copy of each forwarded message you send.

4. Click **OK** to close the dialog box.

CAUTION

Too Much Mail!   If you save all the mail you receive and send, you may accumulate so much mail that you run the risk of running out of disk space. You can and should periodically delete mail from the Sent Items folder by selecting the mail and pressing the **Delete** key; you also need to remove the deleted mail from the Deleted Items folder. See Lesson 4, "Managing Mail," for more information. Alternatively, you can create an archive file of the messages you've sent. The archive enables you to save items on disk or elsewhere on the system. See Lesson 17, "Saving, Opening, and Finding Outlook Items," for details.

Creating Folders

You'll likely want to organize your mail in various folders to make storing items and finding them more efficient. You can create folders within Outlook that make it easier to manage your mail and other items in Outlook.

To create a folder, follow these steps:

1. Choose **File**, **Folder**, **Create Subfolder**. The Create New Folder dialog box appears (see Figure 9.2).

2. In the **Name** text box, enter a name for the folder.

3. Click the **Folder Contains** drop-down arrow, and choose the type of items the folder will store: Mail, Appointments, Contact, Journal, Note, or Task.

4. In the **Make This Folder a Subfolder Of** list, choose the folder in which you want to create the new folder. You can, for example, make the new folder a subfolder of Personal Folders so that it appears in lists with all of the Outlook folders. Or you might want to make it a subfolder of Sent Mail.

5. (Optional) In the **Description** text box, add a comment or brief description of the folder.

6. (Optional) Click the **Create a Shortcut to This Folder in the Outlook Bar** check box to remove the check mark if you prefer not to see the folder in the Outlook Bar. (By default, the check box is checked so that you will see the new folder in the Outlook Bar.)

7. Click **OK** to close the dialog box. The new folder appears on the Outlook Bar and in the Folder List.

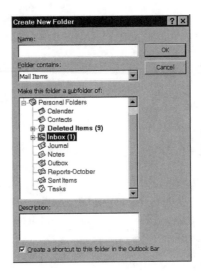

Figure 9.2   Create folders to organize your mail and other items.

TIP   **Add Folder Later**   Even if you choose not to add the folder to the Outlook Bar when you create the folder, you can add it later. You simply choose **File**, **Add to Outlook Bar**. In the dialog box that appears, you can select any folder name in Outlook or on the system and add it to the Outlook Bar by selecting it and clicking **OK**.

CAUTION   **I Want to Delete a Folder!**   If you added a folder by accident or you change your mind about a folder you've added, you can delete it from Outlook. To delete a folder, select it and then choose **File**, **Folder**, **Delete** *foldername*. You also can rename, move, or copy the folder using the commands in the secondary menu that appears when you choose **File**, **Folder**. Be sure to select the folder first.

In this lesson, you learned to save a draft, view sent items, and create folders. In the next lesson, you learn to use the Calendar.

Using the Calendar

In this lesson, you learn to navigate the Calendar, create appointments, and save appointments.

Navigating the Calendar

You can use Outlook's Calendar to schedule appointments and create a to-do list to remind you of daily or weekly tasks. You can schedule appointments months in advance, move appointments, cancel appointments, and so on. And the Calendar makes it easy to identify the days on which you have appointments.

To open the Outlook Calendar, click the **Calendar** icon in the Outlook Bar or select the **Calendar** folder from the Folder List. Figure 10.1 shows the Outlook Calendar.

Outlook provides multiple ways for you to move around in the Calendar and view specific dates:

- Scroll through the schedule pane to view the time of the appointment.
- In the monthly calendar pane, click the left and right arrows next to the names of the months to go backward and forward one month at a time.
- In the monthly calendar pane, click a date to display that date in the schedule pane.
- To view a full month in the schedule pane, select the name of the month in the monthly calendar pane.
- To view a week or selected days in the schedule pane, select the days in the monthly calendar pane.

- To add a task to the Task list, click where you see **Click Here To Add a New Task**, enter a new task, and press **Enter**.
- Use the scroll bars for the Task list pane to view appointments.

Click the left or right arrow to move to
previous or next month

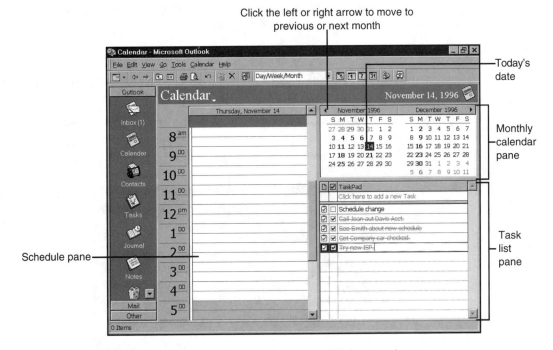

Figure 10.1 You can view all appointments and tasks at a glance.

TIP Change the Date Quickly To quickly go to today's date or to a specific date without searching through the monthly calendar pane, right-click in the schedule pane and choose either **Go To Today** or **Go To Date**.

TIP How About Opening an Outlook Calendar Within Schedule+? If you have Schedule+ (Microsoft's previous PIM program before Outlook), or you are exchanging information with someone who does, you might want to use the *Outlook Driver*. It lets you open an Outlook Calendar from within Schedule+, as long as you have Microsoft Exchange Server. Check out the Microsoft Outlook Web page for more information about this driver and how you can download it for free. See Appendix D for more information.

Creating an Appointment

You can create an appointment on any day well past the year 2000 using the Outlook Calendar. When you create an appointment, you can add the subject, location, starting time, category, and even an alarm to remind you ahead of time.

Follow these steps to create an appointment:

1. In the monthly calendar pane, select the month and the date for which you want to create an appointment.

2. In the schedule pane, double-click next to the time at which the appointment is scheduled to begin. The Untitled - Appointment dialog box appears, with the Appointment tab displayed (see Figure 10.2).

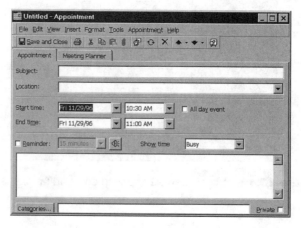

Figure 10.2 Enter all the details you need when scheduling an appointment.

3. Enter the subject of the appointment in the **Subject** text box (you can use a person's name, a topic, or other information).

4. In the **Location** text box, enter the meeting place or other text that will help you identify the meeting when you see it in your calendar.

5. Enter dates and times in the **Start Time** and **End Time** text boxes (or click the drop-down arrows and select the dates and times).

 TIP **Autodate It!** You can use Outlook's Autodate feature: Enter a text phrase such as **next Friday** or **noon** in the date and time text boxes, and Outlook figures out the date for you.

6. Select the **Reminder** check box and enter the amount of time before the appointment that you want to be notified. If you want to set an audio alarm, click the **Alarm Bell** button and select a specific sound for Outlook to play as your reminder.

7. From the **Show Time As** drop-down list, choose how you want to display the scheduled time on your calendar.

8. In the large text box near the bottom of the Appointment tab, enter any text that you want to include, such as text to identify the appointment, reminders for materials to take, and so on.

9. Click the **Categories** button and assign a category to the appointment.

10. Click the **Save** button, and then click the **Close** (X) button to return to the calendar.

The Meeting Planner tab enables you to schedule a meeting with coworkers and enter the meeting on your calendar. See Lesson 11 for more information.

Scheduling a Recurring Appointment

Suppose you have an appointment that comes around every week or month, or that otherwise occurs on a regular basis. Instead of scheduling every individual occurrence of the appointment, you can schedule that appointment in your calendar as a recurring appointment.

To schedule a recurring appointment, follow these steps:

1. In the Calendar folder, choose **Calendar, New Recurring Appointment**. The Appointment dialog box appears, and then the Appointment Recurrence dialog box appears (as shown in Figure 10.3).

2. In the Appointment Time area, enter the **Start**, **End**, and **Duration** times for the appointment.

3. In the Recurrence Pattern area, indicate the frequency of the appointment: **Daily**, **Weekly**, **Monthly**, or **Yearly**. After you select one of these options, the rest of the Recurrence Pattern area changes.

4. Enter the day and month, as well as any other options in the Recurrence Pattern area that are specific to your selection in step 3.

5. In the Range of Recurrence area, enter appropriate time limits according to these guidelines:

   Start Choose the date on which the recurring appointments will begin.

No End Date Choose this option if the recurring appointments are not on a limited schedule.

End After Choose this option and enter the number of appointments if there is a specific limit to the recurring appointments.

End By Choose this option and enter an ending date to limit the number of recurring appointments.

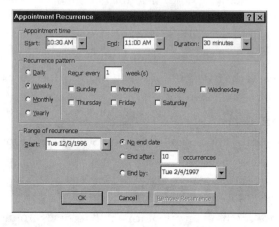

Figure 10.3 Schedule a recurring appointment once, and Outlook fills in the appointment for you throughout the Calendar.

6. Click **OK** to close the Appointment Recurrence dialog box. The Appointment dialog box appears.

7. Fill in the Appointment dialog box as described previously in this lesson. When you finish, click the **Save and Close** button to return to the Calendar. The recurring appointment appears in your calendar on the specified date and time. A recurring appointment contains a double-arrow icon to indicate that it is recurring.

Planning Events

In the Outlook Calendar, an *event* is any activity that lasts at least 24 hours, such as a trade show or a conference. You can plan an event in the Calendar program to block off larger time slots than you would for normal appointments. In addition, you can schedule recurring events.

To schedule an event, choose **Calendar, New Event**. The Event dialog box appears; it looks very much like the New Appointment dialog box. Fill in the **Subject, Location, Start Time**, and **End Time** text boxes. Make sure to check the **All Day Event** check box (that's the only difference between an Event and an Appointment). Click the **Save** button and the **Close** (X) button to return to the Outlook Calendar. The appointment appears in gray at the beginning of the day for which you scheduled the event.

To schedule a recurring event, choose **Calendar, New Recurring Event**. Fill in the Appointment Recurrence dialog box as you learned to in the previous section. When you close the Appointment Recurrence dialog box, the Recurring Event dialog box appears. Fill it in as you would the Event dialog box. Then click the **Save** button and the **Close** (X) button.

To edit an event or a recurring event, double-click the event in your calendar. As with a mail message or appointment, Outlook opens the event window so you can change times, dates, or other details of the event.

In this lesson, you learned to navigate the Calendar, create appointments, and save appointments. In the next lesson, you learn to plan a meeting.

Planning a Meeting

In this lesson, you learn to schedule a meeting, enter attendees for a planned meeting, set the meeting date and time, and invite others to the meeting.

Scheduling a Meeting

Outlook provides a method by which you can plan the time and date of a meeting, identify the subject and location of the meeting, and invite others to attend the meeting. You use the Calendar folder to plan and schedule meetings.

Meeting In Outlook, a meeting is an appointment to which you invite people and schedule resources.

Attendees The people who will be attending your meeting.

Resources Any equipment you use in your meeting, such as a computer, slide projector, or even the room itself.

To plan a meeting, follow these steps:

1. Click the icon for the Calendar folder, and then choose **Calendar, Plan a Meeting**. The Plan a Meeting dialog box appears (see Figure 11.1).
2. To enter the names of the attendees, click in the All Attendees list where it says **Type Attendee Name Here**. Enter the name and press **Enter**. Continue adding new names as necessary.

TIP **Invite More People** You can click the **Invite Others** button to choose names from your Personal Address Book or the Outlook Address Book.

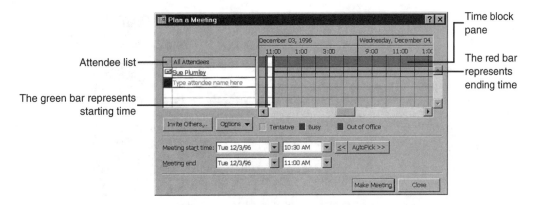

Figure 11.1 Choose the date and time of your meeting as well as the attendees.

3. To set a date for the meeting, open the leftmost **Meeting Start Time** drop-down list and select the date from the calendar, or just type the date in the text box. The ending date (in the Meeting End Time drop-down list) automatically shows the same date you set in the Meeting Start Time date box; you can change the End Time date if you want.

4. To set a start time for the meeting, do one of the following:

- Open the rightmost **Meeting Start Time** drop-down list and select the time.

- Type a time in the text box.

- Drag the green bar in the time-block pane of the dialog box to set the start time.

5. To set an end time for the meeting, do one of the following:

- Open the rightmost **Meeting End Time** drop-down list and select the end time.

- Type a time in the text box.

- Drag the red bar in the time-block pane of the dialog box to change the ending time of the meeting.

6. When you finish planning the meeting, click the **Make Meeting** button. The Meeting window appears (see Figure 11.2), from which you can refine the meeting details, as described in the next section.

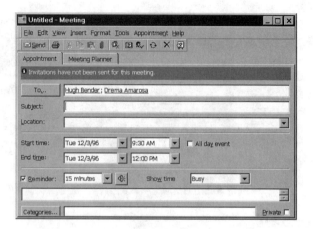

Figure 11.2 Specify the details about the meeting in the Appointment tab of the Meeting dialog box.

Working Out Meeting Details

After you plan a meeting, Outlook enables you to send invitations, identify the subject of the meeting, and specify the meeting's location. You enter these details in the Meeting dialog box.

When you schedule a meeting (as described in the previous section), you finish by clicking the **Make Meeting** button in the Plan a Meeting dialog box. When you do that, Outlook displays the Meeting dialog box with the Appointment tab in front (refer to Figure 11.2).

Follow these steps to specify meeting details for a meeting you've already scheduled.

1. If you did not list the attendees in the Plan a Meeting dialog box, either click in the **To** text box and enter the names of the people you want to attend the meeting, or click the **To** button to select the attendees from an address book.

2. In the **Subject** text box, enter a subject for the meeting.

3. In the **Location** text box, enter a location for the meeting.

4. (Optional) You can change the starting and ending dates and times in the Appointment tab. You also can choose the Meeting Planner tab to view the meeting in a format similar to that of the Plan a Meeting dialog box; make any changes to attendees, time, dates, and so on in the Meeting Planner tab.

5. (Optional) Select the **Reminder** check box, and enter a time for Outlook to sound an alarm to remind you of the meeting.

6. (Optional) Enter any special text you want to send the attendees in the text box provided.

7. When you're ready to send the invitations to the meeting, click the **Send** button. Close the Meeting window by choosing **File**, **Close**.

When you send an invitation, you're sending an e-mail that requests the presence of the recipient at the meeting. The recipient can reply to your message, save your message, and forward or delete the message, just as he can with any other e-mail message. If you want the recipient to reply, choose **Appointment**, **Request Responses**, and the recipients will be prompted to reply to your invitation.

An Invitation Mistake To cancel an invitation after you've sent it, choose **Appointment**, **Cancel Invitation**.

CAUTION

Inviting Others to the Meeting

If you need to add names to your attendees list—either while you're planning the meeting or at some later date—you can use your Personal Address Book or the Outlook Address Book to find the names of the people you want to invite. Additionally, you can choose whether to make the meeting required or optional for each person you invite.

To invite others to the meeting, follow these steps:

1. In either the Plan a Meeting dialog box or the Meeting Planner tab of the Meeting dialog box, click the **Invite Others** button. The Select Attendees and Resources dialog box appears, as shown in Figure 11.3.

2. Open the **Show Names from The** drop-down list and choose either **Personal Address Book** or **Outlook Address Book**.

3. To add a new name to a list, click the **New** button, and then enter the name, e-mail address, phone numbers, and other pertinent information about the name you're adding to the list.

4. Select any name in the list on the left side of the dialog box, and click the **Required** or **Optional** button to specify attendance requirements.

369

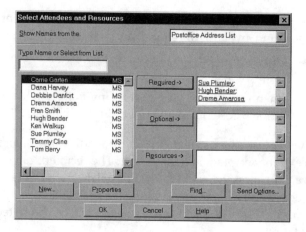

Figure 11.3   Use the address books to specify attendees to your meeting.

 TIP   Reserve Resources   Click the **New** button to add resources to the list; then notify the person who is in charge of those resources of your meeting.

5. Click **OK** to close the dialog box and add any attendees to your list.

Editing a Meeting

You can edit the details about a meeting, invite additional people, or change the date and time of the meeting at any time by opening the Meeting dialog box.

To open the Meeting dialog box and edit the meeting, follow these steps:

1. In the Calendar folder, choose the meeting date in the monthly calendar pane. The date appears in the schedule pane, and the meeting is blocked out for the time period you specified, as shown in Figure 11.4.

2. Double-click the meeting block to display the Meeting dialog box. You can edit anything in the Appointment or Meeting Planner tabs.

 TIP   Any Responses?   Choose the **Show Attendee Status** option in the Meeting Planner tab of the Meeting dialog box to see if the people you invited to the meeting have responded to your invitation.

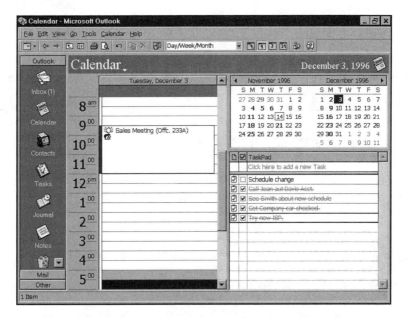

Figure 11.4 Select the meeting you want to edit from within the Calendar.

3. When you're finished, choose **File**, **Close** to close the Meeting dialog box. If you've made changes to the meeting specifics, you should also send a message to your attendees to notify them of the change.

In this lesson, you learned to schedule a meeting, enter attendees for a planned meeting, set the meeting time, and invite others to the meeting. In the next lesson, you learn to create a contacts list.

Creating a
Contacts List

In this lesson, you learn to create and view a Contacts list, and to send mail to someone on your Contacts list.

Creating a New Contact

You use the Contacts folder to create, store, and utilize your Contacts list. You can enter any or all of the following information about each contact:

- Name
- Job title
- Company name
- Address (Street, City, State, ZIP, Country)
- Phone (business, home, business fax, mobile)
- E-mail address
- Web page address
- Comments, notes, or descriptions
- Categories

 TERM   **Contact**   In Outlook, any person or company for which you've entered a name, address, phone number, or other information. You can communicate with a contact in Outlook by sending an e-mail message, scheduling a meeting, sending a letter, and so on.

You also can edit the information at any time, add new contacts, or delete contacts from the list. To create a new contact, follow these steps:

1. Click the **Contacts** button or choose the **Contacts** folder. If you haven't used the list before, the folder is empty.

2. Choose **Contacts**, **New Contact**, or simply click the **New Contact** button on the toolbar. The Contact dialog box appears, with the General tab displayed (see Figure 12.1).

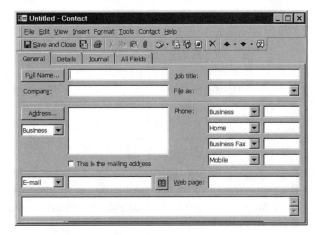

Figure 12.1 You can enter as much or as little information about each contact as you need.

3. Click the **Full Name** button to display the Check Full Name dialog box, and then enter the contact's title and full name (including first, middle, and last names) and any suffix you want to include. Alternatively, you can enter the name in the text box.

4. (Optional) Enter the client's company name and job title.

5. In the **File As** drop-down list box, enter or select the method by which you want to file your contact's names. You can choose last name first or first name first, or you can enter your own filing system, such as by company or state.

TIP **Keep It Simple** The default filing method for contacts is last name first, which makes it easy to quickly find the contact when you need it.

6. (Optional) Enter the address in the Address box and choose whether the address is **Business**, **Home**, or **Other**. Alternatively, you can click the **Address** button to enter the street, city, state, ZIP code, and country in specified areas instead of all within the text block. You can add a second address (for example, a home address) if you want.

7. In the Phone drop-down lists, choose the type of phone number—Business, Callback, Car, Home Fax, ISDN, Pager, and so on—and then enter the number. You can enter up to 19 numbers in each of the four drop-down boxes in the Phone area of the dialog box.

 TIP   **Phone Number Tips**   You can enter phone numbers with or without dashes, spaces, or parentheses. Outlook ignores them anyway. Outlook also ignores any extensions you add to the end of a phone number. Just don't forget to enter the area code, even if it's local.

8. (Optional) Enter up to three e-mail addresses in the **E-mail** text box; in the **Web Page** text box, enter the address for the company or contact's WWW page on the Internet (be sure to use the entire URL, such as **http:// www.microsoft.com**).

9. (Optional) In the comment text box, enter any descriptions, comments, or other pertinent information you want. Then select or enter a category to classify the contact.

10. Open the **File** menu and choose one of the following commands:

    Save   Saves the record and closes the Contact dialog box.

    Save and New   Saves the record and clears the Contact dialog box so you can enter a new contact.

    Save and New in Company   Saves the record and clears the Name, Job Title, File As, E-Mail, and comment text boxes so you can enter a new contact within the same company.

 TIP   **Quick Save and Close**   For an even faster save and close, click the **Save and Close** button on the toolbar. This saves the contact and returns you to the Contact folder view.

You can edit the information about a contact at any time by double-clicking the contact's name in the Contacts list; this displays the contact's information window. Alternatively, you can click within the information listed below a contact's name (such as the phone number or address) to position the insertion point in the text, and then delete or enter text. Press **Enter** to complete the modifications you make and move to the next contact in the list.

Viewing the Contacts List

By default, you see the contacts in an Address Cards view. The information you see displays the contact's name and other data such as addresses and phone numbers. The contact's company name, job title, and comments, however, are not displayed by default. Figure 12.2 shows the Contacts list in the default Address Cards view.

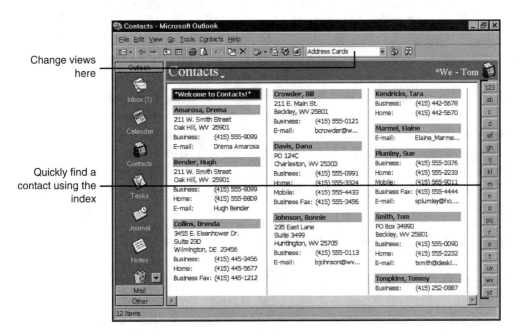

Change views here

Quickly find a contact using the index

Figure 12.2 View your contacts in Address Cards view.

You can use the horizontal scroll bar to view more contacts, or you can click a letter in the index to display contacts beginning with that letter in the first column of the list.

CAUTION

Do I Save View Settings?   Depending on the changes you make to a view, Outlook might display the Save View Settings dialog box to ask if you want to save the view settings before you switch to a different view. If you choose to save the current settings, Outlook lets you name the view and adds that view to the Current View list. If you choose to discard the current settings, your modifications to the view will be lost.

You can change how you view the contacts in the list by choosing one of these options from the Current View drop-down list on the standard toolbar:

Address Cards   Displays File As names (last name first, first name last, and so on), addresses, and phone numbers of the contacts, depending on the amount of information you enter in a card format.

Detailed Address Cards   Displays File As name, full name, job title, company, addresses, phone numbers, e-mail addresses, categories, and comments in a card format.

Phone List   Displays full name, job title, company, File As name, department, phone numbers, and categories in a table, organizing each entry horizontally in rows and columns.

By Category   Displays contacts in rows by categories. The information displayed is the same as what's displayed in a phone list.

By Company   Displays contacts in rows, grouped by their company. The information displayed is the same as what's displayed in a phone list.

By Location   Displays contacts grouped by country. The information displayed is the same as what's displayed in a phone list.

Communicating with a Contact

You can send messages to any of your contacts, arrange meetings, assign tasks, or even send a letter to a contact from within Outlook. To communicate with a contact, make sure you're in the Contacts folder. You do not need to open the specific contact's information window to perform any of the following procedures.

Sending Messages

To send a message to a contact, you must make sure to enter an e-mail address in the General tab of the Contact dialog box for that particular contact.

If Outlook cannot locate the mailing address, it displays the message dialog box shown in Figure 12.3.

Figure 12.3   Outlook cannot send the message until you complete the address in the New Message dialog box.

To send a message from the Contacts folder, select the contact and choose **Contacts**, **New Message to Contact**. In the Untitled - Message dialog box, enter the subject and message and set any options you want. When you're ready to send the message, click the **Send** button. For more information about sending mail, see Lesson 6, "Creating Mail."

Scheduling a Meeting with a Contact

To schedule a meeting with a contact, the contact must have a valid e-mail address. If no address is listed for the contact, Outlook notifies you with a message dialog box and enables you to enter an address within the message dialog box. If the listed address is not found, Outlook responds with the Check Names dialog box, as described in the previous section.

To schedule a meeting with a contact, select the contact and choose **Contacts**, **New Meeting with Contact**. The Untitled - Meeting dialog box appears. Enter the subject, location, time and date, and other information you need to schedule the meeting; then notify the contact by sending an invitation. For more information about scheduling meetings, see Lesson 11, "Planning a Meeting."

Assigning a Task to a Contact

Tasks are assigned through e-mail. Therefore, you must enter a valid e-mail address for the contact before you can assign her a task.

To assign a task to a contact, select the contact and choose **Contacts**, **New Task for Contact**. The Task dialog box appears. Enter the subject, due date, status, and other information, and then send the task to the contact. For detailed information about assigning tasks, see Lesson 13, "Creating a Task List."

Sending a Letter to a Contact

Outlook uses the Microsoft Word Letter Wizard to help you create a letter to send to a contact. Within the Word Letter Wizard, you follow directions as they appear on-screen to complete the text of the letter.

To send a letter to the contact, select the contact in the Contact folder, and choose **Contacts, New Letter to Contact**. Word opens the Letter Wizard on-screen. The Office Assistant asks questions about your letter and gives you information about how to use the Letter Wizard (see Figure 12.4). All you have to do is follow the directions and make your choices.

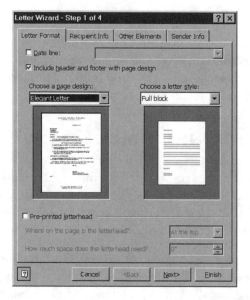

Figure 12.4 Use Word's Letter Wizard to create a letter to a contact.

TIP **How About vCards?** Install Microsoft's new vReader program that lets you make Outlook contacts out of electronic business cards (called vCards) you find on the Web. To learn more about it, connect to your Internet account, open Outlook's **Help** menu, select **Microsoft on the Web, Free Stuff**. This opens your Web browser and displays the Outlook Web page where you can learn more about downloading this free enhancement. (Refer to Appendix D for more information.)

In this lesson, you learned to create a Contacts list, view the list, and send mail to someone on your Contacts list. In the next lesson, you learn to create a task list.

Creating a Task List

In this lesson, you learn to enter a task and record statistics about the task.

Entering a Task

You can use the Tasks folder to create and manage your task list. You can list due dates, status, and priorities, and even set reminder alarms so you don't forget to perform certain tasks.

 Task List   A list of things you must do to complete your work, plan for a meeting, arrange an event, and so on. Various tasks might include making a phone call, writing a letter, printing a spreadsheet, or making airline reservations.

To enter a task, follow these steps:

1. In the Tasks folder, choose **Tasks**, **New Task** or click the **New Task** button on the toolbar. The Untitled - Task dialog box appears (see Figure 13.1).
2. In the Task tab, enter the subject of the task.
3. (Optional) Enter a date on which the task should be complete, or click the down-arrow to open the **Due** drop-down calendar and then choose a due date.
4. (Optional) Enter a start date, or click the down-arrow to open the **Start** drop-down calendar and then choose a starting date.
5. From the **Status** drop-down list, choose the current status of the project: Not Started, In Progress, Completed, Waiting on Someone Else, or Deferred.

6. In the **Priority** drop-down list, choose **Normal**, **Low**, or **High Priority**.

7. In the % **Complete** text box, type a percentage or use the spinner arrows to enter one.

8. (Optional) To set an alarm to remind you to start or complete the task, select the **Reminder** check box and enter a date and a time in the associated text boxes.

9. Enter any comments, descriptions, or other information related to the task in the Comments text box.

10. Click the **Categories** button and choose a category, or simply enter your own category in the text box.

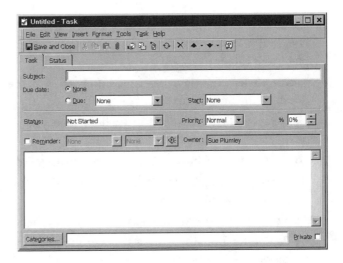

Figure 13.1 Enter data such as subject, due dates, and priority.

 TIP   **Access Denied**   Select the **Private** check box if you don't want others to see information about your task. The task subject appears, but not the details you've entered about the task.

11. Click **Save** and then **Close** when you finish.

TIP **Quick Save and Close** For an even faster save and close, click the **Save and Close** button on the toolbar. This saves the task and returns you to the Task folder.

Viewing Tasks

As in any Outlook folder, you can change how you view tasks in the list using the Current View drop-down list in the Standard toolbar. By default, the Tasks folder displays tasks in a Simple List view. Following is a description of the views you can use to display the Tasks folder:

Simple List Lists the tasks, completed check box, subject, and due date.

Detailed List Displays the tasks, priority, subject, status, percent complete, and categories.

Active Tasks Displays the same information as the detailed list but doesn't show any completed tasks.

Next Seven Days Displays only those tasks you've scheduled for the next 7 days, including completed tasks.

Overdue Tasks Shows a list of past-due tasks.

By Category Displays tasks by category; click the button representing the category you want to view.

Assignment Lists tasks assigned to you by others.

By Person Responsible Lists tasks grouped by the person who assigned the tasks.

Completed Tasks Lists only those tasks completed, along with their due dates and completion dates.

Task Timeline Use to display tasks by day, week, or month. Figure 13.2 shows the tasks assigned within one week.

Save What Settings? Depending on the changes you make to a view, Outlook might display the Save View Settings dialog box asking if you want to save the view settings before you switch to a different view. Generally, you want CAUTION to discard the current view settings and leave everything the way you found it.

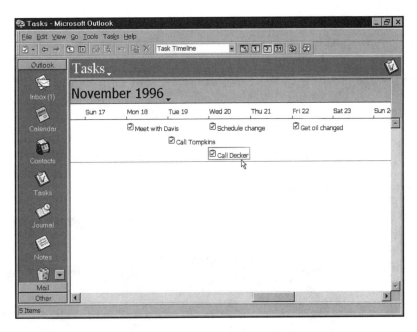

Figure 13.2 Double-click a task in Timeline view to edit it.

Managing Tasks

When working with a task list, you can add and delete tasks, mark tasks as completed, and arrange the tasks within the list. You also can perform any of these procedures in most of the task views described in the previous section. For information about printing a task list, see Lesson 16, "Printing in Outlook."

Figure 13.3 shows the Tasks folder; the following list describes how to manage certain tasks in the list.

- To quickly add a task, click the top row of the task list where it says **Click Here to Add a New Task** and enter the subject and date. You can also add a new task by double-clicking the next available row.

- To edit a task, double-click the task in the list. The Task dialog box appears.

- To mark a task as completed, click the check box in the second column from the left, or right-click the task and choose **Mark Complete** from the shortcut menu. Outlook places a line through the task.

383

- To delete a task, right-click the task and choose **Delete** from the shortcut menu. You can also select the task and press the Delete key on your keyboard.

- To assign a task to someone else, right-click the task and choose **Assign Task** from the shortcut menu. Fill in the name of the person to whom you want to assign the task and click the **Send** button to e-mail him the task request.

- To assign a new task to someone else, choose **Tasks**, **New Task Request**. Create the task as you normally would, but send the task as an e-mail by clicking the **Send** button.

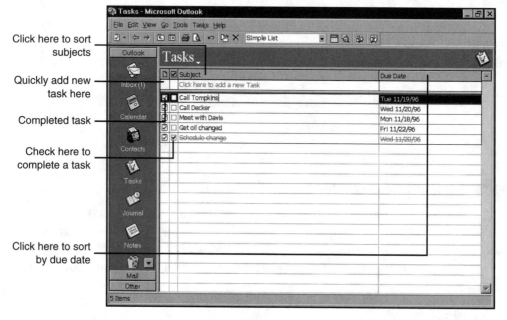

Figure 13.3   Add, delete, and sort the tasks in your list.

 TIP   **Get Rid of the Default Task**   If you don't want to leave the Start up Microsoft Outlook task on your list, right-click the task and choose **Delete**.

Recording Statistics About a Task

You can record statistics about a task, such as time spent completing the task, billable time, contacts, and so on, for your own records or for reference when sharing tasks with your coworkers. This feature is particularly helpful when you assign tasks to others; you can keep track of assigned tasks and find out when they are completed.

To enter statistics about a task, open any task in the task list and click the **Status** tab. Figure 13.4 shows a completed Status tab for a sample task.

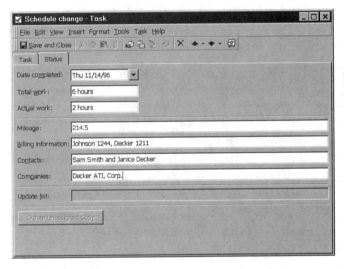

Figure 13.4 Fill in the status of the task so you can share it with others and keep personal records.

The following list describes the text boxes in the Status tab and the types of information you can enter:

Date Completed   Enter the date the task was completed, or click the arrow to display the calendar and choose the date.

Total Work   Enter the amount of time you expect the task to take. When you complete the job, Outlook calculates the actual time spent and enters it in this text box.

Actual Work   Enter the amount of time it actually took to complete the job.

Mileage   Enter the number of miles you traveled to complete the task.

Billing Information   Enter any specific billing information, such as hours billed, resources used, charges for equipment, and so on.

Contacts   Enter the names of in-house or outside contacts associated with the task. Separate multiple names with semicolons.

Companies   Enter the names of any companies associated with the contacts or with the project in general.

Update List   Automatically lists the people whose task lists are updated when you make a change to your task.

Create Unassigned Copy   Copies the task so it can be reassigned; use the button to send a task to someone other than an original recipient. If the task is not sent to someone else, the button is unavailable.

To track tasks you've assigned to others and to receive status reports, follow these steps:

1. In the Outlook dialog box, choose **Tools, Options**. The Options dialog box appears with the Tasks/Notes tab displayed.

2. In the Task Defaults area of the dialog box, check the **Keep Updated Copies of Assigned Tasks on My Task List** check box. This automatically tracks the progress of new tasks that you assign to others.

3. Check the **Send Status Reports When Assigned Tasks are Completed** check box to automatically receive notification upon the completion of assigned tasks.

4. Click **OK** to accept the changes and close the dialog box.

 TIP   Color Your World   You can also set colors to represent tasks within the Tasks/Notes tab of the Options dialog box. Outlook offers 20 different colors from which you can choose for overdue tasks and completed tasks.

In this lesson, you learned to enter a task and record statistics about the task. In the next lesson, you will learn to use the Journal.

Using the Journal

In this lesson, you learn to create journal entries manually and automatically, and to change views in the Journal.

Creating a Journal Entry

You can create a record of various items and documents so you can track your work, communications, reports, and so on. In the Outlook Journal, you can manually record any activities, items, or tasks you want. You also can automatically record e-mail messages, faxes, meeting requests, meeting responses, task requests, and task responses. Additionally, you can automatically record documents created in the other Office applications: Access, Excel, Office Binder, PowerPoint, and Word.

Journal   A folder within Outlook that you can use to record interactions, phone calls, message responses, and other activities important to your work.

Item   An article or object in Outlook, such as a task, appointment, contact, or Journal entry.

You can automatically or manually record items in Outlook's Journal. You can, for example, choose to automatically record your e-mail messages, meeting requests, task responses, and so on. When you automatically record items in the Journal, Outlook records all items you receive. However, if you don't want to record all items, you can have Outlook record only those items you choose by manually adding them to the Journal. For example, you might add only the e-mail relating to one account or one client instead of all the e-mail you receive.

Manually Recording an Entry

To manually create a journal entry, follow these steps:

1. In the Inbox folder (or any other folder in Outlook), select the item you want to record in the journal and choose **Tools, Record in Journal**. The Journal Entry dialog box appears (see Figure 14.1).

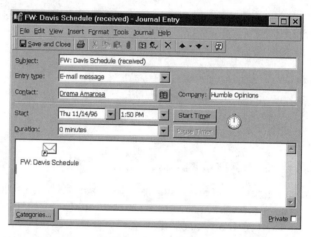

Figure 14.1   Record any Outlook item in the Journal.

2. The Subject, Entry Type, Contact, and Company boxes and other information is entered for you from the selected task, contact, or other selected item. However, you can change any of the statistics you want by entering new information in the following text boxes:

   Subject   Displays the title or name of the item.

   Entry Type   Describes the item based on its point of origin, such as a Word document, Meeting or Appointment, and so on.

   Contact   Lists the name(s) of any attendees, contacts, or other people involved with the selected item.

   Company   Lists the company or companies associated with the contacts.

   Start Time   Displays the date and time of the meeting, appointment, or other item.

Start Timer Like a stopwatch, the timer records the time that passes until you click the Pause Timer button.

Pause Timer Stops the timer.

Duration Enter the amount of time for completing the item.

Text box Displays shortcuts to any text, documents, details, or other information related to the item.

Categories Enter or select a category in which to place the item.

3. Click **Save and Close** to complete the entry.

TIP **Time Your Calls** When making phone calls or meeting with clients, you can create a journal entry to record the event, and use the Start Timer and Pause Timer buttons to record billable time.

If you want to create a new journal entry, but you don't have a contact, task, e-mail, or other related item for the entry, you can manually record a journal entry by following these steps:

1. Change to the Journal folder.

2. Choose **Journal, New Journal Entry** or click the **New Journal Entry** button on the Standard toolbar. The Journal Entry dialog box appears.

3. Enter the subject, entry type, contact, time, and any other information you want to record.

4. When you finish, click **Save** and then **Close**.

Automatically Recording Entries

You can set options to automatically record items and their related contacts and statistics about Microsoft Office documents you create. Suppose you want to keep a record, for example, of all memos you send to your boss. You can record it in the Journal.

To set the options to automatically record journal entries, follow these steps:

1. In the Journal folder, choose **Tools, Options**. The Options dialog box appears with the Journal tab displayed, as shown in Figure 14.2.

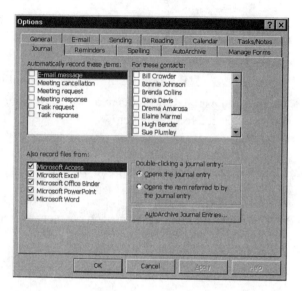

Figure 14.2 Set options for automatically recording items in your Journal.

2. In the **Automatically Record These Items** list, check those items you want Outlook to automatically record in your journal. (The items recorded correspond with those people selected in the list of contacts in step 3.)

3. In the **For These Contacts** list, check any contacts you want automatically recorded in the Journal. Outlook records any items checked in step 2 that apply to the selected contacts.

4. In the **Also Record Files From** list, check the applications for which you want to record journal entries. Outlook records the date and time you create or modify files in the selected program.

 TIP **Automatic and Easy** When you're creating a new contact in Outlook, you can set items to be automatically recorded in the journal by choosing the **Journal** tab in the Contact dialog box and checking the **Automatically Record Journal Entries for This Contact** check box.

Viewing Journal Entries

By default, the Journal folder displays information in the Timeline view and By Type, as shown in Figure 14.3. However, you can display the entries in various views, as described in the following list:

Current View ——

Double-click to
view entries ——

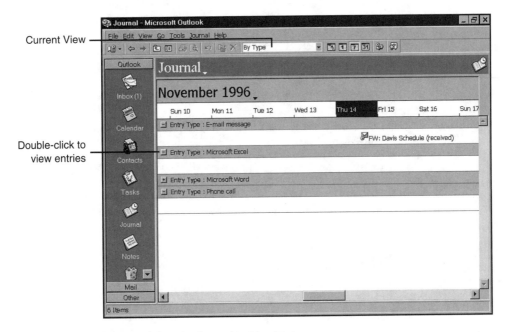

Figure 14.3 View the journal entries by type.

CAUTION

Save Settings? As in other views, Outlook might display the Save View Settings dialog box to ask if you want to save the view settings before you switch to a different view. You're probably getting used to this dialog box by now.

By Type In Timeline view, this option groups journal entries by type, such as e-mail messages, meetings, Word documents, and so on. Double-click a type to display its contents, and then position the mouse pointer over an entry to view its contents or name.

By Contact In Timeline view, this displays the name of each contact that you selected in the Options dialog box. Double-click any contact's name to view recorded entries.

By Category If you've assigned categories to your journal entries and other items, you can display your journal entries by category in the Timeline view.

Entry List Displays entries in a table with columns labeled Entry Type, Subject, Start, Duration, Contact, and Categories.

Last Seven Days Displays entries in an entry list, but includes only those entries dated within the last seven days.

Phone Calls Lists all entries that are phone calls.

TIP **Sort Journal Entries** You can click the heading bar—Subject, Start, or Duration—in any Entry list view to sort the items in that column in ascending or descending order.

In this lesson, you learned to manually and automatically create journal entries and to change views in the Journal. In the next lesson, you learn to create notes.

Creating Notes

In this lesson, you learn to create, sort, and view notes.

Creating Notes

If you've ever used paper sticky notes to remind yourself of tasks, ideas, or other brief annotations, Outlook's Notes are for you. Notes are very similar to paper sticky notes. You can use Notes to write down reminders, names, phone numbers, directions, or anything else you need to remember. In Outlook, all notes are kept in the Notes folder. You have to remember to look at the folder so you can view your notes, unless you drag a note out of Outlook and place it on the Windows 95 or Windows NT desktop.

To create a note, follow these steps:

1. In the Notes folder, choose **Note**, **New Note** or click the **New Note** button on the Standard toolbar. A note appears, ready for you to type your text (see Figure 15.1).

2. Enter the text for your note.

TIP **The Long and Short of It** Notes don't have to be brief. You can enter pages and pages of text if you want. As you type, the page scrolls for you; use the arrow keys and the Page Up/Page Down keys to move through the note text.

3. When you finish, click the **Close** (X) button to close the note.

The text you enter in a note also becomes a title for the note that's displayed in the Notes folder in various views (as described later in this lesson). If you want to give your note an actual title, just create a new note, enter the title text only, and then close the note. Then you can reopen the note and enter as much text as you want, but only the title is displayed in the Notes folder list. Another way to title your note is to type in the title text on the first line, then press **Enter** and proceed with typing in the note text. After the note is closed, the first line you entered appears as the note title.

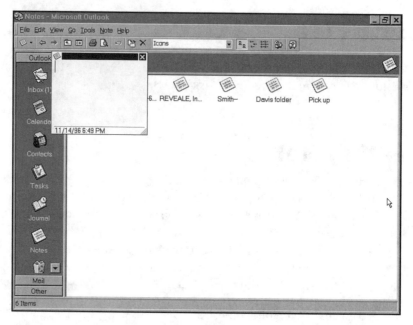

Figure 15.1 A Note automatically includes the date and time it was created.

Setting Note Options

You can change the default color and size of your notes. You also can change the default font used for your notes. To set note options, follow these steps:

1. In the Notes folder, choose **Tools**, **Options**. The Options dialog box appears with the Tasks/Notes tab displayed (see Figure 15.2).

2. In the Note Defaults area of the dialog box, click the **Color** drop-down arrow and select a new default color for your notes. You can change the color to yellow, blue, green, pink, or white. The default is yellow.

3. Open the **Size** drop-down list and choose **Small**, **Medium**, or **Large** for the size of the notes. The default is Medium.

4. If you would prefer not to show the time and date on your notes, deselect the **Show Time and Date** check box.

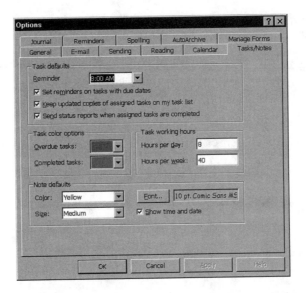

Figure 15.2 Customize your notes.

5. To change the font, click the **Font** button. The Font dialog box appears. Change the font, font style, size, color, and other options, and then click **OK**.

Managing Individual Notes

To open a note, double-click it in the Notes folder. You can edit the text in an open note as you would edit any text. To move a note, drag its title bar. You also can delete, forward, or print notes; you can change the color of individual notes; and you can specify categories for your notes.

Click a note's **Control-menu** button to display a menu with the following commands:

New Note   Creates a new note but leaves the first note open.

Save As   Enables you to save the note and its contents.

Delete   Deletes a note and its contents. (You also can delete a note by selecting it in the **Notes** list and pressing the **Delete** key.)

Forward   Enables you to send the note as an attachment in an e-mail message.

Cut, Copy, Paste   Enables you to select text from the note and cut or copy it to the Clipboard. The Paste command enables you to paste items on the Clipboard at the insertion point in the note.

Color   Choose another color for the individual note.

Categories   Enter or choose a category.

Print   Prints the contents of the note.

Close   Closes the note. (You also can click the **Close** (X) button in the note's title bar.) A closed note appears in the Notes folder.

Viewing Notes

The Notes folder provides various views for organizing and viewing your notes. You can also sort notes in any entry list view by right-clicking the heading bar—Subject, Created, Categories, and so on—and select the Sort method.

The default view is Icons, but you can change the view using the Current View drop-down list in the Standard toolbar. Figure 15.3 shows the Notes folder in the default view.

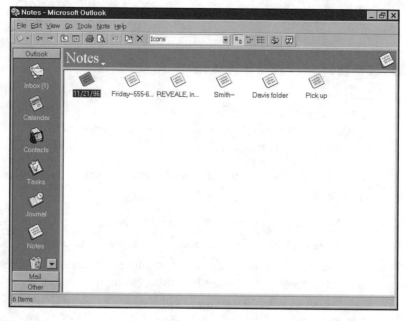

Figure 15.3   This view lists the notes you've written in the last seven days.

You can choose to display your Notes folder in any of the following views:

Icons   Displays the notes as note icons with the message (or a portion of the message) displayed below the icon.

Notes List   Displays the notes in a list, showing the title and note contents in the Subject column, the creation date and time, and the Categories.

Last Seven Days   Displays all notes written in the last seven days, by Subject, creation date, and categories.

By Category   Displays the categories; double-click a category to show its contents.

By Color   Displays notes by their color. Double-click a color to display the notes.

In this lesson, you learned to create, sort, and view notes. In the next lesson, you will learn to print in Outlook.

Printing in Outlook

In this lesson, you learn to print items in Outlook, change the page setup, preview an item before printing it, and change printer properties.

Choosing Page Setup

In Outlook, you choose the print style you will use before you print. Each folder—Inbox, Calendar, Contacts, and so on—offers various print styles, and each style displays the data on the page in a different way.

Page In Outlook, this is the area of the paper that will actually be printed on. You might, for example, print two or four pages on a single sheet of paper.

Print Style The combination of paper and page settings that control printed output.

You can choose from Outlook's built-in print styles, modify the default print styles, or create your own print styles. These lists show the default print styles available for each folder.

The Inbox, Contacts, Tasks, Journal, and Notes use the following two styles:

Table Style Displays data in columns and rows on an 8.5-by-11 sheet, portrait orientation, .5-inch margins.

Memo Style Displays data with a header of information about the message and then straight text on an 8.5-by-11 sheet, portrait orientation, .5-inch margins.

The Calendar folder provides the Memo style, plus the following styles:

 Daily Style   Displays one day's appointments on one page on an 8.5-by-11 sheet, portrait orientation, .5-inch margins.

 Weekly Style   Displays one week's appointments per page on an 8.5-by-11 sheet, portrait orientation, .5-inch margins.

 Monthly Style   Displays one month's appointments per page on an 8.5-by-11 sheet, landscape orientation, .5-inch margins.

 Tri-fold Style   Displays the daily calendar, task list, and weekly calendar on an 8.5-by-11 sheet, landscape orientation, .5-inch margins.

The Contacts folder provides the Memo style, plus the following styles:

 Card Style   Two columns and headings on an 8.5-by-11 sheet, portrait orientation, .5-inch margins.

 Small Booklet Style   One-column page that equals 1/8 of a sheet of paper—so that eight pages are on one 8.5-by-11 sheet of paper with .5-inch margins. Then the portrait orientation applies to the 1/8 pages.

 Medium Booklet Style   One column that equals 1/4 of a sheet of paper—so that four pages are on one 8.5-by-11 sheet of paper. Portrait orientation with .5-inch margins.

 Phone Directory Style   One column, 8.5-by-11 sheet of paper, portrait orientation with .5-inch margins.

 TIP **Page Setup Only Matters in Printing**   No matter how you set up your pages, it will not affect your view of tasks, calendars, or other Outlook items on-screen. Page setup only applies to a printed job.

You can view, modify, and create new page setups in Outlook. To view or edit a page setup, follow these steps:

1. Change to the folder for which you're setting the page.

2. Choose **File**, **Page Setup**. A secondary menu appears that lists the available print types.

3. Select the print type you want to view or edit, and the Page Setup dialog box appears (see Figure 16.1).

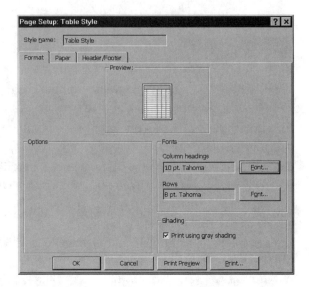

Figure 16.1 Customize the print type to suit your needs.

4. Click the **Format** tab to view or edit the page type, choose options (in some cases), and change fonts.

5. Click the **Paper** tab to view or edit paper size, page size, margins, and orientation.

6. Click the **Header/Footer** tab to view or edit headers for your pages.

Previewing Before Printing

You can choose to preview an item before printing it so you're sure it looks the way you want it to look. If you do not like the way an item looks in preview, you can change the page setup.

Before you display an item in print preview, you must change to the folder containing the item you want to print. Then you can choose to preview the item in any of the following ways:

- Click the **Print Preview** button in the Page Setup dialog box.
- Choose **File**, **Print Preview**.

- Click the **Print Preview** button on the Standard Toolbar.
- Click the **Preview** button in the Print dialog box.

Figure 16.2 shows a calendar and task list in Print Preview. You can change the page setup by clicking the **Page Setup** button; the Page Setup dialog box appears. Click the **Print** button to send the job to the printer. Click the **Close** button to exit Print Preview and return to the Outlook folder.

Mouse pointer changes to a magnifying glass

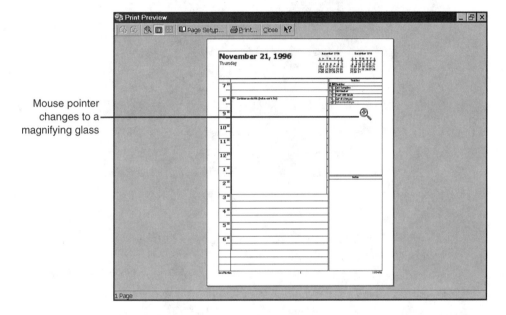

Figure 16.2 Preview the item before printing it.

TIP **Enlarge the View** When the mouse pointer looks like a magnifying glass with a plus sign in it, you can click to enlarge the page. When the mouse pointer looks like a magnifying glass with a minus sign in it, you can click to reduce the view again.

Printing Items

After you choose the print style and preview an item to make sure it's what you want, you can print the item. You can indicate the number of copies you want to print, select a printer, change the print style or page setup, and set a print range.

When you're ready to print an item, follow these steps:

1. Choose **File**, **Print** or click the **Print** button on the Standard Toolbar. The Print dialog box appears, as shown in Figure 16.3.

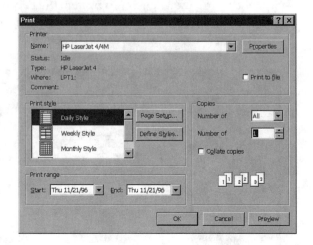

Figure 16.3   Set the printing options before printing the item.

2. In the Printer area of the dialog box, choose a different printer from the Name drop-down list if necessary.

TIP   In a Hurry?   If your computer is on a network and you notice the Status of the selected printer is Busy or Paused, for example, choose a different printer from the drop-down list.

3. In the **Print Style** area, choose a print style from the list. You also can edit the page setup (with the Page Setup button) or edit or create a new style (with the Define Styles button).

4. In the Copies area of the dialog box, choose **All**, **Even**, or **Odd** in Number of Pages and enter the number of copies you want to print. Click the **Collate Copies** check box if you want Outlook to automatically assemble multiple copies.

5. Set the print range with the options in that area. (The Print Range options vary depending on the type of item you're printing.)

6. Click **OK** to print the item.

Setting Printer Properties

Whether you're printing to a printer connected directly to your computer or to a printer on the network, you can set printer properties. The properties you set apply to all print jobs you send to the printer until you change the properties again.

Printer Properties Configurations specific to a printer connected to your computer or to the network. Printer properties include paper orientation, paper source, graphics settings, fonts, and print quality.

Access Denied? If you cannot change the printer properties to a network printer, it's probably because the network administrator has set the printer's configuration and you're not allowed access to the settings. If you need to change printer properties and cannot access the printer's Properties dialog box, talk to your network administrator.

To set printer properties, open the **Print** dialog box (by choosing **File**, **Print**). In the **Printer** area, select a printer from the Name drop-down list, and then click the **Properties** button. The printers' Properties dialog boxes differ depending on the make and model of printer.

Most likely, you will be able to set paper size, page orientation, and paper source by using options on a Paper tab in the dialog box. In addition, you might see a Graphics tab, in which you can set the resolution, intensity, and graphics mode of your printer. A Fonts tab enables you to set options on TrueType fonts, font cartridges, and so on. You might also find a Device Options tab, in which you can set print quality and other options. For more information about your printer, read the documentation that came with it.

How About Printing Schedule+ Files? The Microsoft Outlook Web page has support files you can download that let you print a Schedule+ Calendar from Outlook. To find out more about these files, log onto your Internet account; then open the Outlook **Help** menu and select **Microsoft on the Web**, **Free Stuff**. This opens your Web browser to the Outlook Web page where you can find more information.

403

In this lesson, you learned to print items in Outlook, change the page setup, preview an item before printing it, and change printer properties. In the next lesson, you will learn to manage your files and Outlook items.

Saving, Opening, and Finding Outlook Items

In this lesson, you learn to save items, open items, and archive items in Outlook.

Saving Items

Generally, when you finish adding a new task, appointment, meeting, contact, or other item, Outlook automatically saves that item for you or you're prompted to save the item yourself. You also can save most items in Outlook for use in other applications by using the Save As command. After you save an item by naming it, you can open that same item and edit, print, or otherwise use the saved file in Windows applications that support the file type. You might save an item—a journal entry or appointment page, for example—so you can refer to it later, edit the original, or keep it as a record.

Save As When you save an item using the File, Save As command, you can designate a drive, directory, and new file name for that item, as well as a file type.

File Type A file type is the same thing as a file format. When you save a file, you specify a file type that identifies the file as one that can be opened in specific applications. For example, the file extension .DOC identifies a file type that you can open in Word, and the extension .TXT represents a text-only format you can open in nearly any word processor or other application.

To save an item, follow these steps:

1. In the folder containing the item you want to save, choose **File**, **Save As**. The Save As dialog box appears (see Figure 17.1).

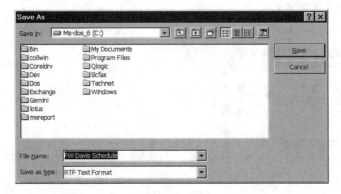

Figure 17.1   Save items as files for use in other programs, as copies of the originals, or for later use.

Why Is Save As Dimmed?   When the Save As command is dimmed, you must first select an item—an appointment, meeting, task, note, and so on—before you can save it.

CAUTION

2. From the Save In drop-down list, choose the drive to which you want to save the file. From the folders on that drive, select the one you want to save to.

3. In the Save As Type drop-down list, choose a file type. You can save the file in the following file types:

Text Only   Saves in an ASCII format that you can use in other applications, such as Word, Notepad, and so on.

RTF Text Format   Saves in Rich Text Format. You also can use this format in Word, Outlook, or Lotus Notes, for example.

Outlook Template   Saves as a template (or style sheet) that you can use as a basis for other items.

Message Format   Saves in a format you can use in your e-mail messages.

Word Document Format   Saves the file in a format that Word can read, using a DOC extension.

4. Enter a name for the item in the **File Name** text box, or accept the default.

5. Click the **Save** button.

Opening and Using Saved Items

After you save items, you can open and use them in Outlook and other applications. If, for example, you saved a contact as a message file, you can insert that file into a message and send the contact's name, address, and other information to someone through an e-mail message. You can save other items, such as meeting information from your calendar, as a text file you can open in Notepad or Word to edit, format, print, or otherwise modify the file.

Opening and Using an RTF File

You can open RTF files in many word processing programs—Word, Notepad, WordPad, and so on. To open an RTF file in another Windows application, choose **File**, **Open**. In the Open dialog box, choose **Rich Text Format** (or **RTF Text Format**) in the **Files of Type** drop-down list. The saved files appear in the file list. (You may need to locate the exact folder containing the RTF file before the file name appears in the file list.) Select the file and click the **Open** button.

RTF Isn't Listed? If RTF isn't listed in the application's Files of Type list box, see if Text Only is listed. You can also save Outlook items as Text Only.

CAUTION

Figure 17.2 shows an e-mail message saved as an RTF file and opened in Word. After opening a file, you can format it, cut or copy items to it, insert objects, print, edit, and otherwise manipulate the file.

Opening and Using a Text-Only File

You open a text-only file in much the same way you open an RTF file. In Notepad, for example, choose **File**, **Open** and choose **Text Documents** as the file type in the Open dialog box. (You may have to first locate the folder containing the text-only file before it's displayed in the file list.) Files saved as text-only do not retain any formatting; however, you can select the text and format it in the destination application.

407

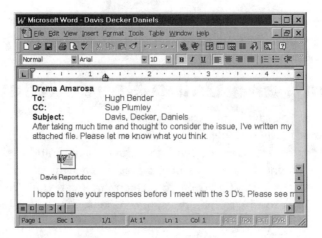

Figure 17.2 Exchanging data between applications makes your work quicker and easier.

Using a Message Text File

After you save an item as a message text file, you can insert the item into an e-mail message to send. Suppose you saved a contact's information or an especially long note that you want to share with someone else; you can insert the file as an object into a message and send the e-mail as you normally would. Then the recipient can open the message and the message file.

TIP **Files as Objects** As described in Lesson 10, you can insert any existing file as an object; therefore, you can insert an RTF, text-only, or message file into a Word document, Excel spreadsheet, mail message, or any other Windows document that supports OLE.

To insert a message file into a message, open the message and choose **Insert**, **Object**. In the Insert Object dialog box, choose **Create from File**. Enter the path and file name and click **OK**. Figure 17.3 shows a message file in the text of an e-mail.

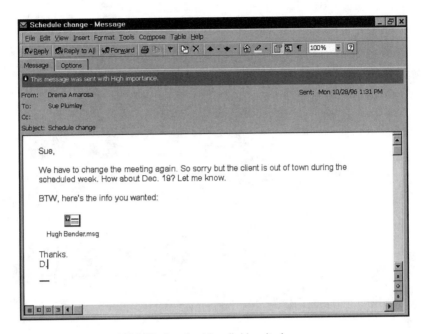

Figure 17.3 Open the MSG file by double-clicking its icon.

Using AutoArchive

You can set an option in Outlook to automatically archive your mail messages into files periodically. The AutoArchive feature cleans your Inbox for you without deleting any messages.

Archive To save items to a file that can be opened at any time and printed, viewed, or otherwise used. You might, for example, want to archive some of your mail messages to keep for your records instead of leaving those messages in your Inbox. Archived items are removed from the folder and copied to an archive file.

To use AutoArchive, follow these steps:

1. Choose **Tools**, **Options**. The Options dialog box appears.
2. Click the **AutoArchive** tab.
3. Click the **AutoArchive Every** *xx* check box to display the rest of the items in the dialog box (see Figure 17.4).

409

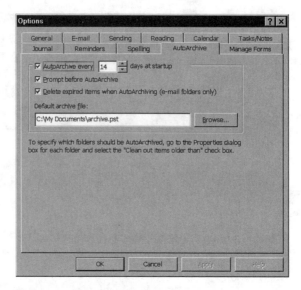

Figure 17.4 Specify options for automatically archiving items into files.

4. Choose from the following options:

AutoArchive Every *x* Days at Startup Enter a number for how often (in days) you want Outlook to automatically archive items. If you enter **14**, for example, when you start Outlook on the 14th day, it automatically archives the contents of your folders into an archive file.

Prompt Before AutoArchive If you check this, Outlook displays a dialog box each time it is about to perform the AutoArchive; you can click OK or Cancel to continue or stop the operation.

Delete Expired Items When AutoArchiving (E-Mail Folders Only)
Check this box to have Outlook delete messages from the Inbox after archiving them.

5. In the **Default Archive File** text box, enter a path to where you want to save the file, and name it (if you don't want to use the default).

6. Click **OK** to close the dialog box.

In addition to setting the AutoArchive options in the Options dialog box, each folder—Inbox, Tasks, Calendar, and so on—has additional AutoArchive options you can set.

To set individual folders' AutoArchive options, follow these steps:

1. Right-click the folder in the Outlook Bar to display the shortcut menu.

2. Choose **Properties**. The item's Properties dialog box appears.

3. Choose the **AutoArchive** tab. Figure 17.5 shows the Inbox's AutoArchive tab.

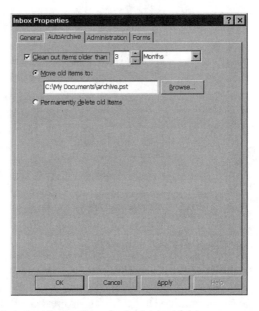

Figure 17.5 Set AutoArchive options for individual folders.

4. Set the options you want in the dialog box. You can change the length of time you want the archived files to be saved before they're deleted or saved to another file, and you can enter a path and file name for the second save.

5. Click **OK** to close the dialog box.

Archiving Manually

You can choose to archive one or two folders or all folders manually whenever you're ready to create an archive file. If you choose to do it yourself, you control exactly how and when archives are created.

To create an archive, follow these steps:

1. Choose **File**, **Archive**. The Archive dialog box appears (see Figure 17.6).

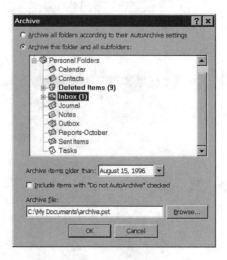

Figure 17.6 Enter settings for manual archiving.

2. Choose one of the following options:

   Archive All Folders According to Their AutoArchive Settings Use this option to save archives of each folder using the settings you select in the AutoArchive tab of the folder's Properties dialog box.

   Archive This Folder and All Subfolders Select this option to archive the selected folder.

3. Enter a date in the **Archive Items Older Than** text box, or select a date from the drop-down calendar.

4. In the **Archive File** text box, enter a path and file name with which to save the file.

5. Click **OK** to archive the selected folder(s).

Retrieving Archived Files

You can retrieve an archived file by importing it to the original file. When you retrieve an archived file, it becomes a part of your Outlook folder just as it was before you archived it.

Follow these steps to retrieve an archived file:

1. Choose **File, Import and Export**. The Import and Export Wizard dialog box appears.
2. Choose **Import from a Personal Folders File (*PST)** and click the **Next** button.
3. In the second Wizard dialog box, enter the path and the file name of the archived file.
4. Select any one of the following options, and then click the **Next** button:

   Replace Duplicates with Items Imported to overwrite any copies of the data with imported items.

   Allow Duplicates to Be Created to create duplicates of the items instead of overwriting them.

   Do Not Import Duplicates to preserve the originals in the folder instead of overwriting them with items from the archived file.

5. In the third Wizard dialog box, choose the folder into which you want to import. (The default is to import the archived item to the Personal Folders area; you may have created subfolders into which you want to import.)
6. Click the **Finish** button, and Outlook imports the archived files.

Deleting Archived Files

The easiest way to delete archived files is by using the Windows Explorer. However, you can also delete files from the Find Files and Folders dialog box or from My Computer (both Windows applications).

To delete an archived file, follow these steps:

1. Open the Explorer and locate the files. Archived files are saved with a .PST extension in the My Documents folder (by default) or any other folder you designate.
2. Open the folder containing the files and select the file(s) you want to delete.
3. Press the **Delete** key, or drag the file(s) to the Recycle Bin.
4. Empty the Recycle Bin by right-clicking the **Bin** and choosing **Empty Recycle Bin**.
5. Close the Explorer by clicking the **Close** (X) button.

Finding Items

Outlook provides a method you can use to locate items on your computer. You can search for messages, files, journal entries, notes, tasks, contacts, appointments, and so on. You can search for specific words, categories, priority, item size, and other criteria that you stipulate. Outlook's Find feature can be especially useful if your folders become full, and locating items on your own is difficult.

 Criteria Guidelines you set in the Find dialog box that Outlook uses to find items, such as messages, contacts, or appointments. Included in the criteria you set may be the date an item was created, the title or subject of the item, or specific text within the item.

To find an item in Outlook, follow these steps:

 1. Choose **Tools**, **Find Items** or click the **Find Items** button on the Standard Toolbar. The Find dialog box appears, as shown in Figure 17.7.

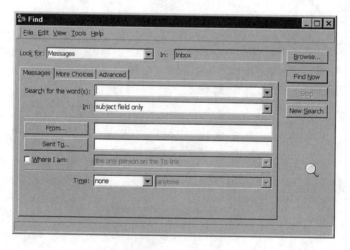

Figure 17.7 Use the Find dialog box to search for messages, appointments, and other items.

CAUTION

My Dialog Box Is Different   The Find dialog box in Figure 17.7 was opened from the Inbox. If you open the Find dialog box from Calendar, Tasks, or any other folder, the options in the dialog box relate to the item for which you're searching.

2. In any Find dialog box, choose the item for which you want to search in the **Look For** drop-down list. You can choose Tasks, Notes, Messages, Journal Entries, Files, Contacts, Appointments and Meetings, or Any Type of Outlook Item.

3. Click the **Browse** button to display the Select Folder(s) dialog box, from which you can choose the folder to search.

4. On the first tab, which is named for the item you select in the Look For list, you can enter specific words to search for, fields you want to search, dates, contact names, file types, and so on. The second tab, More Choices, offers additional options to add to the search, such as item size, category, and so on. Set the options you want on both tabs.

TIP   **Narrow the Search**   The more options you select and specify in the Find dialog box, the more you narrow the search; fewer items will match the search criteria. However, when you select more options, the search could take longer.

5. When you're ready to find the item(s), click the **Find Now** button. The Find dialog box extends to display a list of items Outlook finds that match the search criteria. In addition to the name of the item, the search results also show the folder in which you find the item, along with other item details.

You can perform a new search by clicking the **New Search** button, which clears the text boxes and previously selected options, and entering new criteria. If you want to pause or stop a search that's taking too long, click the **Stop** button.

TIP   **Fast Find**   When you're in the Inbox, an extra Find command appears on the Tools menu: Find All. With the Find All command, you can choose to find all messages related to the selected message or all messages from the sender of the selected message. The Find dialog box appears, displaying a list of the matching messages.

415

In this lesson, you learned to save items, open items, and archive items in Outlook. In the next lesson, you will learn to integrate items between Outlook folders.

Integrating Outlook Items

In this lesson, you learn to use various items in Outlook together (to create a task or an appointment from a mail message or to create a document within Outlook, for example).

Creating a Task from a Mail Message

You can use a mail message to create a task quickly and easily in Outlook. Instead of printing the message and then opening your Task List to add the information, you can create the task by using drag-and-drop copying. For more information about using the Tasks folder, see Lesson 13, "Creating a Task List."

 TIP **You Don't Lose the Message** When you use a message to create another item, Outlook copies the message so that the original message remains in the Inbox.

To create a task from a mail message, follow these steps:

1. Open the **Inbox** folder.
2. Click and drag the unopened mail message from the Inbox window to the **Tasks** icon on the Outlook Bar. The Task dialog box opens (see Figure 18.1).
3. Change the subject or other data if you want, and then set any options for the task (such as due date, priority, reminders, categories, and so on).
4. Click the **Save and Close** button and Outlook adds the task to your list.

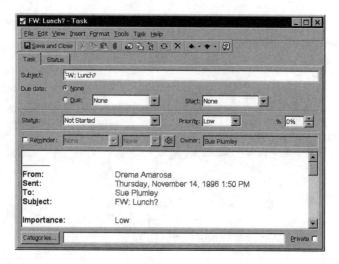

Figure 18.1   Create a task from an e-mail message.

Creating an Appointment from a Mail Message

In addition to creating tasks from messages, you can create an appointment from a mail message. When you create the appointment, you can set a time and date for the appointment, invite attendees to the appointment, create a meeting, and otherwise set options for the appointment. For more information about creating appointments, see Lesson 10, "Using the Calendar."

To create an appointment from a mail message, follow these steps:

1. Open the Inbox and locate the mail message you want to use.
2. Drag the unopened message from the Inbox window to the Calendar folder on the Outlook Bar. The Appointment dialog box opens with some information automatically filled in (see Figure 18.2).
3. Add the location to the appointment and make any desired changes in the **Subject**, **Start Time**, or **End Time** boxes, or in any other of the options.
4. Click the **Save and Close** button to complete the appointment.

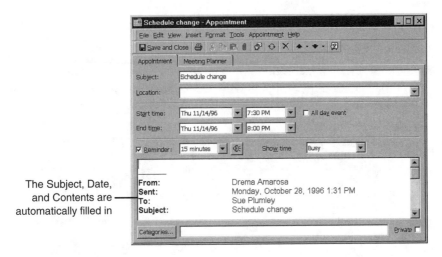

The Subject, Date, and Contents are automatically filled in

Figure 18.2   Create an appointment using the data in a mail message.

Create a Note from Any Item

Just as you can create tasks and appointments from a mail message, you also can create a note from any item in Outlook. Suppose someone e-mailed you information about a product or service that you want to add to a report; you can simply create a note with the information on it. Or suppose you want to call someone at a certain time later in the day. You can create a note from your contact entry so you won't forget.

You can create a note from a mail message, appointment or meeting, contact, task, or journal entry. After you create the note, you can edit the text in the note without affecting the original item.

To create a note from any Outlook item, drag the item into the Notes folder in the Outlook Bar. Outlook creates and displays the note, and you can edit the text if you want. For more information about notes, see Lesson 15, "Creating Notes."

Using Outlook Templates

Outlook includes many templates on which you can base new messages, appointments, tasks, and so on. You use a template when you want to create a new item. The e-mail templates, for example, supply an Untitled Message window with decorative fonts and graphics you can use to add pizzazz to your message.

To use an Outlook template, follow these steps:

1. Choose **File**, **New**.

2. In the secondary menu that appears, select **Choose Template**. The Choose Template dialog box appears with several templates from which to choose (see Figure 18.3).

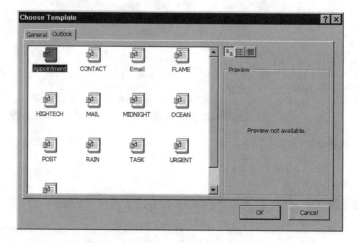

Figure 18.3 Base your new item on a specific template in Outlook.

3. Select the template you want to use and click **OK**. Outlook displays the message, task, appointment, or other window in which you can create your item.

In this lesson, you learned to use various items in Outlook together—to create a task and an appointment from a mail message and to create a document within Outlook. In the next lesson, you learn to customize Outlook.

Publisher 97

Introducing Publisher 97

In this lesson, you learn how to start and quit Publisher 97, what the different parts of the screen are, how to work with PageWizards, how to start with a blank document, and how to save your work.

Starting Publisher 97

Before you can start Microsoft Publisher 97, you must make sure that it is properly installed. See Appendix D in the back of this book for details on program installation.

You start Publisher 97 from the Windows 95 Start menu. Follow these steps:

1. Open the Start menu by clicking the **Start** button.

2. On the **Start** menu, select **Programs**.

3. From the **Programs** submenu, select **Microsoft Publisher**.

The very first time you start the program, Publisher 97 displays a brief introduction. You can press the **Next** button to go through the 11 screens or press **Cancel**. After the Introduction, the Startup dialog box appears, which has three tabbed pages:

- **PageWizard** Use a PageWizard to create your publication. You'll learn how to use the PageWizard later in this lesson.

- **Blank Page** Start a new, blank document in a number of sizes and shapes. Figure 1.1 shows the Full Page chosen under this option.

• **Existing Publication** Open an existing Publisher 97 project. This page will be blank if you've not yet created a Publisher document.

After you have made your selection, click the **OK** button to confirm your choice.

Touring the Publisher 97 Screen

Before you begin creating publications with Publisher 97, it is best to familiarize yourself with the various parts of the screen. Table 1.1 describes a typical opening screen shown in Figure 1.1.

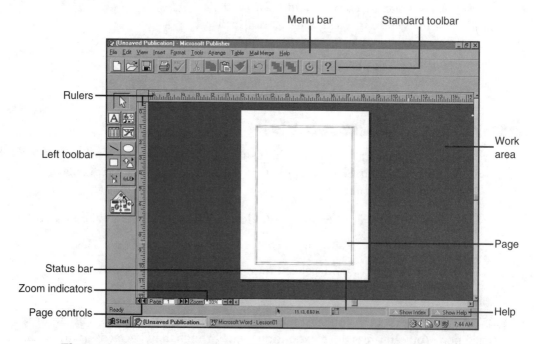

Figure 1.1 Parts of the Publisher 97 screen.

Table 1.1 Parts of the Publisher 97 Screen

Screen Element	Function
Help	Provides on-screen indexed suggestions and technical assistance.
Left toolbar	Enables access to the most commonly used Publisher 97 commands such as Text Frame and Picture Frame.

Screen Element	Function
Menu bar	Allows access to the Publisher 97 menu commands.
Page	Is the primary workspace for creating the publication.
Page controls	Displays current page number and controls access to other pages in the publication.
Rulers	Shows pointer and selected object position for placement.
Standard toolbar	Provides shortcuts to basic program commands.
Status bar	Displays pointer position and dimensions of selected object.
Work area	Used as a "scratch area" for temporary storage of objects.
Zoom indicators	Allows adjustment to the magnification of the publication view, by percentage or by object.

Working with PageWizards

PageWizards are one of the handiest features of Publisher 97. There are over 18 categories of these enhanced template guides covering everything from brochures to origami. Most categories have a wide variety of designs to choose from. Best of all, the PageWizards allow even the most basic beginner to produce high-quality, professional-looking publications.

To develop your first publication using PageWizards, follow these steps:

1. Start Publisher 97.
2. From the **PageWizards** tab of the Startup dialog box, select one of the publication categories by double-clicking your choice. The PageWizard Design Assistant displays the first step in developing your work. An example is shown in Figure 1.2.

   Depending on which wizard you chose, you'll see different options on your first screen. Choices may include:

   - Design options where you can choose an appropriate style by clicking an icon.
   - Mutually exclusive option buttons allow you to make only one choice per screen. For example, you may see a list of form formats such as invoice, fax sheet, or expense report, from which you choose one.

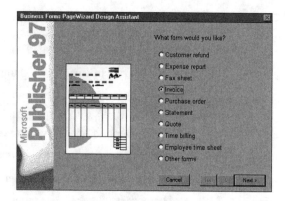

Figure 1.2   The PageWizard Design Assistant for Business Forms.

- Check boxes allow you to choose as many options as you like.
- Text boxes allow you to fill in information specific to your publication. If there is more than one text box on the screen, press **Tab** to move from one box to the next.

3. When you have completed the choices on your screen, click **Next**.

Change Your Mind?   If you change your mind about a selection, you can click the **Back** button to back up one step at a time. Click **Cancel** to end the PageWizard and return to the Publisher screen.

CAUTION

4. Some PageWizards have more design options than others. When you reach the last screen of the PageWizard, click **Create It!**

5. A progress bar shows the percentage completed as the PageWizard creates your publication. When completed, The PageWizard Design Assistant asks if you would like step-by-step help for adding your own text or making changes:

- Select **Yes**, and the Help window opens. You will see a variety of topics under the heading What Do You Want to Do? next to your publication, as shown in Figure 1.3.
- Select **No**, and you have a full screen to continue work on your publication.

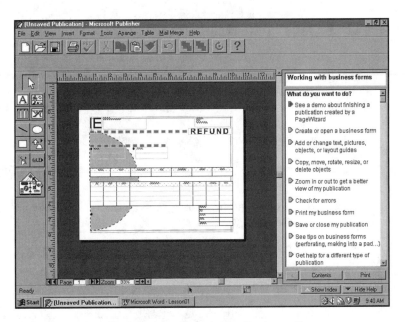

Figure 1.3 The PageWizard Design Assistant for Business Forms.

Starting from Scratch

While the PageWizards are extremely useful, there are times when a simple blank page is the best beginning point. Publisher 97 offers two easy ways to start from scratch:

- Select **File**, **Create New Publication** from the menu bar. From the Startup dialog box, select the **Blank Page** tab and double-click the needed page type.
- Click the **New** button to create a blank letter-sized document.

TIP **Turning Off the Startup Dialog Box** If you prefer not to see the Startup dialog box, you can turn it off. From the **Tools** menu, select **Options**. Click the **Use Startup Dialog Box** option to deselect it. To have the Startup dialog box displayed, just repeat the same steps.

Saving Your Publications

As with all work created on a computer, if a Publisher 97 publication is not saved before the program or publication is closed, the publication will be lost. Publisher 97 warns you if you attempt to quit the program or start a new document without saving changes to your current publication.

To save a file in Publisher 97, follow these steps:

1. Click the **Save** button in the Standard toolbar. The Save As dialog box appears.
2. The first time a publication is saved, you must give it a new name in the **File Name** text box.
3. You can save your publication in a different folder or drive by selecting a different destination in the **Save In** box.
4. Click **OK** to confirm your choices.

The next time you click the **Save** button, Publisher 97 will overwrite your original file with the new version, incorporating any changes you may have made. To save your file under a different name or in a different location, use the **File**, **Save As** menu selection.

Exiting Publisher 97

When you have completed your work in Publisher 97, you quit the program by any of the standard methods:

- Select **File**, **Exit** from the Menu bar.
- Click the **Close** button in the upper-right corner of the Publisher 97 window.
- Use the keyboard shortcut, **Alt+F4**.

In this lesson, you learned how to start and exit Publisher 97, what the different parts of the screen are, how to work with PageWizards, how to start with a blank document, and how to save your work. In the next lesson, you learn how to work with text.

Working with Text

*In this lesson, you learn how to create Text Frames, how to
enter headlines into a text frame, and how to resize and move
the Text Frames.*

Creating Text Frames in Publisher 97

All text—whether a headline or a paragraph—must go into a Text Frame. Text
Frames are created by clicking the text tool (the button containing the large blue
"A" in the toolbox on the left side of the screen) and drawing a rectangle using
the mouse. After you have created a Text Frame, it can easily be moved and
resized.

Only text goes in a Text Frame. Other elements for your publication such as
graphics, tables, or WordArt, must be contained in their own type of frame. For
more information, see Lesson 5 (graphics), Lesson 11 (tables), and Lesson 13
(WordArt).

To lay out your first Text Frame, follow these steps:

1. Start a new, blank publication by clicking the **New** toolbar icon you
learned about in Lesson 1.

2. Click the **Text tool** button and the pointer will become a small crosshair.

3. Click and drag out a rectangle. You can adjust the size and shape later.

4. Release the mouse button.

Handles indicate the Text Frame is selected

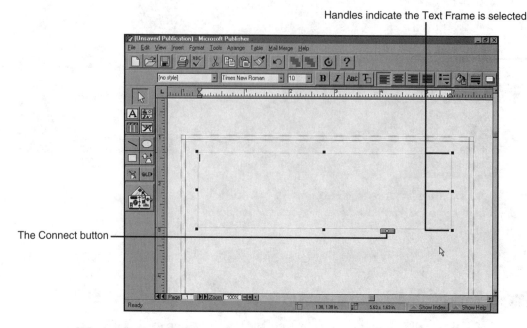

The Connect button —

Figure 2.1 An empty text box.

The button that appears on the bottom right of the Text Frame is referred to as the *Connect button*. The diamond symbol in the center of the Connect button indicates either that there is no text in the box or that all the text fits in the box. You'll learn more about the Connect button and how to control the flow of text in Lesson 4.

Typing Text into the Text Frame

After you have created a Text Frame, you see two cursors: One is the mouse pointer and the other is a blinking vertical bar inside the Text Frame. This vertical bar is the insertion point where text appears when you type.

 TIP **Magnifying the View** To better see what is on-screen, click the word **Zoom** located in the status bar at the bottom of the screen. Select a higher magnification by moving your mouse up the pop-up list and clicking your choice. Selecting **Zoom to Selection** fills the window with the selected object.

Entering text in a Text Frame is easy. Follow these steps:

1. If the insertion point is not blinking in the Text Frame, click in the Text Frame.

2. Type the text you want to appear in the Text Frame. If you type too much text to fit in the frame, the Connect button changes from a diamond shape to an ellipsis (...); in this case, the Text Frame will need to be resized to show the text, described as follows.

3. When you're finished, click anywhere outside of the Text Frame.

CAUTION **Undoing an Accident** The same key combination (**Ctrl+Delete**) used for deleting a single word in Microsoft Word will delete the entire Text Frame in Publisher 97. If this happens, you can cancel your last action by clicking the **Undo** button in the toolbar.

Moving Text Frames

You can easily move your Text Frame into position before or after adding your text.

To quickly move your text on the page, follow these steps:

1. Select the Text Frame by clicking it once.

2. Move your pointer over the border of the Text Frame. The arrow pointer changes into the moving pointer, away from the handles.

3. Click and drag your Text Frame to a new position. As shown in Figure 2.2, an outline of the Text Frame moves with your dragging pointer.

4. When your text is in the correct position, release the mouse button.

TIP **Restricting Frame Movement** To limit the movement of the frame to just up-and-down or just side-to-side, but not both, hold down the **Shift** key while dragging the frame.

The Undo Button

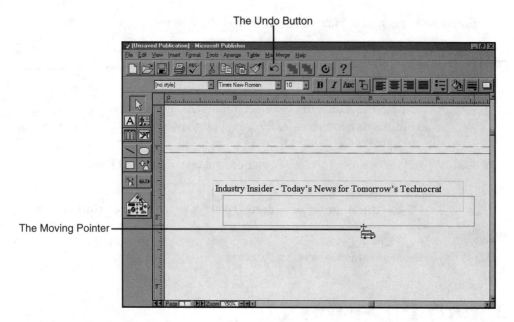

The Moving Pointer

Figure 2.2 Moving a Text Frame.

Resizing the Text Frame

You can resize a Text Frame to accommodate the amount of text you enter.

Follow these steps to resize a Text Frame:

1. Click the Text Frame once to select it (refer to Figure 2.1).

2. Click a handle and drag to resize the Text Frame as follows:

- To increase or decrease the width of a Text Frame, select a handle on either side of the frame.

- To increase or decrease the height of the Text Frame, drag a handle on either the top or bottom of the frame.

- To increase or decrease both the height and the width simultaneously, drag a corner of the frame.

- To resize the box proportionally, drag the corner of the frame while holding down the **Shift** key.

3. When the Text Frame is the shape and size you want, release the mouse button.

In this lesson, you learned how to create Text Frames, how to input text, and how to move and resize Text Frames. In the next lesson, you learn how to format the text you've entered.

Formatting Text

In this lesson, you'll learn how to select a new font; resize a font; and emphasize, color, and align text.

Changing Fonts

All text is rendered in a specific *font*. A font is composed of all the characters in a given typeface. Publisher 97 includes a wide range of fonts that you can use. Generally the bolder, more decorative fonts are more appropriate for headlines while fonts used for paragraphs are chosen for clarity and readability. A few well-chosen fonts will give your publication a professional appearance.

To change the font for a section of text, follow these steps:

1. Highlight your text in a Text Frame by dragging over it.

2. On the Text Formatting toolbar, click the down triangle next to the Font box (see Figure 3.1) and select a font from the drop-down list (use the scroll bar on the right side of the drop-down list to see additional fonts).

3. To try a different font, while your text is highlighted, repeat steps 1 and 2. Once you are satisfied with your new font, click anywhere to clear the highlight.

TIP **Selecting It All** You can easily change the font for all the text in a Text Frame, even if the entire frame is not visible on your screen. From the **Edit** menu, choose **Highlight Entire Story**, and all of the text will be selected. Now follow the steps 2 and 3 outlined above to pick a different font.

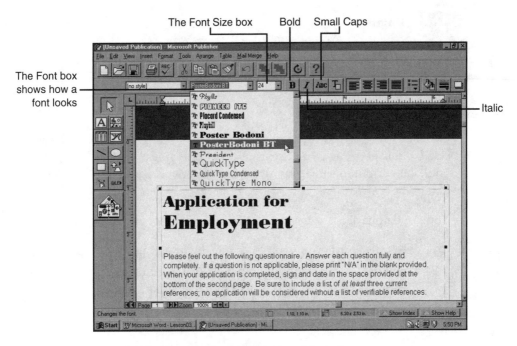

The Font Size box Bold Small Caps

The Font box
shows how a
font looks

Italic

Figure 3.1 A Text Frame with varied fonts and font sizes.

Resizing Fonts

Publisher 97 gives you complete control over the size of the fonts in your publication. You can alter the font size of a paragraph, a line, a word, or even a character. The most professional layout designs use only a few different sizes; too many font sizes in a single publication gives an overly busy appearance and detracts from your message.

To change the size of the font for text in your publication, follow these steps:

1. Select the text to be modified by dragging over it.

2. Choose a new font point size by using one of the following two methods:

- Use your mouse to select a new size from the **Font Size** box on the Text Formatting toolbar, as shown in Figure 3.1.
- Type a new value directly into the Font Size box. You can even type half-point sizes such as 11.5.

3. The selected text is resized. Click anywhere to deselect the text.

435

Points A typographic measurement; there are 72 points per inch. Regular paragraph text is generally 10–12 points while headlines range from 18–72 points.

Using Text Styles

Occasionally, words or phrases in a headline or paragraph need to be emphasized. Publisher 97 allows numerous types of emphasis to be added, including bold, italic and underline among others. Moreover, you can use any combination of these styles.

You can emphasize text in your publication by following these steps:

1. Select the words you want to change by dragging over them.
2. From the Text Formatting toolbar above the editing window (refer to Figure 3.1), you can select one or more styles as follows:
   - **B** for bold
   - **I** for italic
   - **Abc** for small capitals
3. To deselect a style, just click the style button again.
4. When you have completed emphasizing your text, click anywhere to clear the highlighted text.

The Character dialog box provides a wider selection of styles and effects you can add to your text for emphasis. You can change fonts, font sizes, and font color. To access any of these Publisher 97 features, follow these steps.

1. Select the text you want to emphasize.
2. Select **Format, Character** from the menu. The Character dialog box shown in Figure 3.2 is displayed.
3. In the General area of the dialog box, click the drop-down lists to change the font, size, or style of your text. To select any of the available effects, click the name to add a check mark in the box next to name. The Sample area displays a preview of how changes will look.

4. Click **Apply** to change your text and leave the Character dialog box open. Click OK to commit the changes to your text and close the dialog box.

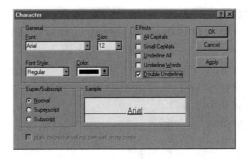

Figure 3.2 The Character dialog box with the double underline effect selected.

Coloring Text

The advent of low-cost color printing has made it possible for small business to produce publications in-house that are highlighted with color. Color, carefully used, enlivens a document overall. As with changes in font and font sizes, the most effective designs are those that use color simply.

There are two different types of color printing in publications: full color and spot color. Publisher 97 can handle full-color printing with resolution up to 600 dpi. Publisher 97 allows up to two spot-color separations to be output to high resolution image setters. For more information on printing, see Lesson 6.

Full Color   Refers to the use of color photographs or an unlimited combination of individual colors.

Spot Color   Used to highlight headlines, captions, or graphic elements. The same spot color is used throughout a document.

By default, all text is initially black. To change the color of any text, follow these steps:

1. Select the text you want to color.
2. Click the **Font Color** icon on the Text Formatting toolbar above the editing window.
3. Select a color from one of the 35 colors displayed in the drop-down option box. The seven most recently used colors are shown in a row across the top of the option box.
4. Click anywhere to clear the highlight and see the text in its new color.

If you click the **More Colors** button in the color drop-down option box, the Color dialog box appears. Each of the seven primary colors is divided into 12 columns. The colors selected for each column are designed to work together in a publication.

If you click the **Patterns & Shading** button in the color drop-down option box, the Fill Patterns and Shading dialog box appears as shown in Figure 3.3. Here, one color is represented with 10 different tints (which add white to the color) and 10 different shades (which add black to the color). Tints and shades are used by layout designers to give a range of color to a publication while only using one additional color to black.

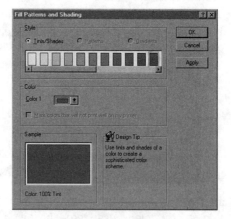

Figure 3.3   The Fill Patterns and Shading dialog box showing the tint end of the color range.

Aligning Text

Alignment of text is a simple but powerful design tool. Any text—headline or paragraph—can be set so that it is even with the left or right margin, centered between the margins, or even with both margins (justified). Generally, centered text is reserved for headlines and columns labels, and paragraphs are either left-aligned or justified; captions can be right-aligned, as can columns of numbers.

To align text, follow these steps:

1. Select the text to be aligned.

2. Click one of the alignment buttons in the Text Formatting toolbar:

- Left-aligned text

- Center-aligned text

- Right-aligned text

- Justified text

3. Click anywhere to deselect the text.

Note that each of the alignment options is mutually exclusive. In other words, text in a single line cannot be both left- and right-aligned. To accomplish this, you need to use the tab alignment feature discussed in Lesson 9.

In this lesson, you learned how to select a new font, resize a font, add styles, and color and align text. In the next lesson, you learn how to import text into a publication.

Importing Text

*In this lesson, you learn how to import text, how to connect and disconnect text frames and how to add **Continued…** notices to guide your readers.*

Importing Blocks of Text

While it is possible to type all of your text directly into your Publisher 97 document, it is far more common, and probably much easier, to import large amounts of text that was previously produced with a word processing program such as Word 97.

Once you have imported your text, you can change its layout by adjusting the Text Frames as described in Lesson 2. As we will see later in this lesson, text can be automatically flowed so that pages are created as needed.

Publisher 97 can import text that was created in Microsoft Word, Microsoft Works, and WordPerfect, or text that was saved in either the plain text or the Rich Text Format. To import any text file, follow these steps:

1. Create a new, blank publication by selecting the **New** button on the toolbar.
2. Create two Text Frames that divide the page vertically, like two columns in a newspaper.
3. Click in the Text Frame on the left side of the page to select this box as the point of insertion. The eight handles will appear to indicate the Text Frame is selected.
4. From the Insert menu, choose **Text File…**.
5. Find the folder in which the word processing file that you want to import is located. Select the file and click OK.

6. If the Text Frame is too small to contain all the inserted text, Publisher 97 asks if you want to use autoflow to place the remaining text:

- If you select **Yes**, Publisher 97 begins the autoflow process by looking for the next available frame.
- If you select **No**, the Text Frame fills with as much text as possible and the symbol on the Connect button changes from a diamond to an ellipsis to indicate the additional text.

7. If you had opted for autoflow, the second Text Frame is now selected and a dialog box asks if you want to autoflow to this frame. Click **Yes**.

8. The text flows into the two existing frames. If there is any text remaining, Publisher 97 asks if you want to create additional text frames and pages:

- If you select **Yes**, Publisher 97 creates as many new pages with Text Frames as needed to finish flowing the text. Publisher 97 tells you how many pages it has created and places your pointer on the final page.
- If you select **No**, text will flow into the second Text Frame where the symbol on the Connect button indicates the additional text, and a Previous Frame button appears on the top of the current Text Frame (see Figure 4.1).

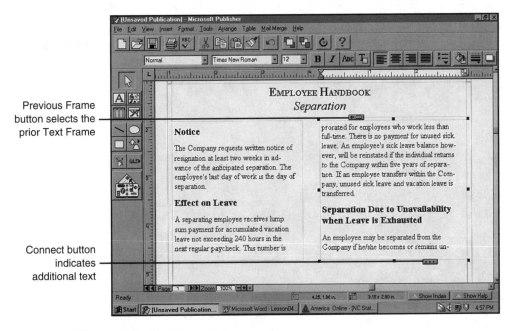

Previous Frame button selects the prior Text Frame

Connect button indicates additional text

Figure 4.1   Text flowed into two columns.

441

Connecting Text Frames

The real power of a page layout program like Publisher 97 comes from its ability to flow text from one Text Frame to another. This is often important to keep paragraphs or sentences from breaking incorrectly. Once you connect text frames, as you change the size or shape of a Text Frame to fit with your layout design, text within one frame automatically shifts or flows to another.

To connect one text frame with another, follow these steps:

1. Import a text file into a Text Frame. Make sure that the text file is large enough to "overflow" the Text Frame—you can tell because the Connect button's symbol changes into an ellipsis when there is too much text for the Text Frame.

2. When Publisher asks if you want to create new pages to autoflow the text, select **No**.

3. Create a new Text Frame, if one does not already exist.

4. Select the Text Frame that contains the text file by clicking it.

5. Click the **Connect** button at the bottom of the Text Frame. The pointer changes into a pitcher for "pouring" the text, as shown in Figure 4.2, when over a Text Frame that can be linked.

6. Click once in the second Text Frame. The next portion of text flows into the Text Frame.

7. If you click again in the first Text Frame, the **Connect button** now displays a chain to indicate it is "linked" to the next Text Frame.

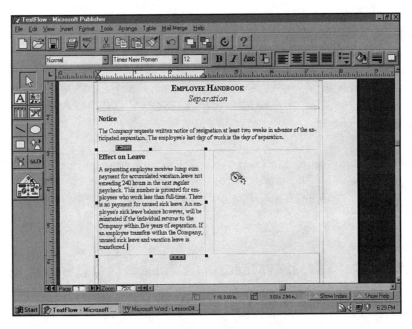

Figure 4.2 One Text Frame is ready to connect to another.

Disconnecting Text Frames

For maximum layout flexibility, Publisher 97 allows you to easily disconnect Text Frames and reconnect them in a new design. When one frame is disconnected from the previous linked frame, the text disappears from view in the disconnected frame. However, all the text is still available in the original frame, ready to be flowed into another Text Frame.

Follow these steps to disconnect one frame from another:

1. Locate the frame to be disconnected and select it.

2. Click the **Previous Frame** button found on top of the selected Text Frame.

3. The Previous Frame is now highlighted. On the bottom of the Text Frame, two buttons are now displayed: the Next Frame button and the Connect button with the linked chain image.

4. Click the **Connect** button to break the link to the next Text Frame.

5. The text in the linked Text Frame disappears (although the Text Frame itself is still available) and the Connect button changes from a linked chain to the ellipsis.

Reflowing the text is done by following the steps in the prior section for connecting Text Frames. You can create a new Text Frame or use any existing Text Frames.

CAUTION

Restoring Lost Text   Publisher 97 does not allow you to disconnect a Text Frame that is in the middle of two other frames. When you break a link between connecting frames, all the text flowing from the connecting frame vanishes. Press **Undo** to recover.

Adding "Continued..." Notices

In larger publications, like newsletters, an extended text piece can flow off one page and onto another. Publisher 97 provides an easy method to help guide the reader through the entire story. Any Text Frame can have a "**Continued on Page X**" line automatically appended where X is the page number of the next linked frame. Publisher 97 also permits a "**Continued from Page X**" line to be included that indicates the previous link.

To add a "Continued on Page..." notice to a Text Frame, follow these steps:

1. Select the Text Frame that the text is flowing from.

2. From the **Format** menu, select **Text Frame Properties**.

3. In the Options section of the Text Frame Properties dialog box shown in Figure 4.3, select "**Continued On Page...**"

The phrase (Continued on Page X) will appear right-aligned at the bottom of the Text Frame, where X is the page number of the linking frame.

To add a Continued from Page... notice to a Text Frame, follow these steps:

1. Select the Text Frame that the text is flowing into.

2. From the **Format** menu, select **Text Frame Properties**.

3. From the **Options** section of the Text Frame Properties dialog box shown in Figure 4.3, select the **Include "Continued From Page..."** box.

4. The phrase "(Continued from Page X)" will appear left-aligned at the top of the Text Frame, where X is the page number of the linking frame.

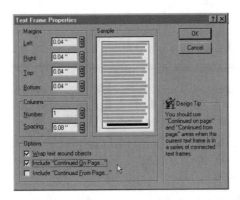

Figure 4.3 The Text Frame Properties dialog box with a "Continued…" option selected.

TIP **Modifying the Continued Notice** You can change the format of either of the "Continued" notices by highlighting them and making your alterations, such as changing the font size or italicizing them. Then, click the **Style** box in the Text Formatting toolbar while it shows either Continued-On Text or Continued-From Text and press **Return**. In the Change or Apply Style dialog box that appears, confirm your choice and press **OK**.

In this lesson, you learned how to import text, how to connect and disconnect text frames, and how to add "Continued…" notices. In the next lesson, you learn how to work with clip art.

Working with Clip Art

In this lesson, you will learn how to create a picture frame and how to insert, move, resize, and crop clip art.

Creating a Picture Frame

Graphics are an essential element for any publication. Carefully selected pictures which are correctly placed can easily be worth the metaphoric "thousand words."

A graphic can be a photograph, drawing, clip art, or something you created with drawing tools. You'll learn more about clip art later in this lesson.

In Publisher 97, every graphic must go into a Picture Frame. Picture Frames contain only graphics.

Clip Art   Graphics that have been previously created, including drawings and photographs, intended to be inserted into documents.

To create a Picture Frame, follow these steps:

1. Start a new, blank publication by clicking the **New** toolbar icon.
2. Click the **Picture Frame** icon (the one that shows a desert scene) from the toolbar on the left side of the screen.
3. Click anywhere on the page and drag out a rectangle. The exact size and shape are unimportant at this point and can be adjusted later.

4. Release the mouse button. The picture frame is displayed with eight handles around it as shown in Figure 5.1.

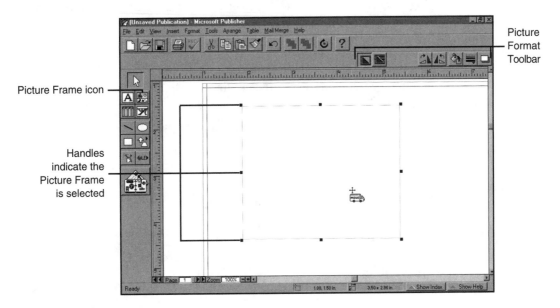

Figure 5.1   A sample Picture Frame.

Inserting Clip Art

Clip art can give your publication a professional appearance with little effort. The Small Business Edition of Publisher 97 includes a gallery of over 5,000 images on the CD-ROM. The Microsoft Clip Gallery is divided into Clip Art (drawings), Pictures (photographs), Sounds, and Videos. Sounds and Videos are used in producing Web pages for publication on the Internet.

Both Clip Art and Pictures are further divided into subject categories to help you to find the right image for your publication. Choosing the right image is important; select an image that conveys both the message of your publication and its tone.

To insert clip art into your publication, follow these steps:

1. Create a Picture Frame as described above. If you have already created your Picture Frame, select it by clicking it.

2. Select **Insert**, **Clip Art** from the menu bar.

447

3. In the Clip Art dialog box, find an image for your publication by scrolling through the available choices using the scroll bar on the right side of the dialog box. You can limit your choices by selecting a category from the list on the left side of the dialog box.

4. Double-click the image you've selected to insert it in the frame.

5. Select one of the following options from the Import Picture dialog box:

   - **Change The Frame To Fit The Picture** will resize your Picture Frame to best fit the image. This option is the default and most often used.

   - **Change The Picture To Fit The Frame** will scale your image to fit the selected frame.

   The Clip Art appears in your Picture Frame, selected and ready to be moved, resized, or cropped.

6. Click **OK** after you have made your choice.

TIP   Searching for Images   The Clip Gallery allows you to search for the correct image by keyword, name, and file type. Click the **Find** button in the Clip Gallery dialog box. Enter the keyword, file name, or file type desired and click **Find Now**.

Moving Clip Art

After you have inserted your Clip Art into your Picture Frame, you can easily move it into the proper position. Publisher 97 provides two methods for moving your images on the page. You can quickly click and drag your image into place and, for more exact placement, you can "nudge" the image pixel-by-pixel.

To quickly move your image on the page, follow these steps:

1. Select the Picture Frame by clicking it once.

2. Move your pointer over the image. The arrow pointer will change into the moving pointer.

3. Click and drag your Picture Frame to a new position.

4. When your image is in the correct position, release the mouse button.

TIP   Placing Images Off-Screen   If you are zoomed in too tightly, you might need to move your image to a portion of the page off-screen; you can still use the click-and-drag method to do this. The screen will automatically scroll when the pointer touches the border of the editing window.

You can nudge your Clip Art into a more precise position by following these steps:

1. Select the Picture Frame by clicking it once.

2. Select **Arrange**, **Nudge Objects** from the menu bar.

3. Click the arrow button corresponding to the direction you want your Picture Frame to move.

4. By default, each click nudges the Picture Frame by 1/100th of an inch. You can adjust the nudge factor by selecting the **Nudge By** check box and entering a new value.

5. The status bar shows your Picture Frame's position relative to the upper-left corner of the page.

 TIP **Nudging with the Keyboard** You can also nudge your pictures by holding down the **Alt** key and pressing one of the arrow keys. You can adjust the nudge factor as described above by selecting **Arrange**, **Nudge Objects**.

Resizing Clip Art

Clip Art can easily be adjusted to fit into your publication. Images can be made proportionally larger or smaller. You can also distort your pictures by disproportionately increasing the width and height.

To resize your Clip Art, follow these steps:

1. Select the Picture Frame by clicking it once.

2. Position your pointer over one of the selection handles. The pointer will change into the Resizer pointer.

3. Click and drag the selection handle to resize the Clip Art. You can get different effects by choosing different selection handles while pressing different keys. Table 5.1 describes the possible combinations.

4. When you are satisfied with your resized image, release the mouse button. You can see the exact measurement of your Picture Frame by looking at the status bar. The measurement is shown in a Width × Height format.

Table 5.1   Resizing Options

Effect	Selection Handle	Keyboard Modifier
Freeform Resizing	Any Handle	None
Proportional Resizing	Any Corner	Shift key
Resizing from Center	Any Handle	Ctrl key
Proportional Resizing from Center	Any Corner	Shift+Ctrl keys

Cropping Clip Art

Images can also be cropped to show a smaller portion of a picture. Cropping can hide extraneous detail and highlight the important sections of your picture without tedious editing. Moreover, cropping a picture in a publication does not permanently alter the original, saved Clip Art image.

Figures 5.2 and 5.3 give a before and after example of a cropped Clip Art picture.

Cropping Tool on the Picture Format toolbar

The Cropping pointer

Figure 5.2   Cropping a picture—before.

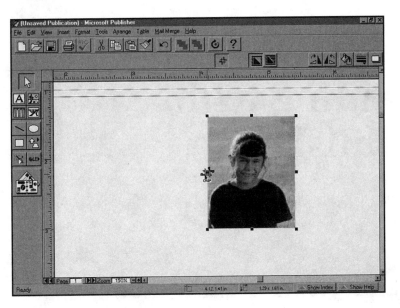

Figure 5.3 Cropping a picture—after.

To crop Clip Art, follow these steps:

1. Select the Picture Frame by clicking it.
2. Select the **Cropping Tool** from the Picture Format toolbar. Your pointer will change into the Cropping pointer.
3. Click one of the selection handles of your Picture Frame and drag across the image.
4. When you are satisfied with your cropped image, release the mouse button.

A cropped image can be uncropped. Simply repeat the above process in reverse and the portion of your image previously cropped is restored.

In this lesson, you learned how to create a picture frame, and how to insert, move, resize, and crop Clip Art. In the next lesson, you learn how to print your publication.

Printing with Publisher

In this lesson, you learn how to print your publication, how to alter your page setup, and how to print double-sided copies.

Printing Your Publication

Publisher 97, like all desktop publishing programs, is primarily about printing. With the exception of its Web page capabilities, all of Publisher 97's focus is on the end-result of generating "hard copy" for publication.

The are two main methods for printing in Publisher 97:

- Select the **Print** icon in the Standard toolbar. This sends one copy of your entire document to your printer without any further prompting.

- Select **File**, **Print** from the **Menu** bar. This opens the Print dialog box, seen in Figure 6.1, which allows you to select the number of copies and which pages of your document to print. After you have selected your options, click **OK**.

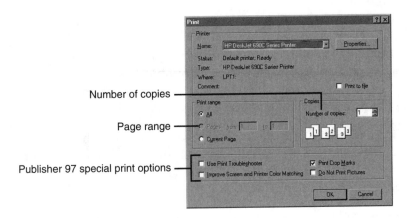

Number of copies ——————

Page range ——————

Publisher 97 special print options ——————

Figure 6.1 The Print dialog box.

The Print dialog b...   is specific to Publisher 97, as seen in
Figure 6.1:

- **Use Print Troubleshooter** activates the Help window with specific printing advice. When this box is checked, the Print Troubleshooter will pop up
  every time you print. Deselect this option to disable this feature.

- **Improve Screen and Printer Color Matching** assures that the colors you
  see on the screen are as closely matched by your printer as possible. This
  feature is Windows 95-specific and works only with printers that have an
  Image Color Matching (ICM) profile. If your printer is not ICM-enabled,
  Publisher 97 informs you that you cannot take advantage of this feature.

- **Print Crop Marks** turns on *Crop Marks* to assure accurate trimming of your
  publication.

- **Do Not Print Pictures** is used for printing draft versions of your publication. The picture is replaced by an outline with a large "X" in the middle.

Crop Marks Small lines used to indicate where your printed page should be
trimmed when your work is smaller or larger than a single page.

Understanding Page Setup

Part of the flexibility of Publisher 97 is its ability to print a wide variety of page setups. Not all publications are best served by printing to an $8\frac{1}{2}\times11$" sheet of paper. Publisher 97 allows a number of special sizes, folds, and labels (capable of printing multiple copies on each sheet).

Selecting **File**, **Page Setup** activates the Page Setup dialog box, shown in Figure 6.2. The primary choice, Choose a Publication Layout, allows you to select from a Normal, Special Fold, Special Size, or Labels layout. Each choice enables a separate set of options:

- **Normal** is used for most layouts including flyers, brochures, and newsletters. Page size is controlled by selecting the **Print Setup** button.
- **Special Fold** is used to make tent cards, greeting cards, and book-fold publications. When selected, you can choose between four different folds and set the size in the Width and Height boxes.
- **Special Size** is used to create a publication that is larger or smaller than a printer page. When selected, you can choose from a variety of sizes for index cards, business cards, posters, and banners. Custom sizes are also available.
- **Labels** is used to create mailing, address, or other-purpose labels. When selected, Publisher 97 displays a list of compatible Avery labels, indicating the Avery number, type, size, and number of labels per page. Labels can be either printed as a single item or multiples on a page.

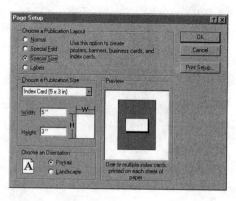

Figure 6.2   The Page Setup dialog box.

All preceding options, with the exception of Labels, allow independent control of the page orientation. The default orientation is Portrait for pages that are printed taller-than-wide. Landscape orientation turns pages on their side so that they are wider-than-tall.

Printing Double-Sided Copies

Certain publications require printing on both sides of a single sheet. Brochures, catalogs, cards, and newsletters are enhanced with duplex or double-sided printing. Some printers can do this automatically; some need the operator to manually feed the paper correctly.

If your printer can print on both sides of paper automatically, follow these steps to enable this option:

1. Select **File**, **Print Setup** from the **Menu** bar.
2. From the Print Setup dialog box, click **Properties**.
3. On the Properties dialog box, click **More Options**.
4. Under Printing on Both Sides, select how the publication is expected to be read:
   - **Flip on Long Edge** is the default and indicates that the publication pages will be turned like a newspaper.
   - **Flip on Short Edge** is used when the publication is intended to be turned from the bottom of the page, like a form on a clipboard.
5. Click **OK** in all three dialog boxes to exit.

Manually feeding a double-sided print job can be tricky. You must first determine how your printer feeds the paper to be printed. Follow these steps to determine how to feed your pages manually (these steps assume that you have a two-page document to print):

1. Using a pencil, write an "X" in the upper-right corner of a sheet of paper.
2. Place the sheet in the manual feed of your printer.
3. Select **File**, **Print**.
4. Click **Properties**.
5. In the Paper Source box, select **Manual Feed**.
6. Click **OK** to confirm your choice.

7. In the Print dialog box, under Print Range, select **Pages**.

8. Type **1** in both the **From** and **To** boxes.

9. Click **OK**.

10. The "X" in pencil on the printed page indicates how the printer feeds your page:

  - If the "X" and the top of your page are in the same position, the printer feeds from top-to-bottom.
  - If the "X" and the bottom of your page are in the same position, the printer feeds from bottom-to-top.

11. Turn the page over and insert in the manual feed of your printer in the right direction.

12. Select **File, Print**.

13. In the Print dialog box, under Print Range, select **Pages**.

14. Type **2** in both the **From** and **To** boxes.

15. Click **OK**.

If your double-sided page prints the way you want, you are ready to print manually. If not, reverse the direction chosen in step 11 and repeat steps 12–15.

In this lesson, you have learned how to print your publication, how to alter your page setup, and how to print double-sided copies. In the next lesson, you learn how to work with Publisher 97's drawing tools.

Using the Drawing Tools

In this lesson, you learn how to create lines, boxes, and ovals, how to work with custom shapes, and how to set rotation, border, and fill options for the objects.

Drawing Lines, Rectangles, and Ovals

Publisher 97 has the ability to create simple shapes including lines, boxes, and ovals. These shapes are used primarily to emphasize text and are not intended to replace clip art created in a graphics program. All three shapes share common characteristics and once you master working with one, you can easily work with any of the others.

To add a line, box, or oval to your Publisher 97 publication, follow these steps:

1. Click any one of the three shape tools in the toolbar on the left side of the screen:
   - **Line** is used to create horizontal, vertical, or diagonal lines of varying widths. Lines can be converted to arrows.
   - **Oval** is used to create oval or circular shapes.
   - **Box** is used to create rectangular or square shapes.
   - **Custom Shapes** is used to create special graphics.

2. Click where you want the upper-left corner of the shape to start and drag to where you want the lower-right corner to end.

3. Release the mouse button. The appropriate Graphic Format toolbar will appear as seen in Figure 7.1.

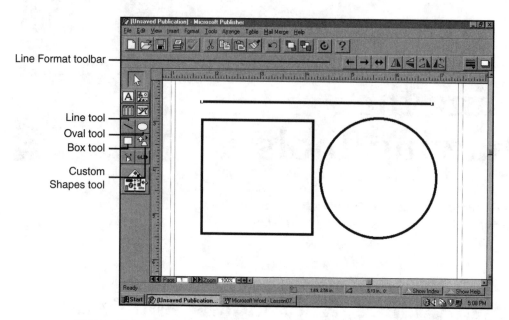

Figure 7.1   Here are some sample shapes you can create with Drawing tools.

While it is possible to eyeball your drawing and get a straight line or a perfect circle or square, Publisher 97 makes such chores a great deal easier. Certain keys pressed in combination with the drawing tools are used to constrain or limit the shapes drawn with the tools. Normally, all objects start drawing in the upper-left corner; the Ctrl key allows the object to be drawn from its center.

Table 7.1 shows which key combinations to use to create each of these effects.

Table 7.1   Drawing Objects

Effect	Graphic Tool	Key Combination
Freeform Drawing	Any Tool	None
Horizontal Line	Line Tool	Shift key
Vertical Line	Line Tool	Shift key
45° Line	Line Tool	Shift key
Circle	Oval Tool	Shift key
Square	Box Tool	Shift key
Any Object Drawn from Center	Any Tool	Ctrl key

Working with Custom Shapes

Publisher 97 makes available a library of 36 custom shapes that can be positioned and sized to your specifications. These custom shapes range from rectangles with rounded corners to advertising splashes to a variety of banner shapes.

To include a custom shape in your publication, follow these steps:

1. Select the **Custom Shapes** icon from the left toolbar. A menu as shown in Figure 7.2 appears.
2. Click the custom shape you want to insert in your publication.
3. The pointer changes into a small crosshair.
4. Move the mouse over the page and click and drag to create the shape.
5. When the shape is at the desired size, release the mouse.

Figure 7.2 Publisher 97's Custom Shapes.

TIP **Altering Drawing Objects** Custom shapes, as well as the line, oval, and box shapes, can be moved and resized just like clip art. The same modifying keys (Shift and Ctrl) apply.

A number of the custom shapes have an additional adjustment capability that allows the object to be reshaped in addition to being resized. When selected, these objects display one or two gray diamonds on their outline, as well as the square black handles. Figure 7.3 shows a Custom Shape being adjusted.

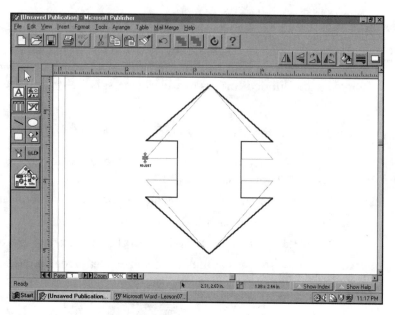

Figure 7.3 Adjusting a custom shape.

To adjust a custom shape, follow these steps:

1. Select a custom shape that has the additional adjustment feature (such as the rounded corner rectangle or the double-headed arrow) and drag to create the shape in your publication. You can see the small gray diamonds in the object (refer to Figure 7.3).

2. Move the mouse over the gray diamond handles on the outline. The pointer changes into the double-headed Adjust cursor.

3. Click and drag the object into a new shape.

4. Release the mouse.

Rotating Drawing Objects

When a drawing object is created or selected, a whole new set of formatting options is enabled. The options vary according to the object, but all can be accessed through the Drawing Format toolbar which appears above the editing window. The Drawing Format toolbar has tools for quickly rotating an object, changing the thickness of the object's outline, and altering the color and type of fill for an object's interior.

To rotate a drawing object, follow these steps:

1. Create or select a drawing object (line, oval, box, or custom shape).

2. In the Drawing Format toolbar, choose one of the four buttons to quickly alter the rotation of the selected object:

- **Flip Horizontal** faces the object in the opposite direction.

- **Flip Vertical** turns the object upside-down.

- **Rotate Right** rotates the object 90° to the right.

- **Rotate Left** rotates the object 90° to the left.

3. Click anywhere outside of or away from the selected object to deselect the object.

TIP **Custom Rotation** To rotate any object by hand, press the **Alt** key while clicking and dragging any of the object's handles. Pressing **Shift+Alt** limits the rotation to every 15 degrees.

Setting the Border Size

When Publisher 97 initially draws an object, all you see is the border or outline of the object. The Border icon on the Drawing Format toolbar allows you to set the thickness of the border and its color.

To change the thickness of an object's border, follow these steps:

1. Select or create a drawing object such as an oval or custom shape.

2. Click the **Border** icon in the Drawing Format toolbar.

3. From the drop-down option list, select an option:

- **None** eliminates the border from view.
- **Hairline** makes the border the thinnest possible width.
- ——————— makes the border thickness 2 points.
- ━━━━━━━ makes the border thickness 4 points.
- **More...** brings up the Border dialog box.

4. If you choose the **More** option from the **Border** drop-down list, the Border dialog box shown in Figure 7.4 opens.

5. Select a new border thickness by clicking one of the images that shows the various widths.

6. If you click the bottom image, the custom border box is activated. Type in a new border thickness. You do not have to type the "pt."

7. Click **OK.** The new border thickness is applied to your object.

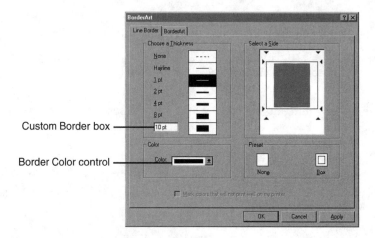

Figure 7.4   The Border dialog box.

Setting the Border Color

You change the color of a border the same way you changed the color of text in Lesson 3.

Follow these steps to change the color of an object's border:

1. Select a drawing object.

2. Click the **Border** icon in the Drawing Tools Format toolbar.

3. Select **More...** to open the Border dialog box.

4. From the Border dialog box, click the arrow next to the current border color.

5. From the drop-down color option box, click the new color.

6. Click **OK.**

Filling a Drawing Object with a Color

So far, all of our drawing objects have been empty, that is, not "filled." Publisher 97 allows you to fill drawing objects with a solid color, a two-toned pattern, or a three-dimensional gradient.

Follow these steps to fill an oval, box, or custom shape with a solid color:

1. Select a drawing object.

2. Click the **Object Color** icon in the Drawing Format toolbar.

3. From the drop-down option box, select one of the following:

- Click a color from those shown to fill the object with a solid color.
- Click **More Colors** to bring up the Color dialog box for a fuller selection of colors as described in Lesson 3.

4. Click **OK**.

Filling a Drawing Object with a Pattern or Gradient

Patterns and gradients can add variety and dimension to the graphics in your publication. Both fill a shape using two colors. Patterns use two solid colors; colors with a high contrast work best for patterns. Gradients blend between two colors; colors with a low contrast work best for gradients.

To fill an oval, box, or custom shape with a pattern or gradient, follow these steps:

1. Create or select an oval, box, or custom shape.

2. Click the **Object Color** icon in the Drawing Format toolbar.

3. From the drop-down option box, select **Patterns & Shading**.

4. The Fill Patterns and Shading dialog box opens. Click one of the option buttons in the Style section:

- **Patterns** displays 17 different designs in a scroll box. Select one by clicking the image. A preview appears in the Sample section.
- **Gradients** displays 44 different designs in a scroll box. Select one by clicking the image. A preview appears in the Sample section.

5. Select the two colors to be used by clicking the option box next to the Base Color example and on the option box next to the Color 2 example.

463

6. Click your color choice. You can click **More Colors** for additional options.

7. Click **OK**.

In this lesson, you learned how to create lines, boxes, and ovals, how to work with custom shapes, and how to set rotation, border, and fill options for the drawing objects. In the next lesson, you learn how to arrange and group items.

Arranging and Grouping Items

In this lesson, you learn how to use the layout and ruler guides, how to line up text and graphics, and how to layer and group objects.

Understanding Layout and Ruler Guides

Page composition often requires precise placement of text and graphics. Publisher 97 uses layout and ruler guides to control text and graphic positioning. A *layout guide* is an adjustable non-printing line that appears on every page of your document; margins are an example of layout guides. A ruler guide is also an adjustable non-printing line which can appear on just one page; a ruler guide might be used to line up blanks on an order form.

In addition to enhancing a publication's professional appearance, these guides make layout much easier. Text, graphics, and other objects can be made to "snap to" a layout or ruler guide so that exact positioning is, well, a snap. Moreover, layout and ruler guides can serve as templates for repeatable projects, such as a newsletter, to ensure a consistent look-and-feel.

Changing the Margin Layout Guide

One of the most common tasks involving layout guides is to change the margins. To adjust the margin layout guides, follow these steps:

   1. Select **Arrange**, **Layout Guides** from the **Menu** bar to open the Layout Guides dialog box shown in Figure 8.1.

2. From the Layout Guides dialog box, you can adjust the Margin Guides one of two ways:

   - Type directly into the margin box. You do not have to type the inch symbol.

   - Click the arrows next to each margin box to increase or decrease the margin by 1/10".

3. Press **Tab** to move from one margin box to the next. The Preview window updates with each Tab press.

4. Click **OK** when you have finished adjusting the margins.

Margin Guides ———

Column Guides ———

Mirrored Guides ———

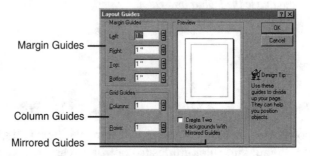

Figure 8.1   The Layout Guides dialog box for margin and column control.

TIP   **Working with Mirrored Margins**   Pages in a publication that are printed back to back often used mirrored guides so that the margins of facing pages match. In the Layout Guide dialog box, click **Create Two Backgrounds with Mirrored Guides** (shown in Figure 8.1) to achieve this effect.

Working with Ruler Guides

Ruler guides are used to help line up objects one page at a time. Easy to set up and easy to adjust, ruler guides provide a tool for creating forms, catalogs, or any other publication that requires various objects to be aligned differently on different pages.

To create and adjust a ruler guide, follow these steps:

1. Hold down the **Shift** key and move your pointer over the inside edge of either the horizontal or vertical ruler. The Adjust pointer appears as shown in Figure 8.2.

2. Click and drag toward the page. A green ruler guide is created.

3. Release the mouse button when the ruler guide is correctly positioned.

4. To adjust a ruler guide on the page, hold down the **Shift** key and move your pointer over the ruler guide until the Adjust pointer appears.

5. Click and drag the ruler guide to its new position.

6. Release the mouse button and the **Shift** key.

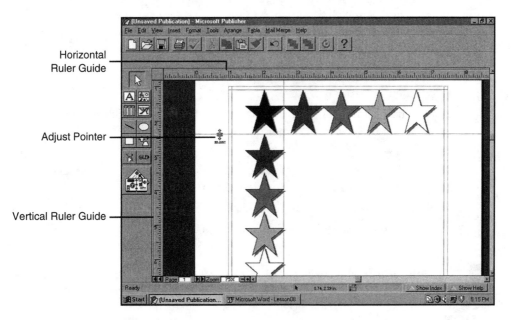

Figure 8.2 Ruler Guides are used to align objects on a page.

Snap To Not Working! If your objects are not snapping to the guides you have set up, click **Tools** on the Menu bar and click the **Snap To** features you want activated: Snap to Ruler Marks, Snap to Guides, or Snap to Objects.

CAUTION

Lining Up Text and Graphics

In Publisher 97, any object—whether text, picture or drawing—can be aligned with any other object or group of objects. Objects can be lined up along their top, bottom, left, or right edges as well as their centers. You can center one object inside of another: For example, a photograph could be centered inside of a gradient-filled box to create a 3-D picture frame. You can also line up or center objects on a page—as if the page were another object.

To align an object to another, follow these steps:

1. Holding down the **Shift** key, click every object you want to align.
2. Select **Arrange**, **Line Up Objects** to open the Line Up Objects dialog box shown in Figure 8.3.
3. From the Line Up Objects dialog box, select from any of the following options, separately or combined with one another:
   - **Left to Right** lines up objects along their left or right edge or along their horizontal center.
   - **Top to Bottom** lines up objects along their top or bottom edge or along their vertical center.
   - **Align Along Margins,** when used in combination with either or both of the other two options, lines up objects on the left, right, top or bottom margins or centered on the page.
4. The Sample section displays a preview of the alignment.
5. Click **OK** when your choices are complete.

CAUTION

Aligning to the Wrong Object!   Publisher 97 generally aligns to the edge of the object that is closest to your alignment choice. For example, objects selected to align to the top align to the top edge of the object closest to the top of the page. For best results, position one element with an edge where you want it and align objects to that edge.

Group button ——

Figure 8.3 Text centered on a Custom Shape.

Layering Objects

Layered objects are a key element in modern desktop publishing design. Publisher 97 can layer text over a picture or a drawing to achieve a more three-dimensional look or it can layer text over text for a shadow effect. Once you have placed one object on top of another, you can arrange the layers to send objects farther away or bring them closer.

To layer one object on top of another, follow these steps:

1. Create or import the objects you want to layer.

2. Move one object on top of another by clicking and dragging it.

469

3. To arrange the layers, select **Arrange** from the Menu bar and choose one of these options:

- **Bring to Front** puts the selected object in front of all the layers.
- **Bring Closer** moves the selected object one layer closer to the top.
- **Send Farther** moves the selected object one layer closer to the bottom.
- **Send to Back** puts the selected object behind all the layers.

TIP   **Layering Text over Pictures**   If you are layering text over a picture, you can make the Text Frame transparent by selecting the text and pressing **Ctrl+T**.

Grouping Objects

Once you have aligned or layered a series of objects, it is useful to group the objects. Publisher 97 treats grouped objects as one object, which makes it easy to move, resize, or rotate a number of objects at once. Grouping a series of objects locks their relative position so you cannot accidentally move one object out of place. Grouped objects can be ungrouped and regrouped at any time.

To group two or more objects together, follow these steps:

1. Hold down the **Shift** key and click every object you want to group.

2. Each time you add an object to the group, the object frame expands to include that object, and the Group button appears with an unlocked image on the lower right of the object frame.

3. Click the **Group** button.

4. Handles appear around the entire object frame. The **Group** button changes to the locked image (see Figure 8.4).

5. To ungroup the objects, click the locked **Group** button.

TIP   **Selecting a Number of Objects**   You can select any number of objects by clicking the **Selection** tool and dragging the Selection box around any objects you want to include in the group.

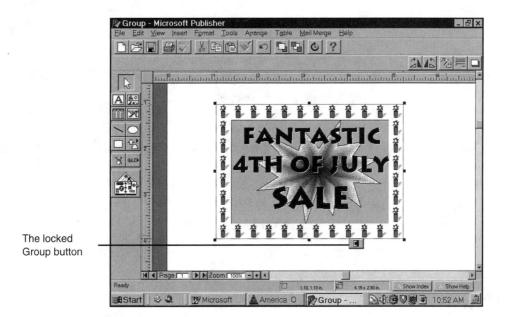

The locked
Group button

Figure 8.4 The Group button changes from unlocked to locked.

In this lesson, you learned how to use the layout and ruler guides, how to line up text and graphics, and how to layer and group objects. In the next lesson, you learn advanced text-formatting techniques.

Using Advanced Text Techniques

In this lesson, you learn how to edit your text, how to use tabs, how to create bulleted and numbered lists, and how to work with styles.

Editing Text

Whether you type all your text directly in Publisher 97 or import it from a word processing program, chances are the text will need to be edited in some fashion. Publisher 97 includes industry-standard tools to cut, copy, and paste your text.

To move or copy any text, follow these steps.

1. Select your text using the click-and-drag method.
2. Click the appropriate icon:

- **Cut**   To move text, click the **Cut** icon (the scissors) on the toolbar. If you select Cut, the text disappears from the screen.

- **Copy**   To copy text, click the **Copy** icon (the twin pages) on the toolbar.

3. Move the insertion point by clicking the pointer in a new location.

4. Click the **Paste** icon on the toolbar (the clipboard).
5. The cut or copied text appears on the screen at the insertion point.

TIP   **Dragging and Dropping**   Text can also be moved quickly with the drag-and-drop technique. After highlighting your text, move the pointer over the highlighted text. The pointer will change to an arrow with the word "Drag" attached. Click and drag your mouse and a "shadow" insertion point appears.

Move the insertion point to a new location and release the mouse button. The text moves to its new place. You can also copy text by holding down the CTRL key when dragging-and-dropping.

Working with Tabs

Tabs control the indentation and vertical alignment of text in a publication. By default, Publisher 97 sets a tab every 1/2" in a Text Frame. You can move, insert, or delete four different types of tabs. You can also use *tab leaders* before any tab.

Tab Leaders   The solid, dotted, or dashed line leading up to a tab, used to connect items on the same line.

Follow these steps to set a tab in Publisher 97:

1. Select the text in a Text Frame that you want the tabs to affect. If you want to affect all the text, select **Edit**, **Highlight Entire Story**.

2. Select the type of tab to be set by clicking the tab symbol on the left side of the ruler:

   - **Left-aligned** causes text to be aligned along the left edge of the text. Left-aligned tabs are the default in Publisher 97.
   - **Right-aligned** causes text to be aligned along the right edge of the text.
   - **Center-aligned** causes text to be centered under the tab stop.
   - **Decimal-aligned** causes text to be aligned according to placement of the decimal or period. Used in aligning columns of numbers.

3. Click once on the ruler where you want the tab to be set. All default tabs to the left of the new tab stop are deleted.

4. To set a tab leader, double-click the tab stop on the ruler to which you want to add leader characters. The Tabs dialog box will appear as shown in Figure 9.1.

5. From the Tabs dialog box, select the desired option under the Leader section by clicking it once.

6. Click **OK**.

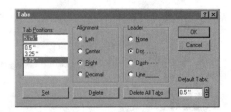

Figure 9.1   The Tabs dialog box allows you to set tab leaders.

Tabs can be moved by clicking and dragging the tab stop on the ruler. To delete a tab, click and drag the tab stop off the ruler and release the mouse button.

Creating Bulleted and Numbered Lists

Lists are a mainstay in many publications: outlines, checklists, and step-by-step instructions like those in this book. Publisher 97 allows quick and easy creation of both bulleted and numbered lists. Bulleted lists are used to set off a series of items in which the order is not important. Numbered lists are used to highlight items where a specific order is necessary. Publisher 97 gives you a wide variety of styles of bullets and numbers to choose from.

To create a bulleted list, follow these steps:

1. Select the text you want to convert into a list. Be sure each item is separated by a paragraph return (the Enter key).

 2. Click the **Bulleted and Numbered List** icon in the Text Formatting toolbar and choose from the following options:

- For a standard bulleted list, select any of the six available bullets by clicking its icon.
- For additional bullet options, select **More** to open the Indents and Lists dialog box.
- Select **None** to turn off the bullets or numbering.

The Bulleted List section of the Indents and Lists dialog box allows you to choose a new bullet, change the size of the bullet, and alter the indentation of each bulleted item.

Follow these steps to create a numbered list:

1. Select the text you want to convert into a list. Be sure each item is separated by a paragraph return (the Enter key).
2. Click the **Bulleted and Numbered List** icon and select **More** to open the Indents and Lists dialog box shown in Figure 9.2.
3. From the Indents and Lists dialog box, click **Numbered List** in the Indent Settings section.
4. Select from the various options:

   Format allows you to change the numbering from Arabic numbers (1,2,3) to lowercase alphabetical (a,b,c) or uppercase alphabetical (A,B,C).

   Separator allows you to select the character that follows the number.

   Start At sets the first number.

   Indent List By sets the amount of indentation.

   Alignment allows the list to be left-, right-, or center- aligned.

5. Click **OK** when you have finished selecting your options.

Figure 9.2 Indents and Lists dialog box showing the Numbered List options.

TIP **Automatic Renumbering** A key advantage to numbered lists is that any time an item is cut, inserted, or moved, Publisher 97 automatically renumbers the list.

Working with Styles

Styles are a powerful publishing tool that help create a consistent look and make publication-wide changes a snap. A *style* is a group of formatting options that are named and saved with a document. Publisher 97 makes it easy to create, use, and modify styles.

Styles can include the font name, size and spacing, paragraph alignment, line spacing, tabs, indents, and list information.

To create a style, follow these steps:

1. Select text that is formatted the way you want your style to appear.
2. Click once in the **Style** box on the Standard toolbar.
3. Type in a new name for the style. Press **Enter** and the Create Style by Example dialog box appears.
4. From the Create Style by Example dialog box, click **OK**.

To apply a style to one or more paragraphs, follow these steps:

1. Select the text you want to apply the style to.
2. Click the down-arrow next to the Style box to see the available styles.
3. Select one style by highlighting and clicking its name.

 TIP **Modifying a Style**   You can easily update a style and alter all the text in a publication at one time. Select text that has the style you want to change applied. Make your format changes. Click in the **Style** box and press **Enter**. From the Change or Apply dialog box, click **OK**.

In this lesson, you learned how to edit your text, how to use tabs, how to create bulleted and numbered lists, and how to work with styles. In the next lesson, you learn all about scanned images.

Incorporating Tables

In this lesson, you learn how to insert a table in your publication, how to resize, add, and delete rows and columns in tables, how to modify a table's borders, and how to merge and split table cells.

Inserting Tables

Tables are a terrific organizational tool that let you present and maintain information in series of columns and rows. Each intersection of a column and a row is called a *cell*; you move from cell to cell by pressing the **Tab** key. In Publisher 97 terms, a cell can be considered a mini-text frame. Tables are used for displaying charts, price lists, and résumés.

To insert a table in your publication, follow these steps:

1. Select the **Table** icon from the left Toolbar.
2. Click and drag out an area for your table to fit into.
3. Release the mouse button and the Create Table dialog box appears as shown in Figure 10.1.
4. From the Create Table dialog box, select any of the following options:

    Number of Rows controls the number of divisions going down a table. Type in a value or click the incrementers.

    Number of Columns controls the number of divisions going across a table. Type in a value or click the incrementers.

    Table Format offers preset formats for a variety of situations. Scroll down the list to see more options; a preview appears in the Sample section.

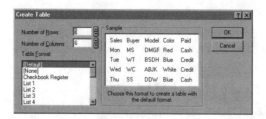

Figure 10.1   The Create Table dialog box has over 20 preset formats.

5. When you have made your choices, click **OK**.

   The table appears with gray borders across the top designating the column selectors and down the left side designating the row selectors. A light gray grid shows the division for each cell.

When created or selected, tables have the same handles that other Publisher 97 objects have and can be sized, moved, or rotated in the same manner.

Resizing Columns and Rows

When the table is first created, Publisher 97 divides the space allocated for the table equally between the specified number of rows and columns. Often you will need to make one column or row larger or smaller than the others in order to get the design you want. Tables are extremely flexible and both columns and rows can be resized easily. Figure 10.2 gives an example of a table that has both columns and rows resized.

Follow these steps to resize a column or row:

1. Create or select a table in your publication.
2. Move the pointer over the column or row selectors between the cell dividers until the mouse pointer changes to the Adjust pointer.
3. Click and drag the column or row to resize it. A dotted grid shows how the rest of the table will be moved.
4. Release the mouse button.

TIP   **Resizing Just the Column or Row**   To keep the table the same overall size and just resize the one column or row you are adjusting, hold down the **Shift** key while you click and drag the column or row into a new position.

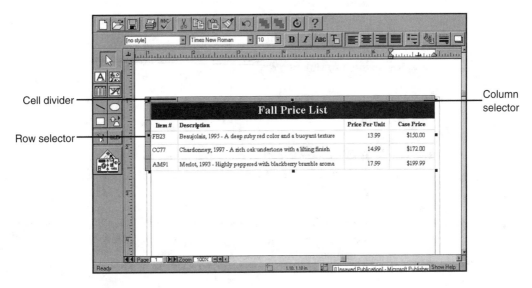

Cell divider

Column selector

Row selector

Figure 10.2 A sample table with resized columns and rows.

Inserting and Deleting Rows or Columns

You are not stuck with your initial choices for the number of columns and rows in your table. Rows and columns can be deleted or inserted at any time.

Follow these steps to insert a row or column:

1. Select your table by clicking it once.
2. Click into a cell next to where you want the row or column to be inserted.
3. Select **Table**, **Insert Rows or Columns** from the **Menu** bar to open the Insert dialog box.
4. From the Insert dialog box, select your options from these two areas:

   Insert Click either Rows or Column and then put in the number to insert, either by typing it directly into the box or using the incrementer arrows.

   Options Choose whether to insert the rows or column before or after your present cell.
5. Click **OK**.

Inserted rows and columns take on the same formatting and size as the current cell.

Follow these steps to delete a row or column:

1. Select your table by clicking it once.
2. Highlight an entire row or column by clicking once on the row or column selector.
3. Select **Table, Delete Row** from the Menu bar to delete a row; select **Table, Delete Column** from the **Menu** bar to delete a column.

 TIP   **Highlighting Multiple Rows or Columns**   You can select any number of rows or columns by clicking the first row or column selector and dragging across other selectors.

Modifying Table Borders

Publisher 97 gives you complete control over all the borders of a table—the border surrounding the entire table and borders for each cell, column, or row. The border's width and color can be individually controlled.

When a table is initially created, the light gray grid lines that divide the cells will not print. To turn on the borders for an entire table, follow these steps:

1. Create or select a table.
2. Select **Format, Border** from the **Menu** bar to open the Border dialog box.
3. From the Border dialog box, in the Preset section in the lower-right, click **Grid**. If you want a border around just the outside of the table, click **Box**.
4. If desired, select a new border thickness by clicking any of the icons in the **Choose a Thickness** section or entering a **Custom Thickness** in the bottom selection.
5. Click **OK**.

Merging and Splitting Cells

Tables often include headings that spread over more than one cell, like the "Fall Price List" title in Figure 10.2. Publisher 97 allows you to merge cells together so that the text can overlap two or more columns. You can only merge cells in the same row.

To merge two or more cells, follow these steps:

1. Create or select a table.
2. Highlight two or more adjacent cells in the same row by clicking and dragging across the cells.
3. Select **Tables**, **Merge Cells** from the **Menu** bar.
4. The grid lines between the cells disappear and all the text in the selected cells is merged into one cell.

You can also split cells that have been merged back to their original configuration. Follow these steps to split a merged cell:

1. Select the table with the merged cell.
2. Click in the merged cell.
3. Select **Tables**, **Split Cells** from the **Menu** bar. The grid lines dividing each cell will be restored and all the text contained in the merged cell is found in the first cell.

In this lesson, you learned how to insert a table in your publication, how to resize, add, and delete rows and columns in tables, how to modify a table's borders, and how to merge and split table cells. In the next lesson, you'll learn how to integrate text and graphics.

Integrating Text and Graphics

In this lesson, you learn how to wrap text around frames and around graphics, how to adjust the flow of text, and how to use custom shapes to create text patterns.

Wrapping Text Around Frames

Wrapping text around other objects—pictures, tables, logos, shapes, and even other text—is one of Publisher 97's most useful capabilities. Newsletters, reports, and catalogs all use text wrapping extensively. Publisher 97 makes the process easy to use with enough options to achieve a wide variety of designs.

As you've seen, all Publisher 97 objects (with the exception of the drawing objects) are contained within frames. Follow these steps to wrap text around a frame:

1. Create or import some text into a Text Frame.
2. Create any framed object:
   - A Text Frame (see Lesson 2)
   - A Picture Frame (see Lesson 5)
   - A Table Frame (see Lesson 10)
   - A WordArt Frame (see Lesson 13)
3. Insert the appropriate object.
4. Move the frame over the text frame you created in step 1.
5. Publisher 97 defaults to wrapping text around a frame. Note that the Wrap Text to Frame button in the Frame Format toolbar shown in Figure 11.1, is selected.

Wrap Text to
Frame button

Wrap Text to
Picture button

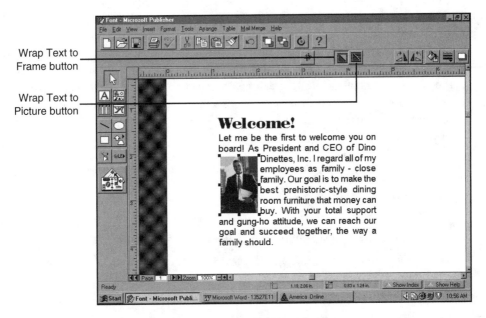

Figure 11.1 Text wrapped around a picture frame.

Publisher 97 automatically wraps text as closely to the frame as possible. When you are wrapping text around a Picture Frame, you can increase the distance between the frame and the wrapped text by following these steps:

1. Select the Picture Frame that the text is wrapping around.

2. Select **Format**, **Picture Frame Properties** from the Menu bar to open the Picture Frame Properties dialog box.

3. From the Picture Frame Properties dialog box, increase the value of any of the Margins—Left, Right, Top, Bottom—by either typing in a number directly into the Margin box or using the arrows.

4. Click **OK**.

CAUTION

Text Won't Wrap! Try clicking the **Text Frame** and selecting **Arrange**, **Send Farther** until it wraps. A Text Frame must be behind the layer of the frame it is wrapping around.

Wrapping Text Around a Graphic

Just as wrapping text around a frame follows the rectangular shape of the frame, wrapping text around a graphic follows the shape of the graphic—whatever that may be. The best graphics to wrap text around are line art (such as drawings and cartoons), ovals, and custom shapes. It is difficult to wrap text around a photograph unless the main image is in the foreground surrounded by a uniform background.

To wrap text around a graphic such as a drawing, follow these steps:

1. Create or import some text into a Text Frame.
2. Create a Picture Frame.
3. Insert your choice of clip art into the frame (see Lesson 5).
4. Move the graphic on top of the text frame. The text will wrap around the Picture Frame.

5. Click the **Wrap Text to Picture** button in the Picture Format toolbar.
6. Move picture as necessary to achieve the desired text-wrapping effect.

Figure 11.2 shows how the previous example (Figure 11.1) would look with the text wrapped to a picture instead of to the frame.

Figure 11.2   Text wrapped to picture follows the curve of the image.

Adjusting the Text Wrap

Publisher 97 gives you the option to adjust exactly how text wraps around a graphic. Sometimes the text flows into places you don't intend it to—Publisher 97 allows you to block the text in one area while allowing it to flow smoothly in all the others.

Follow these steps to adjust how text wraps around a picture:

1. Select a Picture Frame with a clip art drawing.

2. If not already selected, click the **Wrap Text to Picture** button on the Picture Format toolbar.

3. Click the **Edit Irregular Wrap** button on the Picture Format toolbar (shown in Figure 11.3).

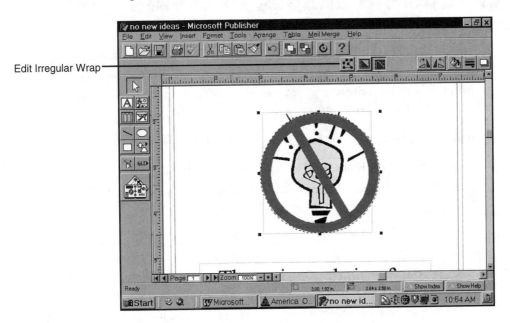

Edit Irregular Wrap

Figure 11.3 Adjusting the way text wraps around a picture.

4. Adjustment handles surround the irregularly shaped object.

5. Position your mouse pointer over any of the handles. The pointer changes to the Adjust pointer.

6. Click and drag the handles to a new position:

- Moving the handles away from the object creates more white space around the object.
- Moving the handles into the object crops the image.

7. Click anywhere to deselect the graphic.

TIP   **Adding or Deleting Handles**   If you need a finer degree of adjustment than the number of handles offers you, you can create additional handles by pressing the **Ctrl** key and clicking where you want the new handle to appear. To delete a handle, press **Ctrl+Shift** and click the handle you want to remove.

Using Custom Shapes to Create Text Patterns

Here's an interesting technique useful for creating eye-catching flyers and posters. In addition to wrapping text around rectangular frames or around irregularly shaped drawings, you can also use Custom Shapes to shape your text so that the text itself appears to become a graphic.

Follow these steps to create a text pattern using Custom Shapes:

1. Create a Text Frame and enter or import your text.

2. Click the **Custom Shapes** button on the left Toolbar.

3. Select one of the Custom Shapes by clicking it.

4. Click and drag out the Custom Shape.

5. Move the Custom Shape over the Text Frame.

6. Select a color from the **Object Color** button on the Picture Format toolbar (see Lesson 7). Choose White if you want only your text shape to be visible.

7. Adjust the Custom Shape by using the standard Resizing handles and the Adjustment handles.

8. From the **Border** button on the Picture Format toolbar, select **None**.

As shown in Figure 11.4, you can make your text assume almost any shape with this technique.

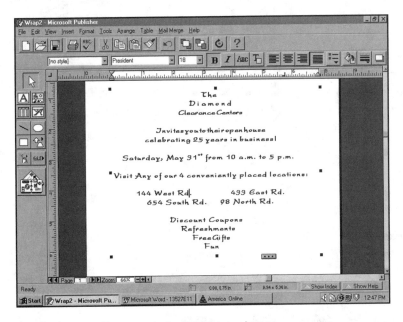

Figure 11.4   A text pattern created with custom shapes.

In this lesson, you learned how to wrap text around frames and around graphics, adjust the flow of text, and use custom shapes to create text patterns. In the next lesson, you learn how to mail merge your publications.

Performing a
Mail Merge

12

*In this lesson, you learn what mail merges are, how
to create an address list, edit your list, set up your main
document, preview your merge, and print your merged
publication.*

What Is Mail Merge?

Mail merge is a process used to generate personalized form letters, labels,
or envelopes. The term *merge* is used because you start with two different
documents—one, a database or list, containing data such as names and
addresses; and the main document, such as a letter, invitation, or card that
you want to send to each person on the list. Both documents are merged to
create a finished product.

Publisher 97 treats every publication as a potential main document which can
be merged with an existing data source or one that is created for that purpose.
Every data source consists of records which consist of categories or fields. One
person's full name and address could be one record while First Name would be
one field. All the records in a data source have the same basic fields whether or
not they are all filled in. You might, for example, have a Country field, but it
would be completed only for customers outside the United States.

TIP   **More on Databases**   Databases are a key component for office computing.
For a more detailed explanation of records and fields, see Part II, Lesson 20.

It is important in creating data sources to have a different field for each category you might want to use independently. For example, if you had one field where you combined City-State-Zip it would be next to impossible to list your addresses by State or do a bulk mailing organized by ZIP code. Using three different fields—City, State, and Zip—allows you to organize and print your information sorted by any or all of the three fields.

Overall, performing a mail merge is a three-step process:

1. Create or open your data source.
2. Make your main document with field codes from the data source.
3. Merge the two documents together.

Creating a Publisher Address List

Publisher 97 provides an easy method for creating data sources: the Publisher Address List. While initially set up for handling names, addresses, and telephone numbers, you can customize the Address List to make it suitable for any other project, such as an inventory list.

As noted previously, every publication is a potential main document—you don't need to do anything special to make your document mail-merge ready, except make sure there's room for the mailing address.

To create a Publisher Address List, follow these steps:

1. From the Mail Merge menu, select **Create Publisher Address List**. The New Address List dialog box, shown in Figure 12.1, opens.
2. Type the information in each field. Press **Tab** to move from one field to the next.
3. When the record is completed, click **New Entry** to add another record.
4. Repeat steps 2 and 3 until you have finished entering your information. You can add, edit, and delete entries later.
5. Click **Close**.
6. The Save As dialog box appears. Enter a file name and location for your new address list.
7. Click **Save**.

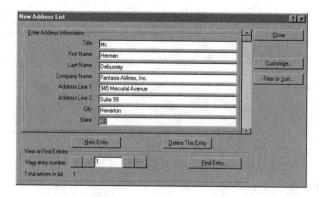

Figure 12.1   The New Address List dialog box with the first record completed.

The Publisher Address List you just created is now linked to the current publication. You can also use it as a data source for any other publication.

Editing Your Data

Once you have created your Publisher Address List, you can edit any of the information it contains. Phone numbers can be updated, misspellings can be corrected, and, when needed, whole records can be added or deleted.

To edit a Publisher Address List, follow these steps:

1. From the Mail Merge menu, select **Edit Publisher Address List**.
2. The Open Address List dialog box opens. Double-click the file name for the Address List you want to edit.

   Your Address List opens in the same type of dialog box that it was created in. You can find the records you want to edit in two ways:

   - To find a record, next to the View Entry Number, type the record number, if you know it, or use the navigation buttons to page through the Address List one record at a time.
   - Click any field to alter any information.

3. To delete a record, click the **Delete This Entry** button. Click **Yes** to confirm the deletion.
4. To add a new record, click the **New Entry** button.
5. Click **Close** when you have finished editing the data.

Is the Data Safe? Publisher 97 never prompts you to save your data after editing your Address List because it automatically saves your changes when

you click Close.

TIP **Finding Records** You can also find a record if you know any part of that record. Click the **Find Entry** button. From the Find Entry dialog box, enter the company name or last name of the record you're looking for in the Find This Text box. Click **Find Next**. The Address List shows the next record that includes your text. From the Find Entry dialog box, click **Close**.

Working with Field Codes

The next step in completing a mail merge is to set up the main document. The best course is to create your publication as completely as possible and then to insert the field codes. Field codes are placeholders that link the main document to the data source. Double angle brackets set off the field codes, for example, <<Company>>.

Follow these steps to insert your Address List field codes in your main document:

1. Create or open a Publisher Address List as described previously.
2. Create or select a Text Frame and place the insertion point where you want the field codes to appear.
3. From the Mail Merge menu, select **Insert Fields**.
4. From the Insert Fields dialog box, double-click the field to include in your publication. The field code will appear at the insertion point in your Text Frame.
5. Add any words, spaces, punctuation, or carriage returns necessary in your main document.
6. Repeat steps 4 and 5 until all needed field codes are inserted in your main document.
7. When finished inserting field codes, click **Close** from the Insert Fields dialog box.

Figure 12.2 shows one example of a completed mail-merge document. Notice the use of bold formatting in the first address line and the use of punctuation (commas and spaces) in the final address line. Field codes can be formatted just like any other text.

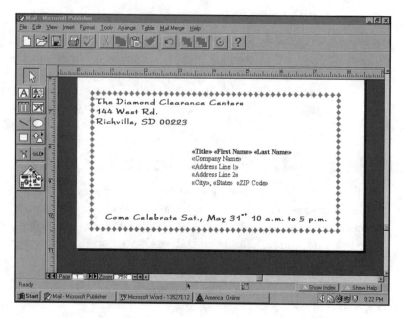

Figure 12.2   A postcard set up for Mail Merge.

Previewing the Merge

Our mail merge is just about complete. It is a good idea to preview your mail merge to make sure you have not accidentally put the wrong information in the wrong field. While it often can slip by unnoticed when you are just editing your information, data in the wrong place stands out like a sore thumb when the merge is previewed.

Follow these steps to preview your mail merge:

1. Open a publication previously set up for mail merge.

2. From the **Mail Merge** menu, select **Merge**.

3. The Preview Data dialog box opens and the data from the first record is displayed in the field codes in your publication. (You can drag the Preview Data dialog box to a new location to see your merged data.)

4. Use the navigation buttons to move through the records or type in a new record number in the box and press **Enter**.

5. Make a note of any errors you see.

6. When finished previewing the mail merge, click the **Close** button. The field codes reappear in the publication.

To correct any mistakes, follow the procedure outlined previously for editing your Address List.

TIP   **Correcting Errors Quickly**   If you discover an error when previewing the mail merge, note the record number along with the nature of the mistake. From **Edit Address List**, enter the record number in the **View Entry Number** to go directly to the problem record.

Printing Your Merged Publication

The final step in a mail merge is printing the publication. Publisher 97 maintains all the print options normally available and adds several that are specific to the mail-merge feature, including the ability to print a test page from your merge.

To print a merged publication, follow these steps:

1. Open a previously set up merge publication.

2. From the **File** menu, select **Print Merge**. The Print Merge dialog box opens as seen in Figure 12.3.

3. In the Print Range section, choose from one of the following options:

    • **All Entries** prints all the entries in your data source.

    • **Entries From...To...** prints a range of entries from your data source starting with the record in the From box and ending with the record in the To box.

4. To print the first merged record as a test, click the **Test** button.

5. To prevent blank lines where there are merge codes but no data, make sure the **Don't Print Lines that Contain Only Empty Fields** box is checked.

6. Click **OK** when you have completed selecting your options and are ready to print.

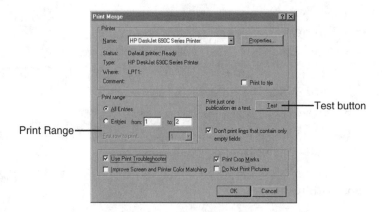

Test button

Print Range

Figure 12.3   The Print Merge has numerous special options.

In this lesson, you learned what mail merges are, how to create an address list, how to edit your list, how to set up your main document, how to preview your merge, and how to print your merged publication. In the next lesson, you learn how to create logos with WordArt.

Making a WordArt Object

In this lesson, you learn how to create a WordArt object, resize your WordArt creation, add special effects, and use your WordArt object on several pages.

Making a WordArt Object

Publisher 97 includes a terrific tool for creating logos and other fancy text objects: WordArt. With WordArt, your text can swirl, cast shadows, and leap from the page. Best of all, your logo is completely adjustable—even to the point of changing the wording. Fancy text objects like WordArt are best used sparingly; transform only your key words into WordArt to achieve the maximum impact.

To create a WordArt object, follow these steps:

1. Click the **WordArt** icon located in the left toolbar.
2. Click and drag out a WordArt Frame the approximate size and shape of your desired creation. Your WordArt Frame can be adjusted later.
3. The phrase Your Text Here appears in the WordArt Frame. The Enter Your Text Here dialog box also opens with the same phrase highlighted in the text box.
4. Type your text to replace Your Text Here. Press **Enter** for additional lines.
5. When you have finished entering in your text, click the Update Display button. Your text replaces Your Text Here in the WordArt Frame.
6. If your text is correct, you can close the Enter Your Text Here dialog box by clicking the **Close** button.

7. To choose a shape for your WordArt object, click the down-arrow of the style box (Plain Text is currently displayed in the style box) on the toolbar.

8. The WordArt shape option list opens. Select a shape from any of the 36 options.

9. Your WordArt object changes shape. Repeat step 8 to try a different shape.

10. You can change the WordArt font by clicking the arrow next to the Font box in the toolbar. Select a Font from the drop-down list of available fonts by highlighting it and clicking once.

11. When you are satisfied with your WordArt object, click the page anywhere outside the WordArt Frame.

Figure 13.1 shows one of the many WordArt shapes that can be applied to text.

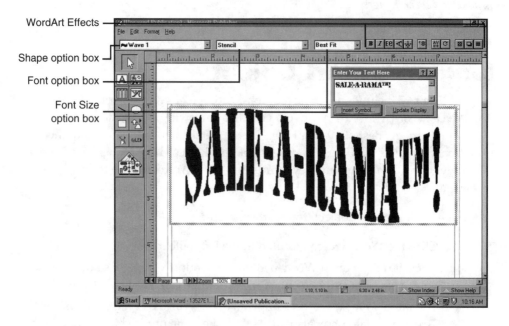

Figure 13.1   A WordArt creation in process.

 TIP   **WordArt Symbols**   You can insert a symbol such as a copyright © or registered trademark ® symbol by clicking **Insert Symbol** button in the Enter Your Text dialog box. From the Symbol dialog box, click the symbol and then click **OK**.

Resizing Your Logo

Instead of asking for a specific font size, Publisher 97 defaults to "Best Fit" when first creating your WordArt object. In other words, Publisher 97 selects the largest font size that fits in your frame. You have two options for resizing your WordArt object: You can specify a font size or you can resize the frame.

Follow these steps to resize a WordArt object by resizing the frame:

1. Double-click your created WordArt object to switch to WordArt creation mode. The Enter Your Text Here dialog box opens.

2. Verify that the Font Size box in the toolbar is set to **Best Fit**.

3. Click anywhere on the page to leave WordArt creation mode.

4. Select your WordArt object by clicking it once.

5. Position your pointer over any of the handles until the Resizer pointer appears. Use one of the following methods to resize your WordArt:

   - To resize the frame proportionally, hold down the **Shift** key and click and drag a corner handle.

   - To resize from the center, hold down the **Ctrl** key and click and drag any handle.

6. When the object is the size you want it, release the mouse button. The WordArt object resizes to fit the new frame dimensions.

Follow these steps to resize a WordArt object by altering the font size:

1. Double-click your created WordArt object to switch to WordArt creation mode. The Enter Your Text Here dialog box opens.

2. Click the arrow next to the Font Size box to display the drop-down list of font sizes and choose the font size you want.

3. Select a size by highlighting it with the mouse and clicking once.

4. The WordArt object resizes to the selected font size. The frame remains the same size.

5. If the font size you have chosen is too large for the frame, the Size Change dialog box appears. Select one of the following options:

   Yes resizes the frame so that your text in the new font size will fit.

   No renders the WordArt object in your new font size without stretching the frame.

6. If you select No in the Size Change dialog box above, portions of your WordArt object will be cut off as shown in Figure 13.2. Your options then are to select a small font size or resize the frame as described previously.

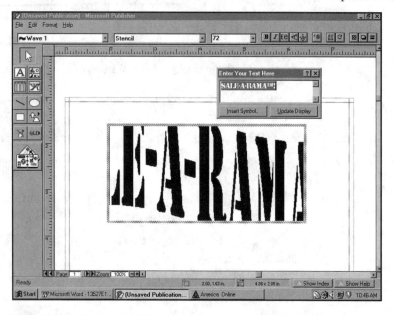

Figure 13.2   A WordArt object with a font size too large for its frame.

Trying Special Effects

WordArt has almost a dozen different options to alter your text, ranging from a standard bold and italic to eight different kinds of shadows. Table 13.1 outlines the various effects and their options. Experimentation with the various special effects is the best way to understand what generates the most suitable look for your particular WordArt object. Often, trying to achieve one effect will lead you to a completely unexpected, but wonderful, result.

To apply any special effect to your WordArt object, follow these steps:

1. Double-click your WordArt object to enter the WordArt creation mode. The Enter Your Text Here dialog box opens.

2. Select any of the WordArt effects, in any combination, from the WordArt toolbar (refer to Figure 13.1). Table 13.1 describes each option.

3. When you have completed applying your special effects, click anywhere on the page to leave WordArt creation mode.

Table 13.1   The WordArt Toolbar Buttons

Special Effect		Description	Options
B	Bold	Makes text bold	Toggle
I	Italic	Makes text italic	Toggle
Ee	Even Height	Makes text all the same height, regardless of capitalization	Toggle
	Stack Letters	Puts letters on top of one another	Toggle
A	Stretch	Stretches text to fit frame	Toggle
	Alignment	Justifies text	Center, Left, Right, Stretch Justify (stretches words), Word Justify (adds spaces between words), Letter Justify (spaces out letters)
AV	Character Spacing	Alters the spacing between characters	Very Tight, Tight, Normal, Loose, Very Loose, Custom
C	Rotation	Rotates text or changes the shape by degree	Rotation (rotates text) and Slider (skews text)
	Shading	Changes the tint or pattern for the WordArt text	24 different patterns and two color choices (foreground and background)
	Shadow	Adds a shadow effect to the WordArt text	8 different shadow types and 35 color choices
	Border	Adds a border around each WordArt letter	7 different border widths and 35 color choices

Copying Your Logo onto Other Pages

Once you have invested a lot of time and energy into creating your WordArt object, you will probably want to use it over and over again. Publisher 97 allows you to store any object you have created in the Design Gallery to use again in this publication or in any other.

To add a WordArt object to the Design Gallery, follow these steps:

1. Select the WordArt object you want to add to the Design Gallery.
2. Click the Design Gallery button located in the left toolbar.
3. From the WordArt Design Gallery dialog box (see Figure 13.3), click the **More Designs** button.
4. From the drop-down option list, select **Add Selection to Design Gallery**.
5. From the Adding an Object dialog box, type in a name for the object and a category name.
6. Click **OK**.
7. From the Create New Category dialog box, type a description (optional).
8. Click **OK**.
9. Your WordArt object appears in the Design Gallery dialog box with the new category name.
10. Click **Close**.

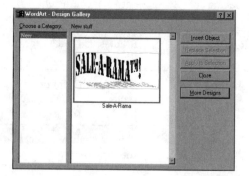

Figure 13.3   The Design Gallery dialog box with a custom WordArt object added.

Follow these steps to insert your WordArt object anywhere in your publication from the Design Gallery:

1. Move to the new page or place in your publication where you want to insert the WordArt object.
2. Click the **Design Gallery** button on the left toolbar.
3. If there are multiple categories in the Design Gallery dialog box, select the Category that contains your WordArt object.
4. Select the WordArt object by clicking it once.
5. Click the **Insert Object** button.
6. The WordArt object is placed in your publication.

Once you have placed a new copy of your WordArt object in your publication, you can move, resize, or alter it however you like.

In this lesson, you learned how to create a WordArt object, resize your WordArt creation, add special effects, and use your WordArt object on several pages. In the next lesson, you will learn how to work with the background.

Creating a Uniform Look with Backgrounds

In this lesson, you learn how to edit the background of a Publisher 97 publication, how to add page numbers, how to work with mirrored layouts, and how to generate a watermark.

Adding Objects to the Background

Certain publications, like newsletters or catalogs, have repeating elements on every page—a logo with the date next to it, or a watermark in the middle of the page, for instance. Publisher 97 handles repeating objects by putting them on the background. Anything put on the background of a publication will be seen on every page of that publication. You create and place objects on the background just as you have been doing on the foreground.

To add objects to the background of a publication, follow these steps:

1. Create or open a publication.
2. From the **View** menu, select **Go to Background**.

   The lower left of the screen now shows the background page symbol as shown in Figure 14.1, instead of the page controls.
3. Add Text, Pictures, WordArt, or any other element that you would like to have repeat on every page of your publication.

4. When you are finished adding objects to the background, from the **View** menu, select **Go to Foreground**.

5. The page controls replace the background page symbol in the lower left of the screen.

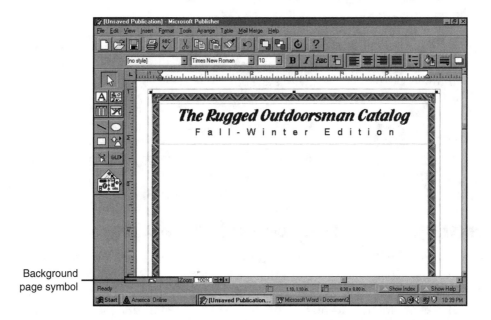

Background page symbol

Figure 14.1 A header and border placed on the background.

Inserting Page Numbers

Page numbers are among the most common objects to be used in background pages. Once you have put the page numbers in place, they automatically increment with every new page. Page numbers can start with any number (not just 1) and be formatted in any way you wish.

Follow these steps to include page numbers in your publication:

1. From the **View** menu, select **Go to Background**.

2. Create a Text Frame where you would like your page numbers to appear.

3. Type any leading text you want, such as **Page.** Be sure to leave a space after any words or else the page number will run into the leading text.

4. From the **Insert** menu, select **Page Numbers**.

5. The symbol for a page number, a pound sign (#), is inserted.

6. Add any additional formatting (centering, italicizing and so on).

7. From the **View** menu, select **Go to Foreground**.

8. The page number is displayed as a number.

You can start your page numbering with a number other than 1. From the **Tools** menu, select **Options**. In the Options dialog box, type in the starting page number next to the Start with Page box.

TIP   **Hide the First Page Number**   You can stop the page number from being displayed on the first page of a publication. From the **View** menu, select **Go to Foreground**, if you are not already there. Then, create a **Text Frame** over the page number to hide it.

Working with Mirrored-Page Layout

In Publisher 97, publications with facing pages can use the mirrored-page layout feature. Often with books or catalogs, you want the odd and even pages to reflect each other with margins and placement of page numbers and other header or footer information. In other words, a report title that appears aligned to the left on the left-hand side page appears aligned to the right on the right-hand side page.

Publisher 97 can mirror the layout guides for facing pages so that the inside margins of facing pages match as do the outside margins. To properly line up your items in your facing page publication, Publisher 97 has a feature that allows you to see both pages simultaneously.

Follow these steps to place "mirrored" information on facing page backgrounds:

1. Create a new or open an existing publication.

2. From the **Arrange** menu, select **Layout Guides**.

3. From the Layout Guide dialog box, select **Create Two Backgrounds with Mirrored Guide** below the Preview section.

4. The Preview displays the new two-page layout.

5. Change margins if necessary.

6. Click **OK**.

7. From the **View** menu, select **Two Page Spread**.

8. From the **View** menu, select **Go to Background**. The page indicator shows symbols for both the Left and Right Background Pages as shown in Figure 14.2.

9. Place your objects on the Left Background Page aligned to the left.

10. Place your objects on the Right Background Page aligned to the right.

11. From the **View** menu, select **Go to Foreground**.

12. If a one-page view is desired, from the **View** menu, select **Single Page View**.

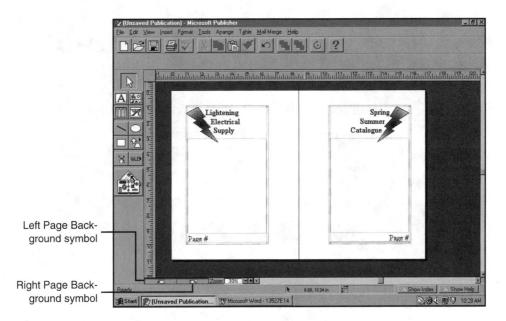

Left Page Back-
ground symbol

Right Page Back-
ground symbol

Figure 14.2   An example of mirrored backgrounds.

 TIP   **Working Across Pages**   When in Two Page view mode, click the **Zoom Indicator** and select **Full Page**. You can select objects on facing pages to align, group, move, or resize. You can also use the Ruler Guides across the pages.

Generating a Watermark

A watermark is an image or text that appears underneath the regular publication text. Some stationery uses company logos as watermarks; or use watermarks to label your publication as a draft or confidential. Because the text or image appears underneath text that must be read, the watermark is usually a light gray or other muted color. Publisher 97 uses the background feature to make watermarks like the ones seen in Figure 14.3.

Figure 14.3 A Publication using both Graphic and Text Watermarks.

Follow these steps to make a watermark:

1. Create a new or open an existing publication.
2. From the **View** menu, select **Go to Background**.
3. Place the text or graphic you want to appear as a watermark on the background page.
4. Recolor the text or graphic to a light gray:
   - For a text watermark, select all of the text. Click the **Text Color** button in the Text Formatting toolbar. Click a light gray color like Silver.

- For a graphic watermark, from the **Format** menu, select **Recolor Picture** or **Recolor Object**. From the Recolor dialog box, select a light gray color like Silver.

5. From the **View** menu, select **Go to Foreground**.

6. Create the necessary Text Frames.

7. Press **Ctrl+T** to make the Text Frame transparent.

8. Enter your text.

In this lesson, you learned how to edit the background of a Publisher 97 publication, how to add page numbers, how to work with mirrored layouts, and how to generate a watermark. In the next lesson, you learn how to print your publication using an outside printer.

Using an Outside Printer

In this lesson, you learn how to change your printer driver, how to set up the outside printer, use the Outside Printer Checklist and InfoSheets, and how to print to an outside printer.

Changing Your Printer Driver

Publisher 97 can print three different kind of publications:

- **Full-color printing** is used when your publication includes a color photograph or black and more than two spot colors.
- **Spot-color printing** is used when your publication includes one or two spot colors (and any of their tints or shades) and black-and-white.
- **Black, White, and Gray printing** (or grayscale) is used when your publication has only graphics with shades of gray (such as a black-and-white photograph) and black and white text.

Depending on the type of printers you have available to you, you might want to switch your printer driver from your default printer to another better suited to the particular publication. If you only have one printer available using its own driver, changing the printer driver will not give your printer additional capabilities; if this is the case, do not attempt to change your printer driver.

Follow these steps to change your printer driver:

1. From the **File** menu, choose **Print Setup**.

2. Click the arrow next to the Name box to list the available printers.

3. Click the printer you want to switch to.

4. Click **OK**.

Printer Driver The software that translates the instructions from Publisher 97 to your printer. Printer drivers are provided by the printer manufacturers and are designed to get the optimum performance from your printer.

Setting Up for Outside Printing

There are two basic reasons for using an outside printer (also known as a service bureau). Either you need better quality (such as higher resolution) than your desktop printer can produce, or you need to print a larger quantity than would be practical or cost-effective for you to do yourself. Preparing your publication to be printed by a service bureau can be tricky and Publisher 97 has provided a number of procedures and aids to make the process as smooth as possible.

Follow these steps to set up for outside printing:

1. From the **File** menu, select **Outside Print Setup**.

2. From the Outside Print dialog box (see Figure 15.1), select the type of printing (full-color, spot-color, or grayscale) by clicking the box next to the description.

If you choose Spot color, a section appears to allow you to select one or two spot colors from drop-down lists.

Figure 15.1 The first screen of the Outside Print Setup dialog box.

3. Click **Next**.

4. Select the printer to use:

   Use Publisher's Outside Driver selects either MS Publisher Imagesetter for either spot-color or grayscale or MS Publisher Color Printer for full-color printing.

   Select a Specific Printer opens the Select Printer dialog box that allows you to choose from available printer drivers as outlined previously.

5. If you have selected Full-Color Printing, click the **Done** button.

6. Select either or both of the two additional options spot-color and grayscale printing offer:

   "Extra" Paper Sizes is chosen when your service bureau needs to print your publication on an oversized sheet to incorporate bleeds or printer marks.

   Show Printer Marks is chosen when your service bureau needs to see crop marks, registration marks, or spot-color names.

7. Click the Done button.

 Bleeds   Any printing that needs to extend to the edge of the trimmed page. A bleed typically overextends the edge of the finished page by 1/2"; the excess is then trimmed away.

Using the Checklist and InfoSheets

Given the complexity of printing to an outside printer and all the variables involved, Publisher 97 includes two handy guides. The first, the Outside Printing Checklist, is a questionnaire designed to help you choose and work with a service bureau. The second, the InfoSheets, are documents created by Publisher 97 with specific information about your publication that will help the service bureau print your job correctly.

Follow these steps to print an Outside Printing Checklist:

1. From the Help section in the lower right of the screen, click **Show Index**.

2. From the Index, in the Type a Keyword box, type **Outside printing**.

3. Under **Outside Printing Services**, click **Outside Printing Checklist**.

4. In the What Is the Outside Printing Checklist pop-up window, click **Click Here to Print a Copy of the Outside Printing Checklist**.

5. Click **Done**.

6. Click **Hide Index** or **Hide Help** to remove the Help windows from the screen.

The first page of the Outside Printing Checklist is reproduced in Figure 15.2. The first section is designed to help you find a printer that can provide all the services you need. The second section guides you through a consultation with the service bureau and helps you ask the right questions.

To print out the InfoSheets with information about your specific publication, follow these steps:

1. If you have not already done so, complete the Outside Print Setup as outlined previously.

2. From the **File** menu, select **Print InfoSheet**.

The InfoSheet contains information helpful to the service bureau, including the number of sheets to print, page size, and colors used in the document. It will also list the fonts and any special effects, such as rotated text, used in the publication.

Following the steps below will help both you and your printing service get the results you want. This checklist assumes you've already read "Printing" in your *Publisher Companion*, and you know what kind of printing you need.

Part A — Call several printing services to find one that meets your needs

---

If you need high-resolution printing (1200 dpi or higher), or spot color printing:

- Tell them what kind of publication you're creating, how many pages it will have, and how many copies you'll need (for example, "I need 500 copies of a 2-page brochure").

Then ask the following questions:

• Can they create output with resolutions greater than 1200 dpi?	Required
• Do they do imagesetting, printing, or both? (Imagesetting creates a film version of a publication, which is then printed by a printing device.)	Service bureau _____ Printer _____ Both _____
• (If your publication uses spot color) Can they print spot color?	Required
• (If your publication uses two spot colors) Can they print two spot colors, or just one?	Required
• Are they familiar with printing from Microsoft Windows? (Recommended.)	____Y ____N
• Do they have Publisher 97? (Recommended.)	____Y ____N
• Roughly how much will it cost to print your publication? They won't be able to give you an exact figure until you've thoroughly discussed the details of your printing job, but they should be able to ask a few questions and give you a general idea.	Estimate_____

For medium-resolution printing (300-600 dpi), or full-color printing:

• Tell them what kind of publication you're creating, how many pages it will have, and how many copies you'll need (for example, "I need 40 copies of a 2-page brochure").	
• (If your publication is full color) Do they have a medium-resolution color printer (300 to 600 dpi)?	Required
• Are they familiar with printing from Microsoft Windows? (Recommended.)	____Y ____N
• Do they have Publisher 97? (Recommended.)	____Y ____N
• Roughly how much will it cost to print your publication? They won't be able to give you an exact figure until you've thoroughly discussed the details of your printing job, but they should be able to ask a few questions and give you a general idea.	Estimate_____

Microsoft Publisher 97   *Outside Printing Checklist*   *Page 1*

Figure 15.2   The Outside Printing Checklist initial page.

Printing to an Outside Printer

Your publication is completed, you've filled out the Outside Printer Checklist, and you are finally ready to send the file to the outside printer. Only one step remains: printing the file.

There is a crucial difference between printing to your desktop printer and printing to an outside printer. In the first instance, the publication is sent directly to your desktop printer. With an Outside Printer, you must first print your publication to a file and then send the file by modem or take on a floppy or removable disk to your printer.

Follow these steps to print your publication for an outside printer:

1. From the **File** menu, select **Print to Outside Printer**.
2. From the Print to Outside Printer dialog box shown in Figure 15.3, click the **Print to File** box, if it is not already selected.
3. Select a different Page Range if desired.
4. If you are printing a book or catalog, click the **Book Printing Options** button:

   Print One Page per Sheet is chosen if you want to print one page per 8.5"×11" sheet.

   Print as Book is chosen if you want to print two or more pages on an 11"×17" sheet.

5. From the Print to Outside Printer dialog box, click **OK**.
6. From the Print to File dialog box, type a file name in the File Name box. Select a different folder if desired.
7. Click **OK**.
8. After printing your publication to the file, Publisher 97 asks if you would like to print a page proof and an InfoSheet. Click **Yes** if you have not already done so.

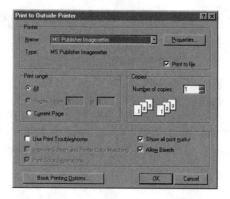

Figure 15.3   The Print to Outside Printer dialog box.

 Page Proof   A representation of your publication as printed by your desktop printer.

In this lesson, you learned how to change your printer driver, how to set up the outside printer, use the Outside Printer Checklist and InfoSheets, and how to print to an outside printer.

Internet
Explorer 4.0

Using Internet Explorer 4.0

1

In this lesson, you learn what Internet Explorer 4.0 is, how to start the program, what the key screen areas are, how the toolbar buttons are used, and how to quit the program.

Understanding Internet Explorer 4.0 and the Internet

Internet Explorer 4.0 is a suite of tightly integrated programs that thoroughly connects you and your computer to the world of information available through the Internet and the World Wide Web. Internet Explorer 4.0 not only acts as a browser to display the data, but helps you to find, incorporate, and interact with it as well. Furthermore, Internet Explorer 4.0 includes all the tools needed for you to communicate your message globally.

How does your computer communicate with the rest of the world? The necessary hardware is called a *modem* and is used to translate signals that come and go over the phone line. The necessary software for interpreting those signals into data that your computer can understand is known as a browser. Internet Explorer 4.0 is the latest generation of Microsoft browser software.

The Internet   A group of computer networks from around the world that are connected to one another. Initially established to share text-based information between universities and research scientists, the Internet has evolved into a more open medium accessible by everyone.

World Wide Web   The Internet's graphic front end, accessed by browsers such as Internet Explorer 4.0.

After your hardware and software are set to go onto the Internet, you need one final link: a connection to the Internet itself. If you are working in an office with a local area network, you may already be connected—check with your manager of information services or other computer consultant. If you are working at home or in a small office, you need to set up an account with an Internet Service Provider (ISP). Some ISPs such as America Online, Microsoft Network, and CompuServe provide additional, member-only services as well as Internet access. Other ISPs specialize in just the Internet connection. The choice is yours.

Starting Internet Explorer 4.0

Before you can start Internet Explorer 4.0, you must install the program on your computer. See installation instructions in Appendix D of this book.

Depending on the type of Internet connection you have set up, you may need to connect to your ISP directly before starting Internet Explorer 4.0. Check with your ISP's technical support department.

Because of Internet Explorer 4.0's tight integration into the Windows 95 operating system, there are numerous ways to start the program. No matter how you have installed the program, you can always start Internet Explorer 4.0 by following these steps:

1. From the Windows 95 taskbar, click once on the Start button.

2. From the Start menu, click **Programs**.

3. From the Programs submenu, click **Internet Explorer** found in the Internet Explorer Suite.

TIP   **Internet Explorer 4.0 Quick Start**   On most Windows 95 desktops, you can double-click **The Internet** icon to start Internet Explorer 4.0.

If you are connected to the Internet, Internet Explorer 4.0 opens your Start Page. Lesson 7 tells you how to customize your Start Page.

Touring the Screen Layout

Before you begin exploring the Internet and other capabilities of Internet Explorer 4.0, take a moment to familiarize yourself with the components of the screen. Table 1.1 describes the different sections of the screen and their uses, as shown in Figure 1.1.

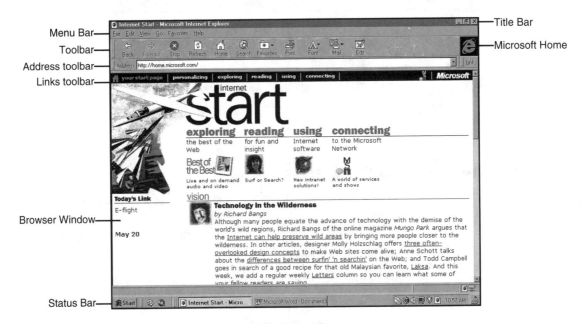

Figure 1.1 Sections of the Internet Explorer 4.0 screen.

Table 1.1 Sections of the Internet Explorer 4.0 Screen

Screen Element	Function
Address toolbar	Displays current Internet address.
Browser Window	Primary display area.
Links toolbar	Provides shortcuts to regularly updated Web pages.
Menu Bar	Allows access to the Internet Explorer 4.0 menu commands.
Microsoft Home	Opens the Home Page for Microsoft.

continues

Table 1.1   Continued

Screen Element	Function
Status Bar	Displays information on connection status.
Title Bar	Displays program and current Web page title.
Toolbar	Provides shortcuts to basic program commands.

TIP   **Customizing Toolbars**   All the toolbars can be moved and resized with a simple click and drag on any bar area not covered by a button.

Exploring the Toolbar

The shortcuts available in the toolbar across the top of Internet Explorer 4.0's screen go a long way toward simplifying your exploration of the World Wide Web. You will find yourself returning to them time and again for both basic and more advanced operations.

Here's a brief outline of the function of each toolbar button, from left to right across the screen:

Back displays the previous Web page.

Forward returns to the most recent Web page (if you have clicked the Back button).

Stop interrupts the transfer of any Web page from the Internet to your computer.

Refresh reloads the current Web page.

Home opens the user-definable start page.

Search opens a list of search engines used for finding a particular topic on the Web.

Favorites contains a dynamic list of your favorite Web pages and the ability to organize them.

Print sends the current Web page to your printer.

 Font is used to alter the default typeface used in displaying Web pages.

 Mail accesses the electronic mail component of Internet Explorer 4.0.

 Edit opens the current Web page in the Internet Explorer 4.0 editor, FrontPad, used for creating and updating Web pages.

 Web Page A document created for the Internet that uses a particular protocol. This protocol, HTTP, allows Web pages to link to one another and to convey not only text, but multimedia such as sounds, graphics, and video.

Web Site A collection of Web pages.

Quitting Internet Explorer 4.0

When you have finished your Internet Explorer 4.0 session, you quit the program by any of the standard methods:

- Select **File**, **Exit** from the Menu bar.
- Click the **Close** button in the upper-right corner of the Internet Explorer 4.0 window.
- Use the keyboard shortcut, **Alt+F4**.

In this lesson, you learned what Internet Explorer 4.0 is, how to start the program, what the key screen areas are, how the toolbar buttons are used, and how to exit the program. In the next lesson, you will learn how to navigate on the World Wide Web.

Navigating the World Wide Web

In this lesson, you learn how to go to a specific Web page, explore a Web site, revisit favorite Web pages, and "surf" the Web.

Going to a Web page

When you first begin to explore the Internet, you start by visiting specific Web pages. The Web page address, or *URL*, could be given to you by a friend or a colleague, or perhaps it is one you jotted down from an advertisement or announcement.

URL   (Universal Resource Locator, pronounced "earl" or "u-r-l"), a unique name used as an address by the Internet. A URL begins with a protocol specification (such as "HTTP://"), followed by the specific Web site name. The last part of the URL designates the type of site; for instance, .com is for commercial, .edu is for educational institutions, .gov is for governmental agencies.

Internet Explorer 4.0, like all browsers, revolves around URLs. Finding, remembering, and managing these Internet addresses are a lot of what Internet Explorer 4.0 is about. Starting Internet Explorer 4.0 takes you to your first URL, the Internet Explorer 4.0 Start Page. Once you are up and running, getting to a specific URL is easy.

Follow these steps to go to a specific Web page:

1. Start Internet Explorer 4.0.

2. The Internet Explorer 4.0 Home Page is loaded. The status toolbar tells you what is happening.

3. When the home page is completely loaded, the status toolbar displays Done.

4. Move the mouse pointer over the **Address** box. The pointer changes into an I-beam shape.

5. Click once anywhere in the Address box to select the current URL.

6. Type the URL. The first letter you type replaces the previous highlighted URL.

7. When you have completed typing the Internet address, press **Enter**.

8. Internet Explorer 4.0 connects to the requested Web page.

Internet Explorer 4.0 remembers URLs that you have visited. The next time you type in the address of a previously visited site, Internet Explorer 4.0 automatically completes the address.

TIP **More Auto-Completion** Most commercial URLs are variations of http://www.*company*.com. If you type just the main part of the Web site address (the *company* part above) and press **Ctrl+Enter**, Internet Explorer 4.0 puts an "http://www." at the beginning and a ".com" at the end, and then connects to your requested site.

Exploring a Web Site

Very few single Web pages exist by themselves in cyberspace. Most are part of a larger structure called a Web site. Because all Web sites are designed independently, there is no common user interface among them. However, most Web sites open with a home page that contains links to other pages within their site.

TERM **Link** Short for a key concept on the World Wide Web: hypertext links. When you click a link, Internet Explorer 4.0 opens that link, whether it is another Web page (in the same or different site) or a downloadable graphic or sound.

Figure 2.1 shows a typical opening page for a Web site. To explore a Web site such as this one, follow these steps:

1. Go to a specific URL by typing an Internet address in the Address box and pressing **Enter**.

2. Move the pointer over the various elements of the page to identify the potential links:

   - Underlined words that are a different color from the rest of the text.
   - Buttons or icons with clear directional signs.
   - Graphic images, possibly surrounded by a border.
   - Portions of a large graphic image.

3. When your mouse pointer passes over a link, the pointer changes to a hand.

4. Click once on any link to go to that Web page.

5. If you want to return to the previous page, click the **Back** button in the toolbar.

6. If you see a link on the new page that interests you, click it to go to that page.

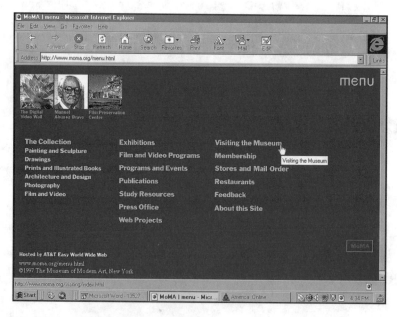

Figure 2.1 The main menu from the Museum of Modern Art Web site (**www.moma.org**).

Exploring a Web site is a combination of following your nose and retracing your steps. Clicking links that lead from one page to another takes you down a particular path. Clicking the Back button on the toolbar brings you back the way you came, one page at a time.

 TIP **Jump Back** If you click the Back button with the right mouse button instead of the left, a drop-down list of recently visited sites appears. You can jump to any listed URL by highlighting it with the mouse pointer and clicking once. The same is true of the Forward button.

Revisiting Favorite Web Pages

After a short time, you will want to revisit Web sites that have valuable information you need to review or are updated frequently with new information. Internet Explorer 4.0 allows you to mark any Web page as a "favorite," and easily return there.

Follow these steps to mark a Web page as a favorite:

1. Go to the Web page you want to mark.
2. Click the **Favorites** button on the toolbar.
3. From the Favorites drop-down list, select **Add to Favorites**.
4. In the Add to Favorites dialog box, Internet Explorer 4.0 places the title of the Web page in the Name box. This is the name this page will be under in your Favorites list. Modify if desired by typing a new name in the box.
5. By default, Internet Explorer 4.0 lists a new entry alphabetically in the Favorites folder. To list your selection in a different subfolder, click the **Create In>>** button.
6. The Add to Favorites dialog box extends to display the available subfolders (see Figure 2.2):
    - To list the entry under an available folder, click that folder to open it.
    - To create a new folder, click the **New Folder** button and type in a new name. Press **Enter**.
7. Click **OK**.

Figure 2.2   Adding a Favorite Web page to your list.

You can accumulate a lot of Favorites over a short period of time, and soon you'll find your Favorites drop-down list so long it can't show all of your choices. It's a good idea to organize your Favorites as you add them. There is a standard Add Folder button in the extended Add to Favorites dialog box that allows you to create folders on-the-fly.

To access a Web page that has been added to your Favorites collection, follow these steps:

1. Start Internet Explorer 4.0.

2. Click the **Favorites** button on the toolbar.

3. Highlight the desired Web page or folder where the favorite is stored, and click the favorite name.

TIP   **Start Menu Favorites**   If you installed the Integrated Shell option, you'll find an additional category on the Windows 95 Start menu after installing Internet Explorer 4.0: Favorites. Click **Start**, then **Favorites**, and then any Web page you want to revisit. If Internet Explorer 4.0 is not already running, it will open and go directly to the requested Web page.

Surfing the Web

So how exactly does one "surf" the Web? The term comes from the practice of jumping from Web page to Web page by following the links available on various Web sites. You can easily start out looking for information on animal vaccinations one minute and find yourself downloading audio clips from the Three Dog Night Web site the next. That's part of the fun—and the distraction—of the Internet. Literally, everything is interconnected.

Although all scenarios vary widely, follow these steps for a demonstration of how surfing the Web can help your business:

1. Click into the Address box and type the URL for the Small Business Administration: **www.sbaonline.sba.gov** and press **Enter**. Internet Explorer 4.0 fills in the missing "http://".

2. From the SBA Home Page, use the scroll bar to move down the screen until you see the listing for Your Local SBA Resources and the multicolor map of the United States.

3. Click once on either the underlined words or the map image to jump to that page.

4. From the Local SBA Resources Web page shown in Figure 2.3, click your regional area.

5. From the regional area map, click your state.

6. From the state map, click a city.

7. Select from the list of available SBA services, including loans, advice, and training.

8. Retrace your steps by clicking the **Back** button at any time.

Obviously, you can continue to follow any of the various paths to get the information you need. There is a vast amount of data on the Web. Finding the right information requires a little patience, but can be very gratifying, if not downright exciting.

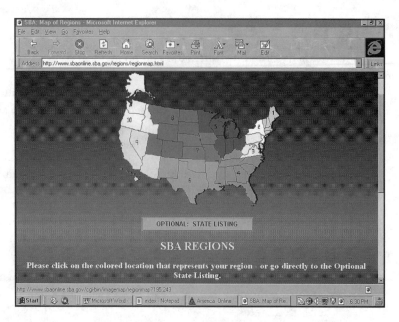

Figure 2.3 A Web page that uses graphics for navigation.

TIP **Business Research?** To find more sites devoted to business issues, check out *The 10 Minute Guide to Business Research* by Thomas Pack, published by Que.

Stopping a Web Page If you encounter a Web page that is taking forever to finish loading, press the **Stop** button on the toolbar. Pages load slowly either because of network delays or because the page has a lot of large graphic files.

CAUTION

In this lesson, you learned how to go to a specific Web page, how to explore a Web site, how to revisit favorite Web pages, and how to "surf" the Web. In the next lesson, you will learn how to search the World Wide Web.

Searching the World Wide Web

In this lesson, you learn how to search the Internet using a search engine, how to search by category, and how to set up your search page.

Starting the Search

The World Wide Web is made up of hundreds of thousands of constantly changing Web sites filled with vast amounts of data. How can you find the information you need? Internet Explorer 4.0 gives you quick and easy access to a variety of different *search engines* for this very purpose.

 Search Engines Web sites devoted to cataloguing and indexing the World Wide Web. When you submit a search for keywords or a phrase, the search engine returns a list of links to Web pages that are relevant to your search.

Internet Explorer 4.0's innovative Search button allows you to see both the list of links returned by your search request and the Web pages connected to those links, as shown in Figure 3.1. With this feature, you can quickly home in on your information without having to constantly use the Back button.

Figure 3.1 The Search bar lists available search engines.

Follow these steps to start a search:

1. Click the **Search** button on the toolbar. The Search toolbar opens in a frame on the left side of the screen.

2. In the Search box, type the keywords for your search in the box.

3. If you would like to use a particular search engine, click the box next to their logo. Currently supported search engines are:

AltaVista (www.altavista.com) indexes more Web pages than most other services, but does not categorize them.

Excite (www.excite.com) searches by concept rather than keyword; Excite includes a directory of reviewed sites.

HotBot (www.hotbot.com) has fill-in-the-blank type boxes for selecting key search criteria like keywords, dates, and places.

Infoseek (www.infoseek.com) categorizes and includes check marks next to sites that have been reviewed by the staff.

Lycos (www.lycos.com) uses WebGuides to highlight specific areas and continuously updates their Top 5% of the Web list.

Yahoo! (www.yahoo.com) uses categories more extensively than the other services, and includes special local search engines for metropolitan areas.

4. Click the **Search** button.

5. A list of responses to your search query is returned in the left frame.

6. Move your mouse pointer over the resulting links. If available, a synopsis of the Web page appears.

7. Select a link and click it.

8. The selected Web page appears in the right frame as shown in Figure 3.2.

9. To clear the search results and submit a new search, in the Search bar, click the words **Click Here to Start a New Search**.

10. To expand the right frame to full-screen, click the **Search** button.

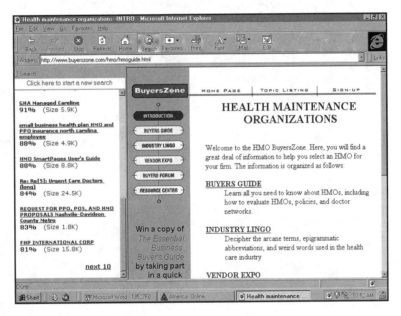

Figure 3.2 The search result on the left link to the Web pages on the right.

Each of the search engines has its own style. Try them all to see which one suits you best.

Using Search Engines

Submitting a single keyword for a search will likely result in thousands of responses. It is best to use multiple keywords to narrow your search.

For example, "computer" will yield over 1.2 million responses; however, "computer technician LAN job NYC" returns only 23 responses.

The opposite situation—restricting the search too tightly—can also be a problem. The phrase "travel magazines" returns far fewer results than "travel magazine" because the former only searches for those sites that indicate they work with multiple publications.

Follow these steps for better results in searching the Web:

1. Click the **Search** button in the toolbar.

2. Use the following techniques in any combination to make your search more appropriate:

   Multiple keywords   Search engines look for documents with any of the words specified. Web pages that contain all of the keywords are listed first. Example: computer technician LAN

   Double quotes   Use double quotes around a phrase to look for the phrase and not the individual words. Example: "white house"

   Plus sign (+)   A plus sign in front of a word indicates that the word must be in the Web page, but not necessarily together. Example: +OSHA requirements +CA

   Minus sign (-)   A minus sign in front of a word indicates that the word must not be in the Web page. Example: python antidote venom -monty

   Capitalization   Enter all queries in lowercase unless a proper name is desired. Example: "White House"

3. Click **Search**.

All the search engines have advice for using the particular system better. Go to the search engine's home page and click pages labeled Tips or FAQ (Frequently Asked Questions).

Searching by Category

Sometimes, the best way to search for information is to start in a particular category and then enter your keywords. Most of the search engines are organized this way—Yahoo!, Lycos, Infoseek, and Excite among them. Searching by category also allows you to explore unanticipated avenues.

Follow these steps to search by category:

1. In the Address bar, type the URL of any of the previously listed search engines.

2. Press **Enter**.

3. Click any highlighted category. Additional subcategories are listed at the top of the page before the pertinent Web sites.

4. Follow the links through any additional subcategories to your desired topic.

TIP   **Favorite Categories**   If you find a category page with a number of links that you want to reference, make it a Favorite for quick access. You can mark any page as a Favorite.

Setting Up the Search Page

After a while, you might find that you prefer one search engine to another. Internet Explorer 4.0 allows you to specify which Web page is to be used as the Search page. You can always revert to the original search page.

Follow these steps to select your own search page:

1. In the Address bar, type the URL of the search engine you want to select as your search page.

2. From the **View** menu, select **Options**.

3. From the Options dialog box, click the **Navigation** tab.

4. From the Navigation tab shown in Figure 3.3, click the arrow to the right of the Page box and select Search Page from the drop-down list.

5. Deselect the **Use IE 4.0 Search** by clicking its box so that the check mark disappears.

6. Click the **Use Current** button.

7. Click **OK**.

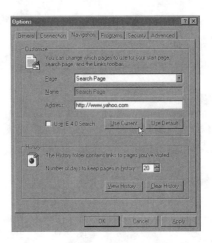

Figure 3.3 The Navigation tab of the Options dialog box.

The next time you click the Search button, the page you specified is loaded. Unlike the Internet Explorer 4.0 default search, the full browser window is used.

Restoring the Search Page Return to the Navigation tab as outlined previously and select Search Page from the Page list. Enable the default search by clicking the **Use IE 4.0 Search** box and clicking the **Use Default** button.

CAUTION

In this lesson, you learned how to search the Internet using a search engine, how to search by category, and how to set up your search page. In the next lesson, you'll learn how to download files.

Integrating Files and Links

In this lesson, you learn how to retrieve a file, decompress downloaded software, capture a picture from the Web, and copy a link into your documents or onto the desktop.

Retrieving a File

In addition to the vast amount of information available for browsing on the Web, there is also an enormous number of files there for the *downloading*. Graphics, software, compressed reports, and entire books—these are just some of the types of files at hand.

 TERM   **Downloading**   Transferring a file from a remote computer to your computer.

Once you have downloaded a file, you can run it on your computer or incorporate it into your work. Internet Explorer 4.0 even allows you to copy a link directly into an open document or onto your desktop.

Most files on the Internet intended to be downloaded are clearly labeled. When you come across a file that you want to download, follow these steps:

1. Click the link to the file to be downloaded.
2. Internet Explorer 4.0 displays a system message telling you that you are about to download a file and warning you about viruses. Click **Save to Disk** and then click **OK**.

3. A Save As dialog box opens. If desired, choose a new place for the downloaded file to be saved by selecting a different folder or drive. Click **OK**. A
   Download File dialog box opens as shown in Figure 4.1.

4. If necessary, you can click the **Cancel** button on the Download File dialog
   box to abort the transfer.

5. You can continue browsing the Web or even quit Internet Explorer 4.0
   while the download is proceeding.

6. After the file has finished downloading, the Download File dialog box
   closes.

Figure 4.1   A download in process.

 TIP   **Easy File Recovery**   A good place to temporarily store your downloaded files is the Windows 95 desktop. An icon is created for your file that's
easy to find. Once you've finished with the file, you can drag it directly to the
Recycle Bin.

Decompressing Software

Many downloadable files are compressed in order to reduce the file size and,
therefore, the download time. Software programs consisting of more than one
file are compressed to keep all the separate files together. Some compressed files
expand automatically when they are opened; others require an outside application.

Currently, the most popular compression scheme for Windows 95 is the ZIP
method. Files that have been compressed using this algorithm have the extension **.zip**; these files are uncompressed with a program such as WinZip or
PKZip. Before you can open a file with a .zip extension you need to install
one of these types of programs. There are widely available on the Web. Two
good sources for decompression programs are **www.tucows.com** and **www.
shareware.com**.

536

Other files use a self-extracting method that automatically expands when opened; these files have an **.exe** or **.sea** extension. No special software is needed to open these files.

Follow these steps to decompress a downloaded file:

1. Locate the file that you have downloaded by opening its folder or using **Find File** from the Start button.

2. Double-click the icon for the file.

3. The file opens with one of the following methods:
   • If the file has a .zip extension, the decompression program will open and decompress or extract the file.
   • If the file has an .exe or .sea extension, the file will open automatically and, if necessary, begin to install itself.

4. If the file has not automatically installed, open the file or folder created when the original download decompressed.

5. Load or install the program as necessary by double-clicking the icon.

 Mirror Sites Some Web sites list several mirror sites from which to download specific software. A mirror site is an exact duplicate of the site you accessed and is used to allow more people to download the software simultaneously.

Capturing a Picture

The graphics on the Web can convey as much information as the text. You can capture almost any image that you see on the Web and transfer it to your computer to view or use offline. There are numerous sites that are devoted to clip art images that are free to use. Be sure to check the copyright limitations on any Web page before using someone else's work.

To capture an image from the Web, follow these steps:

1. Locate the image you want to copy.

2. Move the mouse pointer over the image and click the right mouse button.

3. From the Quick Menu, select **Save Picture As...**, as shown in Figure 4.2.

4. From the Save As dialog box, choose a folder to save the image in and a new file name, if desired.

5. Click **OK**. The image copies to your computer.

Figures 4.2 shows an image in the process of being captured from the Flags of the World site at **http://flags.cesi.it/flags/**. Figure 4.3 shows the same image incorporated into the title page of a report written in Word 97.

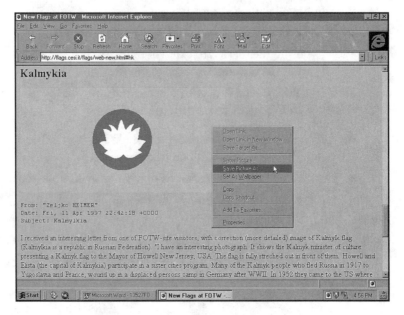

Figure 4.2 A flag image is copied from the Flags of the World Web site.

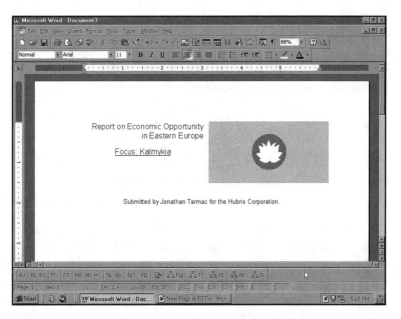

Figure 4.3 The same flag image is inserted into a Word document.

Copying a Link

As the modern world becomes increasingly tied into the World Wide Web, links to Web pages are becoming more prevalent. Already, Web page links can be found on desktops, in electronic mail, and in Office 97 documents. Clicking these links starts Internet Explorer 4.0, if it is not already running, and opens the corresponding Web site.

Internet Explorer 4.0 makes copying and using the links easy. Follow these steps to copy a link from any Web page to the desktop:

1. Go to a Web page that has a link you want to copy.
2. If Internet Explorer 4.0 is maximized, click the **Restore** button next in the title bar to reduce the Internet Explorer 4.0 window.
3. Click and drag your desired link onto the desktop.
4. Release the mouse.

   A shortcut to the Web link is created on the desktop.

If you have Internet Explorer 4.0 and another program such as Word 97 open side-by-side, you can click and drag the link directly into the program.

To copy a link from Internet Explorer 4.0 to another program when they are not side-by-side, follow these steps:

1. Open a Web page with the link you want to copy.
2. Position your pointer over the desired link.
3. Click once with the right mouse button the link to open the **Quick** menu.
4. From the Quick menu, select **Copy Shortcut**.
5. Switch to your other application by clicking once its button in the taskbar.
6. Click the insertion point where you want the link to appear.
7. Click the **Paste** button in the toolbar. The link is copied to your program.

CAUTION

Copy Not Linking?   If you paste a link into Word 97 and the text is there but it doesn't link, the AutoFormat option may be turned off. From the **Tools** menu, select **AutoCorrect**. Click the **Autoformat As You Type** tab and make sure there is a check mark in the **Internet and Network Paths with Hyperlinks** box.

In this lesson, you learned how to retrieve a file, how to decompress down-loaded software, how to capture a picture from the Web, and how to copy a link into your documents or onto the desktop. In the next lesson, you will learn how to view Web pages offline.

Viewing Web Pages Offline

In this lesson, you learn how to browse offline, print a Web page, and save a Web page.

Browsing Offline

While it may seem that there is so much on the Web that you have to stay connected to it 24 hours a day, that's not the way people work. You work the Web to access your research, contacts, and e-mail—and then you go offline for most of the day. Internet Explorer 4.0 combines the best of both worlds with a new feature that allows you to browse your favorite sites offline.

Follow these steps to browse Web pages offline:

1. Go to a Web page that you want to browse offline.
2. From the **Favorites** menu, select **Add to Favorites**.
3. From the Add to Favorites dialog box, specify a new folder to save it in or rename the page if desired.
4. Click **OK**.
5. From the **File** menu, select **Browse Offline** as shown in Figure 5.1.
6. From the **Favorites** menu, highlight the Web page you added to the Favorites collection.

   The Web page displays, complete with any active content, as if you were online.

Figure 5.1 The Browse Offline option is found under the File menu.

CAUTION

Browsing Offline Off? If you keep getting the message that the page you requested is not available offline, the amount of file space reserved for temporary files may be set too low. From the **View** menu, click **Options**. On the **Advanced** tab, click **Settings**. Increase the **Amount of Disk Space to use** by clicking and dragging the slider. Click **OK** here and in the Options dialog box.

Printing a Web Page

Being able to get a printout of your data—no matter what the source—is vital to anyone in business today. Today, much of the data gathered is from the Web. Printing and saving Web pages is extremely helpful if you are gathering sales research, presenting at an out-of-office meeting, or burning the midnight oil putting together a proposal.

Printing a Web page gives you instant hands-on access. Follow these steps to print a Web page:

1. Browse to the Web page you want to print.

2. Click the **Print** button in the toolbar. The Print dialog box opens as shown in Figure 5.2.

3. Select from the following options:

> **Print Range** Because Web pages do not correspond 1-to-1 to printed pages, it is best to leave the Print All box selected.
>
> **Copies** Type the number of copies you want or use the incrementer arrows to print more than one.

Linked Documents Checking **Print all Linked Documents** makes Internet Explorer 4.0 download and print any Web page with a direct link to the current page.

Print What These options activate when the page in question contains *frames*. You can print a portion of a screen by clicking in one frame and selecting **Print Document in Selected Frame**.

4. Click **OK**.

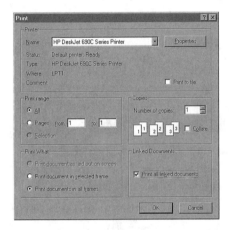

Figure 5.2 The Print dialog box with special Web page options.

CAUTION

Wrong-Way Printing Because the Web is a screen-based medium instead of a page-based one, some Web pages look better printed sideways instead of straight up-and-down. To change the page orientation, from the **File** menu, select **Page Setup**. In the Page Setup dialog box, choose either **Portrait** (the default) or **Landscape** (sideways) in the Orientation section.

Saving a Web Page

If you need to incorporate data you found on the Web into a report or other document, neither browsing offline nor printing the page does the trick. For times like these, you need to be able to save the Web page to your computer's hard drive.

Internet Explorer 4.0 allows you to save Web pages in two ways—as an RTF text file and an HTML file. RTF (Rich Text Format) files are basic text with minimal formatting (bold, centered, and so on). Save your Web pages in RTF format when you want just the text. An HTML file includes the Web page layout as well as the text as it appears on the Web. While saved HTML files show spaces for the graphics, they don't automatically save the images (see Lesson 4 on capturing images).

HTML HyperText Markup Language. HTML is the computer language used to build Web pages. HTML files usually end with either an .htm or .html extension.

To save a Web page, follow these steps:

1. Browse to a Web page that you want to save to disk.
2. From the **File** menu, select **Save As**.
3. From the Save HTML Document dialog box, enter a new folder to save the file in, if desired.
4. Select a file type option by clicking the arrow next to the Save as File Type box as shown in Figure 5.3:

   HTML file (*.htm,*.html) saves as HTML files.

   RTF file (*.doc,*.rtf) saves as a text file.

   Any file (*.*) allows you to save the file with any extension.

5. Type a new file name in the File name box.
6. Click **OK**.

Figure 5.3 The Save HTML Document dialog box showing available file types.

In this lesson, you learned how to browse offline, how to print a Web page, and how to save a Web page. In the next lesson, you learn how to manage your Web information.

Managing Your Information

In this lesson, you learn how to organize your favorite Web pages, view thumbnails of your favorites, and use Smart Favorites, Link Shortcuts, and Quick Links.

Organizing Favorite Web Pages

After you get into the habit of adding Web pages to your list of Favorites, it's hard to stop. Soon your list is at the bottom of your screen, and remembering why you selected every entry is next to impossible. It's time to organize your favorite Web pages.

Internet Explorer 4.0, like Windows 95, uses folders as a primary organizational aid. Folders take up almost no physical hard drive space and they can help you find your files more quickly while avoiding clutter. Internet Explorer 4.0 provides a special tool for arranging your Favorite Web pages: the Organize Favorites dialog box.

Follow these steps to organize your favorite Web pages:

1. From the **Favorites** menu, select **Organize Favorites**.
2. The Organize Favorites dialog box opens, as shown in Figure 6.1, and displays the folders and Web sites selected in Internet Explorer 4.0 and, if you installed the Integrated Shell, favorites selected in other Office 97 programs such as Word 97.
3. When the Organize Favorites dialog box opens, all of the command buttons, with the exception of the Close button, are inactive. Click any file or folder to activate the buttons.

4. From the Organize Favorites dialog box, select any of the following options:

> **Move** opens the Browse for Folder dialog box to display all folders in your Favorites collection. Click any folder to move the selected file there. Click **OK**.
>
> **Rename** highlights the name of selected file or folder. Type in a new name and press the **Enter** key.
>
> **Delete** places the selected file or folder in the Recycle Bin. Before proceeding, Internet Explorer 4.0 asks for confirmation. From the Confirm File Delete dialog box, choose **Yes** to delete, **No** to cancel.
>
> **Open** opens the selected file or folder. This is useful if you don't remember what the Favorite is.

5. To create a new folder, click the **New Folder** button in the dialog box toolbar. Enter the new folder name and press **Enter**.

6. When you have finished organizing your Favorites, click **OK** to close the dialog box.

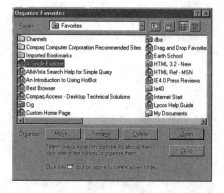

Figure 6.1 The Organize Favorites dialog box arranges all your selected Web sites.

TIP **Dragging Favorites** You can move your Favorites around by clicking and dragging them both in the Organize Favorites dialog box and on the Favorites menu. Just click the Favorite you want to move, drag it onto a folder, and release the mouse button.

Viewing Thumbnail Favorites

After you have organized your Favorites, you still might have trouble remembering what each of the file names means. If you installed the Integrated Shell, Internet Explorer 4.0 provides a visual alternative to often cryptic file names: thumbnails. Thumbnails are basically small pictures used as a reminder.

To view your Favorites as thumbnails, follow these steps:

1. Click in the Address bar and type **c:\windows\favorites**.
2. Press **Enter**. Your Favorites are displayed in the browser window.
3. From the **View** menu, select **Thumbnails**.
4. The view switches to **Thumbnail view** (with a Windows Explorer toolbar) as shown in Figure 6.2.
5. To go to any Favorite shown, double-click the thumbnail.
6. To return to your previous Internet Explorer 4.0 page, click once on the **Back** button in the toolbar.

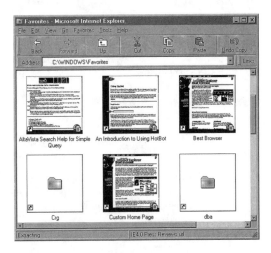

Figure 6.2 A Sample Thumbnail view shows both Web pages and folders.

TIP Thumbnails for Other Folders You can display what's inside other folders besides the Favorites folder. Select a folder you want to display and click once with the right-mouse button to reveal the Quick Menu. From the Quick Menu, select **Properties**. From the Properties dialog box, on the General tab, check **Enable Thumbnail View**.

547

Using Smart Favorites

By now, you may have noticed that some icons identifying some Favorite sites have a small red gleam in the upper-left corner. This gleam indicates that the Web site has been updated since your last visit. Internet Explorer 4.0 uses a system called Smart Favorites to check your favorites to see if there have been any changes.

Smart Favorites cut down on the amount of time spent in checking and rechecking a site to see if the information has been updated. Smart Favorites can also tell you when it was updated. You can use this information to determine whether a site visit is necessary.

To use Smart Favorites, follow these steps:

1. From the **Favorites** menu, look for any Favorites with a red gleam on the icon.

2. Move your mouse pointer over any Favorite with a red gleam.

3. A help tip appears (see Figure 6.3) that displays:

    • The last time you visited the Web site.
    • The last time the Web site was updated.
    • If available, information on what was updated.

4. Click anywhere in the Browser Window to close the Favorite menu.

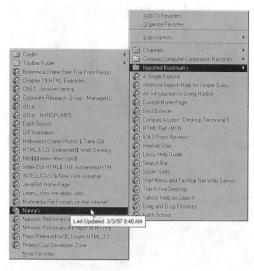

Figure 6.3 Smart Favorites display information about a Web site.

Saving Link Shortcuts and Using Quick Links

Those Web sites you access the most frequently can be set up for one-click access from the desktop or from the Links toolbar. While the Favorites menu is convenient for most repeatedly visited Web pages, there are times when you go to a site again and again; you might need to look up a ZIP code often or keep in touch with a competitor's Web site. Internet Explorer 4.0 has two features for these circumstances: Link Shortcuts and Quick Links.

A *shortcut* is an icon that acts as a pointer to a program or, in this case, a link to a Web page. Shortcuts are usually found on the Windows 95 desktop, although they can exist in any folder.

To create a shortcut to a link, follow these steps:

1. Go to the Web page containing the link you want to create a shortcut to.
2. If your Internet Explorer 4.0 screen is maximized, click the **Restore** button in the title bar.
3. Click the link you want and drag it to the desktop.
4. Release the mouse button.
5. A Link Shortcut is created on the desktop.

To access your Web page via the Link Shortcut, double-click the desktop shortcut. If Internet Explorer 4.0 is open, the Web page loads; if not, Internet Explorer 4.0 will open and then load the Web page.

TIP **Flipping to the Desktop** If you have the Desktop Integration mode turned on, you can bring the desktop to the front just as you would any open window. Click the **Surface/Restore Desktop** icon on the right side of the taskbar.

A Quick Link is a user-specified button on the Links toolbar. Internet Explorer 4.0 has room for up to five Quick Links. To connect a Web site to a Quick Link button, follow these steps:

1. Go to the Web site containing the link you want to make into a Quick Link.
2. If the Links toolbar is not fully visible, click once on the word **Links**.

3. Click your desired link and drag it up to any of the other buttons on the Links toolbar.

4. Release the mouse button. The Quick Link dialog box opens as shown in Figure 6.4.

5. From the Quick Link dialog box, click **Yes** to set the Quick Link to the selected Web address or click **No** to cancel.

6. If you clicked Yes, the name of the Quick Link button changes to your selected site.

7. Click the **Quick Link** button to load the chosen Web page.

8. Click the word **Links** to shrink the Links toolbar.

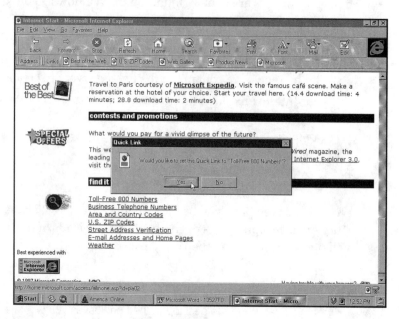

Figure 6.4 Quick Links can give you a custom toolbar.

In this lesson, you learned how to organize your favorite Web pages, view thumbnails of your Favorites, and use Smart Favorites, Link Shortcuts, and Quick Links. In the next lesson, you will learn how to customize Internet Explorer 4.0.

Customizing Internet Explorer 4.0

In this lesson, you learn how to personalize your Start page, select a different Start page, customize your general Web page settings, and choose a different font size for Web pages.

Personalizing Your Start Page

Every time Internet Explorer 4.0 opens, it goes to its Start page. The default Start page is maintained by Microsoft and offers an excellent entry into the Internet. One advantage that this page has over others is that you can get daily headlines (and their links) in a variety of categories. Furthermore, you get to choose the categories and the content providers used. For example, you could pick the Sports and Stock Ticker categories or you could opt for Technology, Money, and Entertainment categories.

Follow these steps to personalize the Internet Explorer Start page:

1. Start Internet Explorer 4.0.
2. From the Microsoft Start page, click the **Personalizing** button located at the top of the Web page.
3. From the Personalizing page shown in Figure 7.1, first click the category under step 1 you want to alter.
4. For each category, different options appear under step 2. Select any desired option by clicking its logo.
5. To step through the categories one at a time, under step 3, click the **Next** button.

6. When you have made all your choices, click the **Finish** button under step 3.

Your Start page is reloaded with your new options enabled.

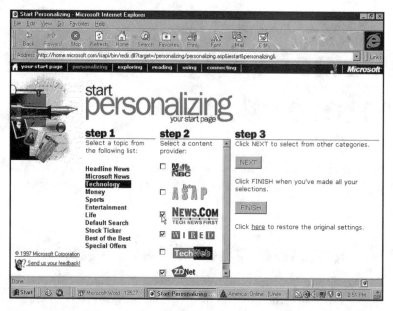

Figure 7.1   Personalizing your Start page to give you the headlines you want.

 Stock Ticker Delay The Stock Ticker option needs a small program called an ActiveX control to run on your start page. After you have clicked the **Finish** button, the ActiveX control downloads and installs into your system. This may take several minutes.

CAUTION

Selecting a New Start Page

There are some circumstances where you might want to choose an entirely different Start page. If your business has its own Web site, you might prefer using that home page as your starting point. Or, you might have a news source specific to your industry that is not available through Microsoft. Internet Explorer 4.0 allows you to choose your own Start page as well as your own Search and Quick Link pages previously covered.

To select a Web site as your new Start page, follow these steps:

1. Go to the Web page that you want to set up as your Start page.
2. From the **View** menu, select **Options**.
3. Click the **Navigation** tab.
4. From the Navigation section, make sure that Start Page is currently listed in the Page box. If not, click the arrow next to the box and highlight **Start Page**.
5. Click the **Use Current** button. The current URL appears in the Address box.
6. Click **OK**.

Tailoring Your Web Page Display

If you enter a Web site with intensive graphics and multimedia elements, the World Wide Web can become the World Wide Wait. Internet Explorer 4.0 allows you to turn off certain elements in order to speed up the downloading of Web pages. You can independently control pictures, sounds, and videos with Internet Explorer 4.0.

Furthermore, Internet Explorer 4.0 lets you customize the colors of your Web browser. Many Web pages, particularly the text-intensive ones, use the browser defaults when displaying background, text, and link colors. Use this feature to reduce eyestrain or increase the contrast between text and background.

To alter your Web browser's display, follow these steps:

1. From the **View** menu, select **Options**. The Options dialog box appears.
2. From the **General** tab, remove the check mark next to the multimedia elements to stop the pictures, sounds, or videos from automatically displaying (see Figure 7.2). Click again to enable them.
3. To change the colors, check **Use Windows Colors** to deselect it.
4. Click the box next to Background to open the **Color** dialog box.
5. Click a desired color, and then click **OK**.
6. Repeat steps 4 and 5 to choose the text color.
7. You can follow the same procedure to alter either of the Visited or Unvisited Link colors.
8. Click **OK**.

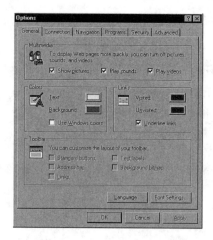

Figure 7.2 Customizing Your Web Browser with the Options dialog box.

Altering the Browser Fonts

With Internet Explorer 4.0, you can alter the size of the font normally used to display Web page text. This is useful when you need to make the text larger for presentation purposes or smaller to see more on a page. These changes are also reflected in any printouts of the page. You can either alter the font size temporarily or specify your new size as the default.

To temporarily alter the size of the default font, follow these steps:

1. Click the **Font** button on the Toolbar.
2. Select one of the five available sizes ranging from Largest to Smallest. Medium is the default.
3. Open a Web page in order to see the resulting changes.
4. Adjust if necessary.

The new font size stays in effect until you change it using the preceding method or until you close Internet Explorer 4.0. Figure 7.3 shows the same Web page using the smallest and the largest available fonts.

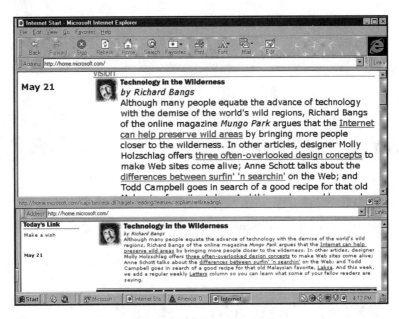

Figure 7.3 The same paragraph in two different font sizes.

Follow these steps to change the default size of your font:

1. From the **View** menu, select **Options**. The Options dialog box appears.
2. From the **General** tab, click the **Font Settings** button.
3. From the Fonts dialog box, click the arrow next to the Font Size box.
4. Select the new default size by clicking one of the options.
5. Click **OK** to close the Font dialog box.
6. Click **OK** to close the Options dialog box.

You can change the default fonts used in displaying Web pages. The Proportional Font is the one primarily used for text. The Fixed-Width Font is used when a monospaced font is required, as with a simplified column layout.

In this lesson, you learned how to personalize your Start page, select a different Start page, customize your general Web page settings, and choose a different font size for Web pages. In the next lesson, you learn how to use the integration features of Internet Explorer 4.0.

Integrating the Desktop

In this lesson, you learn how to browse your computer, switch to Web view, search the Internet through the desktop, and add an Active Component to your desktop.

Browsing Your Computer

A key feature of Internet Explorer 4.0 is the integration between your desktop and the Web. By providing one central interface for exploring the Web and exploring your computer, Internet Explorer 4.0 shortens the learning curve and reduces training requirements. Moreover, Internet Explorer 4.0 uses Smart Toolbars to present different buttons for different circumstances; when you change from searching the Internet to searching your hard drive, the Smart Toolbar changes with you.

No Integration Features? If you don't see any of the features mentioned in this lesson, you probably didn't install the Shell Integration option. See Appendix D for installation instructions.

CAUTION

To browse your computer using Internet Explorer 4.0, follow these steps:

1. Open Internet Explorer 4.0.
2. In the Address toolbar, type the path of a folder you would like to browse—for example, **c:\my documents**.
3. Press **Enter**.
4. Internet Explorer 4.0 displays your folder as shown in Figure 8.1.

5. The Smart Toolbar presents buttons suitable for file and folder exploration:

    Back loads the previous Internet address or folder.

    Up loads the directory one level above the current one.

    Cut moves the selected item to the Clipboard.

    Copy copies the selected item to the Clipboard.

    Paste inserts the contents of the Clipboard.

    Delete puts the selected item in the Recycle Bin.

    Undo Delete returns the previously deleted item.

    Properties opens the Properties dialog box for the selected item.

    View switches between Large Icon, Small Icon, List, and Detail views.

6. Click the **Back** button to return to the previous Internet address.

Figure 8.1 Internet Explorer 4.0 explores your computer.

Switching to WebView

When you open a folder, you get a combination of icons or names representing folders and files. Often, the names themselves are not as descriptive as they could be. Internet Explorer 4.0 adds another option to the regular icon and list views: WebView. WebView allows each folder to have its own customizable format.

Internet Explorer 4.0 demonstrates the possibilities of WebView in two folders: My Computer and the Control Panel. To enable the WebView option, follow these steps:

1. Open a folder by clicking it.

2. In a clear area of the folder, click once with the right mouse button to open the Quick menu.

3. From the **Quick** menu, select **View** and then **Click on Web View**.

4. Depending on the customization of the folder, a different view appears:

   My Computer shows the available and used hard drive space when the mouse is over any hard drive as shown in Figure 8.2.

   Control Panel shows a description of each program when selected by the mouse; a Connect button is also available for reading Microsoft Technical Support through the Internet.

5. To turn off WebView, right-click and select **View**, **Web View** again.

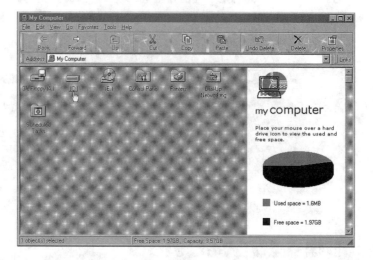

Figure 8.2   The WebView of My Computer shows free hard-drive space.

TIP   **Custom WebViews**   Microsoft provides a Wizard for building custom WebViews online at **http://www.microsoft.com/ie/ie40/integrat/folderwiz.htm**.

Searching the Internet Through the Desktop

Integration is a two-way street—just as Internet Explorer 4.0 allows you to use its browser to explore your computer, it also allows you to search the Internet through the desktop. Not only can you search for keywords and categories as demonstrated in Lesson 3, but you can also search for people's phone numbers, mail addresses, or e-mail addresses.

To search the Internet through the desktop, follow these steps:

1. From the desktop, click the **Start** button in the taskbar.
2. Select the **Find** menu.
3. Select **On the Internet** from the submenu.

    If not already running, Internet Explorer 4.0 opens.
4. Internet Explorer 4.0 connects to Microsoft's All-in-One Search page.
5. Click a category from the left pane of the window.
6. Complete the options that appear in the right pane.
7. Click the **Search** button.

The Business and Finance category, shown in Figure 8.3, has searches for stock market quotes, company Web addresses, package tracking information, and various loan and retirement calculators, among others.

To search for a person's address through the Internet, follow these steps:

1. From the desktop, click the **Start** button in the taskbar.
2. Select the **Find** menu.
3. Select **People** from the submenu.
4. In the Find People dialog box, select from any of the search services listed by clicking its button.
5. Enter the name to search for in the Name box.
6. Click the **Find Now** button. The message `Connecting to Directory Service` is displayed. When the search is completed, all results are shown in the box below showing Name, Email Address, Home Phone, and Work Phone (if available).

7. To add an entry to your Windows address book, select it and click the **Add to Address Book** button. For more information about the address book, see Part III, Lesson 5.

8. Click the **Close** button when you are finished with your search.

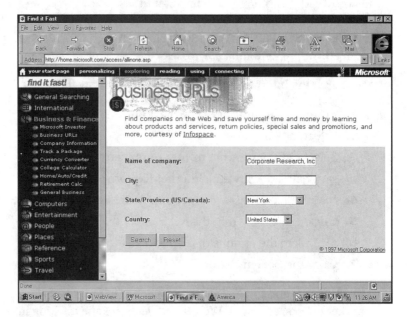

Figure 8.3   You can look up a company's URL online.

Adding a Desktop Component

Desktop Components are another element that link your computer to the Web. Desktop Components are mini-Web pages placed on the desktop, used to display information updated from the Web on a user-definable schedule. Examples of Desktop Components include:

Tickers displaying sports scores, stock quotes, or weather information.

Headline links for news stories or announcements to more detailed information.

Pop-up messages for internal corporate announcements, broadcast over the company network.

Notifications of new mail or public discussion forums.

Pictures of breaking news stories.

Microsoft maintains a gallery of Desktop Components that you can download and install. To add a Desktop Component to your system, follow these steps:

1. Open Internet Explorer 4.0.

2. In the Address bar, type in the following address: **http://www.microsoft.com/ie/ie40/gallery/** and press **Enter**.

3. The Desktop Component Gallery Web page opens. Click any of the components listed to get more information about it. The information page for the Weather Map Desktop Component is shown in Figure 8.4.

4. Click the words **Put It On My Desktop** to download and install the Desktop Component. A message box informs you of the progress of the installation process.

5. When the installation is complete, bring your desktop to the front by clicking the **Desktop** icon in the taskbar.

6. The Desktop Component can be moved by clicking and dragging its upper-left corner and it can be resized by clicking and dragging its lower-right corner.

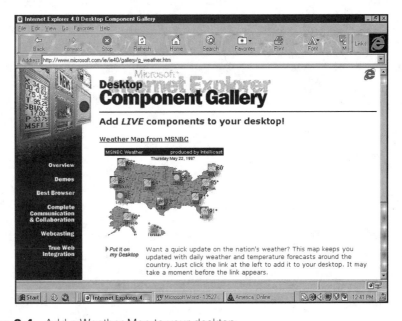

Figure 8.4 Add a Weather Map to your desktop.

To turn off or remove a Desktop Component, follow these steps:

1. From the desktop, right-click over an open area to bring up the Quick menu.
2. From the **Quick** menu, select **Properties**.
3. From the Display Properties dialog box, select the Desktop tab.
4. Select one of the following:
   - If you want to turn off a Desktop Component, click the box next to its name so that the check mark disappears.
   - If you want to remove a Desktop Component, select the component and click the **Remove** button.
5. Click **OK**.

In this lesson, you learned how to browse your computer, switch to Web view, search the Internet through the desktop, and add an Active Component to your desktop. In the next lesson, you learn how to use e-mail.

Communicating with E-Mail

In this lesson, you learn how to compose and send a message, reply to and forward e-mail you receive, attach a file, and use your address book.

Composing and Sending a Message

E-mail in the '90s is becoming what faxes became in the '80s: indispensable. For worldwide business, inter-office, and even personal communication, electronic mail is fast, inexpensive, and convenient. Internet Explorer 4.0 includes a powerful e-mail component called Outlook Express that makes sending all forms of electronic communication—notes, documents, graphics, and even multimedia files—a breeze.

Follow these steps to compose and send e-mail to anyone on the Internet:

1. If it is not already running, start Internet Explorer 4.0.
2. Click the **Mail** icon in the toolbar.
3. From the drop-down option list, click **New Message**. The New Message form opens as shown in Figure 9.1.
4. Type the recipient's e-mail address in the **To:** box; for example, *jsmith@smithco.com*.
5. Press **Tab** to move to the next box.
6. Enter any additional recipients in the **Cc:** and **Bcc:** boxes and press **Tab**.
7. In the **Subject:** box, type in your e-mail message title and press **Tab**.
8. Type your text in the message area. You can use any of the formatting options available in the toolbar above the message area including bold, italic, underline, font (name, color, and size), alignment, and bulleted or numbered lists.

9. To put your e-mail into the Outbox, click the **Send** button (the envelope) in the Outlook Express toolbar.

10. Outlook Express asks if you want to send your e-mail now. Click **Yes** or **No**.

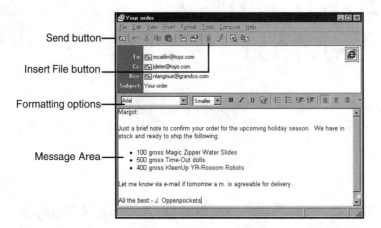

Send button

Insert File button

Formatting options

Message Area

Figure 9.1   The New Mail form, filled out and ready to send.

TIP   **Sending Unsent Mail**   Unsent e-mail goes into the Outlook Express Outbox. Click the **Mail** button and select **Read Mail** to open Outlook Express. Click the **Outbox** folder in the left pane. Select the e-mail to send and click the **Send and Retrieve** button on the toolbar.

Getting and Replying to Messages

After you open up your electronic mail box, you'll be amazed at the number of messages you receive. It is best to respond quickly to your e-mail, as with any communication. Internet Explorer 4.0 makes replying easy and offers a number of other options for e-mail handling as well. But first, you need to know how to get your mail.

To retrieve your mail, follow these steps:

1. From the Internet Explorer 4.0 toolbar, click the **Mail** button.

2. From the drop-down list, select **Read Mail** to open Outlook Express.

3. From the Outlook Express Tools menu, select **Retrieve**.

4. From the submenu, select **All Accounts** or a single account.

5. Any mail received goes into the Inbox. The number of new messages appears in parentheses next to the Inbox in the Folder List as shown in Figure 9.2.

6. To read a message, select it from the Message List. The message opens in the Preview Pane.

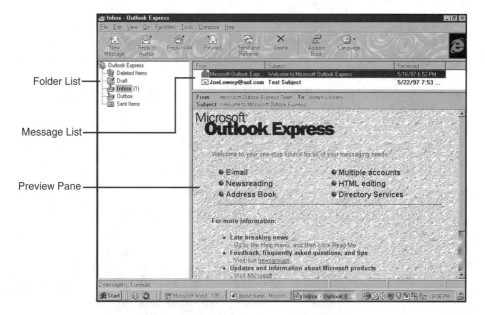

Figure 9.2 Outlook Express displays messages in the Preview Pane.

To respond to an e-mail message, follow these steps:

1. Open Outlook Express, if it is not already running.

2. From the Message List, click the message you want to respond to.

3. Click the **Reply to Author** button on the toolbar.

4. The Reply form opens with the To and Subject boxes filled in. The insertion pointer is in the message area.

5. Type your reply.

6. Click the **Send** button in the Reply form toolbar.

CAUTION

Repeating Messages?   By default, Outlook Express includes the original message after your reply. To disable this feature, from the **Tools** menu, select **Mail** Options. On the **Send** tab, uncheck **Include Message in Reply**. Click **OK**.

Attaching a File

One of the most powerful features of e-mail is the ability to attach any document to your message. This feature has greatly enhanced productivity between working groups by sharing files across the office or the country. Word processing documents, spreadsheets, or graphics all can be sent with equal ease. You only have to be certain that whoever is receiving the files has the capability (or software) to view them.

To attach a file to your e-mail, follow these steps:

1. Compose a new message or respond to a previous message.

2. From the **Message** toolbar, click the **Insert File** button.

3. From the Insert Attachment dialog box, select a file and click **OK**.

4. An icon for the file appears in a box below the message area as shown in Figure 9.3. To send additional attachments, repeat steps 2–4.

5. Click the **Send** button to send the e-mail message with the attachments.

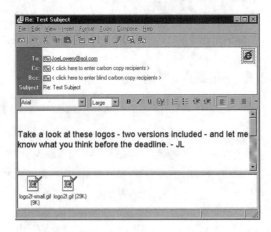

Figure 9.3   An e-mail reply with attachments.

When the e-mail is sent, your message is sent first and then the attached file or files are uploaded. The time it takes to send the entire e-mail message and attachments depends on the size of the files and the speed of the Internet connection.

 TIP **Priority E-Mail** Need to let someone know this e-mail is urgent? Click the "stamp" in the upper-right corner with the Internet Explorer 4.0 logo. A drop-down list gives you High, Normal, and Low priority options.

Using Your Address Book

The Address Book is a key component of any e-mail system. Internet Explorer 4.0 and Outlook Express use the central Windows Address Book found in Outlook and all Office 97 applications. With Internet Explorer 4.0, the Address Book's major emphasis is on e-mail addresses—the often cryptic, hard-to-remember strings of characters that take the form, *jsmith@somewhere.com.*

Follow these steps to send an e-mail message to someone in your Address Book:

1. Click the **Mail** button in the Internet Explorer 4.0 toolbar and then select **New Mail** from the drop-down list.
2. From the **New Mail** form, click the **Address Book** icon (the rolodex card), next to the **To:** box. The Select Recipients dialog box opens as shown in Figure 9.4.
3. From the Name List on the left, double-click the name of the intended recipient.
4. The name appears in the **To:** box.
5. To add additional recipients, repeat steps 3 and 4.
6. Click **OK**.

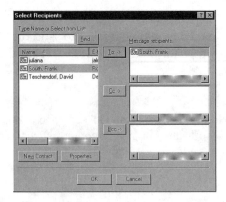

Figure 9.4 The Address Box maintains a list of all your contacts through the Select Recipients dialog box.

In this lesson, you learned how to compose and send a message, reply to and forward e-mail you receive, attach a file, and use your address book. In the next lesson, you learn about security on the Internet.

Protecting Your Web Transactions

In this lesson, you learn how to set your security level, manage security certificates, and use Microsoft Wallet.

Setting Your Security Level

Because of the nature of the Internet as an interconnected series of networked computers, any information you send can pass through many computers before it reaches your intended destination. This fact gives rise to a number of security concerns—not because there has been a rash of "Information Superhighway Robberies," but because the possibility exists that your data (business records, proprietary trade information, or credit card numbers) might be appropriated by unauthorized individuals.

Internet Explorer 4.0 has a wide range of industry-standard security measures in place. For example, most Web sites involving credit card transactions are run on computers known as secure servers. When Internet Explorer 4.0 encounters a secure server, a small lock appears in the status bar.

Internet Explorer 4.0 can prevent certain types of information from loading onto your computer. This is useful to prevent unwanted programs such as viruses from accessing your system. Because of the increasing use of "active content" on Web pages, which requires small programs to be downloaded to your computer, Internet Explorer 4.0 allows you to set the level of security. By default, the security level is set at High.

Follow these steps to alter the security level setting:

1. From the **View** menu, select **Options**.
2. From the Options dialog box, click the **Security** tab (see Figure 10.1).
3. In the Active Content section, click the **Safety Level** button.
4. From the Safety Level dialog box, select from one of the three options:

   High doesn't download certain programs and alerts you to the attempt. Microsoft recommends this setting for the general public.

   Medium warns of any file attempting to load onto your system. Microsoft recommends this setting for developers and expert users.

   None neither warns about nor avoids any file download. Microsoft does not recommend this setting.

5. After you have clicked the option button next to your selection, click **OK**.
6. Click **OK** again to close the Options dialog box.

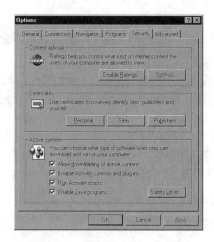

Figure 10.1   The Security tab manages Web transaction safety.

Understanding Security Certificates

When you buy software in a store, it's labeled and shrink-wrapped—you can be fairly certain who the publisher is and that the software has not been tampered with. There are no such guarantees when downloading software over the

Internet, however. Internet Explorer 4.0 recognizes a set of industry-standard security certificates to assure that the software publisher and the software are "as advertised."

Whenever you download software from a secure Web server, Internet Explorer 4.0 first downloads a security certificate. When the software begins to download, Internet Explorer 4.0 checks it against the security certificate to make sure that the software is from the correct publisher and is intact.

If the software appears to have been tampered with, Internet Explorer 4.0 issues a warning. If the software has not been digitally signed (and cannot therefore be verified), Internet Explorer 4.0 asks if you would like to continue the download of unverified software.

You can view and delete the security certificates that are installed on your system during transactions. Follow these steps to manage your security certificates:

1. From the **View** menu, select **Options**.
2. From the Options dialog box, click the **Security** tab.
3. From the Security tab, in the Certificates section, click one of the optional buttons:

   Personal lists certificates that identify you to secure servers.

   Sites lists certificates from secure servers you have visited.

   Publishers lists certificates from publishers that you have accepted. This permits any software from these publishers to be loaded on your system without asking permission.

4. Clicking any of the three Certificate buttons opens its respective list. The Authenticode Security Technology dialog box is shown in Figure 10.2.
5. From the Personal or Sites dialog box, select any certificate listed to enable the View and Remove buttons.
6. To see details of the certificate, click the **View** button.
7. To delete the certificate from your system, click **Remove**.
8. Click **OK** to close the Personal, Sites, or Publisher Certificate dialog box.
9. Click **OK** to close the Options dialog box.

Figure 10.2   This dialog box permits listed publishers to install software on your system.

CAUTION

Certificate Accidentally Removed   If you unintentionally remove a security certificate, you can get it back. The next time you visit a site that requires a particular certificate, the system asks if you would accept the certificate.

Using Microsoft Wallet

As electronic credit card transactions increase, you'll find yourself typing the same 16 numbers (plus expiration date) over and over again. Internet Explorer 4.0 includes a new feature that allows you to hand over a "virtual" credit card for easy-to-use, but safe, electronic transactions. Microsoft Wallet holds any amount of personal and credit card information necessary to do business over the Internet.

To access Microsoft Wallet, follow these steps:

1. From the **View** menu, select **Options**.
2. From the Options dialog box, click the **Programs** tab.
3. From the Programs tab, select one of the two buttons in the Microsoft Wallet section:

    Address Manager allows you to set up your address information so that it will not have to be retyped for every site.

    Payment Manager allows you to input credit card information so that it will not have to be retyped for every site.

4. If you want to change your address information, click the **Address Manager** button. To add new information, click the **Add** button and fill out the form. Click the **Close** button when you are finished.

5. If you want to change your credit card information, click the **Payment Manager** button.

6. Click the **Add** button shown in Figure 10.3, and choose one of the available credit card types.

7. The Credit Card Wizard opens. Click **Next**.

8. Fill out the required information. Click **Next**.

9. Enter a password in the first box. Retype the password in the second box. Click **Finish**.

10. Click **Close** to close the Address or Payment Manager dialog box.

11. Click **OK** to close the Options dialog box.

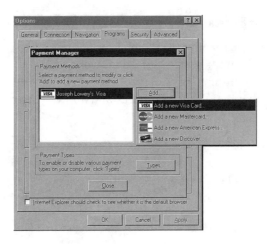

Figure 10.3   Adding a new credit card to the Microsoft Wallet.

In this lesson, you learned how to set your security level, how to manage security certificates, and how to use Microsoft Wallet. In the next lesson, you'll learn how to access Internet Explorer 4.0's Webcasting features.

Webcasting to Your Desktop

In this lesson, you learn how to set up and schedule Subscriptions and how to change the delivery options.

Setting Up a Site Subscription

A big complaint about the Web is how time-intensive it is. If you want to get any new information from a site, you have to go online, browse to the site, see if there is anything new and, if so, capture it. Internet Explorer 4.0 includes a new feature that handles these chores and allows you to reduce your time online considerably: Subscriptions.

Subscriptions go Smart Favorites (covered in Lesson 6) one better. As with Smart Favorites, a red gleam on the site's icon lets you know that the Web page has been updated. However, with Subscriptions, the updated information is also downloaded automatically and waiting for you to browse offline.

Follow these steps to set up a subscription to a site:

1. Browse to a site you want to subscribe to.
2. From the **Favorites** menu, select **Subscriptions**.
3. From the Subscriptions submenu, select **Subscribe**.

    The Subscription dialog box, as shown in Figure 11.1, appears with information about the Web site and Subscription options.
4. Click **OK**.

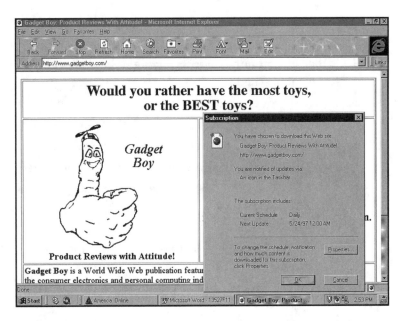

Figure 11.1 Subscriptions deliver Web sites to your desktop.

 TERM   **Webcasting**   Incorporates both Push and Pull technology. *Push* (or Server-Push) refers to the broadcasting of information to a local computer from particular content providers. *Pull* (or Client-Pull) refers to a local computer scheduling information retrieval from a content provider.

Scheduling Subscriptions

You can completely customize your schedule for receiving your Subscriptions. For a Web site with breaking news important to your business, you might want to pull down the information hourly during the week. For a Web site that posts quarterly reports, you could set the schedule so that Internet Explorer 4.0 only visits the site every three months. You can also choose to manually update the Subscription once you have been notified of a change.

To schedule a Subscription, follow these steps:

1. Click the **Favorites** button in the toolbar.

2. From the drop-down list, select **Subscriptions**.

3. From the submenu, select **View All**.

575

4. A new browser window opens displaying the contents of your Subscription folder.

5. In the Subscription window, highlight the Web site whose Subscriptions you want to schedule.

6. Click the **Properties** button from the Subscription toolbar.

7. From the Properties dialog box, click the **Schedule** tab.

8. From the Schedule tab, select from the following options:

> **Daily** checks the Web site each day at a specified time.
>
> **Weekly** checks the Web site every week on a specified day and time.
>
> **Custom** allows you to choose your own schedule for visits to the Web site.
>
> **Manually** allows you to receive notification of an updated page and browse to it on your own.

9. Click **OK** after you have made your selection.

If you choose the Custom option, you open the Custom Schedule dialog box shown in Figure 11.2. There are different options for daily, weekly, and monthly.

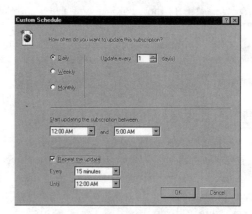

Figure 11.2   Scheduling a Custom Subscription Delivery.

TIP **Changing Default Schedules** You can set the default values for both the Daily and Weekly Schedules. Click the **Favorites** button and select **Subscriptions**, **Options**. Click either the Daily or Weekly tab and reset the default schedule. Click **OK** when you're finished. Make sure your computer is up and running at the time you schedule your Subscriptions or you won't receive the updates.

Setting the Delivery Options

Web pages very seldom exist in total isolation. Usually if one page in a site is updated, others are as well. Internet Explorer 4.0 allows you to determine how many pages "deep" into the site the Subscription is to go—and whether linked pages should be included. You can also set what multimedia elements, if any, are to be downloaded and the time or disk space limit.

To set your Subscription delivery options, follow these steps:

1. Open the Properties dialog box for a selected Subscription as described previously.

2. Click the **Delivery** tab.

3. From the Delivery tab, as shown in Figure 11.3, choose from the following options:

   Number of Pages to Download Select either to download the one page specified or that page plus however many pages deep you would like.

   Amount of Time Spent on Download After selecting, type in a value in the adjacent box or use the incrementer arrows.

   Amount of Disk Space to Allow After selecting, type in a value in the adjacent box or use the incrementer arrows.

   Download Images Deselect to exclude any graphics (default is selected).

   Download Sound and Videos Select to automatically load any associated audio or video elements on the Web page(s).

   Follow Hyperlinks to Other Sites Select to also download (to one page deep) any links on the Subscribed Web page.

4. Click **OK** to close the Subscription Properties dialog box after you have made your selections.

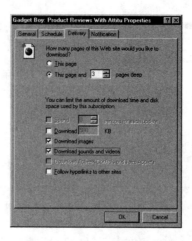

Figure 11.3 The Delivery tab for Subscriptions.

CAUTION

Too Much Space Taken! In the Delivery options outlined previously, the two choices to watch out for are Download Sound/Video and the Follow Hyperlinks. Sound and especially video files can be enormous, and a single Web page can easily have 20–50 links—which would mean 20–50 more pages on your system!

In this lesson, you learned how to set up and schedule Subscriptions and how to change the delivery options. In the next lesson, you learn how to hold a virtual conference with NetMeeting.

Conferencing with NetMeeting

In this lesson, you learn how to place a conference call with NetMeeting, use the chat feature, and work with the Whiteboard.

Placing a Conference Call

NetMeeting, one of the Internet Explorer 4.0 suite of programs, is a complete Internet conferencing system. NetMeeting capabilities include:

- Conferencing with up to 16 individuals via the Internet, using *full-duplex* audio and video.
- Text-based chat sessions permitting both group and individual messages.
- Sharing of applications between participants. For example, two (or more) grant writers could edit an application together in real time using Word 97.
- Visual collaboration through a shared whiteboard, allowing comments as well as graphics.

Full-Duplex The capability for a modem to conduct two-way conversations simultaneously. To check the capacity of your system, from the **Tools** menu, select the **Audio Tuning Wizard**.

To set up an Internet conference call with NetMeeting, follow these steps:

1. From Internet Explorer 4.0's **File** menu, select **New** and then **Internet Call** from the submenu. NetMeeting opens.
2. Click the **Call** button in the toolbar.

3. From the New Call dialog box, enter the e-mail address, computer name, network address, or modem phone number of the person you want to call in the Address box. The Call Using box should be in the Automatic setting.

4. Click **Call**. NetMeeting finds the address you have called.

5. Click the **Current Call** tab on the left side of the screen.

6. When the connection is made, both your name and the name of the person you're calling display in the Current Call window as shown in Figure 12.1.

7. Speak into your computer's microphone. Adjust the sensitivity of the microphone and the volume of the speaker by moving the sliders on top of the window, if necessary.

8. To hang up the call, click the **Hang Up** button in the toolbar.

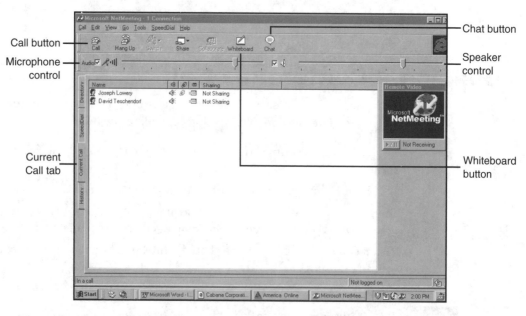

Figure 12.1   Conference calling over the Internet with NetMeeting.

Sending Messages with Chat

Chatting over the Internet is a very effective business tool for sharing ideas among widespread coworkers. Chatting is text-only and, while typing your thoughts may seem a limitation to those used to speaking them, it does overcome the limitations a slow network might bring to voice conferencing.

Moreover, chat conferences can be saved and incorporated into any text document, such as an interview in a newsletter.

To chat with someone using NetMeeting, follow these steps:

1. Open NetMeeting and call one or more individuals as described in the preceding task.

2. Click the **Chat** button in the toolbar. The Chat window opens as shown in Figure 12.2.

3. From the Chat window, type your text into the Message box. Press **Enter** to send the text.

4. Your name appears next to your message in the main chat window.

5. To send a message to everyone in the chat session, make sure that Everyone in Chat appears in the Send To: box.

6. To send a private message, click the arrow next to the Send To: box to reveal the drop-down option list.

7. Click the name of the party to send your private message. Your message appears in italic as a "whisper" to the person indicated.

8. The main chat window scrolls as additional messages are added.

9. To save the entire chat, from the **File** menu, select **Save** and enter the file name in the Save As dialog box.

10. To leave Chat, click the **Close** button in the Chat title bar.

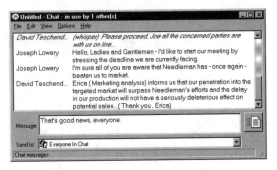

Figure 12.2 Chatting is an effective business tool.

Incorporating the Whiteboard

A shared whiteboard allows team members to visually share their ideas and comments simultaneously—just as if they were all in the same conference room. NetMeeting's Whiteboard feature allows text, drawing, highlighting, and multiple pages. The Whiteboard can be combined with audio, video, and the Chat windows.

To use the NetMeeting's Whiteboard, follow these steps:

1. Open NetMeeting and call one or more individuals as shown previously.
2. Click the **Whiteboard** button in the toolbar. The Whiteboard window opens as shown in Figure 12.3.
3. From the Whiteboard window, select any of the various tools in the left toolbar. To use any of the drawing tools, select the button and drag into the main Whiteboard window to create the shape.

4. To move any object, click the **Select** tool and click and drag your object.
5. To put in text, click the **Text** tool, click into the main Whiteboard window, and begin to type.

6. To add a page, click the **Add a Page** icon.
7. To insert a screen from another program, click the **Select Window** button and then click the screen to be inserted.
8. To leave the Whiteboard area, click the **Close** button in the Whiteboard title bar.

Select Window button ——

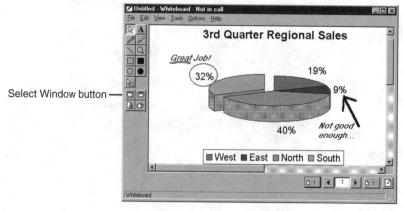

Figure 12.3   The Whiteboard allows visual collaboration.

In this lesson, you learned how to place a conference call with NetMeeting, use the chat feature, and work with the whiteboard. In the next lesson, you learn how to build a Web page.

Building Your Own Web Page

In this lesson, you learn how to start FrontPad, format text, add graphics, save your Web page, browse them in Internet Explorer 4.0, and quit FrontPad.

Starting FrontPad

One of the reasons that the Web has grown so rapidly is that Web pages are easy to make. The language used to construct Web pages, HTML, is easy enough to learn, but Internet Explorer 4.0 comes with its own editor that makes building Web pages even easier. The program, FrontPad, is referred to as a WYSIWYG (What You See Is What You Get) editor which means that you lay out your page as you would in Publisher, and all the coding is handled behind the scenes.

FrontPad is a separate program and can be started by following these steps:

1. Click the **Start** button on the taskbar.
2. Select **Programs**, and then from the submenu, select **Internet Explorer Suite**.
3. From the Internet Explorer menu, select **FrontPad**.

Figure 13.1 shows a FrontPad screen with a new, blank page, and highlights some of the key features.

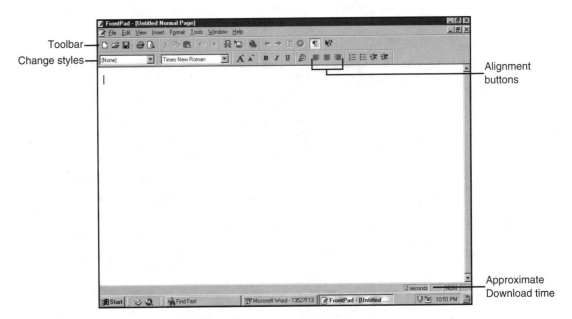

Toolbar

Change styles

Alignment buttons

Approximate Download time

Figure 13.1 FrontPad is Internet Explorer 4.0's editor.

TIP **FrontPad Through Internet Explorer** You can also access FrontPad through the Internet Explorer 4.0 toolbar by clicking **Edit**. This opens FrontPad and loads whatever Web page is currently open in Internet Explorer 4.0. Click the **New** icon in the FrontPad toolbar to start with a blank page.

Formatting Text

A main feature of a Web page is its computer platform independence. A Web page built on a Windows 95 machine can be viewed by a Windows 3.1, Macintosh, UNIX, and any other system with a basic browser. To reach this degree of universal accessibility, text in Web pages uses formatting styles, such as STRONG or SMALL, rather than specific font sizes as in a word processing program. Headings, used for titles and subtitles, can be any one of six different relative sizes (Heading 1—the largest—through Heading 6—the smallest).

Follow these steps to enter and format some text on your Web page:

1. Start FrontPad.
2. Type in your first heading.

3. Select the text you just entered by clicking in front of it and dragging the mouse across the rest.

4. From the Change Styles box in the toolbar, click the arrow to reveal the drop-down option list.

5. From the option list, click a text style choice. Heading 1 or Heading 2 is suitable for a Web page title. The text changes to the selected size.

6. Keeping the text highlighted, click one of the Alignment buttons to make the text align to the Left, Centered or Right.

7. If desired, click the standard Bold, Italic or Underline style buttons.

8. Click anywhere on the blank page to clear the highlight.

Repeat these steps to continue to add text to your Web page, varying the text styles between Headings and Normal.

Adding Graphics

A major World Wide Web innovation was the inclusion of graphics with text. Most browsers currently support only two types of graphics. The first, GIF format, can have up to 256 colors and is used for drawings, logos and illustrations. The second, JPEG, can display millions of colors but takes longer to load because it is compressed; JPEG is primarily used for photographs.

Web graphics are in-line graphics which means they can be placed right next to text. Graphics can be aligned left, center, or right, just like text.

To place a graphic on your Web page, follow these steps:

1. Move the insertion point where you would like to have the graphic appear. If necessary, press **Enter** to move down the page.

2. From the **Insert** Menu, select **Image**.

3. From the Insert Image dialog box, choose the **Other Locations** tab to select a graphic file from your hard drive or from a Web address. Click **OK** when finished.

4. To select from one of the available clip art images, click the **Clip Art** tab and select a category. Click an image to select it and then click **OK**.

5. The image is inserted on the page. To re-align the image, select it and click one of the Alignment buttons in the toolbar.

Figure 13.2 shows a Web page with two lines of text and two images.

Figure 13.2 A Web page with mixed graphics and text.

TIP **Re-use Graphics!** It's a good idea to re-use the same graphic image on the Web site in several places. This gives continuity to a site with no additional download time: once a graphic has been downloaded, it is temporarily cached on the viewers system and can be re-used without re-downloading.

Saving Your Web Page

Once you have spent some time creating your Web page, you have to save it before you see it in Internet Explorer 4.0. Because Web pages and Web sites can be made of many separate files (each graphic is an individual file), you'll probably want to create a folder for each Web site you work on. This also makes it easy to find all the files when it comes time to publish your creation to the Web.

FrontPad allows you to either publish directly to the Internet (or an internal intranet) or to a file. Follow these steps to save your Web page as a file in FrontPad:

1. Click the **Save** button in the toolbar.
2. From the Save As Web dialog box, click the **As File** button.
3. Create a new folder, if necessary, from the Save As File dialog box by clicking on the **New Folder** icon.
4. Type a new name for your Web page in the Name box and click **OK**.
5. FrontPad asks if you would like to copy your graphics to the new directory. Click the **Yes to All** button.

Browsing Your Web Page

You'll want to check your Web page frequently in Internet Explorer 4.0. When you are browsing your creation, you can get an idea of how quickly (or how slowly) your page will load. You can also double-check your links and your graphics to make sure everything is in place. If you are eventually posting your page to the Internet (as opposed to an internal network), look at your Web page with different screen resolutions; you can't be sure what your potential readers are using so it's best to see how your Web page looks under a variety of circumstances.

Follow these steps to browse a Web page previously saved in FrontPad:

1. From the Internet Explorer 4.0 **File** menu, select **Open**.
2. From the open dialog box, click the **Browse** button.
3. Open the folder in which your Web page is saved.
4. Double-click the file name of the Web page you want to browse.

   The page loads and the dialog box closes.

 TIP **Fast Editing** When you are developing your Web pages, keep both Internet Explorer 4.0 and FrontPad open. Move between the two by clicking the program's button on the taskbar. You can quickly see changes made in FrontPad by clicking the **Refresh** button in Internet Explorer 4.0.

Quitting FrontPad

When you have finished your FrontPad session, you quit the program by any of the standard methods:

- Select **File**, **Exit** from the Menu bar.
- Click the **Close** button in the upper-right corner of the FrontPad window.
- Use the keyboard shortcut, **Alt+F4**.

TIP **Publishing your Web Page** For information on how to put your Web page on the Internet, see Part VI, Lesson 10.

In this lesson, you learned how to start FrontPad, format text, add graphics, save your Web page, browse them in Internet Explorer 4.0, and quit FrontPad. In the next lesson, you learn more advanced techniques in FrontPad.

Creating Enhanced Web Pages

In this lesson, you learn how to work with lists, insert hyperlinks, and scroll a banner.

Working with Lists

Text is not all headings and paragraphs. A common method of detailing several items is by using a list. Web pages includes two kinds of lists—bulleted and numbered. FrontPad allows you to choose from different bullet symbols and different types of numbering formats.

Follow these steps to enter your text into a list:

1. In FrontPad, open a previously created Web page or click **New** to create a new one.
2. Move your insertion point to where you want the list to begin.
3. Choose one of the two list options in the toolbar:

    Numbered lists are used when the sequence or the number of items is important.

    Bulleted lists are used when the sequence is not important.

4. The first bullet or number appears with the insertion point indented.
5. Type the first entry in your list and press **Enter**. A new bullet or the next number in sequence appears on the new line.
6. Repeat steps 5 and 6 for every new entry in your list.
7. Click again on the **Bullet List** or **Numbered List** button in the toolbar to end the list.

If you need to add a list item in the middle of your list, place your insertion point at the end of the line above where you want your new item to appear. Press **Enter**. A new bullet or new number (in sequence) appears.

As you can see in Figure 14.1, you can also mix bullets and numbered list items.

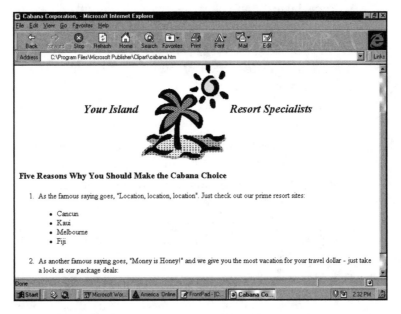

Figure 14.1 A list with both bulleted and numbered items.

 TIP **New List Formats** To change the type of bullet or numbered list, select **Format**, **Bullets and Numbering** from the Menu bar. Click either the **Bulleted** or **Numbered** tab to select your new format.

Inserting Hyperlinks

What makes the Web a web? Hyperlinks! The ability to interconnect various pages of one site to one another and then to an unlimited number of sites around the globe makes the World Wide Web a unique and powerful medium. Adding hyperlinks in FrontPad is very easy; all you need is the full Internet address (the URL).

To add a hyperlink to your Web page creation, follow these steps:

1. In FrontPad, open a previously created Web page or click **New** to create a blank one.

2. Move your insertion point to where you want the hyperlink to appear.

3. Type the text that will represent the hyperlink, either by name (Visit the Sales Department) or by action (Click here to place your order.).

4. Highlight the word or phrase that identifies the hyperlink.

5. Click the **Create Hyperlink** button in the toolbar. The Create Hyperlink dialog box appears.

6. If the hyperlink is to a page already created, click the **Open Pages** tab and double-click the name of the Page from the list.

7. If the hyperlink is to a page that has yet to be created, click the **New Page** tab as shown in Figure 14.2 and complete the boxes:

   Page Title is the plain English phrase that appears in the title bar of a browser when the page is visited.

   Page URL is the Internet address for the page. If the page is going to be in the same folder as the page it is being linked to, you can use just the file name (such as Kauii.htm).

8. If the page is in a different folder or Web site, click the World Wide Web tab. Type the full Internet address (such as http://www.travel.com/kauii.htm) in the URL box.

9. Click **OK** when you're finished.

10. If you created a new page, FrontPad asks which template to use. Double-click the Normal Page for a blank page.

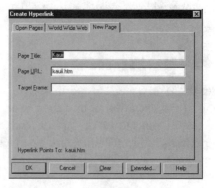

Figure 14.2 Linking one page to another with the Create Hyperlink dialog box.

Scrolling a Banner

One of the special tools available in Internet Explorer 4.0 and FrontPad are marquees or scrolling banners. These eye-catching displays move text across the screen and are best used (sparingly) for special, not-to-be-missed messages.

To add scrolling text to your Web page, follow these steps:

1. In FrontPad, open a previously created Web page or click **New** to create a new one.
2. Move your insertion point to where you want the scrolling banner to appear.
3. From the **Insert** menu, select **Marquee**. The Marquee Properties dialog box is displayed.
4. Type in the text you want to scroll in the box next to Text.
5. You can alter any or all of the following default properties:

   Direction makes the banner come from the left or from the right.

   Movement Speed changes how often the text is updated (Delay) and its speed across the screen (Amount).

   Behavior controls whether the banner will continuously move across the screen (Scroll), move across once and stop (Slide), or move in from one direction and then bounce back in the other direction (Alternate).

   Align with Text moves the text to the top, middle or bottom of the Marquee box.

   Size determines the width and height of the Marquee box. Both can be set to a fixed pixel size or a percentage of the browser screen size.

   Repeat controls how many times the text scrolls across the screen. If the box next to Continuously is deselected, a set number can be entered into the box.

   Background Color is used for setting the background color of Marquee box. Default is transparent.

6. Click **OK** when you have selected all of your options.

After you click OK, you'll see an unmoving version of your text in a Marquee box with a dashed outline. Save your file and then open it in Internet Explorer 4.0 to see the scroll in action.

TIP **Resizing a Banner** To change the size of the text in a scrolling banner, begin by highlighting the entire object. Then click on the Text Styles arrow on the toolbar to select a different Heading size.

In this lesson, you learned how to work with lists, insert hyperlinks, and scroll a banner.

Small Business Solutions

Sharing Office 97 Data

In this lesson, you'll learn how to share data between Office 97 applications, including creating dynamic links and embedding with OLE.

Using Cut, Copy, and Paste

The simplest way to share data between programs is to use the Cut, Copy, and Paste commands. All of the Office 97 programs have these basic commands, and you can use them to move or copy data from one file to another. For example, you can copy a Word document into Publisher, cut a graphic from Publisher and place into an Excel worksheet, or copy Word notes into your Outlook Journal. By using these three basic commands, you can quickly and easily share data between applications with a few simple clicks of the mouse. You can use these commands in just about every Windows program available today. This means you can share data with non-Microsoft Office 97 programs, too.

When you cut or copy data from one application to place into another, you must first select the text or graphic to be copied or moved, then click the **Cut** or **Copy** buttons on the program's toolbar (or select the commands from the Edit menu). This places the cut or copied item into the Windows *Clipboard*, a temporary holding place for data in transit. Next, open the application and click the insertion point where you want the data copied or moved to, then click the **Paste** command button in the toolbar or select it from the Edit menu. The data is placed in its new location.

TIP   **More Cut, Copy, and Paste**   You'll also find the Cut, Copy, and Paste commands located on the shortcut menu when you right-click your Office 97 document.

Unfortunately, the data you cut or copy retains no connection with its file or application of origin, so the data sharing is somewhat limited and static. For a more dynamic method of data sharing, you need to learn how to use Object Linking and Embedding, which is explained in the remainder of this lesson. But remember, if you're looking for a quick and simple swap of data, you can always rely on the Cut, Copy, and Paste technique.

What Is Object Linking and Embedding?

Object Linking and Embedding, or *OLE* for short (pronounced "oh-LAY") is a Windows feature that enables the Windows applications that employ it to transparently share information. OLE is used throughout Windows programs, and the Office 97 Small Business Edition applications are no exception.

With OLE, data you share between programs retains a connection to its place of origin. For example, you might create a quarterly report in Microsoft Word that contains an Excel chart. Each quarter, the Excel data in the chart changes. When it comes time to generate the next quarterly report, you could find the most up-to-date version of the Excel chart and copy and paste it into the report, or you could use an OLE link to automatically update the report with the changes made in each supporting document. Which of these methods seems the easiest route to updating the file? If you chose the latter, you're on your way to full Office 97 integration. But first you need to know the difference between linking and embedding.

What Is Linking?

When you link an object to a container file, any changes you make to the object in its native application are automatically made to the object as it resides in the container file. The object in the container file remains a mirror image of the object in its native application, regardless of how many times you update the original object.

Object   Any snippet of data that you want to link to another document. It can be as small as a single character or as large as a huge report with many graphics.

TIP   **Container file**   The file that's receiving the object. For example, if I'm linking an Excel chart to a Word document, the Word document is the container file.

What Is Embedding?

When you embed an object, you insert a copy of it into your document, in the same way you might with the regular Paste command. A link to the source file is not maintained. However, embedding does offer something that regular pasting does not. When you embed an object into a document, a link is maintained to the original application; you can double-click that object at any time to open the application and edit the object.

A good example of an embedded object would be a company logo, created as Microsoft WordArt, that's embedded as part of a letterhead document created in Word. As an embedded object, all the information about the logo is maintained in the letterhead document, so you do not have to worry about managing or locating a separate file for the logo. When you do need to change the logo, you double-click it to open WordArt and edit the logo.

Linking and Embedding with Paste Special

The easiest way to link and embed is with the Paste Special command on the Edit menu.

When an object is pasted into a document with the regular Paste command, the object is simply dropped in, with no information about its origin. In contrast, when an object is pasted into a document with Paste Special, several pieces of information about the object are stored as part of the container file, including the source file's name and location, the server application, and the location of the object within the source file. This extra information is what makes it possible for the object to be updated whenever the source file is updated.

OLE needs the name of a source file to refer back to later in order to link, so you must save your work in the source program before you create a link with OLE. However, if you merely want to embed and not link, you do not need a named source file. The only information OLE needs in order to edit the object later is the name of the *server application* (the application in which it was created).

Source file   The file from which the information to be pasted originated.

TIP   **Server application**   The native application for the object that's being linked or embedded. For instance, if you embed an Excel worksheet into a Word document, Excel is the server application.

TIP   **Container application**   The application in which the container file (the file to receive the object) is created. For instance, if the container file is a Word document, Microsoft Word is the container application.

To link or embed with Paste Special, follow these steps:

1. Copy the desired object to the Clipboard with the **Edit**, **Copy** command.

2. Open the container file (the file where you want to paste) and position the insertion point where you want it.

3. Select **Edit**, **Paste Special**, and the Paste Special dialog box appears. (The one for Word is shown in Figure 1.1; they are similar in all Office applications.)

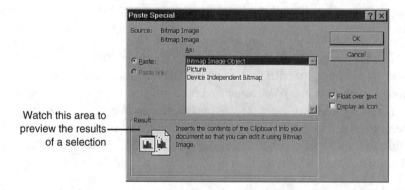

Watch this area to preview the results of a selection

Figure 1.1   The Paste Special dialog box.

4. Choose **Paste** or **Paste Link**, depending on the type of connection you want:

Paste   Pastes the contents of the Windows Clipboard into the document at the location of the insertion point. The link is not maintained, but you can double-click the pasted material to edit it. (This is embedding.)

Paste Link   This option is available if the contents of the Clipboard can be linked back to its source file. With this option selected, a link is created between the source file and the container file. If you have not saved the source file, the Paste Link option is not available.

5. Select the format you want to use from the **As** list. The formats listed change depending on the object type. Some formats you might see include:

Object   A type that ends with the word Object is a recognized OLE-capable format that you can either link or embed. If you want to embed, you should choose a data type that ends with the word *object*. For example, in Figure 1.1, you would choose **Microsoft Word Document Object**.

Formatted Text (RTF)   This data type formats text as it is formatted in the source file. If the text is formatted as bold italic, it is pasted as bold italic. This format does not support embedding.

Unformatted Text   No formatting is applied to the object when this data type is selected. This format does not support embedding.

Picture   This data type formats the object as a Windows metafile picture. It does not support embedding.

Device Independent Bitmap   This data type formats the object as a bitmap picture, such as a Windows Paint image. It does not support embedding.

6. (Optional) If you want to display the pasted object as an icon instead of as the data itself, select the **Display as Icon** check box. This option is only available if you have selected Paste Link. This is useful for pasting Sounds and MediaClips because you can double-click one to play it later.

7. (Optional) If you want the object to appear inline with the rest of the document's text, make sure the **Float Over Text** check box is deselected. When selected, this check box forces the pasted object into the drawing layer of the document, where it can be moved freely over the top of the document.

8. Click **OK**. The object is embedded or linked into the container file, depending on the options you chose.

When deciding which options to select in the Paste Special dialog box, pay close attention to the notes that appear in the Result area. These notes tell you what will happen if you choose OK with the present set of options.

Linking or Embedding an Entire File

If you want to link an entire file to your document, an entire Excel spreadsheet, for example, you can use the Object command. It appears on the Insert menu of most Windows applications.

Unlike Edit, Paste, you do not have to open the source file to retrieve the object. You can perform the entire procedure without leaving the client application. Follow these steps to learn how:

1. Start the client application—the one to receive the object—and then create or open the container file. (Microsoft Word is the client application in this example.)

2. Select **Insert, Object**. The Object dialog box appears.

3. Click the **Create from File** tab at the top of the dialog box. The dialog box changes to show a File Name list box (see Figure 1.2).

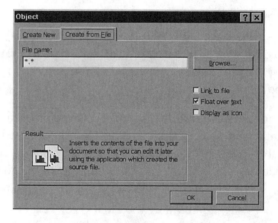

Figure 1.2   Use the Object dialog box's Create from File tab to choose an existing file to link or embed.

4. Click the **Browse** button, and select the name of the file you want to insert and link or embed in the container file. For example, you might use an Excel worksheet. Navigate through the directories and subdirectories to locate the file if it does not appear in the current directory. When you locate the file, double-click it.

5. If you want to link, make sure the **Link to File** check box is selected. This will create an active link between the source file and the destination file. If you merely want to embed, not link, make sure it's deselected.

6. Select or deselect the **Float Over Text** and **Display as Icon** check boxes as desired. (See the descriptions of these controls earlier in this lesson.)

7. Click **OK**. The dialog box closes, and the source file is inserted into the container file.

CAUTION

Whole Files Only   Remember that using the Insert, Object command links or embeds an entire file to the container file. You cannot use this command to link an individual object (such as a range of Excel cells) to the container file. Use the steps in the "Linking and Embedding with Paste Special" section earlier in this lesson for that.

Creating a New Embedded File

The Insert, Object command can also help you create a brand new file and embed it at the same time. (You can't link with this procedure, because to link you must already have a named file that the object is coming from.)

For example, let's say you want to insert an Excel spreadsheet into your Publisher document, but you haven't created the spreadsheet yet. You can do it all at once with the following procedure:

1. Open the container document and position the insertion point where you want the linked or embedded file to go.

2. Select **Insert, Object**, and the Object dialog box appears (see Figure 1.3).

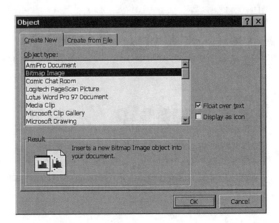

Figure 1.3   Select the type of file you want to create.

3. In the **Object Type** list, select the type of object you want to create.

4. Click **OK**. The application you selected opens within Publisher, and you can create the object.

5. When you're finished working with the object, select **File, Exit and Return to** *application* (the exact name of the command depends on the container application). The object is now embedded in your container file.

Editing Embedded Objects

Editing an embedded object is where the greatest advantage of embedding comes into play. You do not have to remember the name and location of the source file that you used to create the embedded object. You simply double-click the object and the source application starts, allowing you to edit the object.

Follow these steps to edit an embedded object:

1. Open the document containing the embedded object you want to edit.

2. Double-click the object or choose **Edit, Object**. The native application of the embedded object starts and displays the object.

3. Edit the object using the server application's tools and commands.

4. Click a portion of the container document or select **File, Exit and Return to** *application* from the object's native application. The object's native application closes, and you are returned to the container document.

CAUTION

Modified Launch   Some objects perform a function or action when you double-click them, instead of opening the source file for editing. For example, Windows Sound Recorder objects play a sound when double-clicked. To edit objects like this, hold down the **Alt** key and double-click the object.

Editing Linked Objects

Once you have created a linked object, you may want to edit and update the information in the object. At this stage, you'll realize the full benefit of an OLE link because you can edit the object one time, and it will be updated in every document that it is linked to.

There are two ways to edit a linked object. The first is to start at the source file, using the server application to make changes to the object. The second is to start at the container file and let the link information lead you to the correct source file and server application. With the second method, you do not have to remember the name of the source file or even which server application created it. In the next sections, you'll learn how to edit objects using these two methods.

Editing from the Source File

To edit a linked object starting from the source file, follow these steps:

1. Start the server application, and then open the source file that contains the object you want to edit.
2. Edit and make changes to the object.
3. Save the document and close the server application.
4. Switch to (or start) the client application and open the container file. The changes should automatically be reflected in the container file.

If the changes are not reflected, the document may not be set up to automatically update links. Skip to "Managing a Link's Update Settings" later in this lesson to learn how to update the links.

CAUTION

Now You See It, Now You Don't   Some client applications let you edit or make changes directly to the object that is linked to the container file without starting the server application. This can cause problems because the source file is not being changed, only the image of the object. The changes you make to the image will be wiped out when the object is updated via the source file. You will not have this problem with Microsoft Office products, but it may occur with other non-Microsoft applications.

Editing from the Container File

Editing from the container file is quick and easy because you do not have to find and open the server application manually. To edit a linked object from the container file, follow these steps:

1. From the container file, double-click the linked object you want to update. The server application starts and displays the source file.
2. Edit the object in the source file. You can make as many changes to the object as you like.
3. Choose **File**, **Save** in the server application.

4. Choose **File**, **Exit** in the server application. You're returned to the container file, which reflects the changes you made to the linked object.

If double-clicking the object does not start the server application, open the Links dialog box by choosing **Links** from the **Edit** menu. Select the link you want to edit and click the **Open Source** button. The server application starts and displays the source file.

Managing a Link's Update Settings

Once you have created a linked object, you can control when changes to the source file are updated in the container file(s). You can update a link manually or automatically. If a link is set to be updated manually, you must remember to follow the update steps each time you change the source file that contains the linked object. With the automatic setting enabled (the default update setting), the changes you make to the source file are automatically updated each time you open the container file.

To set a linked object to be manually updated, follow these steps:

1. Open the container file that contains the object link you want to update.

2. Choose **Edit**, **Links**. The Links dialog box appears (see Figure 1.4). For the linked objects in your document, the list indicates the link name, the path name of the source file, and whether the link is set to update automatically or manually.

Figure 1.4   You can control each individual link in your document from the Links dialog box.

3. Select the link you want to update.

4. Change the Update setting to **Manual**.

5. Update the link by clicking the **Update Now** button in the Links dialog box. The object is then updated with any changes that were made to the source file.

6. Click **OK** to close the dialog box.

7. Choose **File**, **Save** to save the document and the changes to the link settings.

With the link set for manual update, you must repeat step 5 of this procedure each time you want the linked object to reflect changes made in the source file.

Locking and Unlocking Links

In addition to setting link update options to manual and automatic, you can lock a link to prevent the link from being updated when the source file is changed.

To lock or unlock a link, follow these steps:

1. Open the document containing the linked object.

2. Choose **Edit**, **Links**. The Links dialog box appears (refer to Figure 1.4).

3. Select the link you want to lock.

4. To lock the link, select the **Locked** check box. To unlock the link, make sure the check box is empty.

5. Click **OK** to close the dialog box.

A locked link will not be updated until it is unlocked.

Breaking Links

If at some point you decide that you want a linked object in your document to remain fixed and no longer be updated by its source file, you can break (or cancel) the link. This does not delete or alter the object; it merely removes the background information that directly ties the object to its source file. The object becomes like any other object that was placed by Windows Copy and Paste operation.

To break or cancel a linked object, follow these steps:

1. Open the container file that contains the object whose link you want to break.

2. Select **Edit, Links** (or **Link Options** in some applications). The Links dialog box appears, showing linked object information.

3. Select the link name of the object you want to break.

4. Click **Break Link** (or **Delete** in some applications). A warning box may appear, cautioning that you are breaking a link. Click **OK** or **Yes** to confirm your choice.

In this lesson, you learned how to create and manage OLE links and embedding. In the next lesson, you'll learn how to use Office 97 tools to create a small business plan.

Creating a Small Business Plan

2

In this project lesson, you learn how to assemble a small business plan using Office 97 programs.

What Makes a Good Business Plan?

One of the hardest parts of starting a small business is putting together a comprehensive business plan. On the other hand, a good business plan can really help you organize, strategize, and define your small business goals and directives. This makes it easier for investors, banks, and employees to understand your business, products, and ideas. You can use Office 97 tools to create a professional business plan you can share with others.

A good business plan should contain several key elements. Assuming you're presenting your plan to potential investors or funding sources, it's important you build a plan that is both easy to follow and communicates precisely. The following elements should be included:

Title Page and Table of Contents   A good plan always includes front matter that clearly titles and outlines your plan.

Executive Summary   Briefly summarize each integral part of your business plan. Like the table of contents, the summary organizes your plan and briefly tells the reader what it's all about. It's usually a good idea to save this part of your plan for last so you can better summarize the other parts of the plan.

Product or Service Description   Use this part of the plan to clearly identify your products or services, prices, and how the product differs from like products on the market.

Market or Industry Analysis   Describe the market's need for your product or services. Research the market and provide background information on market size, scope, and growth rate. This particular part of your plan may take the longest amount of work; however, you'll find plenty of information at your local library or bookstore, and on the Internet.

Identify the Competition   Here's another part of the plan that requires research. Find out who your competition is, what your impact will be on their market, and identify their strengths and weaknesses—then convey this information in your business plan.

Management Team   In this part of the plan, outline how your business will be run, the types of skills you're looking for in people you will hire, responsibilities for each position, and business advisors who may be working with you.

Operations or Manufacturing Plan   Describe the processes, equipment, and materials needed to set up and maintain your operating or manufacturing procedures. Include types of production, locations, international and licensing prerequisites, and anything else that's needed to generate your product or services.

Marketing Strategy   Explain how you're going to get the word out about your company or product. What's your sales approach? Are you going to use direct marketing, catalogs, or phone sales? Describe what types of advertising you plan on using or ways you can increase public awareness.

Financial Analysis   In this section of your plan, present your financial information. Show how much investment is required, when you'll break even, and when you'll be able to pay back investors. Nitty-gritty financial data, such as a projected income statement (3 to 5 years in the future), balance sheet, and cash flow analysis should be included. Use charts, graphs, and tables to clearly lay out your financial information.

Conclusion   This final section includes another summary of your material, plus actions you want a potential investor to take.

Business Plan Tips

One of the purposes of your business plan is to clearly state points of interest to your audience. Potential investors or advisors who will read your plan won't spend a lot of time wading through endless pages of repetitive information or lengthy paragraphs that focus on irrelevant information. The plan should capture the reader's attention and quickly get to the point. For that reason, here are a few tips for you to consider when compiling your own business plan:

- Keep the text clear and concise. A plan that's too lengthy will turn off the reader, but one that's easy to read and keeps the coverage brief is infinitely more appealing.

- Support your opinions with facts. Make sure you do your research thoroughly.

- Organize information in easy-to-read tables, charts, and graphs. It's much easier to convey important data when it's visually organized. Take advantage of Excel's charting features to create simple charts and graphs to present financial or numerical data.

- Summarize your information often; don't let the reader draw his or her own conclusions.

- Make sure your material is consistent and doesn't conflict with other paragraphs in your plan.

- Treat your competition with respect when referring to them in your plan, and avoid trivialities. Don't forget: The competition was there first, so they must be doing something right. What can you do even better?

- Be sure to use the most up-to-date information in your plan, particularly when analyzing a turbulent marketplace.

- Keep your writing focused and on track. If you wander far from your main thoughts, you'll appear without direction, and so will your business ideas.

- Don't sprinkle technical terminology throughout your plan unless you're absolutely sure the reader will know the terms as well. Instead, keep the language simple and precise.

- Concentrate on presenting the data that matters the most: product, price, quality, availability, and competition.

 TIP **Need Help?** The Internet is a great source of help when it comes to small businesses. You'll find plenty of Web sites online that can help you assemble business plans, locate and download accounting software, offer loads of advice, and more. To learn how to access the Internet and use a Web browser, check out Part V of this book.

Creating a Business Plan with Office 97

As you learned in Lesson 1 of this part of the book, you can integrate all of the Office 97 products to work together. To create a detailed business plan, you may want to type your text in Word, and import financial data from spreadsheets you create in Excel. Use these steps to help you:

1. Prepare your business plan in Word. You can choose to create the plan from scratch or base it on a preexisting template. Figure 2.1 shows an example of a plan created from scratch.

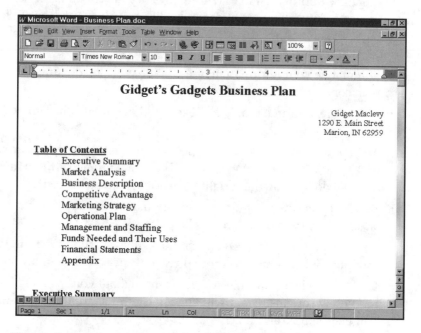

Figure 2.1   Create the text portions of your business plan in Word.

TIP   **Can I Use a Template?**   Word has several templates you might customize to create a business plan, or you can check out the templates included in the Small Business Edition ValuPack (see Appendix B for more information). You can also check Microsoft's Web site (**http://www.microsoft.com**) for templates you can download.

2. Use Word's format commands to design your plan to suit your needs or audience. Limit yourself to two complementary font styles, and be sure to use a legible font size.

3. When you're ready to insert financial data into your plan from an Excel worksheet, move the insertion point to the location in your document where you want to insert the data.

4. Switch to Excel, and open or create the financial worksheet from which you want to copy the data.

> **TIP**   **How Do I Make a Financial Report?**   Part II includes lessons for using Excel to create worksheets of all kinds, as well as charts and graphs. Remember, you can use the Small Business Financial Manager to create reports. Turn to Lesson 23 in Part II for more information.

5. Select the data you want to include in the business plan. If it's a chart you're including, be sure to select the entire chart.

6. Open the **Edit** menu and select **Copy**, or click the **Copy** button in the toolbar.

7. Switch back to your Word document. Open the **Edit** menu and select **Paste Special**, so you can insert the copied worksheet data as a link. If you choose to link the data, any changes you make to the original file (Excel) will automatically be reflected in the business plan document (Word).

> **TIP**   **What's a Link?**   Refer to Lesson 1 in this section of the book to learn more about linking and embedding data in your Office 97 programs.

8. The Paste Special dialog box, shown in Figure 2.2, asks how you want the copied data pasted. Click the desired format (usually RTF) in the **As** list, and then click the **Paste Link** option. Click **OK**.

9. The data appears as a table inside your Word document. To change the position of the table, click inside the table, and drag the margin and column width markers, as desired.

> **TIP**   **Use the AutoFormat Command**   Keep in mind that you can quickly change the look of your table by using the AutoFormat command. Right-click anywhere inside the table, and click **Table AutoFormat**. You can then pick from a list of table designs.

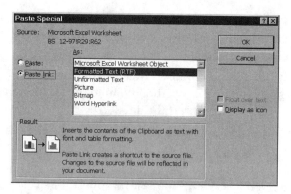

Figure 2.2 The Paste Special dialog box.

10. Continue building your document, inserting Excel data as needed (see Figure 2.3). When finished, be sure to save the document, as well as any spreadsheets you created in Excel.

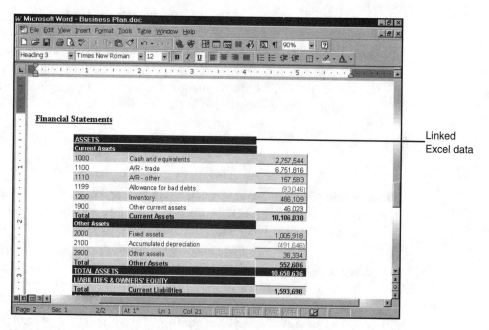

Figure 2.3 A finished business plan in Word that uses Excel charts and tables.

TIP **Unlinking Data** To learn how to break links you've created in Office 97, refer to Lesson 1 in this part of the book.

Have a business advisor or knowledgeable friend read over your plan before presenting it to potential investors or lenders. And most importantly, keep your business plan up-to-date; it should evolve along with your business. Investors will periodically refer to the plan to compare your performance.

TIP **Trouble?** If you run into trouble creating a business plan, you may want to consider business-planning software, programs designed to give you structure by asking you questions and letting you "fill-in-the-blanks" with information related to your own business ideas. Just remember that this type of software only produces a cookie-cutter type of plan. If your idea warrants something more original, it's best to build the plan yourself.

In this project lesson, you learned the basics of building a business plan using Office 97 programs. In the next lesson, you'll learn how to create a mass mailing.

Creating Mass Mailings

In this lesson, you learn how to merge Outlook's Address Book with a form letter you create in Word 97.

Performing a Mail Merge

Mass mailings are a popular way of advertising or seeking new clients. You can also use mass mailings to contact your entire client base to distribute the same information or notify potential clients about a new service. There are dozens of ways you can use mass mailings for your small business.

Office 97 makes it easier than ever to merge an electronic address book with a form letter to create mass mailings. You can even print mailing labels to go with the letters. You can perform a mail merge using Word, Excel, and Publisher, along with your Outlook Address Book. In the rest of this project lesson, I'll focus on using Word 97 to create a form letter and merge with an Outlook Address Book. Just remember, you can use other Office 97 programs (and even non-Microsoft programs), too. For example, you can create a form letter in another Office program and use the steps outlined in this lesson to merge the letter with an address database.

Building the Form Letter

Start your mail merge project by first composing the form letter you want to use. Open Word and create the letter, using a template or typing a letter from scratch. Leave out any information that can be merged from the Address Book data source. For example, omit the name and address. That data can be inserted from the data source—your Outlook Address Book.

Leave the form letter on your screen and proceed to the next set of steps. (You can save the letter now if you like; select **File**, **Save** and give the form letter a name.)

TIP   **Got an Address Book?**   You'll need an electronic address book in order to perform a mail merge. If you haven't created one yet, refer to Lesson 5 in Part III of this book. You'll find steps for creating an address book using Outlook 97.

Using the Mail Merge Helper

Armed with the form letter and the data source (the Outlook Address Book), you're ready to start creating mass mailings using the Mail Merge Helper dialog box. Follow these steps:

1. With the Word form letter opened on your screen, display the **Tools** menu and select **Mail Merge**. The Mail Merge Helper dialog box appears, as shown in Figure 3.1.

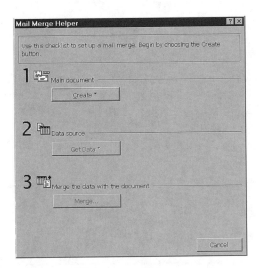

Figure 3.1 The Mail Merge Helper dialog box.

2. Under Main Document, click the **Create** button, choose **Form Letters**, then click **Active Window**. This instructs Word to use the open document as the main document in the mail merge.

3. Under Data Source, click the **Get Data** button (see Figure 3.2). There are four options to choose from to use as the source data for the mail merge (select **Use Address Book** for this example):

- **Create Data Source** lets you create a Word table with the data you want to merge with your form letter.

- **Open Data Source** lets you use an Excel spreadsheet, another Word file, a text file, or a database file (created in Microsoft Access, FoxPro, or another database program) as the data source.

- **Use Address Book** lets you use an existing electronic address book (from Outlook or Schedule+) as the data source. After selecting this option, choose the address book source you want to use.

- **Header Options** lets you use a file containing data fields and another containing data entries.

TIP Using Another Address Book Source? If you want to use a Word table as your data source, refer to Lesson 17 in Part I. If you want to use an Excel spreadsheet, refer to Lessons 4 through 6 in Part II.

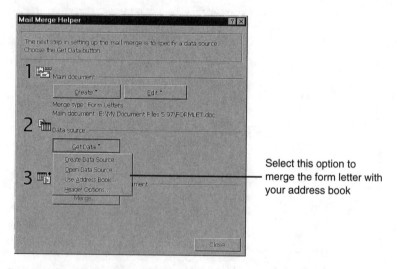

Select this option to merge the form letter with your address book

Figure 3.2 Click the **Get Data** button to display data source options.

4. If you select Use Address Book, you'll be prompted to choose the source (Outlook) of the address book and the Outlook profile you want to use. You'll also be prompted to select **Edit Main Document**. This returns you to the form letter, and the Mail Merge toolbar appears on-screen (see Figure 3.3).

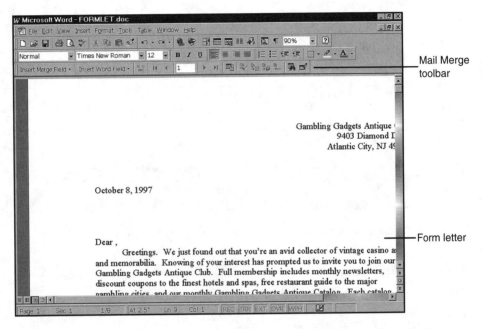

Figure 3.3   You are returned to the form letter to start entering data fields for the mail merge.

5. Now it's time to start placing data fields into the form letter to hold pieces of data from the address book. Place the insertion point where you want a field inserted. For example, click where you want to insert a person's name into your letter (see Figure 3.4).

6. Open the **Insert Merge Field** drop-down list in the Mail Merge toolbar and select the field you want to insert (see Figure 3.4).

7. The field code is inserted into your letter (such as <<First_Name>>). Take a look at Figure 3.4 to see an example. The field code pulls specific data from your address book and inserts it into the letter when merged.

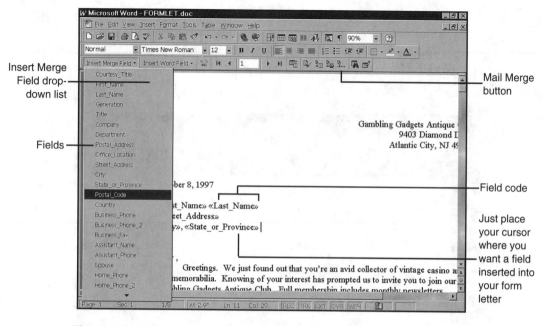

Figure 3.4 The field code is inserted into your form letter.

8. Continue repeating steps 5 through 7 to place all the necessary field codes into your form letter. Be sure to add punctuation or spacing between codes as necessary. For example,

    <<First_Name>> <<Last_Name>>
    <<Street_Address>>
    <<City>>, <<State_or_Province>> <<Postal_Code>>

9. When ready to merge the data from the data source (Outlook) with the Word form letter, click the **Mail Merge** button on the Mail Merge toolbar (see Figure 3.4).

10. The Merge dialog box appears, as shown in Figure 3.5. Use the following options to control how the data source (Outlook) and main document (form letter) are merged:

    • **Merge To** lets you merge to a new document, printer, or even an e-mail application.

- **Records to Be Merged** lets you choose a range of records from the data source to merge.
- **When Merging Records** instructs Word on inserting blank lines if a particular record in your address book is blank.
- **Query Options** opens another box with options for sorting merged letters or letters from a range of address records.

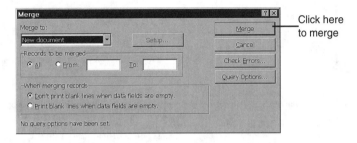

Click here to merge

Figure 3.5   The Merge dialog box.

11. Select the necessary options from the Merge dialog box, if needed, then click the **Merge** button.

12. If you merge into a new document, as shown in Figure 3.6, Word opens a new document window and displays all the merged letters where you can then choose to print them. Use the scroll bar to scroll to view each letter.

If you merge to your printer, Word starts immediately printing the letters.

TIP   **Save It!**   Be sure to save the new document file if you want to wait and print the letters at a later time.

If anything went wrong with your merge, such as field codes that didn't come out the way you wanted them, simply close the merge file and edit the codes on the form letter.

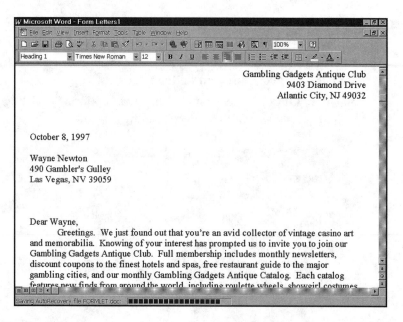

Figure 3.6 The form letter and address data fields are merged.

Creating Mailing Labels

Once you've created a mail merge for mass mailing, you'll probably need to create address labels to go with the letters. You can use the same steps you used for merging a form letter with an address book. Instead of choosing **Form Letters** in step 3, choose **Mailing Labels**. When you then select the data source in step 4, the Mail Merge Helper dialog box displays the Label Options box (see Figure 3.7). From there, you can choose a type size and style for the labels. Make your choices and click **OK**.

Figure 3.7 The Label Options dialog box.

Next, the Mail Merge Helper opens the Create Labels dialog box, as shown in Figure 3.8. Click the **Insert Merge Field** button and select the fields you want to include on the mailing labels. Don't forget to add punctuation between codes. Click **OK** when finished and go on to merge the labels with the data source (see the previous mail merge steps for more details).

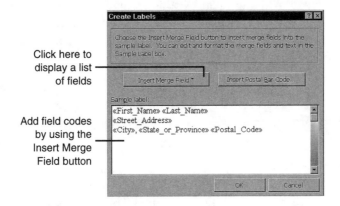

Figure 3.8 The Create Labels dialog box.

In this lesson, you learned the basics of performing a mail merge. In the next lesson, you'll learn how to create a practical business form with Excel.

Building a
Custom Invoice

*In this lesson, you learn how to create a custom invoice for use
with your small business.*

Creating an Invoice

Like most small business owners, you probably have to bill your customers
before they'll pay you. Although handwriting an invoice is legal, it makes your
company look like some fly-by-night operation. And preprinted invoice forms
may not be the perfect solution, either. The answer? Create your own custom
invoices in Excel!

Office 97 comes with an Invoice template. All you have to do is adjust the
invoice so it fits your needs, and then fill in the blanks. The steps in this first
project walk you through creating a custom invoice for your own personal
needs.

If you are not happy with the Invoice template, you can create your own invoice
from scratch and save it as a template. Use the **File, Save As** command; click the
Save as Type drop-down list and then **Template**. Then click **Save**.

If you are basically happy with the invoice template but want a few additions
such as new text, a different term agreement, and so on, don't hesitate to add
and delete elements from the existing template. Once you have made the
changes, select the **File, Save As** command; click the **Save as Type** drop-down
list and then **Template**. If you want to give a new name to your template, type
the name in the **File Name** text box and click **Save**. If you want to overwrite the
existing template, simply click **Save**.

TIP   **Sending Your Invoice**   Once you have an invoice, you can print it and send it by standard mail, e-mail, or fax (if you have a fax modem). To fax or e-mail the invoice, open the **File** menu, point to **Send To**, and choose the appropriate command: **Mail Recipient** or **Fax Recipient**.

Creating an Invoice with the Invoice Template

Before you can start filling in an invoice with your own data, you must first create the invoice in Excel. Follow these steps to build an invoice based on the Office 97 Invoice template:

1. Open the **File** menu and select the **New** command. The New dialog box appears.

2. Click the **Spreadsheet Solutions** tab and then click the **Invoice** icon. Click **OK** to continue.

CAUTION   **Macro Warning**   Whenever you open a template that contains macros, such as the Invoice template, Office 97 displays a warning. If you think that your system may have been infected by a macro virus (if you share files with other people), you can click **Disable Macros** to prevent the macros from running. However, if you disable the macros, the template won't do everything it is designed to do. To load the macros, click **Enable Macros**. If you commonly share Office 97 documents, purchase a good anti-virus program, such as McAfee AntiVirus or Symantec, and use it.

3. The Invoice template appears on-screen, as shown in Figure 4.1. You will also notice a new floating toolbar called Invoice. Before you begin typing information on the template, you need to make some custom changes, such as adding your company name. Click the **Customize** button in the top-right corner of the Invoice template.

TIP   **Move It!**   To move the floating toolbar out of the way so you can see more of the screen in the steps, drag its title bar out of the way. When you release the mouse button, the toolbar appears relocated.

4. You'll see a screen that says Customize Your Invoice (see Figure 4.2). In the **Type Company Information Here** area, type your company name and address in the appropriate text boxes.

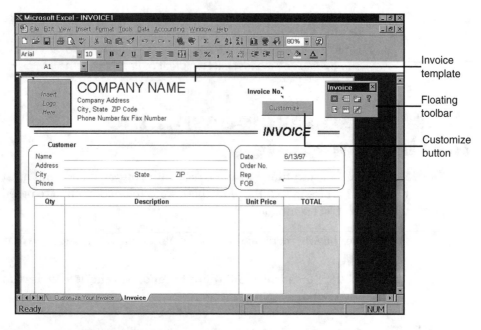

Invoice template

Floating toolbar

Customize button

Figure 4.1 The Invoice template.

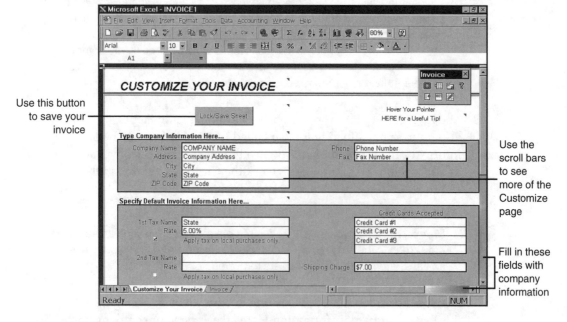

Use this button to save your invoice

Use the scroll bars to see more of the Customize page

Fill in these fields with company information

Figure 4.2 The Customize Your Invoice page.

5. In the **Specify Default Invoice Information Here** area, enter pertinent information such as your state's tax rate, what credit cards you accept, and shipping charges. Select the check boxes that apply to your situation.

6. Scroll down the page a bit to find the Formatted Information area. Notice the company name shows the information you entered in step 4. If you want to change the font or font size, click the **Change Plate Font** button at the bottom of the invoice. The Format Cells dialog box appears, as shown in Figure 4.3. Make any changes in the dialog box you want and click **OK**.

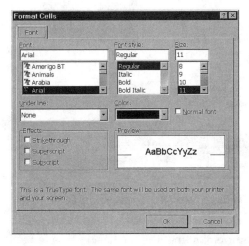

Figure 4.3 The Format Cells dialog box lets you change the font and size of the company name.

7. If you would like to add your company logo or a graphic to the invoice, click the **Select Logo** button at the bottom of the invoice. In the Insert Picture dialog box, select the file that contains your logo or the graphic you want to use and click **Insert**.

8. When you finish making the selections for customizing the Invoice template, click the **Lock/Save Sheet** button at the top of the invoice.

9. In the Lock/Save Sheet dialog box (see Figure 4.4), click the **Lock and Save Template** option button and click **OK**.

10. In the Save Template dialog box (see Figure 4.5), type a name for your customized template in the **File Name** text box and click **Save**. This doesn't overwrite the original invoice template, but creates another version of the template for you to use in the future.

Figure 4.4   The Lock/Save Sheet dialog box.

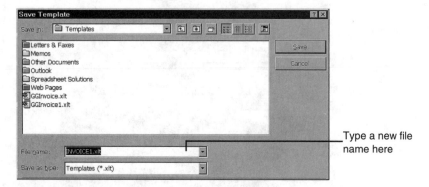

Type a new file name here

Figure 4.5   The Save Template dialog box.

11. Excel prompts you that the file has been saved and instructs you to begin use by choosing **File**, **New** and opening the templatem (see Figure 4.6). Click **OK**. You'll notice that the information you entered when you customized the form, such as your company name and address, now appears on the invoice. Close the invoice by selecting **File**, **Close**.

Figure 4.6   A box appears telling you the file has been saved.

To fill out an invoice, follow the instructions in the next set of steps in this lesson.

Filling Out the Invoice

After creating an invoice, you're ready to start filling it in. Don't forget that you can use data from other programs in your invoice, and link and embed data as needed (see Lesson 1 in this part of the book). For example, you can use an address from Outlook or a graphic from Publisher.

To use data from another source, put the Copy and Paste commands to work for you. Open the source program, such as Outlook, and copy the data you want to use in the template into Windows Clipboard. Return to the template file and paste the data into the appropriate cell. Use the Paste Link command to link the data (see Lesson 1 in this part of the book to learn more about linking data).

Use these steps to help you fill in your invoice:

1. Select **File, New**, then click the template you saved in the previous set of steps; click **OK**.

2. Start filling in the invoice. In the **Customer** area of the invoice, click the line you want to fill in and begin typing. Continue until you fill in all of the customer information (see Figure 4.7).

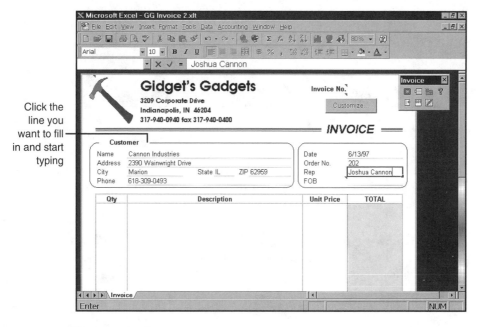

Figure 4.7   The customized Invoice template.

3. To the right of the Customer area, Excel adds the current date (if you want to change it, click the field and type the new date). To fill in the remaining fields, click the field and begin typing.

4. To fill in the body of the invoice, click the **Qty** field and enter your quantity per item. Enter a description of the item in the **Description** field and the individual price per unit in the **Unit Price** field. Excel automatically calculates the amount and places it in the Total field (see Figure 4.8).

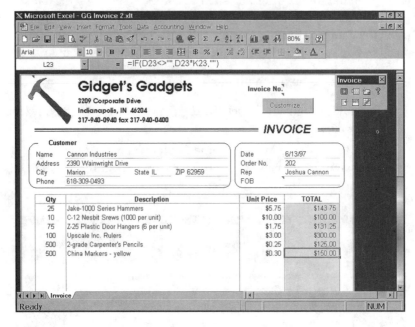

Figure 4.8 Excel totals your amounts for you.

5. Continue entering your invoice information. Excel displays the grand total automatically at the bottom of the invoice after adding the shipping charges and taxes (see Figure 4.9).

TIP **Comment Notes** Anytime you see a little red triangle-shaped dot next to a cell, the cell includes a *comment* with helpful information on filling in the information. To see the comment, point at the red dot.

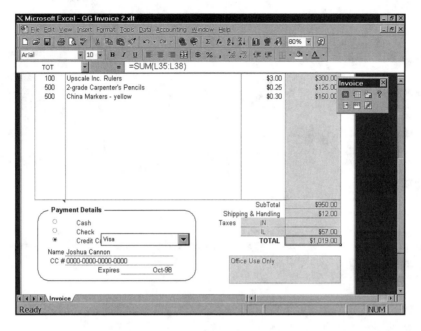

Figure 4.9 Excel also displays the grand total for you.

6. Fill in the **Payment Details** information areas as needed.

7. (Optional) In the **Office Use Only** area, fill in any information necessary.

8. If you want special text on the invoice, double-click inside the **Insert Fine Print Here** box, drag over the existing text, and type your new text.

9. To add a closing statement to your invoice, double-click inside the **Insert Farewell Statement Here** box, drag over the existing text, and type the desired text.

> **TIP** **Preview Your Invoice!** To see a preview of your invoice as you create it, click the **Print Preview** button on the toolbar.

10. When you finish your invoice, remember to save the invoice as an Excel workbook with the **File**, **Save** command as you normally would save a workbook. You can also print it or send it via fax or e-mail.

In this lesson, you learned how to create a custom invoice. In the next lesson, you'll learn how to create a quarterly report that updates itself.

Creating a Quarterly Report that Updates Itself

5

In this project lesson, you learn how to create a quarterly report that will update itself anytime your data changes.

Create a Quarterly Report that Updates Itself

When you create a status report in Word, you usually maintain the structure from the last status report and simply update the data for a new report. If you use Excel data in the status report, you can save yourself some time by linking the data to the Word report once instead of copying the data each time you need to update the report. That way, anytime you make a change to the data in the Excel worksheet, that change will appear in the status report in Word.

Once you understand how to link an Excel worksheet to a Word document, you can apply that knowledge in many ways, especially saving yourself the work of retyping existing information. Here are a few examples:

- You can automate the monthly creation of a status report that contains a summary chart from a company data worksheet. If anyone makes changes to the data worksheet, your status report will include those latest sales figures automatically.

- You can create a memo that informs team members of the project status and link the memo to a schedule you have created in Excel, so that your memo will contain the latest mission-critical dates.

- You can create business inventory reports much easier by simply including the inventory worksheet portions directly on the business report.

- You can create a will that links to your net worth worksheet. Any changes to your assets or liabilities portion of the Excel worksheet can generate an updated document in Word automatically the next time you open it.

TIP   **Inserting Data**   When inserting data from an Excel worksheet, keep in mind that you don't have to copy and paste the entire worksheet. You can paste only the portion you need. The steps in this lesson show an example in which you can omit entire columns from the worksheet by hiding those columns before selecting the data.

Paste Worksheet Data so It Updates Itself

To link data from Excel into a Word report, follow these steps:

1. Prepare your report in Word; then when you're ready to insert Excel worksheet data, move the insertion point to the location where you want to insert the data.

TIP   **Inserting a Worksheet**   Another way to insert an Excel worksheet into Word is with the Insert Microsoft Excel Worksheet button on the Standard toolbar. Use this button to define the spreadsheet size.

Select the number of cells you want to use, then a portion of an Excel worksheet appears within the Word window and Excel's toolbars appear at the top of the Word window. You can proceed to enter data in each cell. Click anywhere outside of the spreadsheet cells to display the Word toolbars again. Any data you entered in the worksheet will appear as a table in the Word document.

2. Switch to Excel, and open or create the worksheet from which you want to copy the data.

3. In this example, I want to present the income and expenses for only the second quarter, but my spreadsheet shows both quarters. To hide the first quarter numbers, drag over the column letters B, C, and D at the top of the worksheet (see Figure 5.1).

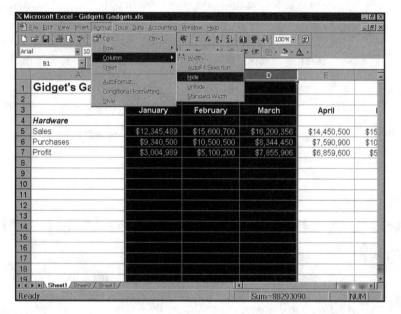

Figure 5.1 You can hide data in Excel that you don't want to link with Word.

4. To hide the selected columns, open the **Format** menu, point to **Column**, and click **Hide**.

5. Excel hides the selected columns (see Figure 5.2), so you can copy the data in columns A, E, F, and G as a single unit. Drag over the data you want to copy.

6. Open the **Edit** menu and select **Copy**, or click the **Copy** button in the toolbar.

7. Switch back to your Word document. Open the **Edit** menu and select **Paste Special**, so you can insert the copied worksheet data as a link.

8. The Paste Special dialog box, shown in Figure 5.3, asks how you want the copied data pasted. Click the desired format (usually **RTF**) in the **As** list, and then click the **Paste Link** option. Click **OK**.

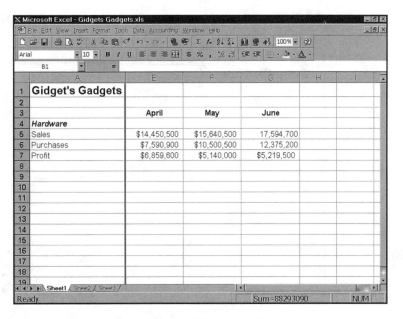

Figure 5.2 Columns B through D are hidden in this figure.

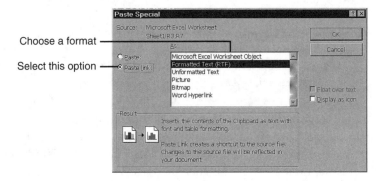

Figure 5.3 The Paste Special dialog box.

What's RTF? *RTF (rich-text format)* inserts the Excel data as formatted text. Microsoft Excel Worksheet Object inserts the data as a picture, making it a little less manageable.

9. The data appears as a table inside your Word document (see Figure 5.4). To change the position of the table, click inside the table, and drag the margin- and column-width markers, as desired.

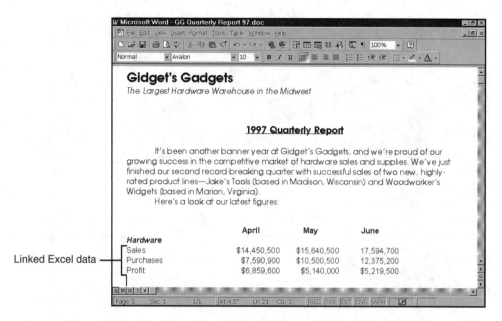

Linked Excel data ——

Figure 5.4 The linked Excel data appears as a table in the Word document.

TIP **Use the AutoFormat Command** Keep in mind that you can quickly change the look of your table by using the AutoFormat command. Right-click anywhere inside the table, and click **Table AutoFormat**. You can then pick from a list of table designs.

10. To find out how the link updates itself, try a little experiment. Switch back to your Excel worksheet, and change one of the numbers. In Figure 5.5, the April sales amount was changed from 14,450,500 to 13,450,500. Be sure to press **Enter** after typing your change, or the link will not update.

11. Switch back to the table in your Word document, and look at the number you changed in your Excel worksheet. As expected, the new entry was automatically inserted into the table, as shown in Figure 5.6.

Change the data in Excel and the change will be reflected in Word

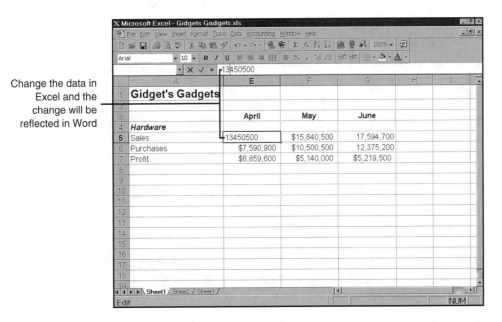

Figure 5.5 When data is linked, any changes made to the source file are reflected in the container file.

Linked data is updated

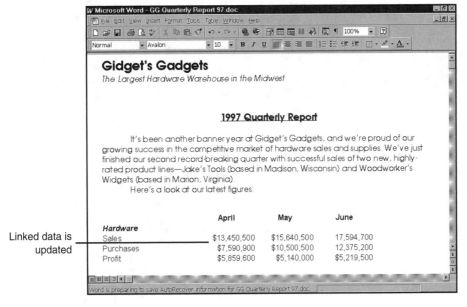

Figure 5.6 Notice Word now reflects the changes made in step 10.

Now anytime you change the data in Excel, those changes will be reflected in your Word quarterly report.

CAUTION

Warning! If you hide columns as shown following the previous steps and then you unhide the columns, you might run into trouble if you update the link later. When you update the link (using **Edit Update Link**), Word assumes that you want the hidden columns inserted as well.

TIP **Unlinking Data** To learn how to break links you've created in Office 97, refer to Lesson 1 in this part of the book.

In this lesson, you learned how to link data from an Excel spreadsheet into a Word 97 report. In the next lesson, you'll learn how to create a newsletter using Office 97 programs.

Creating a Newsletter

In this lesson, you learn how to lay out a newsletter in Publisher, how to import text written in Word, and how to wrap text around images imported from the Clip Art Gallery.

Laying Out the Newsletter

A newsletter is a combination of text and graphics. The text is created in either Word or Publisher. The graphics can be an image from the Clip Art Gallery, a digitized picture on your hard drive, or a chart from another program such as Excel. You can even cut and paste a map from the AutoMap Streets Plus program.

When you lay out a newsletter, it's best to work from the background to the foreground. First, put in the elements that repeat: those that repeat in every issue like your logo and masthead and those that repeat on every page such as headers and footers. Don't forget to lay out any repeating graphics such as borders or rules.

Next lay out your basic column structure. Keep it to two or three columns—more than that, and the page becomes too cluttered. Whether each column is the same size or varied is a matter of taste; unequal columns are less conservative. Don't worry about placing your graphics at first; Publisher 97 can easily flow text around inserted graphics at any point.

To start laying out your newsletter, follow these steps:

1. Open Publisher 97.
2. Open a new blank page by clicking the **Blank Page** tab of the Startup dialog box, selecting **Full Page**, and clicking **OK**.

3. If your newsletter is longer than one page, from the **Insert** menu, select **New Page**. Enter the number of additional pages you want, and click **OK**.

4. From the **Arrange** menu, select **Layout Guides**. Enter the number of columns you want in the Grid Guides section. For a newsletter with facing pages, select **Create Two Backgrounds with Mirrored Guides**.

5. From the **View** menu, select **Go to Background**.

6. If your newsletter is longer than one page, from the **View** menu, select **Two Page Spread**.

7. Create text boxes to hold repeating elements such as headers or footers with page numbers, newsletter name, date, and so on. Figure 6.1 shows the beginning of a sample newsletter with a header added for one page.

8. Add any watermark or other graphic element for the background such as borders or lines between columns.

9. From the **View** menu, select **Go to Foreground**.

10. Create any elements that repeat from issue to issue such as main logo or masthead. Figure 6.2 illustrates the placement of our example newsletter's main logo.

11. Save your newsletter by clicking the **Save** button in the toolbar. In the Save dialog box, change the folder, if necessary, and type in a new file name. Press **Enter** to close the dialog box.

Figure 6.3 shows a the first page of a sample newsletter. Portions of the background image were masked with white rectangles to create the design. A header is covered on the first page by the logo but because it was placed in the Background, it appears on subsequent pages. Text boxes overlapping background elements were made transparent by selecting them and pressing **Ctrl+T**.

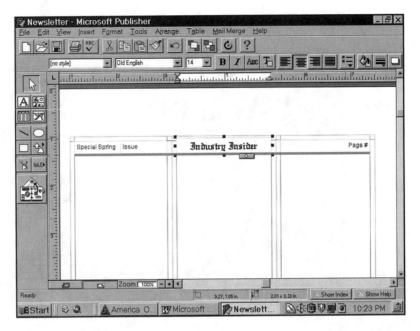

Figure 6.1   A Background header holds information that repeats on every page.

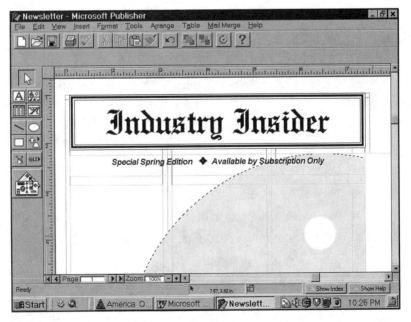

Figure 6.2   The main logo and subtitle are placed in the foreground on the first page.

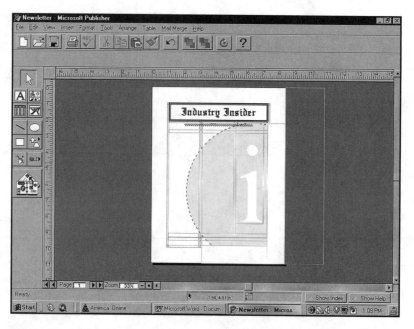

Figure 6.3 Newsletter background and repeating elements in place.

Preparing and Importing Text

For anything longer than a paragraph or two, it's best to write your articles in Word and import them into Publisher. Not only does this give you the flexibility and power of a dedicated word processor, but it also allows many people to contribute articles while one person controls the final layout. Finally, you can assign styles in Word that can be imported and modified in Publisher.

Follow these steps to prepare your text in Word and import it into Publisher:

1. Open Word.
2. Type your text for an article.
3. Apply styles to the headings, subheadings, and paragraphs as described in Part IV, Lesson 11.
4. Click the **Spelling and Grammar** button on the Standard toolbar to proof your article.
5. Click the **Save** button to store your document. Close the document.
6. Open or switch to Publisher.

7. If it is not already loaded, open your previously saved newsletter.

8. Click the **Text Frame** button and lay out your frames on each page for the text to flow into. Follow the column guides previously set up.

9. Use the page controls to go to the first page.

10. Click inside the first text frame where the imported text is to go.

11. From the **Insert** menu, select **Text File**.

12. From the Insert Text File dialog box, double-click the article's file name.

13. If the article doesn't fit in one frame, Publisher asks if you would like to autoflow the text into the next frame. Click **Yes**.

TIP **Changing Styles** Publisher automatically imports styles associated with a text file. Modify your text's format globally by selecting **Text Styles** from the **Format** menu. Select the style to change from the drop-down list and click **Change This Style**.

Figure 6.4 shows the next step in our newsletter's development with text imported from Word and styled in Publisher.

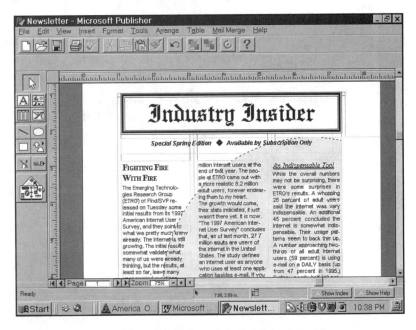

Figure 6.4 Text imported from Word flows into Publisher's text frames.

Wrapping Text Around Pictures

You need pictures or graphics to break up the text and keep the reader attracted to the page. Publisher automatically wraps text around any new filled-in object placed on top of it. Text that is "pushed out of the way" by a photograph or artwork moves down the text frame.

In Publisher, you can either wrap text around the rectangular frame of the picture or around the picture itself. This effect works best with clip art that has a simple background. One good place to use this technique is between two columns so the words wrap irregularly on both sides of the clip art.

Follow these steps to wrap text around a picture:

1. Open your previously saved newsletter in Publisher.
2. Click the **Picture Frame** button on the left toolbar and drag out an area in your newsletter for a picture.
3. From the **Insert** menu, select **Clip Art**.
4. Double-click a picture or drawing from those already in the Clip Art Gallery, or click the **Import Clip** button to use another file.
5. Publisher asks if you want to resize the picture or the frame. In most cases, it is best to resize the frame. Your graphic is then imported.
6. Move your picture frame into position by clicking and dragging the mouse on the frame.
7. To wrap a text irregularly around clip art, select the clip art and click the **Wrap Text to Picture** button in the Picture Format toolbar. (See Part IV, Lesson 10 for more on wrapping text around graphics.)

Figure 6.5 shows the inside spread of our newsletter with imported photographs, clip art, and a pull quote.

In this lesson, you learned how to lay out a newsletter in Publisher, import text written in Word, and wrap text around images imported from the Clip Art Gallery. In the next lesson, you'll learn how to lay out an advertisement.

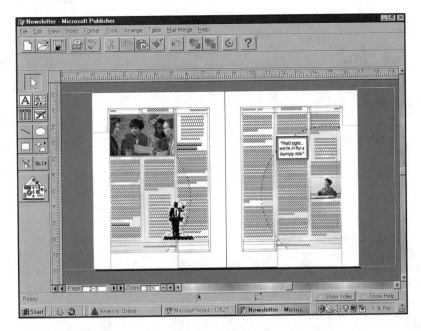

Figure 6.5 Text wraps easily around any photograph or clip art.

Laying Out an Advertisement

In this lesson, you learn how to start a brochure with a PageWizard, how to add spot color to your brochure, and how to mail merge your brochure to an Excel- or Word-created address list.

Setting Up Your Brochure with PageWizard

One of the most difficult steps in laying out a brochure is figuring out what goes where when dealing with folds. Publisher's PageWizard greatly simplifies the process and makes the initial brochure layout a breeze.

To set up a brochure using PageWizard, follow these steps:

1. Open Publisher.
2. From the **File** menu, select **Create a New Publication**.
3. From the **PageWizard** tab, double-click **Brochure**.
4. Select a style of brochure from the selections shown in Figure 7.1. Classic, Flashy, and Modern have the most layout options. Click **Next**.
5. From the next screen, choose the type of fold: Top or Side. Click **Next**.
6. From the next screen, click **Yes** to include a picture on the front. Click **Next**.
7. From the next screen shown in Figure 7.2, choose your inside layout: Mostly Text, Text and Pictures, or Mostly Pictures. Click **Next**.
8. From the next screen, click **Mail** if you plan to mail your brochure. Click **Next**.

9. Publisher tells you how many pages the brochure uses to print. In most cases, it uses two: one inside and one outside. Click **Next**.

10. Click **Finish** to have PageWizard create the brochure based on your choices. To change a choice, click the back arrow.

11. After the brochure is created, Publisher asks if you want step-by-step help for adding text and picture. Select **Yes** or **No** and then click **OK**.

If you select **Yes**, the Help screen opens next to your brochure with topics on working with brochures. There is even a short demo on how to finish a publication started by a PageWizard.

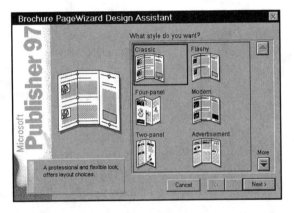

Figure 7.1   There are 17 brochure templates to choose from.

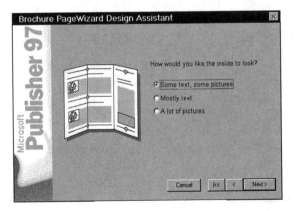

Figure 7.2   The inside layout gives you three different looks.

Figure 7.3 shows the inside spread of a tri-fold brochure as completed by the PageWizard. In this particular design, the text frames on the left go across two panels of the brochure.

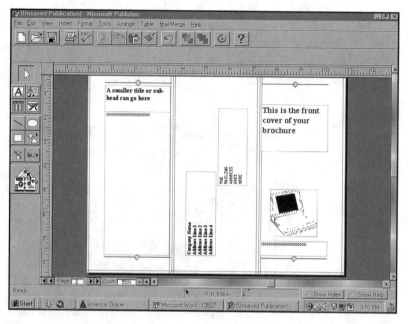

Figure 7.3   A brochure as generated by PageWizard, prior to being customized.

Customizing a Brochure

After the PageWizard has built your brochure template, you need to customize it by putting in your information and artwork. If you're just starting out designing brochures, keep the format as set up by the PageWizard and change only the text.

In most cases, Publisher uses phrases like "Replace this text with your own" or "This is the front cover of your brochure" to provide you with some direction. When you are replacing the generic text and pictures with your own, it's a good technique to start with the cover and work your way through the brochure.

Follow these steps to begin customizing your brochure:

1. Follow the steps in the previous section to use PageWizard to create a brochure or open a previously saved one.

2. Use the page controls to move to the page with the cover of your brochure.

3. Click the **This Is the Front Cover of Your Brochure** text frame once. Note that all of the text is highlighted. Type your own heading.

4. To replace a picture, select the graphic. From the **Insert** menu, select **Clip Art** and double-click your new artwork.

5. Move to the inside page of the brochure and repeat steps 3–5 for every text and picture frame.

6. Move the final outside panel of your brochure and replace the company information with your own.

7. If you plan to mail merge this brochure, follow the instructions at the end of this lesson. If you plan to use labels, delete the address information by clicking it once and pressing the **Delete** key.

8. Save your brochure by clicking the **Save** button in the standard toolbar.

When you've completed the brochure, choose **File, Print Preview** and take a look at it before you print it. Figure 7.4 shows a customized version of the brochure template shown in Figure 7.3 as it would print. You can temporarily hide the layout lines by selecting from the **View** menu **Hide Boundaries and Guides**. Restore them by selecting from the **View** menu **Show Boundaries and Guides**.

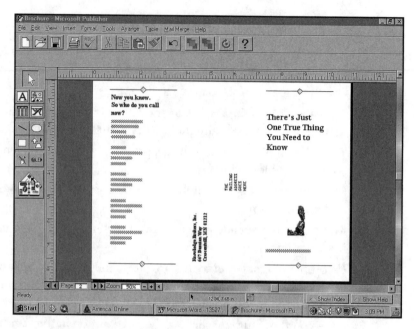

Figure 7.4   A customized PageWizard brochure.

Adding Spot Color

If your budget permits, color is a great way to make a brochure stand out. Spot color is a far less expensive option than full color but can be extremely effective. You can get more visual variety when using spot color by taking advantage of Publisher's tint/shade capability. Remember, you can only use up to two spot colors per publication in Publisher; any more, and you must print in full color.

Spot color can be used to highlight key words, company names, and slogans. Publisher has a handy feature which allows you to recolor any clip art, including full-color photographs, with a spot color. All the contrast and shading is retained through use of the spot color's tints—it's like looking at a black-and-white photo, except black has been replaced with your color.

To add spot color to your brochure, follow these steps:

1. Open your previously saved brochure in Publisher.
2. Highlight any text you want to change by clicking and dragging over it.
3. Click the **Text Color** button in the Text Format toolbar.
4. Select a color by clicking it.
5. Highlight other text you want in the same color.
6. Click the **Text Color** button in the Text Format toolbar.
7. To color clip art in the spot color, first select your clip art.
8. From the **Format** menu, select **Recolor Object** or **Recolor Picture**.
9. Select your color from the **Recent Colors** box.
10. You can also add new ovals, rectangles, or custom shapes in your spot color as shown in Figure 7.5.

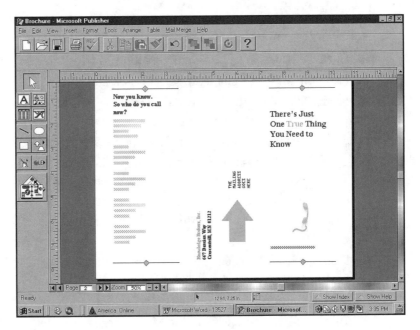

Figure 7.5 Spot color can be added to text, clip art, and custom shapes.

Mail Merging Your Brochure

Not only can Publisher work with internally created address lists, but it can also import address lists created in Excel or Word. Whenever possible, it's a great idea to reuse your existing database of addresses. Aside from eliminating the workload of reentering all those names and addresses, when you have one central source for all your mailing information, it's much easier to make additions, deletions, and corrections.

 TIP   **Importing Outlook Address Lists**   If you want to import your Outlook address lists, you must first convert the file to either Excel or Access.

Follow these steps to mail merge your brochure using a list previously created in Excel or Word:

1. Open your previously saved brochure.
2. Click the text box containing the mailing address information.
3. From the **Mail Merge** menu, select **Open Data Source**.
4. From the Open Data Source dialog box, click the **Merge Information from a File I Already Have** button.
5. Select your file from the Open Data Source dialog box.
6. To find an address list created in Word, click the arrow next to the **Files of Type** box and select **Microsoft Word Address Lists (*.doc)**.
7. To find an address list created in Excel, click the arrow next to the **Files of Type** box and select **Microsoft Excel (*.xls)**.
8. Click **OK**.
9. From the **Mail Merge** menu, select **Insert Fields**.
10. Double-click the field name to insert it. Add any necessary punctuation or carriage returns.
11. To preview the merge, from the **Mail Merge** menu, select **Merge**.
12. Use the arrows on the Preview Data dialog box, as shown in Figure 7.6, to view different records.
13. To print your merge file, from the **File** menu, select **Print Merge**. Select your options and click **OK**.

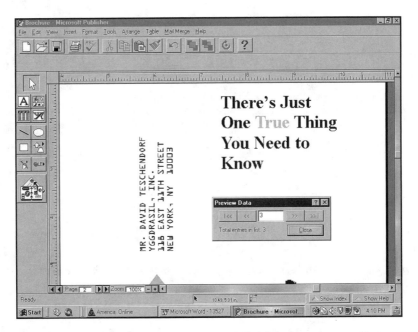

Figure 7.6 Excel-created data is merged into a Publisher brochure.

In this lesson, you learned how to start a brochure with a PageWizard, how to add spot color to your brochure, and how to mail merge your brochure to an Excel- or Word-created address list. In the next lesson, you'll learn how to prepare office documents for the Web.

Preparing Office Documents for the Web

In this lesson, you learn how to prepare Web pages in Word, divide large documents into separate Web pages, insert hyperlinks, and export spreadsheets from Excel for the Web.

Preparing Web Pages in Word

The entire Office 97 suite of programs is geared to interface easily with the World Wide Web. Word now makes short work of the previous chore of making existing office documents Web-ready. Excel can convert its data and charts into formats accessible by anyone on the Internet.

When preparing existing office documents for publication on the Web, there are a few key differences between traditional publishing and online publishing. The first difference is that Web pages are separated by subject, not by page length. There are no page numbers in cyberspace, or headers and footers. Any important information contained in the header or footer must be moved into the main document.

Another difference between a regular word processing document and a Web page is that Web pages currently have no equivalent to the tab character. If you leave tabs in the front of paragraphs, some browsers replace the tab with a single space, making your paragraphs uneven.

Follow these steps to convert existing office documents into Web pages:

1. Start Word.

2. Open the existing document you want to convert into a Web page.

3. From the **View** menu, select **Headers and Footers**.

4. Move any vital information from the headers or footers into the body of the document by cutting and pasting the text as shown in Figure 8.1.

5. From the **Edit** menu, select **Replace**.

6. In the Find and Replace dialog box, click the **More** button.

7. Click the **Special** button and select **Tab Character** from the option list as seen in Figure 8.2 to go in the **Find What** box.

8. Leave the Replace With box empty and click the **Find Next** button.

9. Find and replace all tabs at the beginning of each paragraph. Do not select **Replace All** unless you are sure no tabs are used except at the beginning of each paragraph.

10. From the **File** menu, select **Save as HTML**.

11. From the Save As HTML dialog box, select the folder where you want to save your Web page, and type a name in the **File Name** box. Click the **Save** button.

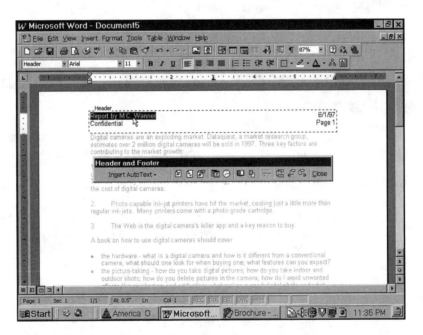

Figure 8.1 Vital information from headers or footers needs to be moved into the body of an HTML document.

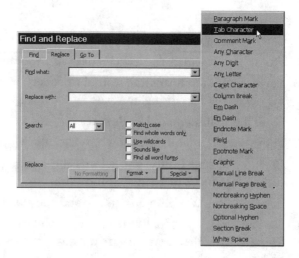

Figure 8.2 Tab characters can be eliminated with Find and Replace.

CAUTION

Avoid Name Conflicts In selecting a name for your Web page, use a lowercased, one-word name (no spaces or punctuation). Many Web servers are UNIX-based machines, and avoiding uppercased or mixed-cased names— and names with spaces—eliminates a potential conflict.

Dividing a Large Document into Several Web Pages

In a long office document, major sections often begin on a new page. On the Web, each page (and therefore each major subject) is a separate file. While the choice is up to you, it's best to divide a large multi-section document into several Web pages.

If your document needs to be divided into separate Web pages, follow these steps for each section that is to become a Web page:

1. At the beginning of a section, press the **F8** key to turn Extend Selection mode on.

2. Move to the end of the section.

3. Click the **Cut** button in the toolbar.

4. Click the **New** button in the toolbar.

5. Click the **Paste** button in the toolbar.

6. From the **File** menu, select **Save as HTML**.

7. From the Save As HTML dialog box, select the folder where you want to save your Web page, and type a name in the **File Name** box. Click the **Save** button.

Inserting Hyperlinks to Other Web Pages

Hyperlinks are the key to Web pages. Every page must be linked, at the very least, to your Web site's home page. A Hyperlink can be a word or a phrase (such as "Home" or "Index of Links"), or a picture such as a button or other graphic image.

Hyperlinks use a file's Internet address or URL to locate the file. When you are linking separate Web pages to form a Web site, most documents are in the same folder and you can refer to the Web page just by its file name (**benefits.htm**) as opposed to its full Web address (**http://www.yourcompany.com/benefits.htm**). The first page—the default home page—in any folder is named *index*.

To insert a Hyperlink to another Web page, follow these steps:

1. Save your converted documents as HTML as noted in the previous section.

2. Place your insertion point where you want the hyperlinks to appear.

3. To use text as a Hyperlink, type the words or phrase you want to represent your home page.

4. To use a picture as a Hyperlink, from the **Insert** menu, select **Picture**, and then **Clip Art** from the submenu. Select a picture, and click the **Insert** button.

5. Select the words or picture and then from the **Insert** menu, select **Hyperlink**.

6. From the Insert Hyperlink dialog box as shown in Figure 8.3, type in or browse to the main Web page. If the page has not been created yet, type **index.htm**.

7. Click **OK**.

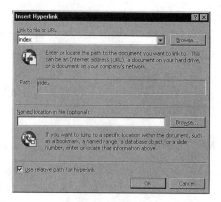

Figure 8.3 Insert a Hyperlink into a Word file.

Using Excel Data on the Web

Excel 97, just like Word 97, allows you to convert office documents to a Web page format. When a spreadsheet is converted to a Web page, the data becomes a fixed table, and all calculations display the current value. Be sure your spreadsheet is in its final form before you begin the conversion process.

Excel uses the Internet Assistant Wizard, shown in Figure 8.4, to assist in the process. Follow these steps to convert the spreadsheet into a stand-alone Web page:

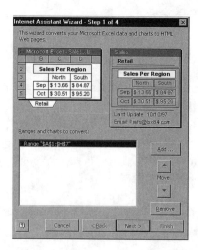

Figure 8.4 The first window of the Internet Assistant Wizard.

1. Start Excel.

2. Open the existing spreadsheet you want to convert into a Web page.

3. From the **File** menu, select **Save as HTML**. The Internet Assistant Wizard opens, highlighting the first data range in the spreadsheet.

4. To add additional data ranges, click the **Add** button and then click and drag the new range. Click **Next** when you are finished.

5. From the next window, make sure the **Create an Independent Ready-to-View HTML Document...** option is selected. Click **Next**.

6. From the next window, enter the following elements in the corresponding boxes:

   - **Title** becomes the title of the Web page.
   - **Header** information is placed on the first line before the data.
   - **Description Below Header** is text that goes between the header and the data.
   - **Horizontal Line Boxes** when checked, place lines before and/or after your data.
   - **Last Update On** defaults to today's date; put in any date you want.
   - **By** is the name of the person responsible for the data.
   - **E-mail** is the e-mail address for the person listed.

7. Click **Next** when you have finished filling out the options.

8. From the next window, first select the code language in which to create your Web page. US/Western is the default.

9. If you are working with an existing FrontPage 97 Web site, click the **Add the Result to my FrontPage Web** option.

10. Enter the path and file name of the new Web page. Click the **Browse** button to find a different folder.

11. Click the **Finish** button.

Figure 8.5 shows a spreadsheet that has been converted to a Web page. All the formatting, including background coloring, was retained.

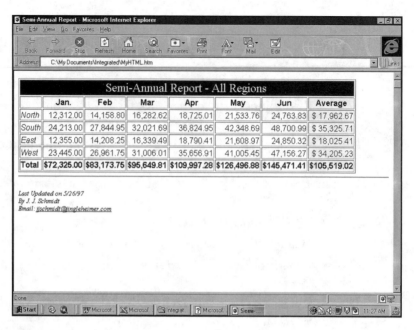

Figure 8.5 A converted spreadsheet.

In this lesson, you learned how to prepare Web pages in Word, how to divide large documents into separate Web pages, how to insert hyperlinks, and how to export spreadsheets from Excel for the Web. In the next lesson, you'll learn how to design Web pages in Publisher.

Designing Web Pages

In this lesson, you learn how to change your Web page's background, insert a map from the AutoMap program, and add special features to your Web page.

Changing Background Colors and Textures

If you don't specify the background of your Web page—the color of the paper, if you will—the page uses whatever the viewer's system defaults to, usually white or a light gray. Not only can you make the background a specific color, but you could also put either a texture or a picture in the background.

Whenever you change the background, you must make sure there is the right amount of contrast between whatever is in the foreground and your new background. If, for example, you put a medium green background under forest green text, it will be difficult to read. Likewise, if you use a neon green text over a hot yellow background, the text seems to vibrate and detracts from your message.

Pictures in the background are repeated or tiled to fill the browser window. This is how textures are created. As with pure colors, you must make sure that your background does not overwhelm or obscure the information in the foreground.

Finally, be sure to take notice of the Hyperlink colors against your new background. Again, the right amount of contrast is important or else your hyperlinks will disappear.

The following procedure assumes that you have created a Web page and saved it as an HTML document (as shown in Part V, Lesson 13). To change the background of a Web page, follow these steps:

1. Open Internet Explorer 4.0.
2. From the **File** menu, select **Open**.
3. From the Open File dialog box, click the **Browse** button to locate your file. Click **OK** when you have selected it.
4. Click the **Edit** button in the toolbar to open FrontPad.
5. In FrontPad, from the **Format** menu, select **Background**.
6. From the Page Properties dialog box, click the **Background** tab, as shown in Figure 9.1.
7. From the Background tab, to change the color, click the arrow next to the **Background** box.
8. Select a color from the drop-down list.
9. If necessary, change the Text and Hyperlink, Visited Hyperlink, and Active Hyperlink colors by clicking the arrows next to their respective boxes.
10. To insert a picture into the background, click the **Background Image** box and type in the path and file name, or click the **Browse** button.
11. When you have completed your selection, click the **OK** button on the Page Properties dialog box.

In the example shown in Figure 9.2, a background picture has been added to create a texture. Notice that while the line of pebbles seems to blend into the texture, the center cartoon of the island does not. The pebbles were saved with the transparency option turned on and the cartoon was not. Use a graphic program such as Microsoft Image Composer to achieve this effect.

TIP   **Both Image and Color**   You can have both a background image and a background color. The color shows through where the image is transparent.

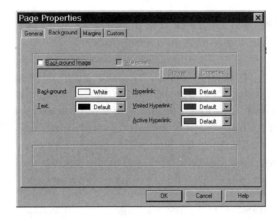

Figure 9.1 You can add a color or an image to the background of a Web page.

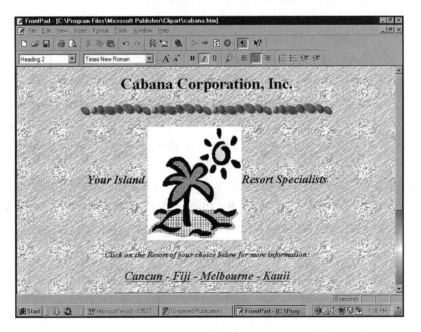

Figure 9.2 A repeating background image adds texture to a Web page.

Inserting a Map from AutoMap Streets Plus

Many organizations include a local or regional contact on their Web page to generate additional business from the global market that the Web reaches. A map to lead customers to your place of business is a useful addition to any Web site. One handy graphic resource included in Small Business Edition of Office 97 is Microsoft's *AutoMap Streets Plus* (see Appendix A for more information on this program). Using the cut-and-paste features of Office 97, you can easily insert a map into your Web page using FrontPad.

Follow these steps to insert a map from AutoMap Streets Plus:

1. Open FrontPad.
2. Create a new Web page or open an existing one that you want to insert your map into.
3. Place your insertion point where you want the map to appear.
4. Open AutoMap Streets Plus.
5. From the **Street Plus** main menu, click the **Find an Address** button.
6. From the Find dialog box, type in your address information and click **OK**.
7. Click and drag a rectangle around the area of your map you want to use. Release the mouse button.
8. Click inside the rectangle to zoom in.
9. Click the map with the right mouse button to open the Quick menu.
10. From the **Quick** menu, select **Copy**.
11. Press the **FrontPad** button on the taskbar.
12. From the FrontPad toolbar, click the **Paste** button.
13. The map is converted to a GIF file and inserted into your Web page as shown in Figure 9.3.

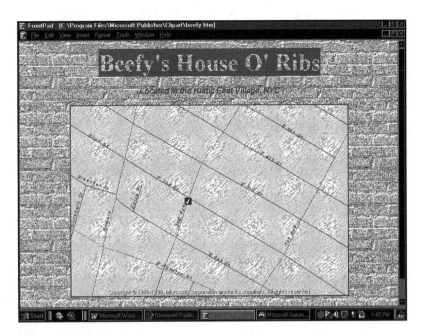

Figure 9.3 A map from AutoMap Streets Plus on a Web page.

Adding Special Web Features

FrontPad allows you to include a number of special Web features in your Web page, no matter what the source of your document is. One of the most valuable additions is a *mini-search engine*. The bigger search engines, like Yahoo! or AltaVista, help you to find subjects over the entire World Wide Web. A mini-search engine looks for a match on only your Web site—and can be a great benefit to your visitors to help them find anything on your site.

Please note that this procedure works only with FrontPage Web sites. FrontPage adds additional support files to enable this search object and other WebBot components.

Follow these steps to add a Search object to your Web site:

1. Start FrontPad.
2. Open a Web page from a previously created FrontPage Web site.

665

3. Place your insertion point where you want the search object to appear.

4. From the **Insert** menu, select **WebBot Component**.

5. From the Insert WebBot Component dialog box, double-click **Search** in the list of available WebBots.

6. From the WebBot Component Properties dialog box as shown in Figure 9.4, fill out the available options:

- Label for Input changes the text for the Search box.
- Width in Characters sets the size of the Search box.
- Label for "Start Search" Button changes the text on the Search button.
- Label for "Clear" Button changes the text on the button that clears the Search box.

7. Click the **OK** button when you have finished.

8. A search object is inserted into your Web page; the dashed border is not visible when the saved Web page is viewed through a browser such as Internet Explorer 4.0.

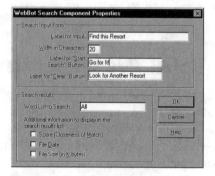

Figure 9.4 The mini-search engine Properties dialog box.

In this lesson, you learned how to change your Web page's background, how to insert a map from the AutoMap program, and how to add special features to your Web page. In the next lesson, you'll learn how to publish your Web pages on the Web.

Placing Your
Web Document
on the Web

In this lesson, you learn how to create a multiple-page Web site in Publisher, add hyperlinked hot spots to pictures, and publish your completed Web site on the Internet.

Creating a Web Site in Publisher

Publisher has a PageWizard for building both single-page and multiple-page Web sites. All of the pages created in the larger Web site are connected to one another, and they all share a common look and feel. This is very important in Web site design as it unifies your Web site and makes it easier for a visitor to navigate through the site.

Follow these steps to create a multiple-page Web site with Publisher:

1. Open Publisher.
2. From the **File** menu, select **Create New Publication**.
3. From the **PageWizard** tab of the Startup dialog box, double-click the **Web Site** icon.
4. The Web Site PageWizard Design Assistant opens. On the first window, as shown in Figure 10.1, select whether your Web site is intended for business, community, or personal use. Click **Next**.
5. In the next window, select either a one-page or multiple-page site. Click **Next**.

6. In the next window, select the boxes next to the pages you want created in your Web site as shown in Figure 10.2. Each selection creates an additional interconnected Web page. Click **Next**.

7. In the next window, select the style of Web site from the available options. Click the icon of your choice and click **Next**.

8. In the next window, choose from a Plain, Solid, or Textured background and then click **Next**.

9. In the next window, choose the type of Navigation buttons for your Web site from Text Only, Buttons and Text, or Icons and Text. Click **Next**.

10. In the next window, type the title for your home (main) page. Click **Next**.

11. The next three screens ask for address and phone information to put on the Web site. Fill out as desired and click **Next**.

12. The final screen appears. You can click the back arrows at this time to change any of your selections or click **Create It!** to make the Web site.

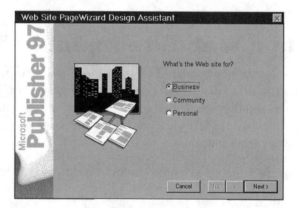

Figure 10.1   The Web Page Design Assistant can lay out an entire Web site for you.

After your new Web site has been created, you can see how it looks on the Web. Click the **Preview Web Site** button on the toolbar to load your site into Internet Explorer 4.0. Figure 10.3 shows an example site browsed for the first time. Notice the use of placeholder text and the working hyperlinks.

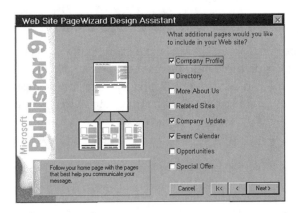

Figure 10.2 Choose the Web pages to be included in your site.

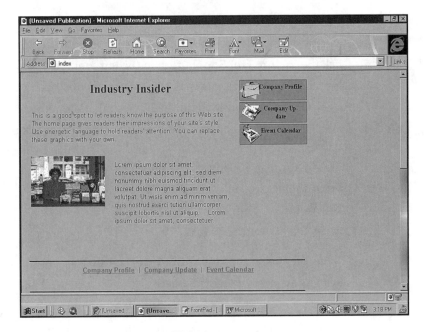

Figure 10.3 A first look at a new Web site.

Adding Picture Hot Spots

A *picture hot spot* is a area on a picture that, when clicked, activates a Hyperlink. An entire picture could be one hot spot, such as navigation buttons, or one picture could contain multiple hot spots. For example, a page on your executive committee could contain a group photo with a hot spot for each person that links to his or her own department. Publisher has an easy-to-use Picture Hot Spot tool that appears when you are creating a Web site.

To add a picture hot spot to your Web site, follow these steps:

1. Open your previously created Web page or site in Publisher.
2. Use the page controls to move to the page where you want to add the hot spot.
3. Select the picture to add the hot spot to.
4. If necessary, use the zoom control to **Zoom to Selection**.

5. Click the **Picture Hot Spot** button in the left toolbar.
6. Click and drag a rectangle over the area on the picture to create a hot spot.
7. Release the mouse button and the Hyperlink dialog box opens.
8. In the Hyperlink dialog box, choose where the Hyperlink is to be connected:
   - An address already on the Internet
   - Another page in your Web site
   - An Internet e-mail address
   - A file on your hard drive
9. Fill out the box in the **Hyperlink Information** section.
10. Click **OK** when you have finished.

Publisher draws a resizable rectangle around the picture hot spot as shown in Figure 10.4. Click the **Preview Web Site** button to see your hot spots in action.

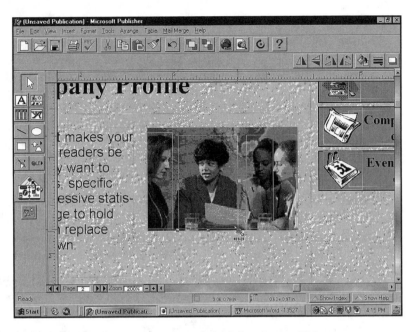

Figure 10.4 Picture hot spots are hyperlinked to separate Web pages.

Publishing Your Web Site

The final step in creating your Web site is publishing it on the Web. *Publishing on the Web* means that the Web pages and all the associated files (such as graphics or sounds) are transferred to a Web server. The *Web server* could be an Internet Service Provider that hosts Web sites for individuals or small businesses, or it could be a members-only directory for one of the larger online services like America Online or CompuServe. Or it could be your company's own internal Web server. Once all the files are on the Web server, anyone connected to the Web—if they know your Web address—can view your Web site.

It is highly recommended that you publish your Web site in the early stages of its development. Viewing a site on the Web is a different experience than viewing from your local hard drive. First, you can see just how long your pages take to download. Second, you can make sure that all the files necessary were transferred to the Web site. Finally, you can make sure that all of your hyperlinks are working correctly. Make the necessary corrections and republish your site to see the changes.

Microsoft includes the Web Publishing Wizard as part of the Small Business Edition ValuPack. If you have not installed it yet, do so before proceeding with the next section. See Appendix B for more details. You must also have arranged with your Internet Service Provider or other Web server to host your Web site.

Follow these steps to publish your Web site on the Web:

1. Open Publisher.

2. Open the Web site you want to publish to the Web.

3. From the **File** menu, select **Publish to Web**.

4. After Publisher generates your pages for the Web, the Web Publishing Wizard opens as shown in Figure 10.5.

5. From the Web Publishing Wizard, select the name of your Web server by clicking the arrow next to the **Web Server** box. Click **Next**.

6. If your Web server is not on the list, click the **New** button. In the top box of the New Server window, enter a descriptive name for the server. In the bottom box, enter the server's Web address. Click **Next**.

7. In the next window, click the **Finish** button to complete the process.

8. If your system does not automatically log on, the Dial-Up Networking dialog box opens. Click the **Connect** button. The Web Publishing Wizard informs you when the process is complete.

Figure 10.5 The Web Publishing Wizard connects to your Web server.

In this lesson, you learned how to create a multiple-page Web site in Publisher, add hyperlinked hot spots to pictures, and publish your completed Web site on the Internet.

Appendixes

Using Microsoft Automap Streets Plus

In this appendix, you'll learn how to locate addresses and plan out routes with Microsoft's Automap Streets Plus program.

What Is Streets Plus?

Microsoft Automap Streets Plus is a detailed map of streets from cities and towns all around the United States and Canada. With over 5 million miles of roads, you can use the program to locate addresses and plan the best route possible. For example, if your business requires a lot of travel, you can use Streets Plus to help you quickly locate an address or landmark anywhere in the U.S. or Canada (depending on which map you've installed). You can easily mark places you've been or places you need to go using electronic pushpins.

Or perhaps you and your family are planning a vacation driving down the coast or heading out west—you can use Automap Streets Plus to chart your course. You'll find useful tools for zooming in and out of the map for a better view, and tools for marking and saving a route you want to take. As you'll soon see, the program is perfect for planning trips or charting courses around home or across the country.

Installing Streets Plus

To install Microsoft Automap Streets Plus, follow these steps:

1. Place the program's CD-ROM into the appropriate drive. The Setup program will immediately start itself and open the Setup window.

2. From the Setup window, click **Continue** or press **Enter** to start the installation procedure.

3. In the next box that appears, type in your name and click **OK**.

4. A confirmation box appears. If the information is accurate, click **OK** to continue.

5. The next box displays your product ID number. It's a good idea to write this number down and keep it with the program's manual or registration information. Click **OK** to continue.

6. In the next box that appears, shown in Figure A.1, you can designate which folder or drive you want to install to by clicking the **Change Folder** button and selecting a new destination. By default, the program installs to your main drive in the Program Files folder. When you're ready to start installing the files, click the large **Install and Run** button.

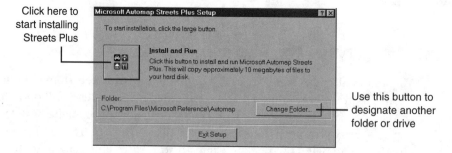

Figure A.1 When you're ready to install the Streets Plus files, click the **Install and Run** button.

7. Next, Setup prompts you to choose a program group name. In most instances, the default group (Microsoft Reference) is fine. Click **Continue**.

8. Setup begins installing the program files. When the installation is complete, another box appears stating that the procedure was successful. Click **OK** to exit the Setup program. You're now ready to use Streets Plus.

Opening and Exiting Streets Plus

There are two ways to open Streets Plus:

- Place the Automap Streets Plus CD-ROM into the appropriate drive on your computer. Streets Plus automatically opens onto your screen, as shown in Figure A.2.

- You can also open the **Start** menu, select **Programs**, **Microsoft Reference**, and **Automap Streets Plus**.

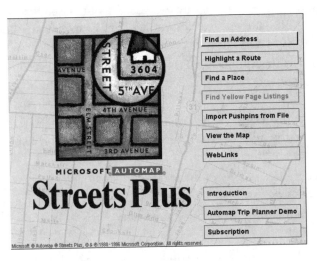

Figure A.2   The Streets Plus home screen.

CAUTION

I Get an Error Message!   If you have too many programs left open when you start Streets Plus, you may get a message prompting you that your computer is running low on virtual memory. Simply close any open programs to free up memory.

Once the Streets Plus home screen appears, you can select from the various options, such as viewing the map or finding an address. By default, Streets Plus always opens with the home screen first. To select an option, simply move your mouse pointer over the appropriate button and click. Many of these options are also available from the menu bar or toolbar after opening the Streets Plus map. Here's a rundown of the Streets Plus options found on the home screen:

Find an Address   Use this option to find a specific address on the map. You can look up business or residential addresses and pinpoint their exact locations.

Highlight a Route   Plan out a route by highlighting your way from point A to point B on the map. You can then save the route to use again.

Find a Place   This option lets you look up places, such as cities, museums,

677

parks, airports, mountains—you name it. You can even find detailed information about a place, such as an address or phone number.

Find Yellow Page Listings   If you've purchased Streets Plus Deluxe or the ABI Yellow pages, you can look up listings from phone books across the country and find their exact location on the map.

Import Pushpins from File   Use this option to exchange pushpins with other Streets Plus users. For example, you can import your salesperson's pushpins to help you coordinate territories or districts.

View the Map   A click on this option opens the map in full view (zoomed out to the fullest). From there, you can home in on a specific area, city, or state using the map tools.

WebLinks   Many of the locations listed on the map are also available as Web sites.

Introduction   This option gives you a brief tour of the Streets Plus features.

Automap Trip Planner Demo   Use this option to run a demo explaining how to use the Automap Trip Planner.

Subscription   This option displays information about upgrading the Streets Plus maps when new ones are available.

In most cases, after you select an option on the home screen, the Streets Plus map opens onto your screen. You can exit the program anytime by using any of these methods:

- Click the **Close** button in the upper-right corner of the Streets Plus window.
- Open the **Options** menu and select **Exit Streets Plus**.
- Press **Alt+F4** on the keyboard.
- Click the **Control-menu** icon and select **Close**.

TIP   **Start Up Without the Home Screen**   If you prefer Streets Plus to open right up without going through the home screen each time, you can do so. Open the **Options** menu, select **Streets Plus Options**, and then deselect the **Show Home Screen When Streets Plus Starts** option and click **OK**.

Viewing the Map

To see a full-screen display of the map, click the **View the Map** button on the Streets Plus home screen. This opens the map window, as shown in Figure A.3. The window displays a bird's-eye view of the map, along with its major highways.

Figure A.3 A full-screen view of the map.

By default, the map opens in Terrain view, which includes topographic features. Depending on your monitor, this may make your screen display a little busy and difficult to read. Thankfully, there are three more view modes you can apply. To change the map view, follow these steps:

1. Open the **View** menu and select **Map Display**. This opens the Map Display dialog box, shown in Figure A.4.
2. A quick click on the **Map Styles** tab brings the four map view modes to the front of the dialog box.
3. To change to another view mode, click the appropriate option button, and then click **OK** to exit the box and apply the view.

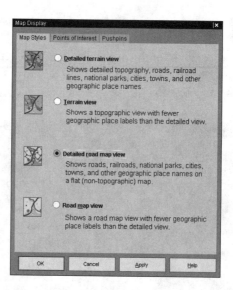

Figure A.4   The Map Display box lets you change your view of the map.

The two road map views are the easiest to read on-screen. They are also easier to read when printed out in black-and-white. Figure A.5 shows what the map looks like using the detailed road map view.

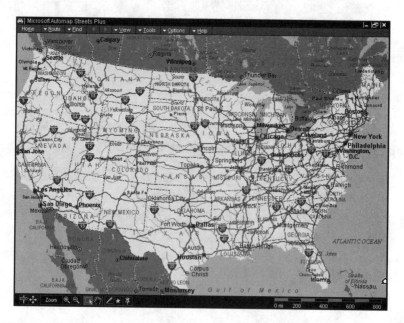

Figure A.5   The same map showing the detailed road map view.

TIP   **Rather Use Kilometers?**   If you prefer kilometers over miles, you can change the mileage scale to reflect kilometers instead. Simply open the **Options** menu, select **Streets Plus Options**, and choose **Kilometers**. Click **OK** to exit the options box.

Using the Map Tools

Automap Streets Plus employs many of the on-screen elements that you're familiar with from other Windows 95 programs, such as a menu bar and toolbar buttons. The menu bar offers nine commands to help you move around the map and perform various tasks. Here's a brief explanation of each menu command:

Home   Click this menu command to return to the Streets Plus home screen (refer to Figure A.2).

Route   You'll find several commands in this menu for planning a route on the map. (Learn more about this feature later in this appendix.)

Find   This menu offers commands for locating specific addresses and places on the map. You'll learn more about using these features coming up.

Undo/Redo buttons   Click the left-pointing arrow to undo your last command. Click the right-pointing arrow to redo your last command.

View   Open this menu to change your view of the map, such as zooming your view or changing view modes.

Tools   Display this menu to find useful map tools such as a measuring tool and a map legend for explaining the various symbols and colors on the map.

Options   This menu has commands for printing, copying, and exiting the program, as well as a command for changing program settings.

Help   Use this menu to find online help with your Streets Plus questions.

Many Streets Plus commands found on the menus are also available as toolbar buttons at the bottom of the Streets Plus window. A simple click is all it takes to activate a tool, which is much faster than opening a menu. Table A.1 explains what each tool button does and how to use the tools in conjunction with the map.

Table A.1   Streets Plus Tool Buttons

Tool	Function
	Opens the Find an Address dialog box
	Opens the Find a Place dialog box
	Opens the Zoom Slider control for changing the zoom perspective
	Zooms in (closer) with each click
	Zooms out with each click
	Zooms in to a specific area you click
	Drag to move around the map
	Use to highlight a route on the map
	Locates points of interest on the map
	Use to mark a place on the map with a pushpin

If you ever have any doubt about what a particular tool button or menu item does, hover your mouse pointer over the item and a ToolTip box appears with a brief description. On the other hand, if this feature annoys you, you can turn it off. To do so, open the **Options** menu, select **Streets Plus Options**, and deselect the **Always Show ToolTips** option. Click **OK** to exit the options dialog box.

Finding an Address or Place

Ready to look up an address or locate a special place on the map? Streets Plus can help you look up an address just about anywhere. However, keep in mind that the map you're using may not reflect brand-new neighborhoods or developments.

Updating Maps If your business depends on accessing the most current addresses available, you should update your Streets Plus map frequently. To learn more about keeping your map up-to-date, click the **Subscription** button

CAUTION on the Streets Plus home screen for more information.

To find an address, follow these steps:

1. From the Streets Plus home screen, click the **Find an Address** button. You can also open the **Find** menu and select **Address**. This opens the Find an Address dialog box, shown in Figure A.6 (the map appears in the background).

2. Type in the street address you're looking for, the city name, and select a state from the State drop-down list. Keep in mind that you don't necessarily have to type in the exact address; sometimes simply the street name will do. If you know the ZIP code, enter it in the ZIP code field.

TIP **Yes, You Can Use Abbreviations!** You can use abbreviations for street names, such as St for street or Ave for avenue. For a comprehensive list of allowed abbreviations, click the **Help** button in the Find an Address dialog box and read about specific abbreviations.

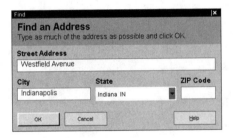

Figure A.6 The Find an Address dialog box.

3. When you're ready to locate the address on the map, click the **OK** button or press **Enter**.

4. If you're looking for an address in a large urban area, another dialog box may appear (see Figure A.7). For example, a particularly long street that runs for several blocks may include several ZIP code zones. When Streets Plus displays the Address Match dialog box, narrow down your search by clicking the street name that most closely matches the one you're looking for, and then click **OK**.

683

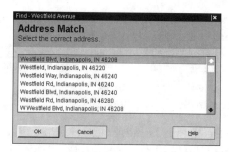

Figure A.7 Streets Plus displays this dialog box to help you narrow your search.

5. When Streets Plus finally finds the address on the map, as shown in Figure A.8, a note bubble appears on the map noting the address and a pushpin marks its location on the map.

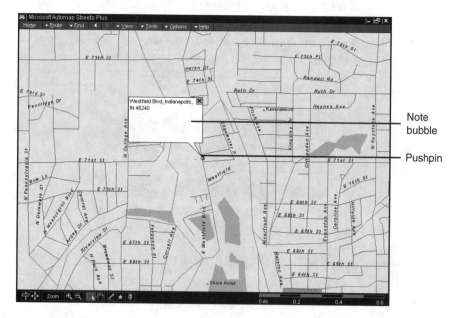

Figure A.8 Streets Plus marks the spot with a pushpin and a note bubble displaying the address.

TIP **Using the Note Bubble** You can type additional text into the note bubble on the map, or edit existing text as needed. Simply click inside the note bubble and change the information as needed.

Once you've found an address, you can use the Zoom tools to move in or out for a different perspective. You can also mark the spot with a permanent pushpin so you can find it again later. You'll learn more about using the pushpin feature later in this appendix.

TIP **Can I Print Out the Address?** To print out the portion of the map you're currently viewing on-screen, open the **Options** menu and select **Print**. This opens the Print dialog box. Click the **Print** button to print out a copy of the map.

Finding a Place on the Map

You can also look up places on the map. What constitutes a place? A place can be a city, park, mountain, airport, anything that's a landmark or location of distinction. To find a place, follow these steps:

1. Open the **Find** menu and select **Place**. (From the Streets Plus home screen, click the **Find a Place** button.)

2. This opens the Find a Place dialog box, shown in Figure A.9. Type in the name of the place you're looking for, and then click the **Locate** button.

Figure A.9 The Find a Place dialog box.

3. If you're looking for a place in a large urban area, another dialog box may appear (see Figure A.10). Narrow your search by clicking the place that most closely matches the one you're looking for, and then click **OK**.

4. Streets Plus finds the location of the place on the map, as shown in Figure A.11.

Streets Plus marks the place with a place symbol on the map. To learn more about what a symbol denotes, open the Map Legend. Pull down the **Tools** menu and select **Map Legend**. This displays a small box containing all the various symbols used on the map. You can scroll through and find out what each symbol signifies. To close the legend, click the **Close** button in the upper-right corner of the Map Legend box.

Figure A.10 Streets Plus displays this dialog box to help you narrow your search.

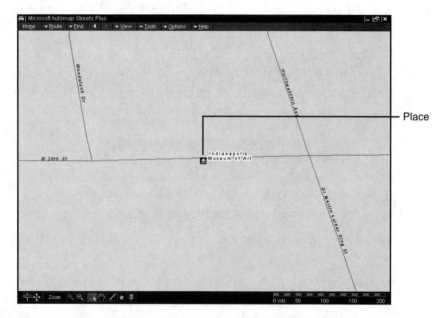

Figure A.11 Streets Plus marks the spot with a symbol on the map.

Finding Points of Interest

Another great tool to utilize is the Streets Plus Points of Interest feature. Use this tool to find out what types of restaurants, lodging, and museums are in the area. For example, let's say you must visit the Indianapolis Museum of Art on business. Use Streets Plus to look up hotels and restaurants in the vicinity. You can even find phone numbers and exact addresses to help you with your trip planning.

To look up points of interest:

1. Click the **Points of Interest** button on the toolbar, or open the **Find** menu and select **Points of Interest**.

2. Click the map where you want to find points of interest. Streets Plus opens the Points of Interest dialog box, as shown in Figure A.12.

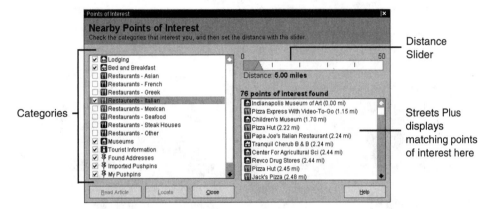

Figure A.12 The Points of Interest dialog box lets you find out more about places in an area.

3. The left side of the dialog box lists categories. Click the category you want listed. A check mark will appear beside the category name.

 TIP **How Do I Unselect a Category?** If you change your mind about the category you chose, simply click the category name again to deselect it. This removes the check mark from the category's box.

4. After selecting categories to list, drag the distance slider to mark how far away from the place on the map that you want to go to locate the points of interest you specified.

5. Streets Plus lists the points of interest that match the categories and distance you specified. To learn more about a particular point of interest, double-click it to open an article that may list an address or phone number. (Click **Close** to return to the Points of Interest dialog box.)

6. To find the exact location of a point of interest listed, simply select the item and click the **Locate** button.

7. Streets Plus finds the place on the map, as shown in Figure A.13.

Original place specified on map

Point of interest

Figure A.13 Streets Plus marks points of interest with symbols.

TIP **Where Am I?** To get a quick look at what area of the map you're viewing, including longitude, latitude, and time zone, open the **Tools** menu and select **Location Sensor**. This opens the Location Sensor box displaying the appropriate data. To close the box, click **Close**.

Planning a Route

There are plenty of instances where you'll want to mark a route on the map—for example, if you need to show a client directions to your business, or if you need to show employees where the next off-site business meeting is, or if you and your family are planning a trip. The Streets Plus routing feature can help you visualize the way to go. With the routing commands, you can highlight a route on the map, save it for future use, and even print it out.

To highlight a route, use these steps:

1. Click the **Highlighter** tool button (the button with the pencil icon), or open the **Route** menu and select **Highlight a Route**. (If you're starting from the Streets Plus home screen, click the **Highlight a Route** button.)

This opens the Highlight a Route box and the mouse pointer takes the shape of the Highlighter tool, as shown in Figure A.14.

Highlighter tool

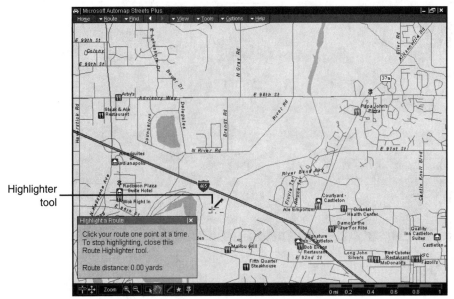

Figure A.14 To start marking a route, first open the Highlight a Route box.

2. Find the starting point of the route you want to mark and click the mouse pointer in place. You may need to zoom in your view of the map to clearly mark your route.

3. Drag the Highlighter tool to the next intersection or point in the route and click. Continue dragging and clicking one point at a time until you reach the final destination point.

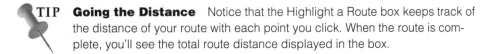

TIP **Going the Distance** Notice that the Highlight a Route box keeps track of the distance of your route with each point you click. When the route is complete, you'll see the total route distance displayed in the box.

4. When finished, click the **Close** button in the Highlight a Route box to finish the route. The route appears higlighted on the map, as shown in Figure A.15.

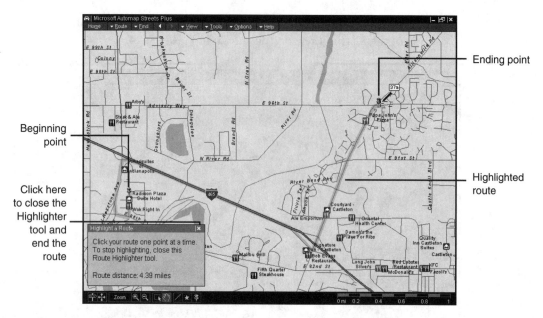

Figure A.15 The route appears highlighted on the map.

TIP **I Made a Mistake!** To undo the section of the route you just did, click the **Undo** arrow (left-pointing arrow) on the menu bar and try again.

If you change your mind about the route, you can easily clear it from the screen and start another one. Simply open the **Route** menu and select **Clear Route**.

TIP **Need to Measure?** If you ever want to measure the distance between two (or more) points on the map, open the **Tools** menu and select **Measuring Tool**. A Measuring Tool box appears on-screen, and the mouse pointer takes the shape of a tiny ruler. Click the first point on the map, and then click the second point. The Measuring Tool box displays the distance between the two points. To close the tool, click the **Close** button in the upper-right corner of the Measuring Tool box.

Saving and Printing a Route

After highlighting a route, you can save it or print it out. When you save a route, it's saved in the Automap Streets Plus Routes file format (.asr) and you can open it again when needed. You can even share the file with other Streets Plus users.

To save a route, follow these steps:

1. Open the **Route** menu and select **Save** or **Save As**. This opens the Save As dialog box, shown in Figure A.16.

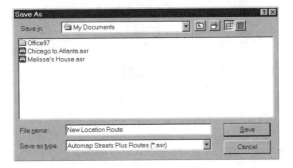

Figure A.16   You can save a route just like you save other Windows 95 files.

2. Type in a name for the route, choose a folder where you want the file stored, and then click the **Save** button.

 TIP   **Opening a Saved Route**   To open a saved route, pull down the **Route** menu, select **Open,** and locate the file you want to open.

To print a route:

1. Open the **Options** menu and select **Print**. This opens the Print dialog box, shown in Figure A.17.
2. To add titles to your printed map, make sure the **Yes** option is selected.
3. Type map titles into the appropriate Map Title fields.
4. When you're ready to print the map, click the **Print** button. Streets Plus prints out your map, including the route you specified.

To make the best use of the highlighted route and colors, printed maps are easier to read when printed on a color printer.

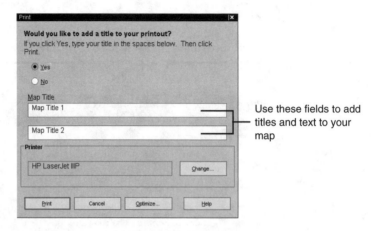

Use these fields to add titles and text to your map

Figure A.17   The Print dialog box.

Marking Your Map with Pushpins

When you look up addresses and places on the map, you may want to save the spot so you won't have to look it up again. You can do this using pushpins. Electronic pushpins act the same way that real pushpins do—tacks you stick on a wall map marking a spot. Electronic pushpins let you add symbols, labels, or a note describing the location along with the pushpin icon. You can even organize your pushpins into sets. For example, you might want all the pushpins in one of your sales territories grouped together, or all the pushpins marking your favorite city spots together. You can then choose to display certain pushpin sets on the map when needed.

To mark a spot with a pushpin:

1. Click the **Pushpin** tool button at the bottom of the Streets Plus.
2. Next, click the place on the map where you want the pushpin to go. It's best to zoom in a bit so you can see the location clearly.
3. The Pushpin Properties box appears, as shown in Figure A.18. Type in a name for the pushpin in the Name box.
4. To associate a symbol with the pushpin, click the **Choose Symbol** button and select a symbol from the palette that appears.
5. To add a note bubble to the pushpin, or a longer note, choose the appropriate Pushpin Type option. When you exit the properties dialog box, you can type in text pertaining to the pushpin.

Type in a name for
the pushpin here

To associate a
symbol with the
pushpin, click here
and choose a symbol

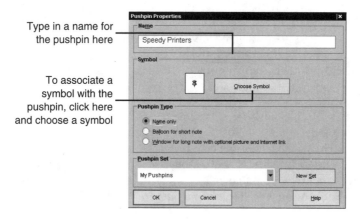

Figure A.18   The Pushpin Properties dialog box.

6. To group the pushpin with another set of pushpins, select a specific set using the drop-down arrow. To start a new set, click the **New Set** button and type in a name, and click **OK**. The new set is added to the drop-down list.

7. Click **OK** to exit the Pushpin Properties box, and the pushpin appears on the map, as shown in Figure A.19.

Figure A.19   The new pushpin appears on the map.

After you place a pushpin on the map, you can display a shortcut menu of commands you can use to display labels, move, or delete the pushpin. You can use the menu to reopen the Pushpin Properties box and make changes to the pushpin properties, or hide the entire pushpins set. To display the shortcut menu, right-click over the pushpin you want to change.

TIP **Importing Pushpins** You can import pushpins created by other Streets Plus users. For example, you can import your sales director's pushpins to help you coordinate territories or districts. From the Streets Plus home screen, click the **Import Pushpins from File** option, or if the program is already opened, pull down the **Tools** menu, select **Pushpins**, **Import Text File**. This opens a dialog box for retrieving the file.

Using the Small Business Edition ValuPack

In this appendix, you'll learn about the various features and tools available in the Office 97 Small Business Edition ValuPack.

Working with the ValuPack

Along with the many great applications that are included with the Microsoft Office 97 Small Business Edition is a collection of useful tools and mini-applets called the ValuPack. You may have noticed the ValuPack while installing the other Office 97 components (see Figure B.1). The ValuPack has a mix of small programs and other information that can help you get more out of Microsoft Office 97, as you can see from the partial list displayed in Figure B.2. Some of the components may be of more value to you than others, depending on your type of business.

Click here to open the ValuPack

Figure B.1 You'll find the ValuPack located among the other Office 97 programs.

To take a peek at all the ValuPack has to offer, you must open the AUTORUN.EXE file on your Office 97 CD-ROM. Follow these steps:

1. Insert the Office 97 CD-ROM into the appropriate drive.

2. The Setup program will automatically open the start window (shown in Figure B.1) when you insert the CD.

3. Next, click the **ValuPack** button. This opens a Help window, shown in Figure B.2, listing the various ValuPack components.

Click a button to learn more about a component

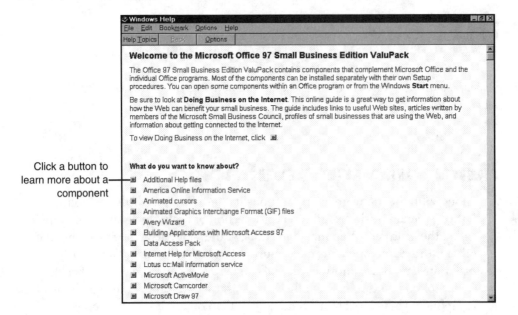

Figure B.2 The ValuPack Help window.

4. From the Help window, you can read more information about each component by clicking the button next to the component you want to know more about. (Use the scroll bar to view more of the list.)

Looking at the ValuPack Components

Some of the ValuPack components can be installed directly from the Help window, while others simply display additional information about how to use the component or Web links that take you to other sites containing more information. Since there are quite a few items listed, here's a rundown of each of the ValuPack features:

Additional Help files   If you're interested in more advanced Office techniques, such as using Microsoft Map or the Microsoft Office Binder, you can install additional Help files to assist you. This ValuPack component tells you how.

America Online Information Service   If you're an AOL member, you can use Microsoft Outlook as your e-mail editor in conjunction with your AOL account. The ValuPack feature has a link for downloading the America Online Information Service for free.

Animated cursors   Install this component to turn your mouse pointer into an animated cursor when using the Office 97 programs.

Animated Graphics Interchange Format (GIF) files   If you design your own Web page, you might want to check out this ValuPack component. It lets you add animated GIF (picture) files to your Web page for viewing with a browser such as Internet Explorer or Netscape Navigator. The animated GIFs are stored in the **Animgifs** folder on the Office 97 CD-ROM or diskette set.

Avery Wizard   If you use Avery Dennison products with your small business, you'll find the Avery Wizard a very useful tool. It helps you print your data onto a variety of Avery labels for mailing or organizing your work.

Building Applications with Microsoft Access 97   If you use Microsoft Access 97, you can access an online Web guide to help you develop database solutions.

Data Access Pack   Advanced users who work with ODBC and IISAMs drivers can use this data pack to help import (and export) data from other applications into Microsoft Access databases.

Doing Business on the Internet   This online guide offers you more information about conducting business on the Internet and the World Wide Web. It has links to business-related Web sites, and other business information.

Internet Help for Microsoft Access   Here's another tool for helping Access 97 users take full advantage of the program's Internet features.

Lotus cc:Mail Information Service   If your office uses cc:Mail as its e-mail system, this ValuPack tool lets you change your e-mail client to Microsoft Outlook while still using the cc:Mail postoffice.

Microsoft ActiveMovie   Download this digital video technology tool that lets you play back ActiveMovie multimedia clips and even view such files on the Internet.

Microsoft Camcorder   Use this tool to record computer sounds and actions to create a movie others can view. For example, you can record a tutorial that teaches how to use an application or perform a particular computer task.

Microsoft Draw 97   If you use a lot of illustrations and graphics with your small business, the Microsoft Draw 97 program can help you create professional graphics fast. Download this tool to use with Word, Excel, Outlook, or Publisher.

Microsoft Internet Explorer 3.0   This ValuPack feature helps you install version 3.0 of Microsoft's popular Web browser, Internet Explorer. Part V of this book covers versions 3.0 and 4.0. Of course, you'll need an Internet account (service provider) in order to use the browser, regardless of which version you install.

Microsoft Office 97 sounds   Care to add some fun sound effects to your Office 97 programs? Install new sounds with this component.

Microsoft Office 97 Upgrade Wizard   If you are updating from previous versions of Office, you can use this tool to help remove old Office files you no longer need, which can often free up memory on your computer.

Microsoft Office Binder templates   Microsoft's Binder feature lets you group related Office files to keep your work organized. Use the Binder templates to create specific kinds of Binders, such as Marketing Plans.

Microsoft Office Far East support   If your small business involves international communications, you can use the Far East support files to help you convert documents from English to Japanese, Korean, and Chinese.

Microsoft Office templates, forms, and wizards   To help you speed up your work, use Microsoft's premade templates and forms to create documents in Word, Excel, and more.

Microsoft Outlook import and export converters   Use Microsoft's converters to import data from non-Microsoft programs into Outlook. For example, you can convert Act! 2.0 files into Outlook notes.

Microsoft PowerPoint Custom Soundtrack   If you're using Microsoft's PowerPoint program, you can use this feature to add music soundtracks to your slide show presentations.

Microsoft PowerPoint Viewer   Installing this tool will enable you to view PowerPoint slide show presentations without having PowerPoint installed on your computer.

Microsoft Publish to ActiveMovie Stream Format   This tool lets you place PowerPoint presentations utilizing audio and visual effects onto the Internet or an internal intranet.

Microsoft TrueType fonts   Need more fonts? You can easily install new fonts to use with your Office 97 programs. Just follow the instructions listed in this ValuPack feature.

Too Many Fonts!   Be careful about installing too many fonts on your computer. They do tend to take up space, and you may not use them all the time.

CAUTION

Microsoft Web Publishing Wizard   Have you created your own Web page yet? Use the Web Publishing Wizard to help you copy files from your computer to a Web server with the greatest of ease.

Microsoft Word 97 converter   If you plan on exchanging Word files with users that have earlier versions of the program, such as Word 6.0, you can install the Word 97 converter and convert Word 97 files into file types that older Word programs can handle.

Microsoft Word Viewer   If you want to exchange a Word file with someone who doesn't use Word, you can distribute the file with a copy of Microsoft's Word Viewer program.

Presentation and World Wide Web page textures   Looking for an interesting background texture for your Web page or Publisher document? Check out these extra page texture JPEG files found in the **Textures** folder on your Office CD-ROM or diskette set.

Software patches   You'll find a few software patches that might be useful in the **Patch** folder on your CD-ROM or diskette set. For example, there's a patch for default file extensions for Microsoft Works.

Timex Data Link Watch Wizard   Own a Timex Data Link Watch? Export your schedule or other important Outlook data onto your Timex Data Link Watch—a handy way to carry your important information with you at all times.

Windows 95 Primer

Microsoft Windows 95 is a graphical operating system that makes your computer easy to use by providing menus and pictures from which you select. Before you can take advantage of it, however you must learn some Windows 95 basics.

A First Look at Windows 95

You don't have to start Windows 95 because it starts automatically when you turn on your PC. After the initial startup screens, you arrive at a screen something like the one shown in Figure C.1.

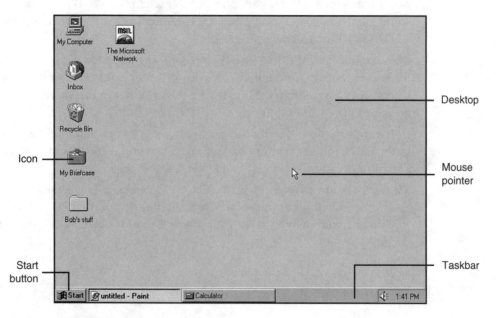

Figure C.1 The Windows 95 screen.

Parts of the Screen

As you can see in Figure C.1, the Windows 95 screen contains many special elements and controls. Here's a brief summary:

- The background on which all the pictures and boxes rest is the *desktop*.
- The *taskbar* shows a button for each window and program that is open. You can switch between open windows and programs by clicking the taskbar button for the one you want. (Notice how the open programs look on the taskbar in Figure C.1.)
- The *Start button* opens a menu system from which you can start programs. To use it, you click the **Start** button, and then you click a selection in each successive menu that appears.
- The *icons* that appear on your desktop give you access to certain programs and computer components. You activate an icon by double-clicking it.
- The *mouse pointer* moves around the screen in relation to your movement of the mouse. You use the mouse pointer to indicate what you want to select or work with.

You'll learn more about these elements as you work through the rest of the appendix.

Using a Mouse

To work most efficiently in Windows 95, you need a mouse. You will perform the following mouse actions as you work:

- **Point**   To move the mouse so that the mouse pointer is on the specified item. The tip of the mouse pointer must touch the item.
- **Click**   To move the pointer onto the specified item and press and release the left mouse button once. Unless you're told to do otherwise (for example, to right-click), you always use the left mouse button. Clicking usually selects an item.
- **Double-click**   To move the pointer onto the specified item and press and release the left mouse button twice quickly. Double-clicking usually activates an item.
- **Drag**   To move the mouse pointer onto the specified item, press and hold down the left mouse button, and move the mouse to a new location. Unless you're told to do otherwise (for example, to right-drag), you drag with the left mouse button.

Controlling a Window with the Mouse

Windows are the heart of the Windows 95 program. Windows 95 sections off rectangular areas called *windows* for particular purposes, such as running a program. You control a window using the techniques described in Figure C.2.

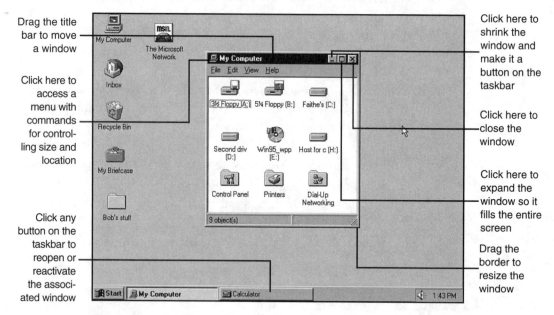

Drag the title bar to move a window

Click here to access a menu with commands for controlling size and location

Click any button on the taskbar to reopen or reactivate the associated window

Click here to shrink the window and make it a button on the taskbar

Click here to close the window

Click here to expand the window so it fills the entire screen

Drag the border to resize the window

Figure C.2   You use your mouse to control windows.

Scroll Bars   If your window contains more icons than it can display at once, scroll bars appear on the bottom and/or right edges of the window. To move through the window's contents, click an arrow button at either end of a scroll bar to move in that direction, or drag the gray bar in the direction you want to move.

Getting Help

Windows 95 comes with a great online Help system. To access it, click the **Start** button and click **Help**. You see the box shown in Figure C.3.

Figure C.3   Windows offers several kinds of help.

This box contains three tabs (Contents, Index, and Find), each of which provides you with a different type of help. The Contents tab appears on top first. To move to a tab, click it. Here's how to use each tab:

- **Contents**   Double-click any book to open it and see its sub-books and documents. Double-click a sub-book or document to open it.
- **Index**   Type the word you want to look up, and the Index list scrolls to that part of the alphabetical listing. When you see the topic that you want to read in the list, double-click it.
- **Find**   The first time you click this tab, Windows tells you it needs to create a list. Click **Next** and then **Finish** to allow this. When Windows finishes, you see the main Find tab. Type the word you want to find in the top text box. Then click a word in the middle box to narrow the search. Finally, review the list of Help topics at the bottom, and double-click the one you want to read.

When you finish reading about a document, click **Help Topics** to return to the main Help screen, or click **Back** to return to the previous Help topic. When you finish with the Help system itself, click the window's **Close** (X) button to exit.

Starting a Program

Of the many possible ways to start a program, this is the simplest (see Figure C.4):

1. Click the **Start** button.

2. Point to **Programs**.

3. Point to the program you want to start (such as Microsoft Excel) and click, or point to the group that contains the program you want to start; then click the program name.

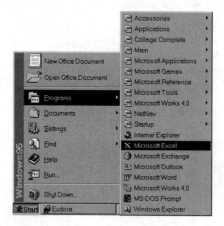

Figure C.4 Work through the Start menu and its successive submenus until you find the program you want to start.

Another way to start a program is to open a document that you created in that program. The program automatically opens when the document opens. For example, double-click a document file in My Computer or Windows Explorer, or click the **Start** button and select a recently used document from the **Documents** menu. Windows immediately starts the program in which you created the file and opens the file.

You can also start a program by double-clicking its shortcut icon on the desktop. *Shortcut icons* are links to other files. When you use a shortcut, Windows simply follows the link back to the original file. If you find that you use any document or program frequently, you might consider creating a desktop shortcut for it. To do so, just use the right mouse button to drag an object out of Windows Explorer or My Computer and onto the desktop. In the shortcut menu that appears, select **Create Shortcut(s) Here**.

Using Menus

Almost every Windows program has a menu bar that contains menus. The menu names appear across the top of the screen in a row. To open a menu, click its name. The menu drops down, displaying its commands (see Figure C.5). To select a command, you click it.

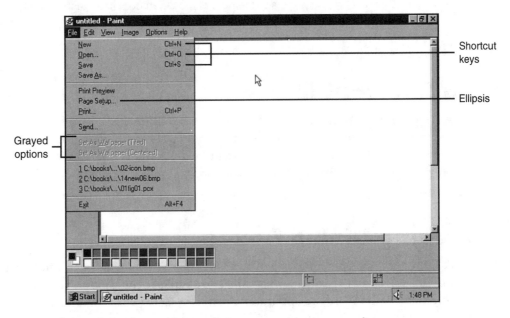

Figure C.5 A menu lists various commands you can perform.

Usually, when you select a command, Windows 95 executes the command immediately. However, the following exceptions break that rule:

- If the command name is gray (instead of black), the command is unavailable at the moment and you cannot choose it.
- If the command name is followed by an arrow (as the selections on the Start menu are), selecting the command causes another menu to appear, from which you must make another selection.
- If the command is followed by an ellipsis (three dots), selecting it will cause a dialog box to appear. You'll learn about dialog boxes later in this appendix.
- In the Office 97 programs, you'll find tiny icons in the front of some menu commands. Those icons represent the equivalent toolbar button you can use to perform the same task or command. It's a good idea to learn to recognize the equivalent toolbar button because it's much faster to click the toolbar rather than opening a menu and then selecting a command.

 TIP   **Shortcut Keys**   Key names appear after some command names (for example, **Ctrl+O** appears to the right of the **Open** command, and **Ctrl+C** appears next to the **Copy** command). These are shortcut keys. You use these keys to perform the command without opening the menu.

Using Shortcut Menus

A new feature in Windows 95 is the *shortcut menu*. Right-click any object (icon, screen element, file, or folder, for example), and a shortcut menu like the one shown in Figure C.6 appears. The shortcut menu contains commands that apply only to the selected object. Click any command to select it, or click outside the menu to cancel.

Navigating Dialog Boxes

A *dialog box* is the operating system's or program's way of requesting additional information or giving you information. For example, if you choose **Print** from the **File** menu of the WordPad application, you see a dialog box, similar to the one shown in Figure C.7. (The options it displays will vary from system to system.)

 Dialog Box   A type of box that a program displays when it needs more information from you or when it needs to give you information. It's the closest thing to a "dialog" that you can have with your program.

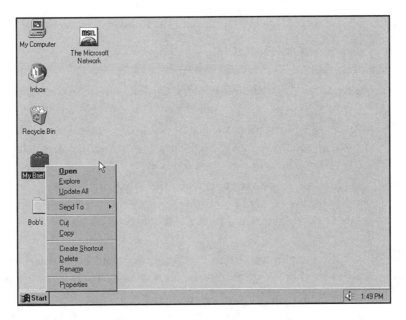

Figure C.6 Shortcut menus are new in Windows 95.

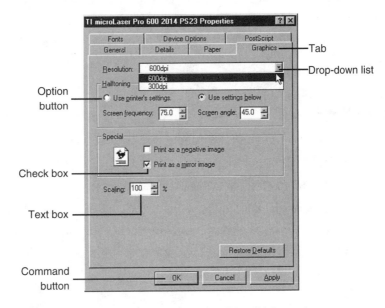

Figure C.7 A dialog box often requests additional information.

Each dialog box contains one or more of the following elements:

- *Tabs* bring up additional "pages" of options you can choose. Click a tab to activate it.

- *List boxes* display available choices. Click any item on the list to select it. If the entire list is not visible, use the scroll bar to find additional choices.

- *Drop-down lists* are similar to list boxes, but only one item in the list is shown. To see the rest of the list, click the drop-down arrow (to the right of the list box). Then click an item to select it.

- *Text boxes* enable you to type in an entry. Just click inside the text box and type. Text boxes that expect numeric input usually have up and down arrow buttons (increment buttons) that let you bump the number up or down.

- *Check boxes* enable you to turn individual options on or off. Click a check box to turn it on or off. Each check box is an independent unit that doesn't affect other check boxes.

- *Option buttons* are like check boxes, except that option buttons appear in groups and you can select only one. When you select an option button, the program automatically deselects whichever one was previously selected. Click a button to activate it.

- *Command buttons* perform an action, such as executing the options you set, closing the dialog box, or opening another dialog box. To select a command button, click it.

From Here...

If you need more help with Windows 95, I suggest that you pick up one of these books:

The 10 Minute Guide to Windows 95 by Trudi Reisner

The Complete Idiot's Guide to Windows 95 by Paul McFedries

The Big Basics Book of Windows 95 by Shelley O'Hara, Jennifer Fulton, and Ed Guilford

Installing Office 97 Small Business Edition

If you haven't yet installed the Microsoft Office 97 Small Business Edition onto your computer, the steps in this appendix will show you how.

Installation Steps

To install Microsoft Office 97 Small Business Edition, follow these steps:

CAUTION

Close All Programs! As a precaution, you should close any open applications before starting the Office 97 installation.

Try the Upgrade Wizard Office 97's ValuPack feature comes with an Upgrade Wizard you can use to help upgrade from previous versions of Office programs. Open the ValuPack to read more about this feature (see Appendix B for more information).

1. Insert the Office 97 CD-ROM into the appropriate drive.
2. The Setup program will automatically open the start window (shown in Figure D.1) when you insert the CD.

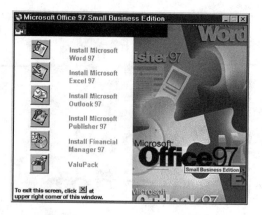

Figure D.1   With the Small Business Edition, you have the option of choosing which Office 97 applications you want installed.

3. Click the Office 97 application you want to install. This opens the Setup program that walks you through the installation procedures.

4. From the Welcome window, click **Continue** or press **Enter**.

5. In the next box that appears, type in your name and organization, then click **OK**.

6. A confirmation box appears. If the information is accurate, click **OK** to continue.

7. The next box asks you for an 11-digit CD key. You'll probably find the number on the back of your CD case. Type in the number and click **OK** to continue.

8. The next box displays your product ID number. It's a good idea to write this number down and keep it with the program's manual or registration information. Click **OK** to continue.

9. Setup prompts you to select a destination folder in which to store the program, as shown in Figure D.2. By default, the program installs to your main drive in the Program Files folder. If that's okay, click **OK** to continue. To designate another folder or drive, click the **Change Folder** button and specify another destination.

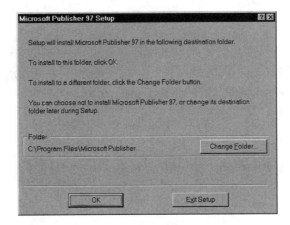

Figure D.2   Designate where you want the program files stored.

10. The next box, similar to the one shown in Figure D.3, prompts you to select a type of installation: Complete or Custom. For most users, the Complete Installation is the best choice. Click the large button next to Complete Installation to continue.

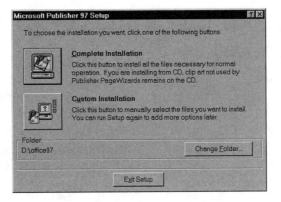

Figure D.3   Select which type of installation you want to perform.

TIP   **Can I Reinstall?**   If you're running low on disk space, use the Custom install to choose which files you want to load onto your computer's hard disk. You can always reopen the Setup program and reinstall files when necessary.

11. Setup begins installing the program files in earnest. When the installation is complete, another box appears stating that the procedure was successful. Click **OK** to exit the Setup program and return to the start window.

12. You can now choose to install another Office 97 program or exit the start window by clicking its **Close** button. If you choose to install another program, repeat steps 1 through 12.

Installing the ValuPack   For more information about installing the various features of the Small Business Edition ValuPack, refer to Appendix B.

CAUTION

What About Uninstalling?   To uninstall any of the Office programs, open the **Start** menu and select **Settings**, **Control Panel**. Double-click **Add/Remove Programs**. From the dialog box that appears, select the application you want to remove and click the **Add/Remove** button. You may have to insert the Office 97 CD-ROM to help uninstall the program.

Finding and Installing Office 97 Enhancements

Be sure to visit Microsoft's Web site (**http://www.microsoft.com**) for additional enhancements you can download and use with your Office 97 programs. For example, you can download numerous enhancements for Outlook that can help you expand the way you use the program, such as installing an E-Mail Forms Fix Utility that lets you switch between using Microsoft Exchange and Outlook as your e-mail client. Check the Web site frequently for new programs that might be useful to you.

For more information about Office 97 enhancements available, open your Internet account and visit the Office 97 Web pages. With Office 97's new Web capabilities, you can log onto the Web from any of the Office 97 programs. Follow these steps:

1. Connect to your Internet account.

2. Open an Office 97 program's **Help** menu and select **Microsoft on the Web**, **Free Stuff**.

3. Your Web browser opens on-screen to the Microsoft Free Stuff Web page. From there you can select a product and follow the links to learn more about an enhancement and find downloading instructions.

4. Once you've downloaded an enhancement program, be sure to check any READ.ME files for installation instructions. Depending on the program, you may be able to install by double-clicking the file name.

TIP   **Downloading Tips**   For more information about downloading files with Internet Explorer, refer to Lesson 5, "Viewing Web Pages Offline," in Part V of this book.

Installing Internet Explorer 4.0

Internet Explorer 4.0 is the latest version of Microsoft's Internet software. In addition to an upgraded World Wide Web browser, there are numerous other components which can be installed.

First, you can choose to install Internet Explorer 4.0 with or without the Integrated Shell. The Integrated Shell extends the capabilities of your Windows 95 desktop—see Lesson 8 of Part V for further details. If you install the Integrated Shell and decide it is not for you, you can use Add/Remove Programs in the Control Panel to remove it.

Second, you can choose from three different installations:

- **Standard Installation** includes Internet Explorer 4.0, Outlook Express (an e-mail program, covered in Lesson 9 of Part V), and multimedia enhancements.

- **Enhanced Installation** includes the preceding and FrontPad, a Web page authoring program, discussed in Lesson 13 of Part V; and NetShow, an Internet presentation program.

- **Full Installation** includes the preceding and NetMeeting—audio and video conferencing software (see Lesson 12 of Part V).

Follow these steps to install Internet Explorer 4.0:

1. Insert the Internet Explorer 4.0 CD-ROM into the appropriate drive.

   The first Internet Explorer 4.0 installation screen opens on your desktop.

2. From the first installation screen, click the button next to either **Install Internet Explorer 4.0 Suite with Integrated Shell** or **Install Internet Explorer 4.0 Suite**. You can also click the **Release Notes** button to see the latest information.

3. A confirmation box appears. If you're ready to proceed, confirm your choice by clicking **Yes**.

4. The Microsoft license agreement appears. After you have read the license, click **Yes** to continue.

5. The Internet Explorer 4.0 Active Setup window, shown in Figure D.4, opens. Choose the installation option you prefer by clicking the down-arrow and selecting one of the three choices described previously: Standard Installation, Enhanced Installation, or Full Installation. Click **Next** to continue.

6. A box asking you to confirm the path for the installation appears. Click **Yes** to confirm.

7. Internet Explorer 4.0 begins the preliminary installation process. A box shows the progress of the installation. When completed, Internet Explorer 4.0 asks you to close any programs still running. Save any open documents and close all programs. Click **Next** on the Internet Explorer 4.0 Active Setup screen when you are finished.

8. Internet Explorer 4.0 needs to restart the computer to complete the installation. Click **Yes** to continue.

   After your computer is restarted, the setup continues. Various boxes, depending on your installation choices, appear informing you of the progress.

9. When the installation is complete, if you have chosen to install Internet Explorer 4.0 with the Integrated Shell, your screen looks like Figure D.5.

Figure D.4 Choose your installation option from the Internet Explorer 4.0 Active Setup dialog box.

Figure D.5 Internet Explorer 4.0's Integrated Shell enhances your desktop capabilities.

Index

ISP (Internet Service
Provider), 518
italics, assigning to fonts, 36
Item command
(Outlook), 353
items (Outlook)
attaching to e-mail
(Outlook), 352-353
finding, 414-416
notes, creating, 419
saving, 405-407

J-K

Journal (Outlook), 387-390
automatically recording
entries, 389-390
manually recording
entries, 388-389
viewing entries, 390-392
Journal Entry dialog box
(Outlook), 388-389
justification, 44-45

keyboard
Backspace key (Word), 12
Delete key (Word), 12
Font Size list, accessing, 35
moving the cursor
(Word), 14
navigating Excel
worksheets, 142-143
keys (shortcut keys),
assigning to symbols, 91-93

L

Label Options
dialog box, 623
landscape orientation
(printing documents), 57-58
layering
graphics (Publisher 97),
469-470
text (Publisher 97), 469-470
laying out newsletters
(Publisher 97), 639-642

layout guides
(Publisher 97), 465
margin layout guide,
465-466
mirrored guides, 466
mirrored-page layout
feature, 504-505
Layout Guides dialog box
(Publisher 97), 466
Lease Analysis worksheet
(Excel), 298-300
legends (charts), 255
Letter Wizard (Word),
378-379
line breaks, 45-46
line spacing, changing, 50-51
Line Up Objects dialog box
(Publisher 97), 468
lines, adding to publications
(Publisher 97), 457-458
Link Shortcuts (Internet
Explorer), 549
linked objects
breaking links, 607-608
editing, 604-606
from container files,
605-606
from source files, 605
locking/unlocking
links, 607
update settings, 606-607
linking
entire files, 602-603
Excel worksheets to Word
documents, 632-638
hiding data, 634-635
Object Linking and
Embedding, 598-599
Paste Special command,
599-601
links, 523
copying (Internet
Explorer), 539-540
Links dialog box, 606-607
Links toolbar (Internet
Explorer), 519

lists
automatic lists, 86
bulleted lists, 84, 474
adding new items, 88
changing format, 88
creating, 84-86
removing, 87-88
inserting into Web pages
(FrontPad), 590-591
multilevel lists, 86-87
numbered lists, 84, 475
adding new items, 88
changing format, 88
creating, 84-86
removing, 87-88
Location Sensor box
(Automap Streets Plus), 688
Lock/Save Sheet
dialog box, 628
locking/unlocking links
(linked objects), 607
Lotus cc:Mail, 324
Lotus cc:Mail Information
Service (ValuPack), 697
Lycos Web site, 530

M

macro viruses, 268
macros, 267
magnifying worksheet
views (Excel), 144
Mail button (Internet
Explorer), 521
Mail group folders
(Outlook), 315
Mail Merge Helper dialog
box, 617-622
mail merges, 488-489
brochures, mail merging
(Publisher 97), 652-653
field codes, 491-492
mass mailings
form letters, building,
616-617
Mail Merge Helper
dialog box, 617-622
mailing labels, creating,
622-623

s

Complete and Return this Card
for a *FREE* Computer Book Catalog

Thank you for purchasing this book! You have purchased a superior computer book written expressly for your needs. To continue to provide the kind of up-to-date, pertinent coverage you've come to expect from us, we need to hear from you. Please take a minute to complete and return this self-addressed, postage-paid form. In return, we'll send you a free catalog of all our computer books on topics ranging from word processing to programming and the internet.

Mr. ☐   Mrs. ☐   Ms. ☐   Dr. ☐

Name (first) ☐☐☐☐☐☐☐☐☐☐☐☐   (M.I.) ☐   (last) ☐☐☐☐☐☐☐☐☐☐☐☐☐☐☐☐☐☐

Address ☐☐☐☐☐☐☐☐☐☐☐☐☐☐☐☐☐☐☐☐☐☐☐☐☐☐☐☐☐☐☐☐☐

☐☐☐☐☐☐☐☐☐☐☐☐☐☐☐☐☐☐☐☐☐☐☐☐☐☐☐☐☐☐☐☐☐

City ☐☐☐☐☐☐☐☐☐☐☐☐☐☐   State ☐☐   Zip ☐☐☐☐☐ ☐☐☐☐

Phone ☐☐☐ ☐☐☐ ☐☐☐☐   Fax ☐☐☐ ☐☐☐ ☐☐☐☐

☐☐☐☐☐☐☐☐☐☐☐☐☐☐☐☐☐☐☐☐☐☐☐☐☐☐
☐☐☐☐☐☐☐☐☐☐☐☐☐☐☐☐☐☐☐☐☐☐☐☐☐☐

...ng factors for

....ok .... ☐
.... ☐
.... ☐
.... ☐
.... ☐
.... ☐
.... ☐
.... ☐
.... ☐
_____ ☐

...book?

...g catalog .... ☐
.... ☐
.... ☐
.... ☐
.... ☐
_____ ☐
_____ ☐
.... ☐

3. How many computer books have you purchased in the last six months?

This book only .... ☐   3 to 5 books .... ☐
2 books .... ☐   More than 5 .... ☐

4. Where did you purchase this book?

Bookstore .... ☐
Computer Store .... ☐
Consumer Electronics Store .... ☐
Department Store .... ☐
Office Club .... ☐
Warehouse Club .... ☐
Mail Order .... ☐
Direct from Publisher .... ☐
Internet site .... ☐
Other (Please specify): _____ ☐

5. How long have you been using a computer?

☐ Less than 6 months   ☐ 6 months to a year
☐ 1 to 3 years   ☐ More than 3 years

6. What is your level of experience with personal computers and with the subject of this book?

	With PCs	With subject of book
New	☐	☐
Casual	☐	☐
Accomplished	☐	☐
Expert	☐	☐

Source Code ISBN: 0-7897-1352-7

JOHN LEWIS EDINBURGH TEL 0131-556-9121

'80   1   8436   021   018   03/02/99

books
6 63001   1   15.49
6 63001   1   27.49

          TOTAL   42.98

          CASH   45.00
          CHANGE   2.02

T REG NO GB 232 4572 80

7. Which of the following best describes your job title?

- Administrative Assistant ☐
- Coordinator ☐
- Manager/Supervisor ☐
- Director ☐
- Vice President ☐
- President/CEO/COO ☐
- Lawyer/Doctor/Medical Professional ☐
- Teacher/Educator/Trainer ☐
- Engineer/Technician ☐
- Consultant ☐
- Not employed/Student/Retired ☐
- Other (Please specify): _____ ☐

8. Which of the following best describes the area of the company your job title falls under?

- Accounting ☐
- Engineering ☐
- Manufacturing ☐
- Operations ☐
- Marketing ☐
- Sales ☐
- Other (Please specify): _____ ☐

9. What is your age?

- Under 20 ☐
- 21-29 ☐
- 30-39 ☐
- 40-49 ☐
- 50-59 ☐
- 60-over ☐

10. Are you:

- Male ☐
- Female ☐

11. Which computer publications do you read regularly? (Please list)

_____
_____
_____
_____
_____
_____
_____
_____
_____

Comments: _____
_____

Fold here and scotch-tape to mail.

BUSINESS REPLY MAIL
FIRST-CLASS MAIL PERMIT NO. 9918 INDIANAPOLIS IN

POSTAGE WILL BE PAID BY THE ADDRESSEE

ATTN MARKETING
MACMILLAN COMPUTER PUBLISHING
MACMILLAN PUBLISHING USA
201 W 103RD ST
INDIANAPOLIS IN 46290-9042

NO POSTAGE
NECESSARY
IF MAILED
IN THE
UNITED STATES